Outsiders Within

Outsiders Within

Writing on Transracial Adoption

Jane Jeong Trenka
Julia Chinyere Oparah
***and* Sun Yung Shin**
Editors

University of Minnesota Press
Minneapolis
London

First published in 2006 by South End Press

First University of Minnesota Press edition, 2021

See page 307 for copyright and original publication information for specific works reprinted in this volume.

Published by the University of Minnesota Press
111 Third Avenue South, Suite 290
Minneapolis, MN 55401-2520
http://www.upress.umn.edu

ISBN 978-1-5179-1053-2 (pb)

A Cataloging-in-Publication record for this book is available from the Library of Congress.

Printed on acid-free paper

To the transracial/national adoptee holding this book: We are grateful *Outsiders Within* has found its way into your hands. It is our gift to you. We hope that you will find something here that will stretch your imagination, something that will offer you a perspective that you didn't see before. May these essays and memoirs offer you guidance, camaraderie, and perhaps a roadmap for your long journey. May they give you the courage to share your own story with someone who comes after you.

Contents

Part Six: Speaking for Ourselves

Preface

Julia Chinyere Oparah, Sun Yung Shin, & Jane Jeong Trenka

We came together to dream *Outsiders Within* into being over fifteen years ago in response to the infantilization and silencing of transracial adoptees. We wanted to rewrite dominant narratives about transracial adoption and, above all, we were driven to disrupt the debate that presented us as either multicultural ambassadors for colorblind love or damaged victims. Rather than staying within the confines of the existing arguments for or against transracial adoption, we chose to reveal and challenge the forces that transform children into adoptable commodities.

We conceptualized *Outsiders Within* as a gift to adoptees who were dealing with feelings of racial isolation and racial trauma on their own and who would find in the pages of this book companionship and community. We were also speaking to a wider audience of adoptive parents and siblings, adoption agency workers, policymakers, and opinion shapers in the hope that our stark critiques of the racism, colonialism, imperialism, and white savior complex inherent in transracial adoption would challenge liberal ideas about saving babies from dangerous and negligent others. Finally, we wanted to reclaim the member of the adoption triad who is most often demonized, blamed, and invisibilized—first mothers—and imagine the possibility of solidarities between adoptees and our first families based on an understanding of shared histories of oppression and of the stigma and coercion experienced by our first mothers.

Did we succeed in those ambitious goals? *Outsiders Within* remains the only book of its kind, emphasizing, through the writings and artwork of Native American, black, Asian, and Latinx adoptees and allies, the intersectionality of adopted people's lives. In the years since its publication, the book has found its way into the hands of thousands of adoptees of color. Adoptees whose journeys have passed through all seven continents have found within the book a new way to understand how birth and racial traumas continue to impact their lives, their relationships with families of origin and adoption, and their connections to communities of color. We have received correspondence from adoptees for whom reading *Outsiders Within* was a life-changing experience and their first opportunity to access a broader adoptee community. Beyond that, the book has provided a powerful counter to a mainstream media narrative that is still focused on rescuing infants and the obstacles facing waiting adoptive parents. By speaking out, the contributors introduced a wide readership to the powerful presence and voice of adult adoptees of color. And the contributors' astute and relentless critique of the complicity of the adoption industry with white supremacy, genocide, and empire pushed all parties involved to examine the workings of privilege, power, and money in the lives of adoptees, adopting families, and our communities of origin.

In 2012, *Outsiders Within* was translated and published by KoRoot with a new preface by Jane Jeong Trenka in South Korea, a country that has sent over 200,000 adoptees around the globe. That edition expanded the reach and impact of the book and bolstered efforts to encourage Korean society to redress the inequalities, prejudice, and violence embedded within the Korean adoption system and the violation of the human rights of women and children. The Korean edition was part of a broader activist movement that has won significant gains.

A coalition of internationally adopted people, unwed mothers, first parents, and their allies started to work to revise South Korea's Special Adoption Act in late 2008. It was wholly revised in 2011 and enforced in 2012 to prioritize family preservation over adoption. Among other provisions, it installed a seven-day waiting period before relinquishment so adoption agencies were no longer able to coerce pregnant women into giving up babies still in the womb. In addition, the process of birth family search was given legal parameters to make the process fairer for adoptees instead of leaving the process up to the daily whims of social workers at private adoption agencies. The law provided the legal foundation for the establishment of Korea Adoption Services, which is a quasi-central authority over adoption matters, including birth family search; under the administration of liberal President Moon Jae-in, the body was moved under the umbrella of the newly established National Center for the Rights of the Child. Other laws that were changed by this coalition led to the expansion of support for single parents, particularly for younger unwed mothers; private adoption agencies being banned from owning or operating unwed mothers' homes as baby factories for the profitable international adoption industry; and "Single Parent Day" being legislated as a national holiday and celebrated for the first time on May 10, 2018. Celebrating single parents raising their own kids a day before May 11 symbolized the government's prioritization of family preservation over adoption, as the government had already legislated May 11 as "Adoption Day" several years prior. This activism to change legislation and social perceptions in order to preserve families has led to an increase in unwed mothers raising their own children and a decline in intercountry adoption. Only 303 children were sent from South Korea for intercountry adoption in 2018, contrasting with the 916 who were sent overseas in 2011, the year before complete revision of the adoption law.

However, South Korea has yet to ratify the Hague Convention on Protection of Children and Co-operation in Respect of Intercountry Adoption; birth families, including siblings, have no legal right to search for relatives; and the vast majority of adoption records still lie in the hands of private adoption agencies and orphanages and are regarded as their private property rather than property of the people whose information they hold. Because there is still no legal mechanism to compel orphanage owners to hand over these records—though they are encouraged to voluntarily cooperate with Korea Adoption Services—the human right to identity remains out of reach, not only for internationally adopted people but also for the majority of late-discovery domestically adopted people and those who aged out of orphanages. Much legislative work and change in social perception are still absolutely necessary to address these issues, guarantee nondiscrimination against all members of society, including QLGBT people, and discourage, instead of valorize, the practice of anonymous child abandonment at churches.

Globally, intercountry adoption has declined significantly since this book was first published. Adoptions to the United States, which brings in the most children internationally for adoption each year, peaked in 2004 with 22,989 children and declined thereafter, with only 4,058 going to the United States in 2018.[1] While more than 400,000 children live in foster care in the United States, many white adoptive families prefer children from outside the United States, both because they fear ties to black and Latinx communities of origin and because of the different racialization of Asian adoptees in particular, who, as Kim Park Nelson points out in this volume, are considered "culturally enriching." The intercountry adoption industry uses the severing of adoptees' ties to their first families to produce a fantasy of a "clean slate" as a selling point, rendering their mothers socially dead.

The shortage of "clean slate" babies as a result of changes in international adoption practices is being filled by the international surrogacy industry. Facilitated by assisted reproductive technologies, as well as laws that diminish the rights of surrogate mothers and recognize babies carried by surrogate mothers as the legal children of the people who contracted the surrogacy services, poor (including white) and black women in the United States and women in the global South have become the new source for families (including Asian families) wishing to parent a child without the complexities of racial difference or familial ties. Our hope is that today's readers will find that the critical tools in this book are still relevant today as they seek to unpack the intimate racialized politics of foster care, adoption, and surrogacy.

Outsiders Within has had a meaningful impact, yet, like any political project, it also has had its silences and failures. When we wrote the preface, the editors articulated our vision of building a "global transracial adoptee community." In some ways, that community has come into existence. For example, when we created an *Outsiders Within* Adoptee Community Facebook page to solicit ideas from transracial adoptees for this preface, over 350 individuals, mostly adoptees from around the world, joined the community in less than a week. Books and artistic and activist communities by and for adoptees of color have sprung up. But we also recognize that this book is a very imperfect basis for panracial solidarity among adoptees. Raised by parents who chose to adopt from overseas, sometimes to avoid bringing black children into their families and/or to avoid dealing with birth families, Asian and Latin American intercountry adoptees are often brought up in environments saturated with anti-blackness and in communities where they have little opportunity to create social connections with black people. Yet we paid insufficient attention to the deep work of unpacking internalized anti-blackness that would need to happen for true, lasting solidarities to emerge between differently racialized and situated adoptees of color. Our efforts to decolonize our experiences lacked sufficient grounding in First Nations perspectives, and we did not sufficiently frame the contributions of non-adopted people in the volume, such as Heidi Adelsman, who wrote about her adopted brother's life and death from the standpoint of a white witness. All this is a reminder that the work is never done and that we must continue to evolve our analysis and our activism.

Nevertheless, we remain deeply committed to the original vision of this book. *Outsiders Within* is not a comprehensive or exhaustive documentation of transracial adoption. Yet, despite its imperfections, its fearless anticapitalist and feminist of color critique continues to provide an important lens for understanding how children circulate within ideologies and structures of race, gender, sexuality, nation, and global capitalism. We hope that the contributors' critical perspectives will gain renewed relevance as they help us to unpack contemporary crises. For example, what does the media and political focus on COVID-19 as an obstacle to the family formation of white prospective adoptive parents say about the value of the lives of women and children in China, India, Colombia, and beyond? How does the Trump administration's inadequate response to the pandemic reveal the inconsistencies in U.S. federal policies that profess to preserve families and reduce the number of children entering the foster care system while funding Christian adoption agencies?

President Trump's executive order "Strengthening the Child Welfare System for America's Children," signed in the midst of nationwide shelter-in-place orders in June 2020, advocates family reunification without tending to the root causes that lead black and brown mothers to relinquish their children. In specific, it fails to redress the disproportionate impact on black, Latinx, and Native families hardest hit by job loss, illness, and death—impacts that will likely fuel an upsurge in families unable to care for their children. At the time of writing, the Centers for Disease Control were reporting an infection rate for African Americans and Native nations as five times that of whites, with continuing rises in infection rates resulting in unimaginable disruption for families of color. In light of the global circulation of the virus, and its disproportionate impact on U.S. communities that already lose children to adoption, we wonder how the pandemic may permanently shift adoption norms and practices and what possibilities there are for policy and advocacy focused on supporting women of color in raising their children.

As we close this preface, the killings of George Floyd, Ahmaud Arbery, and Breonna Taylor and the subsequent worldwide protests are foregrounding the precarity of black life, creating a sense of urgency and even impatience for the editors. We find ourselves asking: How are transracial adoptees speaking out now that we have claimed our voice? Are we speaking not only about our rights and histories, our families of origin and journeys to reclaim our identities, but also about the anti-blackness in our adoptive families and communities? Are we taking action to combat police killings and disproportionate infection and death rates in low-wage black, Latinx, Southeast and South Asian, and Native American communities? We hope that this book will encourage all members of the adoption community to ask difficult questions and to talk to each other about the things we would rather leave silent. As we do so, we build courageous and self-determined communities even as we work to build a world in which people of color have the resources and support to parent their children, and children have a right to their stories, their families and ancestors, and their communities of origin.

Finally, the editors extend their sincere thanks to editor Erik Anderson at the University of Minnesota Press, who made this second edition a reality, and to award-winning author Shannon Gibney, who not only brought this book to the attention of the University of Minnesota Press but also shepherded it to South End Press, which published the first edition. We remain deeply grateful to you both for your faith and commitment.

1 "Adoption Statistics," U.S. Department of State—Bureau of Consular Affairs, Travel.State.Gov, accessed April 26, 2020, https://travel.state.gov/content/travel/en/Intercountry-Adoption/adopt_ref/adoption-statistics1.html?wcmmode=disabled.

INTRODUCTION

Julia Chinyere Oparah, Sun Yung Shin, & Jane Jeong Trenka

We on the periphery, learning and watching from the outside, have a particular power with revolutionary roots.

—Kim Diehl

For those Chinese girls we see with their "forever families" on urban sidewalks; for those Korean kids growing up on farms in rural America; for those African American kids single-handedly integrating small-town schools in British Columbia; for the children bought with the bribes of American dollars; for our sisters who have been kidnapped and sold; for the children who are deemed "unadoptable"—we must witness.

This book is a corrective action. Over the past fifty years, white adoptive parents, academics, psychiatrists, and social workers have dominated the literature on transracial adoption. These "experts" have been the ones to tell the public—*including* adoptees[1]—"what it's like" and "how we turn out." Despite our numbers and the radical way we have transformed the color and kinship of white families, the voices of adult transracial adoptees remain largely unheard. Our cultural production has been marginalized and essays discussing our personal experiences of adoption have remained undistributed and largely unknown.

There are many reasons for our slim output, not the least of which is that transracial adoption is fundamentally an isolating experience. Adoptees of color may fear that expressing our opinions will estrange us from our white families, friends, and colleagues. We have become accustomed to protecting our loved ones from the harsh realities of our experiences with racism, loss, and trauma. Still others of us have been silenced through assimilation into white environments, and only in middle age—after careers and families have been firmly established—do we reach a point where we can acknowledge and heal from the pain of isolation and alienation. There is an enormous amount of internal, emotional work—some of it "unlearning"—that must be accomplished before we can even think about transforming our personal experience into inspiration for political action.

It is commonly pointed out that transracial adoptees have only recently "come of age" and therefore we should not be surprised by a paucity of writings by adult transracial adoptees. Yet there are many transracial adoptees who could be grandparents themselves. Among them are the indigenous people of North America and Australia, the Japanese orphans of World War II, and the children of the Korean War. So it is a fallacy to conceptualize transracial adoptees as perpetually sitting on the cusp of adulthood, one foot forever hanging in childhood. That said, it is not until recently that a *critical mass* of transracial adoptees has reached adulthood. This is largely due to the mass emigration of Korean children sent abroad for adoption, which peaked in the mid to late 1980s. Not only are there up to 200,000 Korean adoptees scattered throughout the world, according to some estimates, but also thousands of people who were adopted out of China, Vietnam, and India; Guatemala and Colombia; Ethiopia and Liberia; African American and Chicano/Latino communities in the United States; and the indigenous nations of Australia and the Americas—to name but a few of the "sending" communities, with more added to the list every year.

Since the 1980s, the dramatic increase in *transnational* adoption has generated a *transracial* adoption boom. According to the US Department of State, a growing number of US citizens are choosing to adopt children from overseas due to a perceived reduction in the number of healthy infants available for adoption within the country.[2] In 1992, the United States issued 6472 "orphan" visas for internationally adopted children. Ten years later, the figure had risen to 20,099. Most of these children came from East Asia, Eastern Europe, and Latin America. As the authors in this book suggest, this shift in adoption patterns is also due to the valuing of European, Latin American, and Asian children over black children, and prospective adopters' desire to adopt children who do not come with the "baggage" of home communities and potentially interfering family members nearby. While the United States is the largest adoption industry "consumer," thousands of children are also brought to Western Europe, Canada, and Australia for adoption each year.

Discussions about adoption have typically separated adoptees who were adopted across racial lines within their country of origin (often referred to as "transracial" adoptees) from those who were adopted transnationally (referred to as "international" or "intercountry" adoptees). This separation prevents us from recognizing our commonalities as a source of solidarity. It also suggests that the problems facing transnational adoptees are primarily related to finding a family and adapting to a new country, rather than to the traumatic experiences of racism, marginalization, and discrimination, both systemically and on the personal level, within our adoptive communities.[3] Increasingly, many of us who have been described in the adoption literature as intercountry or international adoptees have decided to redefine ourselves as *transracial* adoptees. This redefinition emphasizes how relentless our racialization has been throughout our lives. In this book, we use the term "transracial adoption" to highlight the connections between adoptees of color, whether we were adopted domestically or internationally. At the same time, we seek to honor the multiplicity and complexity of the adoption stories gathered together under this umbrella. There is no homogenous transracial adoptee story, no single political line. Yet taken together, our writings create a hopeful vision of a different world, where children of color are neither sold nor expendable, our mothers and families neither erased nor exploited.

who knows? adoption and the politics of knowledge

Writing about transracial adoption raises critical questions about the motivation of the author. Does it matter if the author is a white adoptive parent of children of color or a social worker involved in the adoption industry, like so many of the "experts" writing on the subject? As people of color who for so long have had our histories told and distorted by others, we know that it does indeed matter. Authors never write from a completely impartial place—our vision always reflects our social location in relation to gender, ethnicity, nationality, political perspective, and involvement in the adoption triad. Knowledge production is always marked by this locatedness. Theorist Patricia Hill Collins has asserted that an "outsider within" standpoint enables black women to gain unique insights that may not be available to those who share the worldview of the dominant community in which they operate.[4] Being within—yet excluded from—the dominant discourse is an incentive to create knowledge that goes against the grain. Who then is best positioned to write about transracial adoption? Who occupies the position of "outsider within"?

In a treatise on what he labels the "tragedy of race matching," Randall Kennedy argues that adoptees do not have a unique perspective on race, family, and adoption. Pointing to the differences of opinions among adoptees, some of whom ardently support transracial adoption while others condemn the practice, Kennedy concludes that there is no greater insight associated with the experience of being raised across racialized lines.

> Some observers will be tempted to defer to these witnesses because they bear a supposed "authority of experience." One difficulty, however, lies in determining which of them to defer to, since adoptees' opinions conflict. An even more fundamental challenge consists in deciphering, evaluating, and making use of the asset that is deemed to endow adoptees with their special wisdom—namely, their experience. In reading memoirs and other accounts by adoptees, one encounters not the raw experience of interracial adoption but rather an interpretation of it.[5]

While the essays, poems, and visual art in this anthology confirm that there is no singular "adoptee experience" or "adoptee perspective," this should not lead us to discount the voices of transracial adoptees in favor of more authoritative "experts." Nor should it blind us to the emergence of a body of work by transracial adoptees and our allies that is highly critical of the colorblind rhetoric used by many supporters of the practice. Rather than seeking to discredit the perspectives of critical adoptees—or looking for token adoptees who can be deployed to support positions within the existing debate—we seek to embrace the heterogeneity and multiplicity of the global transracial adoptee community, to shift the terms of the debate, and to open up new avenues for exploration. That is the challenge of this volume.

There are two dominant and competing discourses on race and adoption. On one hand, some scholars and social workers claim that transracial adoption damages children of color, leading to low self-esteem, identity crises, and difficulty relating to their communities of origin. This perspective was particularly prevalent among the black and indigenous social workers who actively promoted same-race placements from the 1970s onward. On the other hand, public opinion—backed by recent studies undertaken by scholars wishing to disprove the centrality of racial identity—asserts that "love" and swift placement into a stable family are the key factors in a child's development. This research denies that children of color adopted into white families suffer from problems related to self-esteem or racial isolation and asserts, to the contrary, that they acquire the advantage of an ability to move with comfort within both white and minority worlds. Proponents of same-race placements are therefore accused of taking a politically motivated separatist stance that promotes racial divisiveness and ignores both the plight of waiting children and the empirical evidence that transracial adoption works. Opposing this rigid adherence to racial thinking, advocates of transracial adoption depict transracial adoptive families as sites of hope for a multicultural utopia. As Rita Simon asserts,

> The studies show parents and children, brothers and sisters, relating to each other in these transracial families as if race was no barrier to love and commitment.... In a society torn by racial conflict, these studies show human beings transcending racial difference.[6]

Transracial adoptees swim in the murky waters between these conflicting accounts. On one hand, we resist being defined as victims condemned to half-lives between cultures, without meaningful connections to our families or communities. Our willingness to work through seemingly irresolvable tensions with our adoptive families, our ability to (re)build connections to communities and families of origin, and our successful efforts to create new identities authentically based on our experiences are testimony that we can indeed survive and thrive. On the other hand, our experiences of racism, isolation, and abuse and our struggles with depression, addiction, and alienation indicate that adoption across boundaries of race, nation, and culture does indeed exact a very real emotional and spiritual cost. We live within this constant paradox, aware that our very lives are acts of transgression. The immutability of our bodies—born in one place and raised in another, speaking different languages, nourished from different tables—are manifestations of the uneasy and often violent clash of the ideologies of race and nationality. Adoptees of color are therefore outsiders within the two powerful discourses on transracial adoption. Yet we refuse to be limited by the terms of reference of the current debate. Instead, the contributors to this volume choose to ask different questions altogether.

beyond the adoption triad: race, colorblindness, and backlash

The impact and significance of transracial adoption is not limited to the families in the so-called adoption triad—birthmother, adoptee, and adoptive parent. In fact, transracial adoption has become a potent symbol in the battle to rearticulate racial meanings and policies in the post–civil rights era. Three decades ago, black and indigenous social workers in the United States and Britain, concerned about the one-way traffic of children of color into white families, fought successfully for the implementation of race-matching policies that would place children into families with the same racial origins. In the past decade, these policies have been attacked and discredited as essentialist, outdated, or racist. Critics have pointed to the large number of children of color awaiting families, arguing that permanency is far more important than race. They have questioned the placement of multiracial children with any white parentage into families of color, arguing that this ignores the complexity of the children's racial origins. And they have suggested that same-race placements infringe upon the rights of white adoptive parents, denying them the opportunity to adopt children purely on the basis of their race.

The battle over same-race placements occurs against the backdrop of a broader debate over the continuing significance of race, as well as the morality and legality of measures designed to provide redress for racial inequalities. In the United States, neoconservative organizations such as the American Civil Rights Institute and the Campaign for a Colorblind America have presented themselves as the true inheritors of the legacy of Dr. Martin Luther King, Jr., rearticulating civil rights rhetoric in defense of those they portray as the new disadvantaged minority: whites. In this context, King's demand that people be judged by the content of their character, not the color of their skin, is mobilized against government interventions designed to redress racist exclusion. Affirmative action, in particular, has come under fire, with California as the testing ground for the neoconservative colorblind agenda. The passage of the California Civil Rights Initiative, Proposition 209, outlawed affirmative action by government agencies, leading to a dramatic decline in the numbers of black and Latino students admitted to the University of California system. A significant success for Ward Connerly's American Civil Rights Institute, Proposition 209 has been followed by a series of legal challenges to affirmative action programs nationwide. But the attack on progressive racial remedies does not stop there. Proposition 54, the Racial Privacy Initiative, which aimed to outlaw the collection of racial statistics by all government agencies (other than law enforcement), was brought to the California ballot in spring 2004. If implemented, the initiative would have prevented state agencies from identifying the race of adoptable children and prohibited the collection of statistics demonstrating racial discrimination in government programs ranging from housing to education. Although it was defeated, the 43 percent support that Proposition 54 received indicates that a large minority of voters in this bellwether state are convinced that people of color receive unfair racial preferences and that the solution to racism is keeping state agencies from acknowledging the existence of racial categories. In effect, any acknowledgment of race is being recast as "racist."

While affirmative action has been the most visible site of the swing toward a colorblind agenda, transracial adoption has also earned the attention of the neoconservative lobby. In the context of adoption, colorblind ideology represents both children of color and white potential adoptive parents as victims of racial ideologues. Children are being forced to wait in foster homes and institutions, we are told, because of a social category they neither perceive nor understand. White parents are being penalized because of their race and denied the opportunity to build families. In this narrative, the Multiethnic Placement Act (MEPA) and the subsequent Interethnic Placement Provisions (IEP)—passed during President Bill Clinton's administration—are presented as a necessary legal defense of the right of children and potential adopters to be united regardless of race.[7] In this sense, the attack on same-race placements can be seen as the testing ground for the later assault on affirmative action. The underlying common sense notion that "love sees no color" provides a useful ideological framework for the reframing of the racial script so that those seeking to assert that race matters are recast as segregationists or ideologues. This narrowing of the discussion to a debate between two camps impoverishes our understanding of transracial adoption. It also prevents us from considering other possibilities.

How would the proposed remedies change if we asked about the right of low-income parents to receive adequate economic support to keep their children, the right of women with addictions to receive treatment and continue their parental roles, or the right of children not to have their mothers taken away and put behind bars? How would the debate change if we considered the right of mothers in the global South and nations surviving the aftermath of war to food, housing, health care, and education for themselves and their children? The contributors to this volume do not limit their concerns to the terms of the existing debate. They do not seek to present either exemplary stories of successful adoptions or cautionary tales of disastrous events. Instead they reveal transracial adoption as the intimate face of colonization, racism, militarism, imperialism, and globalization. In so doing, they direct our attention to the need for long-term solutions embedded in struggles for economic, racial, and global justice that address the root causes leading to children of color being removed from their families or surrendered for adoption. They call on us to demand justice for an entire community, rather than claiming to save a single child.

And so, counterintuitively, we discover that the alternative to transracial adoption is not same-race placement after all. Instead the real alternative is found in welfare policies that support poor mothers of color rather than penalizing them, criminal justice policies that strengthen and heal communities rather than destroying them, and international policies that prioritize human security over profits. This book is about transracial adoption and much more. This complex web of narratives about loss, love, belonging, alienation, home, and exile deeply enriches our understanding not only of transracial adoption but also of the dynamics of race, politics, and the global economy that shape all of our lives.

the contents

Outsiders Within is organized in six parts that map out a journey for the reader. The reader is welcome to take a more eclectic route, to pick and choose the stories and essays that most appeal to her. However, we believe that reading the contributions in the order presented here will generate a rich conversation among diverse authors as they paint a portrait of the many faces of transracial adoption. The journey on which we invite you to embark is not unlike our own adoption journeys as we seek to find meaning in the departures and arrivals, attachments and losses that make up our lives. For even as we learn more about our communities and countries of origin, and the social, political, and economic inequities that mark our journeys away from (and sometimes back to) them, we also struggle with the details of our lives and loves. In this book, we interlace personal accounts, critical analysis, and creative expression, creating a multifaceted dialogue. We hope that by placing personal narratives alongside critical analysis, and poetry and visual art alongside prose, this volume will challenge the privileging of the rationalistic, "expert" knowledge that excludes so many adoptee voices.

part one: where are you really from?

In Part One, transracial adoptees share their struggles to come to a sense of belonging and identity despite the racism and cultural dislocation they have experienced. This part of the book takes its title from a question that has been casually thrown at many of us throughout our lives. Although it appears to be an innocent question, "Where do you come from?" carries the implicit rejection "you are not like us" and underlines the assertion "you do not belong here." We have been taught that to belong means to forget the past, to silence our truths and try to fit in. We are encouraged to adapt and "move on" from our beginnings by forgetting the past. But as Soo Na tells us in the first chapter, it is only by rejecting this denial and silencing of our stories of origin and survival that we can begin to heal the dis-ease inherent in our experiences of loss and dislocation.

Identity is a complex, shifting, and contested area for transracial adoptees who grow up seldom seeing ourselves reflected in family members, schoolmates, or neighbors. How, in the absence of black mothers, aunts, grandmothers, and cousins to school us, do black adoptees reconcile our own curly hair and dark skin with the racist sexualized imagery of black women that bombards us? Jeni Wright's essay will remind many transracial adoptees of our struggles to come to terms with the physical markers of our difference within our own families, and of the physical evidence of our maligned or exoticized African, Asian, Native, or Latin American ancestries.

The two final chapters in this section reveal that for some, the experience of transracial adoption has brought opportunities for emotional and spiritual growth. Kim Diehl explains how her unique perspective as an outsider within has led her into beloved community with others through community organizing and spirituality. Mark Hagland shares how he has navigated between the dual traps of compulsory heterosexuality and assumed Korean cultural identity to construct an authentic, integrated identity that reflects the complexity of his history and contemporary reality.

part two: how did you get here?

Proponents of transracial adoption often invoke the aphorism "love sees no color." The second part of the book shifts our attention from the color of love to the color of money by foregrounding the politics and economics of adoption. The selections here encourage us to consider the ways in which current social and economic policies fuel transracial adoption. Sun Yung Shin opens the section with a poem that evokes the expendable rural women of Korea who provided the cheap labor that fueled the so-called Asian economic miracle and who also provided the children whose bodies fueled the Korean adoption phenomenon.[8]

Essays by Dorothy Roberts, Ellen Barry, and Laura Briggs turn the spotlight onto the United States and provide a trenchant critique of the systemic racial inequality in its child welfare and criminal justice systems. Their chapters show how welfare reform, a conservative "family values" policy agenda, and the rise of the prison-industrial complex have undermined civil rights and devastated African American and Latino families. The authors challenge us to consider reforming the child welfare and correctional systems and providing working-class families with living incomes as real alternatives to the current focus on "freeing" children of color for adoption into white families.

Kimberly Fardy's short narrative reveals the intimate impact of these interlocking systems. As a queer woman of color, as the daughter of an incarcerated father and a teenage mother on welfare, and as a survivor of sexual assault, racism, and homelessness, Fardy has much to tell us about survival and strength in the face of dehumanizing state policies.

The final chapters in Part Two move our focus to the politics and economics of adoption on the international level. Kim Park Nelson's examination of the international adoption industry reveals troubling motivations among both adopters and facilitators involved in the $1.5 billion cross-border "trade" in foreign babies. As one of El Salvador's niños desaparecidos (disappeared children), Patrick McDermott reveals the complicity of the international adoption industry in providing a market for trafficked children. His essay illustrates the ways in which the stories about *how we got here* may be nothing more than comfortable fictions, masking traumatic histories of violence and oppression.

part three: colonial imaginations, global migrations

Part Three uncovers the colonial roots of transracial adoption. The section opens with two reflections on colonization and indigenous identities and struggles, reminding us that all conversations about transracial and transnational adoption in North America begin with colonial takeovers of the land and the creation of settler societies. Shandra Spears's poem can be read as an Indian woman's quest for both a history and a future, truncated by the psychic violence of cultural genocide. But indigenous peoples have not stood idly by while their children have been removed and assimilated into the dominant society. Heidi Kiiwetinepinesiik Stark and Kekek Jason Todd Stark demonstrate that struggles over child welfare have been a key component of movements for decolonization.

There are clear ideological and historical continuities between the adoption and assimilation of Indian children and the "rescue" and relocation of children from the postcolonial South to the dominant North, as well as East to West. By examining the case of adoption from Korea following the Korean War, Tobias Hübinette challenges us to consider the relationships between US empire, anticommunism, and the global movements of children. No bid for empire would be complete without religious forerunners. Long a tool of colonialism, Christian missionaries have justified domination through narratives of saving "Third World" souls. Jae Ran Kim uses her personal history to highlight this general historical dynamic in the Korean adoption boom, drawing on the tale of her return to the Christian orphanage in Daegu where she was left as a child.

part four: growing through the pain

Some commentators have suggested that transracial adoptees are the new face of multiculturalism, as Hübinette points out, acting as "bridges between cultures, symbols of interethnic harmony, and embodiments of global and postmodern cosmopolitans." But as Donna Kate Ruskin reminded us in *This Bridge Called My Back,* a classic volume of writings by women of color in the United States, there is an immense psychic and emotional cost involved in becoming a bridge:

> I've had enough
> I'm sick of seeing and touching
> Both sides of things
> Sick of being the damn bridge for everybody....
>
> I'm sick of filling in your gaps
>
> Sick of being your insurance against
> The isolation of your self-imposed limitations
> Sick of being the crazy at your holiday dinners
> Sick of being the odd one at your Sunday Brunches
> Sick of being the sole Black friend to 34 individual white
> people[9]

For many transracial adoptees, the pain of loss and unbelonging generated by our living in the borderlands of racial, national, and cultural identities produces a kind of spiritual sickness. It is a malaise that expresses itself in depression, rage, grief, rootlessness, and addictions. Some of us feel pressured to censor our own pain as an act of loyalty toward our adoptive families, fearing that it would cause *them* too much pain if we express our feelings of loss and grief. In the face of racist assumptions that we do not belong, or that a multiracial family cannot "work," we throw ourselves into maintaining a model family, proclaiming how wonderful our adoptive lives have been. But for many of us, it is only by facing the pain, without judgment or self-censorship, that we can transform it into healing. Part Four of this book is about the growth and transformation that comes from facing the losses we have experienced. The section opens with contributions by Shannon Gibney, Beth Kyong Lo, and Bryan Thao Worra that explore the themes of yearning, trauma, and healing. These writings reveal the complicated feelings that many of us share about our families and our pasts and explore the journey from denial to personal transformation.

The next three chapters investigate different aspects of the struggles often involved in transracial adoption. John Raible explores the sometimes difficult relationships between adoptees and our families, suggesting ways adoptive families can become "transracialized." Ron McLay's memoir surveys the terrain of healing from addiction and abuse. His journey to sobriety through a twelve-step program and his commitment to facing his troubled history, beginning to heal, and learning to love in a healthy way demonstrates the hope and strength that lies in our adoption stories.

Ron McLay survived. In assembling this collection, the editors had to struggle with how to include the stories of those who did not. We know that many transracial adoptees are accomplished artists, activists, and writers. But what about those who did not overcome the trauma and losses of their lives? In this volume, we also wish to honor the adoptees who have lost to drugs and alcohol, who are locked away in prisons and mental institutions, and who have taken their lives. The final two chapters in Part Four explore dying, grief, and mourning. Heidi Lynn Adelsman tells the story of her adopted brother's struggle with racism, imprisonment, and AIDS. The story of his life and death reminds us why this volume is so urgent. Finally, Rachel Quy Collier considers the intense losses that are associated with our adoptions and suggests a new way of thinking about adoption, denial, and grieving.

part five: journeys home?

Where is home? Is it with the families that raised us? For many adoptees of color, loving our parents or siblings does not prevent us from feeling that we are missing pieces of ourselves. As young children, we search in vain for someone who resembles us, who can show us our connectedness to the rest of humanity. As adults, the search for our original families, for our birthparents, or for our original communities furthers our journey toward the yearned-for home. Yet our returning—whether to the embrace of a birthmother, or to the now strange scents and sounds of our "homeland"—presents us with more questions than answers. For this reason, *Journeys Home?* is written not as a statement but as a question. With each "homecoming" another phase in our journey is just beginning.

All adoptees are faced with the dilemma of whether to search for our birthmothers and the possibility of another rejection if we do find them. Even if we do find our birthmothers after spending years searching, we may find ourselves filled with complicated feelings of anger or resentment for the original betrayal of our abandonment, perceived or real. Intensely emotional and unpredictable, our reunion stories have become fodder for public consumption, sparking curiosity and voyeurism. Gregory Choy and Catherine Ceniza Choy's essay on the film *Daughter from Danang* encourages us to think critically about the politics of such representations.

Our journeys home often involve building connections with other adoptees who share our experiences, as well as with our countries or communities of origin. Ami Inja Nafzger writes about her successful efforts to form an organization of overseas adopted Koreans, dedicated to creating understanding and acceptance of adoptees by Korean nationals and government agencies.

Adoptees seek such understanding whatever the cultures to which we return. Sometimes we find it. Closing this section is Julia Chinyere Oparah's poem about her journey to her birthfather's compound in southeastern Nigeria. There she discovers a relationship to the red earth of Igboland that is a deeply spiritual one, suggesting that, for all their complexities, our journeys home can be profoundly healing.

part six: speaking for ourselves

In creating this book, the editors envisioned a space where we adoptees could speak for ourselves—not as spokespersons for the pro- or anti-transracial adoption lobbies, as the face of multiculturalism and the possibilities for a colorblind future, or as evidence of the caring face of US interventions overseas—but as witnesses of our own truths. Part Six, the final section, focuses on the emergence of a transnational movement of transracial adoptees who have come together to heal and to speak out. This activism is fueled by our determination to define our realities for ourselves—instead of allowing our experiences to be defined by outside "experts."

Kirsten Hoo-Mi Sloth, vice president of Denmark's Korea Klubben, and Indigo Williams Willing, founder of Adopted Vietnamese International, begin this section with critiques of the dominant paradigm in adoption research. Writing against mainstream assumptions that adoptees of color should be encouraged to assimilate and to feel "the same" as their families, Sloth and Williams explore the complex, multiple identities that transracial adoptees develop as adults.

The last three chapters highlight examples of adoptee organizing. Transracial adoptee organizations create spaces for sharing our grief, learning from each other's journeys, demanding change, and speaking our truths freely, without self-censorship. Perlita Harris's essay shares conversations among members of ATRAP, the Association for Transracially Adopted People, in London, England. Sunny Jo describes the emergence of enclaves of Korean adoptees and adoptee-run organizations clustered around specific geographic centers, including Seoul, Stockholm, Brussels, San Francisco, and the Twin Cities of Minnesota. This global, multilingual community is based on personal odysseys of discovery, fluidity, and border-crossing. In this sense it is a community of outsiders within, a multilocal community vibrant with creativity and (re)invention.

We close the book with a memoir by Sandra White Hawk, founder of the US-based First Nations Orphans Association (FNOA). Through FNOA, White Hawk shares the gift of healing with other adoptees, inviting them to "come home" by connecting with Indian spirituality through Indian advocacy and support groups, elders, ceremony, and song.

moving on

In this book, we are united across national borders by our experience. We are united here in our passion to be heard and to end the self-censorship and denial that have silenced us. Many of the scholars, writers, and artists gathered in this anthology are involved in building a global transracial adoptee community. We are gathered together to struggle collectively for dignity and self-determination. We are determined to make connections between personal struggles and broader movements for peace and social justice. We are committed to challenging the use of transracial and transnational adoption as a panacea to social ills rooted in colonial histories and contemporary global inequalities. Moreover, we reject the idea that the increasing popularity of transracial adoption heralds the dawning of a new era beyond race and racism.

If one overriding theme emerges from the writings gathered here it is this: To reclaim our birthright as human beings—not as objects of exchange—and to transform our personal stories into collective action for social change, we must understand our historical connections to past generations, our past and future connections to our countries and families of origin, and our current connections to each other. In expanding the discussion of transracial adoption beyond the black/white binary, we hope to build understanding among adoptees of diverse ethnic and national origins, as well as building understanding between adoptees and non-adopted people of color and between adoptees of color and our white allies.

The editors come to this work as feminists of color. Our definition of feminism includes a commitment to reproductive justice for all. At the heart of our adoptions are the reproductive choices of our mothers—choices that were most often made in the context of limited options. For us, reproductive rights can never be reduced to the right to a safe and legalized abortion or freedom from dangerous contraceptives or forced sterilization. Instead, we must work to create and sustain a world in which low-income women of color do not have to send away their children so that the family that remains can survive. Our feminism demands that we critique a global system that bequeaths power to some mothers but not to others. It calls on us to reconsider the myths that we have been told about our birthmothers and to challenge ourselves to move past our own pain to see the limited survival choices given our mothers and communities that led to our adoptions. Although our stories lie at the intersection of feminist and global economic justice movements, white feminists and feminists of color alike have largely overlooked transracial adoption as a site of struggle. This volume is a platform for transracial adoptees to be heard, but within these pages there is also a call for a global response: It is critical—at a time when right-wing political forces are achieving global dominance—that a real transnational feminist solidarity be created, one that leads women to fight for each others' most basic human rights *to parent their own children* and that rejects transactions that pit (birth) mother against (adoptive) mother.

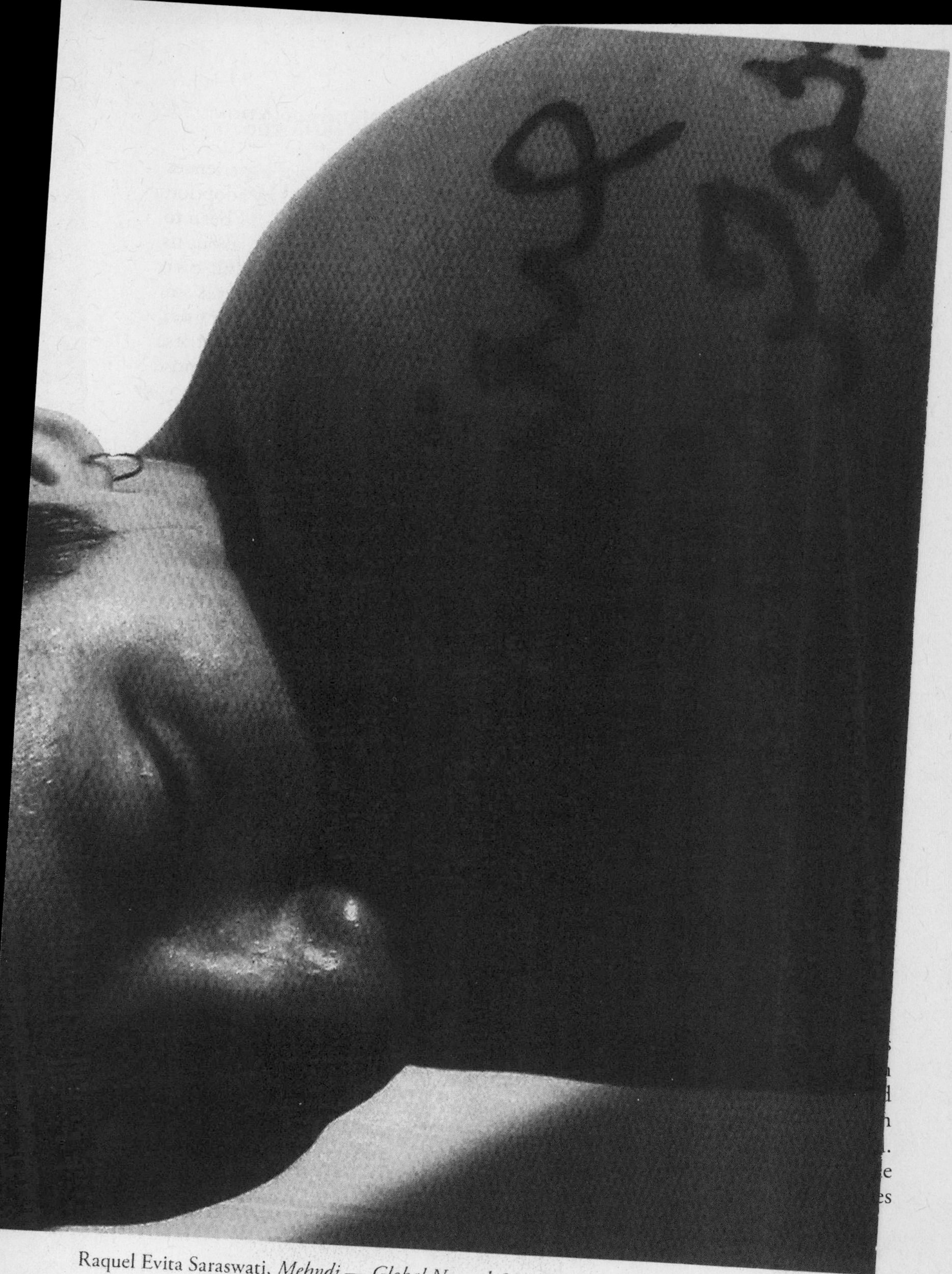

Raquel Evita Saraswati, *Mehndi — Global Nomad,* 2004, digital photograph (subject Anh Đào Kolbe)

PART ONE

WHERE ARE YOU REALLY FROM?

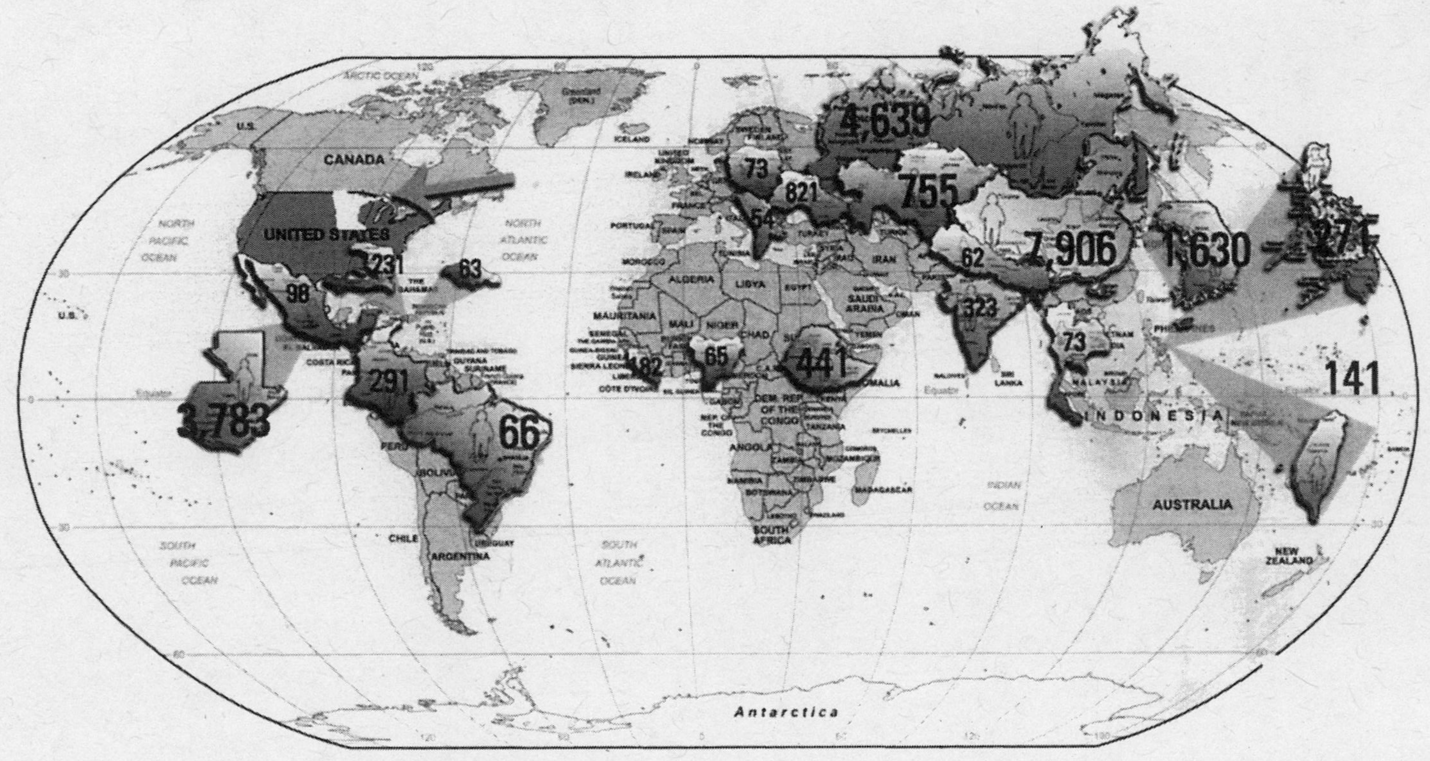

The United States is the world's largest importer of children of color and children from economically struggling former Soviet bloc countries. The US Department of State reports nearly 22,000 children entering the United States for adoption in 2005, an increase of 210% from 15 years ago (http://travel.state.gov/family/adoption/stats/stats_451.html#). *Map by Val Grimm.*

1 GARLIC AND SALT

Soo Na

shadow conversations

Umma. Bong Ok. Female birthperson. Our pain has been ascribed national borders. We have been distracted by nationalism. We have been distracted from our pain, from our stories, through the usage of arbitrary tracts of land, divided by war, famine, and imperialism. But I don't need a country in order to love, miss you, umma, to be Corean, to be mixed, any more than I need a doctor to tell me my heart's pumping to know I am alive. These things comfort us, people telling us the obvious. And it is these things that distract us. I want you. I wanted you all my life, and I am projecting my longing for you onto a country. But my love is not limited by arbitrary lines drawn on a Mercator projection. No, not by any stretch of my skin toward yours.

Thank you, Bong Ok, for sending me photos of me as a child, of my Hundred Day Celebration, of you and the aunts. These photos give me pieces of a life filled with pain, trauma, men, and whispered love. How many times have I imagined you? I'm not crazy; my life in Corea is not in my head. There's Garami, my (half) brother in Corea, whose story is entwined with my own. I'm not crazy, even when my North American parents give me threatened, closed looks as I describe my life in Corea. These same parents want me to believe that my life "began" when I got off that one-way plane from Corea in 1990. But I lived there for six years before landing here, in North America.

You were 19 when your mother died. I am 19, and although neither you nor Virginia, my mother in North America, have died, I wonder how losing a mother by death compares to the losses of mother(s) and umma(s) by transplantation.

There are deeply conservative roots in how I judged you, Bong Ok. I am sorry. I have judged you with a borrowed imperialistic white eye that also turned on me. I, in so many words, blamed you, the woman, for the physical abuse we both experienced. Blamed you because you could not keep us both safe from institutionalized patriarchy, economic exploitation, and colonialism. In my therapist's haste to allow me to admit my pain, she told me you were not a mother. But you are my umma. And you love me. Like I love you.

For years, I practiced cutting you out of my heart, or tried to, until I found out that the beating of my heart determines my humanity, and that cutting is cutting, and cutting means being alone in pain. Calling you "birthperson" dehumanized you the object, and also me, the namer. I projected so much onto you, blamed you for things out of your control, institutional things. I am sorry. You hurt me. I wanted to hurt you. In our hurting, we did not notice that we were stolen from each other.

Somebody (maybe my therapist, maybe mom, maybe me) taught me to distrust your story, to believe that somehow your story obliterated my own, my stories, reminders of that which became synonymous with my "Coreanness." Reading your letters to me from Corea, I approached your recall with the sternness of a lawyer during a cross-examination, trying to measure up my stories with yours, your memory with mine, not because we never existed, but because my family here refused to listen to me, denied parts of my memory, which feels the same as denying all of it. My stories were hypothetical and easily dismissible to my parents. My memory, like yours, was suspect and faulty. But, I ask, why would we lie about pain? I am horrified by the juridical language created to talk about the cruelty of people to themselves and each other, the conscious cutting off of emotion when admitting a part of people's very real capacity for inflicting pain on each other. Of using words like "birthperson" instead of "birthmother." Of denying the fact that you gave birth to me. Of that sticky embroilment between physical birth and emotional birth. Of love. But, wait. Untangle those words, that coercion, from our stories and we are still intact. I see us.

I realize now that my distrust of your stories was not about you. It was about my parents' denial of our collective stories, of all our stories—ummas and children, families and entire countries, separated. Children and young people shipped, flown, carried, and brought to North America, Belgium, England, France, the Netherlands, Canada, and other beaming family destinations. (It seems things are always "happening" to young people, to children, to "unwitting and unwilling" mothers.) Perhaps, implicated, is your denial of my stories.

We have both been silenced by suspicion, afraid to reveal our stories because we know that they can be used against us as "proof" that we could not have been a family. No. We were, if imperfect, a family, you and me and the men you allowed access to your body. I, noticer, talker, and storyteller in my family, was silenced with psychiatric medication, which is what people give you when they are unwilling to change the conditions that create dis-ease. I am still blamed with bringing depression and hardship into my family. And so, you see, Bong Ok, we have been abused by this house in the same way, you and I.

We were poor in Corea. Not in pain. Not in love. In North America, my family is solidly middle-class. I have a place to sleep. I have food in my belly.

I have light in my room, in my house. I have indoor plumbing. No more running out in the night with a candle to the outhouse. No more fear of falling through the hole in the wooden shack where we shat, pissed, vomited. But. I am still afraid of the loud flush of toilets, gurgling water splashing up in an invisible spray. I have things in North America. But things do not hold you when you are alone.

I am still negotiating with you, umma. I am realizing that our stories weave together, that acknowledgment of your story does not mean a necessary preclusion of my own. Something has been shattered. Some door flung open that I will never close. And I will lose some people when I acknowledge the door, while others will accompany me to the other side. And I cannot forget the people who are waiting there, people I have been holding my breath to see.

⧉ ⧉ ⧉

Your visa was denied when you tried to visit in 1998.

"Why?" I asked Virginia.

"Oh, customs thought she might be a liability. They think she wants to stay here forever."

I miss you. I see you between the lines of your letters to my parents in North America. And you have denied parts of my story. But I no longer blame you for your story:

> *January 14, 1997*
>
> *Dear Parents of Soo Na,*
>
> *Respectable parents of Soo Na, I would be grateful if you could read this letter of a sinner with generosity.*

I wonder if you wrote the expository life story letter for my parents and not for me. If you made the video for them and not for me. A transposed audience for whom you performed in order to access me. You understand that, sometimes, love is a performance.

> *Dear Soo Na and parents, may I ask you a favor? I have a favorite English vocabulary "UNDERSTANDING," which I think has a meaning of know well the character of and have a sympathetic feeling towards me.*
>
> *P.S. Please ask me to come to you if it helps Soo Na's treatment. I would like to meet her even for one day, oh no for one hour would be fine, too. Is she still cute, good and a cry baby? Are her fingers still thin and weak? Does her neck is still long? And do her eyes small? She sings well a song of "Daddy and Pastel Crayon"? [sic]*

Now I see that you felt grateful to my parents, so you wrote the letter. This was the only way to get to me. So you acted grateful. So you were deferential. See what we do for love? You never forgot me.

ᄅ ᄅ ᄅ

Whose hands were the invisible hands translating these letters between us, these oceans? Bong Ok, do you fetishize North America, white people, and power, like I do? I do not hide my colonization. And that is the only way I know how to unlearn what has been foisted onto me, without my consent. To this day, I struggle with being a person of color who grew up in a white family whose members deny their white privilege by denying the existence of white supremacy and instead tell me that racist people are "ignorant," and I should therefore ignore them, superior in my silence. Silence is not superior.

I go through the house, slowly accumulating, concentrating photos of the Corean family and me in my room. Am I slowly "disappearing" my Corean family stories from this house? Is this a reactionary hoarding or simply my way of surviving my parents' denials? Concentrating my weaker, diluted, nearly forgotten stories, metanarratives, with the ones I am too familiar with. With this house in North America. No house is free from ugliness. I believe that, at root, ugliness is just the fear of suchness (to borrow from Trinh Thi Minh-ha), of seeing things as they are. It is also the fear of judgment. Ugly is a value judgment ascribed to pain, what is painful to notice, see, acknowledge, accept, and change.

I've been eating a lot of "Corean" food. That means holding my breath while eating because the food is so spicy, nose running, mouth on fire. That means eating lots of red pepper, garlic, salt, capsicum, and white rice. Dried persimmons and tdok, sweet white rice cakes filled with red bean paste. You, my umma, Bong Ok, spoke with me today as I drove home, even though you didn't really. Even though you weren't really here with me. I asked you why you left me. I told you that, no matter how much Corean food I eat, it will never be you on the other side of my full belly. That, even if I expand into infinity, the food inside my belly will never materialize into you, and you will not suddenly tuck your hand through my belly and crawl out to hold me. I realize that I eat tdok because I want to be closer to you. I realize that through food, I realize you. It is not you, though. I have been wondering why I have been eating to the point of gross fullness. I realize now that I have been looking for you—Bong Ok, umma—on the other side of my fullness.

When did I stop being Soo Na? When did you stop being Bong Ok? I was created, molded, into Sonia. You were reified in my mind, first as umma, then as mother, then I, with therapy and my own hands, cut you away with the word "birthperson." When did our names, our stories, become contradictory, contrary, clashing? A friend once said that you don't lose your identity just because you take a wrong turn on a highway. It's not your fault that you are confused. It's the fault of the people who made the highway. It's the fault of the people who told you that there were only two exits on the highway, and you were caught between the two, told you that they were mutually exclusive, set up the highway system in the first place.

With my two bowls of kimchee and white rice, buckwheat noodles with green onions, two pairs of black chopsticks—one for serving, one for eating with—my mother and I regard each other coolly in the kitchen. This evening, I feel as though I was adopted all over again, I feel a stranger in the house. A guest who is passing through and living here temporarily, in a transitional home until I find my own place. Part of my silence at home symbolizes being re-adopted. Because I know that, when I first arrived, I did not speak English. In a way, my silence (but not the purpose of it, I want to make very clear) reminded me of my adoption, except this time I am nineteen and not six. This time I speak English and un poquito de español. Y yo puedo decir yobosayo y kamsahamnida. And I can say "hello" and "thank you." I did not forget how to say my Corean name, how to say umma, uppa. How to count to ten. I cannot understand Corean anymore. My heart still flutters, though, when I hear it. My ears perk up when I think I hear the familiar, jangling syllables.

I wondered, as my mother and I passed each other tensely in the house, how similar this was to when I first arrived. How I no longer try to figure out what this new parent wants from me, how I can best capture them in my needy child's net of indispensability. No young person ever forgets the burden of garnering approval from an older person, and it can unfortunately become an ageless task. But my silence is, in a way, reclaiming the lack of agency I had when I first arrived in North America, continued my life in this house. Acknowledging the way my name was slowly anglicized into Sonia from Soo Na, the way my name was taken away. The way my language, my food was slowly taken away, and later meted out to me in palatable "culture bites," the child of multiculturalism. And of course the palatability was defined by my parents, since I was the difference and I lived it. And how my parents want to believe that my life "began," that I was "born," in North America from a plane's exit door, a painful admission of their unwillingness to see me whole. It's funny that when I ate meat, my favorite meal was meatloaf with mashed potatoes and lots of gravy. I still crave it sometimes. And I can see the sweetness with which my mother bought a frozen vegan dinner of "meatloaf" with mashed potatoes, peas, and corn. Mom was trying to buy me something she knew I liked, before I became vegan. I see the sweet things she tries to do, but it is hard to admit them when you are also being hurt in ways that Virginia, mom, will never understand, does not want to hear about, will not acknowledge. That my thoughts around adoption, around Corea, around food and knowledge and agency, will never be truly accepted. Because I am not white. I am not white.

Desire makes life complicated. I keep repeating words to myself, words like "outgrowth," "moving beyond." But I am only fronting pseudo-transcendence of my adoption. I will never forget being adopted.

speaking the unspoken

So much of my life has been lived through speaking in the third and second person, or silence. I am trying to talk in the first person singular—in the I. And I am trying to think about the first person plural—the we. I am tired of our separated and silenced stories. I want all of us here, because we need all of us here in order to survive. I am thinking about the stories of mental illness stretched out behind me, the women whose blood courses through mine. Of Bong Ok, who drank wine to fall asleep, living with Hepatitis B. She, almost dead from an abusive ex-husband, was living with a man who raped her while she slept and asked for her body even as she struggled to drink down a spicy raw fish soup. This in a styrofoam cup, which she passed on to me, her firstborn child, a girl, as her "lover" looked on disapprovingly, jealously. She is a woman who contemplated suicide, who found safety in (g)od and (j)esus and being "born again" in (t)hem.

And of an entire family, an entire country, split in two, in a perpetual state of war: the north, "Communist," with starving people, intensive regimentation of daily life; the south, militarized, thriving on economic exploitation of women's bodies through a burgeoning military industrial (hetero)sex complex. Southern Corea with rising partner violence, brutal state repression of unionizing, and yongban (owning class) ownership of 80 percent of the country's family-owned corporations. Both sides of the country hungering for the annihilation of the vivisecting line, its forced state of unwholeness as a result of the 38th parallel. Everyone is implicated. Only in the overlap of the "two" countries, and the implication of North American imperialism in dividing the country (its communist hunts, its toppling domino theories that did not take into account that people, too, would be toppled), only in remembering, can pain be acknowledged and healing begin.

It is interesting the men Bong Ok knew in her life, and how she, now a born-again Christian, passes on a man as a savior, tells me in her letters, "Love Jesus." First, a father who kept multiple houses with multiple women. Then, a brother who sold the house from under her and her two sisters when first her mother died and then her father left. Shortly followed by a litany of lovers, the first objects of sex. Then a husband, followed by a daughter, then divorce. Finally, a new marriage, which coincided with finding (g)od, (j)esus, and the missionaries that go to Corea in search of new converts. Christian missionaries being a form of colonialism that isn't always so bad ... isn't so bad if you keep in mind that people need some hope these days. That this world has no values anymore.

Then you will see that, really, the Corean people need these missionaries, those adoption agencies. Oh, those children! Coreans simply do not know how to take care of their own children. They let them starve, they let them get abused, they let them smoke cigarettes and run the streets, filthy and unbathed. They let them go for days on end, unsupervised. Because they don't even know that eating dogs is primitive. They are ignorant of the rational fact that they should sleep on mattresses raised up from the floor. That taking off one's shoes at the door is a weird custom that should be discarded with the next day's toilet contents. That Corean people are short and stupid, speak that funny language. That, really, they need those 37,000 American troops over there just so they don't kill each other off. After all, those troops, like any good influence, emanate a sense of democracy, which the Coreans would otherwise lack. The Corean War, the Forgotten War, gave those people the right to vote, to protest. America did that. They need American soldiers at the (de)militarized zone because those crazy communists in northern Corea will try to come into the democratic south, and then who knows what will happen?

Those communists aren't too far away from China, which isn't too far from Russia, which used to be the Soviet Union, a union with nuclear capabilities. Recall the Cold War, the nuclear arms race, the race to the moon, Chernobyl. Half-lives and buried radioactivity, soot-covered factories, aching lungs, mouths covered with cloth, hundreds of people sucking on air when the last shift is done. Those core-ee-uns wearing silk, drinking lots of tea, and smelling like garlic. Those Coreans who bury their food. (I once asked Virginia, "Who invented kimchee?" And she said, "Maybe it was a mistake. You know, somebody buried it for too long, and dug it up after forgetting about it and decided to eat it.") Those Corean people who enjoy working without pay. And then, oh! Those Corean mothers who let their children get abused, who don't know any better! Who ask to be raped! Whose mothers that lived before them didn't know how to take care of them, either!

Their pathological families were doomed for failure, and no wonder they drink so much soju and smoke so many cigarettes. They're going to die off any day now, just slowly killing themselves. It's not as though they're white. It's not as though they live in America. (G)od bless 'em, they try so hard, but they just can't get capitalism right. They even needed an IMF bailout in 1997, that little dragon of the east.

But then there are social services to worry about, the "illegitimate" children to worry about, and the economy to worry about. Mental illness, han, colonialism and deprivation, living off of millet, barley, and rice. Economy-size six, eight, and twelve packs of Spam, mechanically separated meat and by-products, left over from World War One (or was it World War Two?), that North America passes off as food in its processed food business, now passed on to Corean people, who buy it up. (But how much of consumption is a choice? Think of farm subsidies, the recent suicide of Corean farmer Lee Kyung Hae in Cancún, México, in protest of the World Trade Organization summit. Bong Ok's husband is a farmer, hires himself out with his tractor to work people's fields. Then there are "free" trade "agreements," offshore sweatshops, tariff-free zones.) And, recently, I heard a radio announcement about a proposal to bury nuclear waste on a fishing island off of, but a part of, the Corean peninsula. The Corean fisherpeople are afraid that it will wreck business: "Who will want to eat raw fish when you have radioactive waste buried right next to where it was harvested?" asked one man. The person narrating the report added, "It will take 35,000 years for the nuclear waste to lose its radioactivity." Yes, some of these subatomic particles have half-lives that are more than 1000 times our short lives. Some have half-lives of over millions of years. I ask, if the 37,000 US troops refused to engage in imperial occupation 50 years ago, would there be a need to bury 35,000 years' worth of radioactivity?

Between bitterness, sadness, longing, and white supremacy; between misogyny and the mental illness industry, classism, imperialism, and neo-colonialism; missionaries and Christianity, Taoism and Buddhism, neo-Confucianism and Shamanism; murder, repression, and oppression; between adoption and the ocean, entre la espada y la pared, between the devil and the deep blue sea, between therapist's words of advice, imbibed pills, anticonvulsants, injections in the fleshy part of the butt, we have these words.

It's not romantic. This is not an elegy for a working-class struggle survival story. But it is survival. And I am not going to turn this into "Evita"-style cinematics. There is nothing beautiful about this. There is nothing histrionic about the stories and memories of people. This cannot be appropriated. This cannot be aggrandized.

I need garlic and salt.
Yes garlic and salt
Salt for my wounds
Garlic for to make the ugliness palatable.
Yes garlic and salt.

2 LOVE IS COLORBLIND

Reflections of a Mixed Girl

Jeni C. Wright

memory #1

I'm nine years old and have just finished taking one of my first showers by myself. I am going to look for Q-tips for my itchy ears when it happens: I catch a glimpse of myself in the foggy medicine cabinet mirror. It happens suddenly, the way you run over a small animal. I move closer, wiping the steam away with the edge of my towel, and start to weep.

My face looks like it belongs in the National Geographic movie on Africa we watched in social studies last week, the one Mrs. Dunbar had to turn off in the middle—she hadn't known there would be bare-breasted women in it. The boys I play kickball with at recess didn't talk about anything else all week.

I lean over the sink so my nose is almost touching the glass and mouth to the ugly girl staring back, *you look like an ugly African bush girl,* over and over until my breath clouds over my face. I start to write "jungle bunny" in the steam but I am crying too hard to finish. Why hadn't anyone told me I was so ugly? I don't even look like a real girl. Opening the medicine cabinet, I reach past the Q-tips for my father's little black comb. My quest to comb my curly short afro flat to my scalp keeps me in the bathroom for close to an hour. It feels like forever, especially because in the end I fail. That night I write in my diary until my fingers ache as bad as my scalp. The first sentence of my entry is, "It's a good thing I'm smart because no one is ever going to marry me."

memory #2

Ten years later, I come home from college and find my little sister Mary with three matted dreadlocks where her long curls had been. They are true locks, the kind you cannot get rid of unless they are cut out at the root. I discover all this while kneeling over the side of my parents' bathtub, ready to wash Mary's hair so my mother can "do something with it" for church the next day. As soon as I unravel her bun, I see the damage. I am furious. Fingers entangled in the tangled growth, I yell for my mother. By the time she arrives, her cheeks red with concern and the exertion of stair-climbing, I have a chorus of accusations waiting.

Accusations are easy to make when you were adopted by white parents and you yourself did not come into the world with white skin. For a long time I was angry. Angry that people stared at my family, angry that my parents had never experienced racism, angry that I had to struggle with the intricacies of racial discrimination by myself. Angry that no one looked like me—not my parents, not my Vietnamese brother, not my white sister, not my classmates, not the kids in my neighborhood.

卍 卍 卍

I hid a children's book catalogue in my room for two years because there was a picture of a child model who had my exact features, down to the curly hair, light brown skin, and pink lips. When *The Cosby Show* came on the air, I watched it religiously, trying to pick up clues about black people. *The Souls of Black Folk* and *Invisible Man* were on my bookshelf by the time I was thirteen. I wanted to know about "my people."

memory #3

What I had been told about race by my parents could be summed up in three words—Love Is Colorblind. My mom hand-stitched that ideal into the quilt hanging in my childhood bedroom. It is a beautiful ideal but one I had learned the limits of by first grade.

A little girl stands in the aisle of the school bus and declares that she cannot sit next to me because of my skin color. I don't tell anyone when I get home but apparently the bus driver does, because the girl's mother shows up with her daughter at my house that afternoon to offer an apology. And here's what I recall most strongly: the door closing behind the contrite woman and her daughter and my mother turning to me and saying "you should have told her, *well I don't want to sit next to fat girls!*"

My mother starts crying and I end up sitting in her lap with my arms around her, trying to be comforting. Even as I do it I know that this is not the way it is supposed to be. My mother's anger at seeing her daughter hurt has overtaken her ability to make things right. She arms me with a petty remark and weepy wishes that the world was a different place.

My wish is that instead she had given me the gift of a simple acknowledgment: that our home may be colorblind but outside sometimes wasn't. And that was unfair. And it was OK to feel sad or mad about that. But no matter what, she would always love me, and so would everyone else in our wonderful, multicolored family.

I was teetering on the edge of adolescence when my sister Mary was adopted as an infant. Even though I was barely twelve when she came home, the neighbors at first wondered if I had given birth to her, because we looked like "real sisters."

I found out a few years later that she was biracial like myself, though her white mother was Greek, not Polish-German like mine, and her father was from Haiti, not New Haven. The only thing I really cared about though was that I had a family member who looked like me.

I promised myself she would not suffer the way I had.

At the very least they would learn how to do her hair.

memory #4

That day when I discover Mary's three matted dreadlocks, my heart hardens against the years of love my parents have provided. What matters shrinks to the space of that cramped bathroom where my accusations overflow all the way up to the damp ceiling.

When my mother enters the bathroom, I turn and yell like it is my knotty hair being pulled apart.

Why didn't you take care of her hair?! Why didn't you comb her hair? Why didn't you take care of her hair, she's gonna have to cut it all off, start over, cut it off, she's gonna have to cut it all off!

What happens next: My mother becomes frightened. I start sobbing breathlessly. And Mary screams for all of us.

She sits in the tub howling, shaking her head so violently her three stiff bundles of hair tremble. She starts yelling, *I don't want to cut it off, I'm gonna be ugly, I'll have no friends, no one's gonna like me, I'LL BE UGLY!*

Water splashes over the side of the tub and I know I have to leave. My knees ache and everything else aches and I know that if I stay there with shampoo in my eyes and my snot dripping into the tub and my mother pressed up against the sink... I will drown, and not in water either.

I get up off my knees and run to my room. And even after I leave I can still hear my sister's voice, only this time it's screaming, *I hate my hair!*

Afterwards in my room, I remember my campaign to convince my mother that my sister's hairstyle mattered. I thought I was protecting my sister when I hounded my mother to grow Mary's hair out: Did she want Mary to be mistaken for a little boy the way I had been? Did she want her to be teased?

I assumed the victory was mine when Mary's afro was long enough to be put into ponytails. Then I went away to school and left my mother to carry the torch. She dropped it without knowing what it was.

⧉ ⧉ ⧉

During vacations I hauled my sister off to the bathtub to attend to hair that hadn't been properly combed in months. My mother claimed she couldn't handle all the crying, a line that made me grit my teeth and turn away.

When Mary got older, I told her, with anger in my voice, *you're not white, you don't have straight hair like your friends, you can't just leave it alone and it'll be fine. It gets tangled, you have to take care of it.* She resented me and my words, but she resented her hair even more.

I could see her desire every time a shampoo commercial came on. The glistening long straight hair, flowing across the screen, rippling like sunshine, was too much for me to see reflected in my sister's eyes. I looked away instead. The pain in her eyes made her eyes look too much like mine.

It was hard to explain this pain to my parents. It took a long time, longer than it did to realize how terrified I was of seeing myself in my little sister. That happened about three years ago, around the time I took a pair of scissors to my head and cut off most of the hair I had spent ten years growing. The hairdresser I went to afterwards to even it out gave me a cut so short I couldn't look in the mirror for a full week.

The person I saw when I finally looked was not the little girl who believed herself to be too ugly to marry anyone.

I saw a woman who knew what it was like to be on the outside, a beautiful woman who had developed the love to tell the people who loved her how that felt.

3 POWER OF THE PERIPHERY

Kim Diehl

Being a transracial adoptee may be the most radicalizing force in my life, one that has coursed through me with an intense and raw power. I see parts of myself in so many humans. I share the pain and victories of other displaced, abandoned, and re-birthed people. We on the periphery, learning and watching from the outside, have a particular power with revolutionary roots.

"Solidarity" is more often spoken than practiced. But as a mixed-race transracial adoptee, I simply can't afford to mess around with something so essential to my well-being, to squander a relationship because it no longer serves a strategic purpose or the person has different values than me. Without a birth family or ancestral roots to show me who I came from, I have looked to other marginalized and displaced people for guidance and wisdom.

My thirst for solidarity is directly connected to living on the margins as a not-quite black, raised by white people, bisexual Christian. I am accustomed to living on the outside of identities, cultures, and communities. I have had to create my own communities and, as fun and lighthearted as this creating was at times, I have also been compelled to seriously confront the heaviness of isolation.

About 10 years ago, on a cold winter day, I knelt on my bed and asked the Creator to please give me a community of women, preferably black women. That was my prayer. I needed to feel whole and I needed a cadre of kick-ass women to help me get there. My loneliness was 20 years old and I was starving for community.

My desperate prayer was answered that summer and the following year as I became more involved in community organizing. My longtime feelings about justice came together with women with similar concerns who made me comfortable and encouraged me to be my quirky self. No one called my humor, sexuality, and speech "white." Prayer life and spirituality became central in my life and a community of strong Yoruba, pagan, and Christian healers embraced me. My fascinating journey of loving and healing myself began. I was no longer starving.

power in the periphery

As I learn more about the history of adoption in the United States, I realize how profoundly and intimately the political forces of women's rights, children's rights, and the narrowly framed family values movement have impacted my life. To counter the religious Right's strategy of stripping resources from already debilitated public services while giving tax breaks to adoptive parents, we have to ask broader questions about family structures. Who gets labeled a family member and who is property? Who really benefits from adoptions? Are children's rights taken into consideration during the adoption process?

These are questions from the margins, where the traditional is rolled around, challenged, and turned inside out. Edward Said, the Palestinian writer/activist, wrote in his 1996 book, *Representations of the Intellectual,* that the periphery is "where you see things that are usually lost on minds that have never traveled beyond the conventional or comfortable." In the periphery is where I discover forgiveness and hope. In the periphery is where I struggle with rejection and dislocation. This unconventional place is also where I make connections and explore contexts for my life.

stamp of approval

I was one baby in the United States who was not taken from my black parents through misuse of vagrancy laws so my labor could be rented out to white families. I, fortunately, did not have to live in a crowded orphanage and my birthmother probably was not fined for having illegitimate me, nor sent to prison. I was not lifted from my home country in a plane that made it, or in a plane that crashed. The agency I was placed through probably had more legal accountability and checks and balances than those operating at the turn of the century. I was not one of the Japanese children forcibly removed to internment camps. I was not one of the thousands of indigenous children to be separated from her family and sent to a school to be beaten for speaking my native tongue.

My separation as a brown child from my birthmother was much more sanitized and devoid of blatant political connections. However, I did not have any power in the decision to seal my records; I did not have any power in the decision to take federal money away from social service programs that might have prevented family breakup; I did not have any power in the decision to make it a child placement agency policy to ignore race; I did not have any power to keep from being the physical embodiment of a political process that stamped its approval on transracial adoptions in a country founded on the enslavement and oppression of people of color.

dislocation

When I was seven weeks old I was given to my adoptive family, the Diehls. I have a photo of my mother, who is holding me while I stare at her face: my eyes squinting, eyebrows furrowed, and mouth stern. My expression tells the story of little babies dropped on stoops, babies whose hearts are glad to be in arms again but are broken from separation. Thirty years later, I pass my reflection and my gaze is serious, solemn, even when I feel relaxed. I am still that infant, displaced and confused, but I am also that infant, glad to be held, safe in a process of healing.

My first nine years were spent in Miami, Florida, a place where the wind is always speaking through the trees, bodies of water rise and fall with the tides, and many languages, colors, smells, and political struggles coincide. It is also a place where political refugees and displaced families float ashore with the hopes of restarting their lives.

My childhood was set against the backdrop of an expanding Cuban community led by upper-class, professional Cuban-born immigrants who ran from Fidel Castro's communist government in the 1960s. Twenty years later, after successfully infusing a conservative, Catholic-influenced political agenda into local Miami politics, the city became forcibly integrated with new Cuban immigrants who fled in a one-time legal exodus from the port of Mariel. Over 125,000 Cubans bolted for New York City, Tampa, and Miami during the Mariel Boat Lift, which lasted from April through September of 1980. Of this group, most were working class, not former landowners or business people. Some were former prisoners or patients in mental hospitals. That summer, a great class and culture clash unfolded in Miami.

I was five, getting ready to start kindergarten and still talking to my imaginary friends. I didn't understand the Mariel Boat Lift, but I saw the long lines at homeless shelters, noticed my brother and his friends talking more and more about The Cubans, overheard adults mentioning Castro, boats, rafts, and jobs. Tensions had already been ebbing and flowing, but that summer I detected an edge when I heard Spanish-speakers talking in the mall, in the grocery store, and in the post office. I knew something was up because my parents told us we were never to use the word "spic" even though I'd already heard my brothers' friends say it. Much later, when I read about the Boat Lift in high school, I felt a strange sense of familiarity with the people who left Cuba. Different circumstances and decisions impacted their lives, but I began to understand my own displacement in the context of the Mariel Boat Lift.

Now, when people talk about their displacement and feeling stuck, I get it. I get how we love our safe harbors and resent them at the same time. I know the complicated feelings and not having any way to get rid of them except tolerating them to the point of using the inherent contradictions as sources of power. This way, I feel free and uninhibited to "talk shit" about white people but go home and eat happily at my parents' table. It hurts to be a woman of color and be part of a family with white privilege. It also feels liberating to have that perspective and know firsthand how white people move through the world instead of its being a mystery.

secondhand ancestry

My family took a vacation to the United Kingdom when I graduated high school. We were celebrating my parent's 25th year of marriage. They had been researching their ancestry and wanted to explore the place where some of the Diehl relatives came from. During their time of research, I felt a gnawing in my spirit for knowledge. Once again, I found myself on the outside. This time, I stood on the sidelines of one of the most important parts of our human existence: ancestry.

At the time, I had just started dreadlocks. My new twists were just two weeks young and I was leaving for college in two months. I was ready to fly, though my race analysis was still tender and pink, like the new skin over a wound. Itching for any connection to blackness, African cultures, and multiracial people who looked like me, I stood in London's parks, marveling at all the public space, my eyes absorbing as much as they could hold. I saw mixed race couples too numerous to count and I felt myself, an 18-year-old woman, discovering identity. My hair was locking and would soon become thick ropes of entangled curls, heavy, and full. I was starting to feel free.

The second week, we drove out of the city and headed north into Scotland. We were traveling to the towns of my mother's and father's ancestors. My brother, mother, and father, giddy with excitement, scoured maps to find the easiest route to the cemeteries where we could read headstones that bore the names of these ancestors. Deep in my body lived an inconsolable emptiness. My new sense of freedom transformed into rage. I was tired of secondhand ancestry, relying on the Scottish-Germans to navigate my route to cemeteries with headstones and markers that were supposed to fill me with a sense of belonging. Standing in the streets of those sleepy towns, my heart broke. And I had no one, not even an imaginary friend, to console me. I didn't even have words, just feelings of abandonment and some new twists on my head.

Notorious for mood swings, I swerved into gloom and tried to break up the party. I answered their questions with grunts and, finally, to my family's relief, I took a solitary walk. Later, as we ate lunch in a Chinese restaurant, I tried to imagine my search for ancestry. Which cemeteries hold my people? What roads and rivers did they travel? In a random town in Scotland, imagining my people's struggles, desires, and triumphs, I started a journey that I am on to this day.

My search is slow, filled with waiting lists, frustration, and over-intellectualization. I apply political spin to the process: *I am not a political refugee but a product of a series of political decisions that evolved, shifted, and disappeared over the course of US history. In a sense, I am a product of public and private interventions that took me from one family and a temporary harbor to, finally, a permanent home. This, after a lot of paperwork, financial exchanges, and laws guided me into my family's arms.*

I also use the waiting periods as opportunities to prepare myself for the next stages. In the last two years, I have taken on depression, that eggshell fragile temperament whose real name is Anger.

I have a few transracially adopted friends and we walk with a companion called Melancholy. We disappear for periods of time and cannot be reached. I've learned this is a survival mechanism that keeps us intact while struggling with displacement and isolation. Melancholy has kept me awake many nights in my life. To calm myself I turned to music. At nine, I discovered "Eleanor Rigby" on my parent's Beatles album and I spun the record endlessly, replaying that depressing, stark, raw song over and over: *Look at all the lonely people; where do they all belong?* At that point, it was the closest I could get to feeding my blues. If I had known about Muddy Waters, Robert Johnson, Etta James, or Nina Simone, I'd have played them too, crying with the familiarity of being an outcast, hungry for some alienation music to be my companion.

In college, I made friends with other southern black women who gave me a nickname, "Turtle," like how I'd heard other black people refer to their cousin, "Snookie" or "Lee Lee." My nickname meant I belonged, I had people. My friends knew I periodically left and returned, sometimes with a friendly but distant manner that reminded them of turtles. I have worked hard at staying present but I also have my familiar, comforting turtle shell to climb into whenever I need it. My shell is a place of refuge and retreat, but as I heal and feel whole, I allow others to join me, opening myself to the world. I think it means I'm relating to myself, emerging from my reclusive spot, sharing and living openly.

My separation from ancestral roots, from blood relatives, and from knowledge about moving through the world as a woman of color has often been a lonely struggle. Having to fumble my way alone through mixed identities, horrible self-esteem about my African hair and body, and alienation from people of color communities was wounding.

I learned very early how to lie in order to feel like I fit in. My imaginary world collided with truth and I chose the safety of denial. I remember in preschool or kindergarten lying to a classmate about not being adopted when it was obvious to anyone with sight that I did not look like my German- and Scottish-descent family. I told her my grandmother had curly hair (from regular perms), so that's where I got my curly hair. I clutched at whiteness because the people who raised me were immersed in white culture. The church we went to every Sunday and sometimes during the week was entirely white, except for one other family with adopted children of color. The record collection my parents owned was mostly white, except one Harry Belafonte and one Bill Cosby record.

Each lie brought me further away from myself and I could feel rocks piling on my chest, heavy and sharp. I burned with humiliation every time someone asked, "What are you?" I didn't want to be black because I was becoming injected with light-skin privilege and white supremacy. I knew black people were rarely accepted into honors classes, libraries, vacations to Peru and Mexico, museums, and power. I didn't have the words to explain why, but I knew blackness in the United States would not open elite doors to a world I could move through as a white-ish person partially shielded by my family's all-white privilege.

I tried to believe I was white because I could not imagine any alternatives, could not belong to any communities that looked like me, and certainly could not bear rejection from black communities if I chose to identify as black. It wasn't just that I was alone. I had to form an analysis about racism while being lovingly embraced by white people.

Because, despite all that separates us, I have a fairly close relationship with my family. While my sexuality is certainly a tense issue, we call each other on the phone, exchange emails, and visit one another. My mother and I have grown especially close in the last ten years and I see parts of her in myself. Sometimes I say a word and the voice I hear is my mother's. My signature is starting to look like hers and occasionally I use hand gestures that mirror my mother's. I respect her ways and how she's accepted mine. She is good at forgiving and forgetting. She gets angry and she lets us know she's pissed off, but I've never seen her hold a grudge. She takes me to the African American art museum in her small Florida town and brings me to the Zora Neale Hurston Festival in Eatonville. She does these things for herself. She likes to spend time with me and she makes me feel wanted.

My parents know grief and through their experiences I have learned some important lessons about dealing with my own losses. Years before I was born, their three-year-old daughter passed away from a blood disorder. My mother has spoken to me about it a few times, saying it was devastating. Saying if she could do it over again, she would have tried to deal with it more quickly, instead of retreating.

I, like most other people, especially transracial adoptees, am still developing my extensive toolkit for survival and healing. Instead of retreating, I have my compass to navigate through painful abandonment struggles; a chisel to shape my analyses about racial identities and race relations; a screwdriver to connect identities fused together by years of living in the undeniable intersections of family, politics, community, and religion.

I look at my toolkit and it is filled with liberating techniques and gifts that help me maneuver as a multiracial, bisexual, spirit-filled southern woman. It also has dusty, sharp edges that scrape me when I least expect it, and I am forced to examine and file down those edges (usually named denial, invisibility, shame, and helplessness) to make my life flow more smoothly. I believe I live the legacy of every multiracial person, each adoptee, particularly transracial adoptees, of transforming the wounds of separation into marks of compassion, intensity, and joy. We are the colonized and the colonizers and we have a special place in this world.

Tracey Moffatt, *Early Theft, Draw A Map,* 2004, colour inkjet print on archival paper, 118 x 75cm

4 FINDING THE UNIVERSAL

Reflections on a Multi-Prismed Identity

Mark Hagland

I remember reading an interview with a well-known African American lesbian activist several years ago. This activist was asked a question something like, "How do you prioritize your identities? Are you a woman first, or black, or gay?" And the activist, to her credit, responded by saying, essentially, "Well, honey, it's not as though I can walk out the door and leave one of my identities behind. I'm all three, and my identities all go wherever I go." I'm paraphrasing, of course, but I was struck by the simplicity and power of her response to what has probably been a frequent line of inquiry into her sense of identity.

Like that activist, I often find my multiple identities, and their relations with one another, coming into play in my daily life and in my interactions with people from a very broad range of backgrounds and experiences. As a person with multiple identities—among other things, I am a man, an American, an Asian American, an adult Korean adoptee, a gay person, a partnered gay person, the father of a daughter, a twin, the brother of a transgendered woman, a journalist, and a spiritual seeker—I constantly find myself referencing one or more of my identities in relation to each other and to the mainstream society, as I navigate daily life and continue to construct and evolve my own overall identity.

I've come to believe that my diverse identities strongly inform, enlighten, and ultimately strengthen one another. For example, I have long said that the experiences of being a Korean adoptee and of being a gay man are very similar. I am hyperaware, on a day-to-day basis, of my difference from most of society in both cases, and of the multiple assumptions people make regarding racial, ethnic, and sexual identity that impact how they view and interact with me personally. Naturally, I become aware of pressures to conform to broad societal norms and expectations, pressures that vary depending on the context. For example, when I am in public with my beautiful five-year-old daughter, people tend to assume I am heterosexual; when I am socializing with a group of gay men in a big-city restaurant, a different set of expectations seems to apply; and when I find myself with Asian Americans who are clearly culturally Asian, an entirely different set of expectations comes to the fore. In every case, it is one or at most two slices of myself that I am aware are visible, while of course the rest of me is still there, sometimes uncomfortably aware of my difference from others in the social context of the moment.

Indeed, I find that there is another, very specific way in which being a gay adult is analogous to being an adult Korean adoptee. All the Korean adoptees I've met have expressed a profound awareness of their difference in the world, and of the need to consciously evolve their sense of identity toward a place of integration and harmony. Gay men and lesbians face the same conundrum: like transracial adoptees, they find themselves compelled to consciously construct an identity, often struggling through isolation and confusion to reach clarity and peace. (My twin, who identifies now as a transgendered woman, says the same thing is true for transgendered people.)

The fact that the two identities are similar in certain ways means to me that we can learn from one another and strengthen and support one another through our experiences. Being a Korean adoptee has been life-shaping and remains extremely important, but so has being a gay man, and a twin, and now a parent. My experience tells me that there is universality in the particular, that we as Korean adoptees (and indeed, all transracial adoptees) should feel connected to others who have also experienced profound difference.

When I attended my first mini-gathering of Korean adoptees in Minneapolis in the fall of 2000, I was intensely insecure beforehand about how I would be accepted by the other adoptees. I feared that, despite our commonalities, I might be ostracized or marginalized because of my sexual orientation. To my great relief, I found I was fully embraced. Indeed, the adult Korean adoptee community as it is now evolving is one of the most accepting of personal diversity of any of the communities to which I "belong" as a member of various categories. Adult Korean adoptees know what it means to have been emotionally and socially isolated and marginalized. I grew up in Milwaukee in the 1960s as though I were a Martian in a spaceship; when I discovered the adult adoptee community on the cusp of my 40th birthday, it was as though I'd happened upon a convention for Martians in spaceships!

Of course, sorting out all my identity choices has been an ongoing task and, indeed, one I will keep at all my life. That is why I believe the notion of "constructed identity" is so important for me and for my readers to consider. In contrast to most middle-class, white, heterosexual American males, for example, who likely do not face such questions, those of us from groups that register as "other" inevitably face issues around our identity, and generally are compelled to work toward resolution of those issues. For individuals who find ourselves working through a thicket of identity issues, uncomplicated, unquestioning self-definition is not possible. I am profoundly "other" in my society, and thus find identity construction a psychological and intellectual imperative, if I am to find some internal peace navigating my way in society.

Being the father of a young child, I am constantly being made aware of such things. My daughter loves to play with her mother's lipstick and is surprised to find that "Only mommies wear lipstick, not daddies" (of course, some daddies actually do wear lipstick, but that's a whole different discussion!), and that those people at the mall (other Asians) look like Daddy, but they're speaking a different language. Indeed, my daughter, being a delightful blend of ethnicities (including Korean, Iranian, Irish, and German), will inevitably find herself faced with the task of constructing a racial and ethnic identity for herself from the one I've constructed for myself. I will, of course, do everything I can to help her become able to embrace her self-definition.

The gap between one's self-definition and the identity attributed to one by others has been at the heart of what I call my "cognitive dissonance" as a Korean adoptee—the fact that people have always identified me with Asian societies and Asian cultures, even though I was raised in Milwaukee by parents of Norwegian and German descent. Their categorization of me causes complications both when whites and other non-Asians are involved, and when culturally-Asian Asians are involved.

To cite just one example, some 20 years ago my twin and I went to a Korean film being shown as part of the Chicago International Film Festival. The audience turned out to be at least 90 percent Korean, which surprised us a bit, as audiences at most festival films were broadly representative of Chicago's diverse population. When a middle-aged Korean woman squeezed past me in our row and said, "Excuse me," in Korean, a phrase I didn't know or understand at the time, I responded in English. This apparently astonished her, causing her to gasp. Ever since, I've referred to that woman's expression as the "astonished Korean lady face." I've seen it again—many times.

At KADapalooza, the Korean adoptee mini-gathering held in Los Angeles in the spring of 2001, our hosts put a humorous twist on all this, handing out T-shirts that said "Stealth AZN" on them—the slogan referring to the fact that most people who encounter adult Korean adoptees tend to make huge assumptions about our cultural identity. Those assumptions (branding us as culturally Asian, though most of us grew up in very non-Asian cultural environments, creating identities that are very distinct and unusual in American or European societies) are similar to the broad and intense assumptions of heterosexuality that complicate the lives of gay men, lesbians, and bisexuals in our society. Often, these societal assumptions meet and intersect, creating situations rife with potential confusion. For example, when I am in public with my young daughter, most people assume that I am culturally Asian, that I am married, and that I am heterosexual, none of which is true. Yet most of the time it is neither readily possible nor appropriate to expend a lot of energy clarifying my situation.

moving toward integration

On a far more profound level, all my experience as a member of diverse, often highly marginalized, categories in society has compelled me to consciously develop an integrated (rather than merely composite) identity, one that encompasses all of who I am and brings me to a level of self-acceptance and self-actualization that will allow me to be at peace and in harmony in the world.

Has this been difficult? Of course it has. Has it been intellectually challenging? Certainly. Yet I honestly believe that the challenges I've faced in my life because of my Korean adoptee identity and other identities have been a wonderful spiritual gift. Simply in being who I am and living as I do, I know that I cause many people I encounter in my personal and professional life to question their assumptions about a wide range of issues, including race, sexual and gender orientation, genetics and environment (nature versus nurture), life relationships, and family. Is that not a gift that all of us transracial adoptees end up giving to the world, whether we desire to give it or not?

The potential transracial adoptees possess for enhancing mutual understanding and compassion is powerful. Somehow, I can't help but believe that we were meant individually and collectively to be teachers of a sort, to use our individual and collective experiences to bring greater understanding of identity to our society. But consider an alternative stance: my taking the position "You can never understand me if you are not a Korean adoptee."

The ultimate extension of this kind of thinking leads to wars, conflicts, and misunderstandings on all levels, from the global to the interpersonal: "You are not black/you are not Serbian/you are not a Muslim/you are not a Mormon/you are not disabled/you are not a vegetarian," ad infinitum. In other words, my specialness makes me better than you, and also sets me up as a victim/blessed, and so on, whereas you, being white/Croatian/Hindu/non-Mormon/able-bodied/meat-eating, keeps you from understanding me as a human being. The emotional logic of such self-positioning is devastating to human and inter-group interaction, yet we see such emotional logic being played out every day in news reports from across the world.

By definition, I will never know what it is to be a woman, to be African American, to be disabled, or to be deaf. But our strength as humans lies in our ability to extend beyond our tiny self-worlds and see the deep humanity and the divine spark in one another.

So my plea to my adoptee brothers and sisters is this: let us use our unusual, our exceptional, experiences as transracial adoptees to further mutual understanding among all human beings, to join with all other "others" in celebrating the universality of our humanity in our particulars. By doing so, we will make life easier both for other Korean adoptees, and for everyone. For in the end, I am both uniquely myself and also one tile in the mosaic of humanity. And I lose nothing as a tile in acknowledging the exquisite glory of the mosaic.

PART TWO

HOW DID YOU GET HERE?

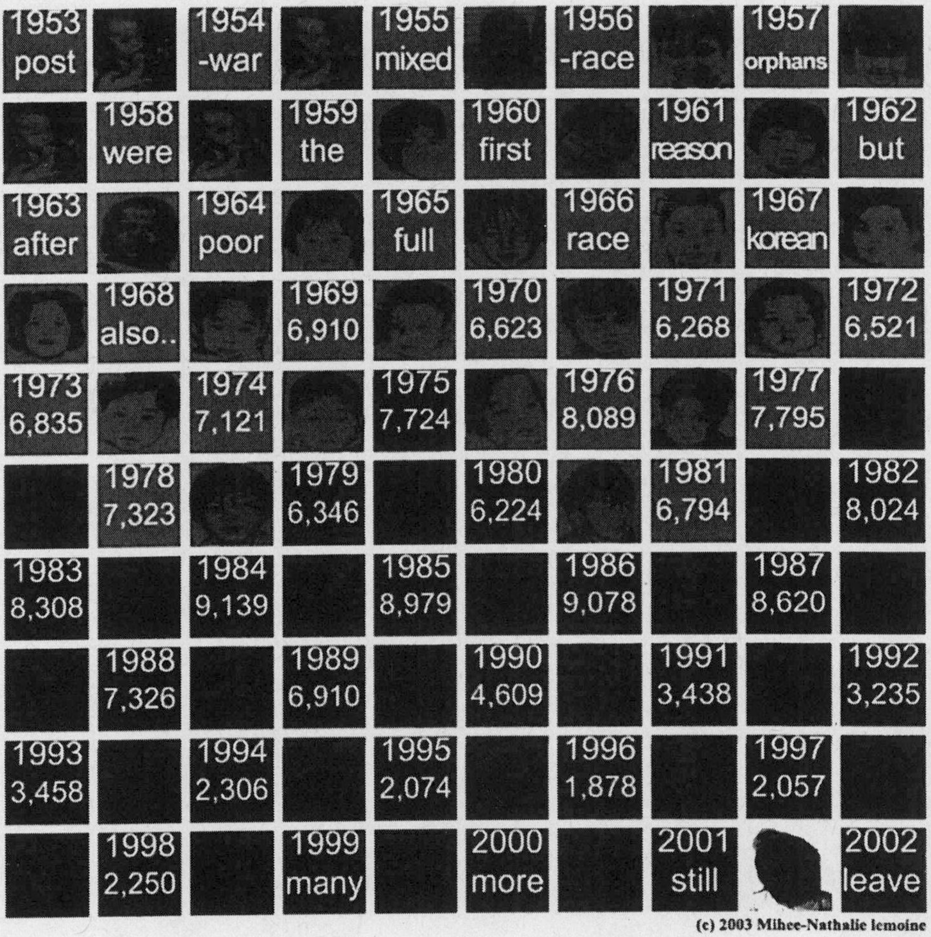

1953 post
1954 -war
1955 mixed
1956 -race
1957 orphans
1958 were
1959 the
1960 first
1961 reason
1962 but
1963 after
1964 poor
1965 full
1966 race
1967 korean
1968 also..
1969 6,910
1970 6,623
1971 6,268
1972 6,521
1973 6,835
1974 7,121
1975 7,724
1976 8,089
1977 7,795
1978 7,323
1979 6,346
1980 6,224
1981 6,794
1982 8,024
1983 8,308
1984 9,139
1985 8,979
1986 9,078
1987 8,620
1988 7,326
1989 6,910
1990 4,609
1991 3,438
1992 3,235
1993 3,458
1994 2,306
1995 2,074
1996 1,878
1997 2,057
1998 2,250
1999 many
2000 more
2001 still
2002 leave

(c) 2003 Mihee-Nathalie lemoine

Mihee-Nathalie Lemoine, *50 Numbers*, Seoul 2003, digital image

5 ECONOMIC MIRACLES

Sun Yung Shin

Also this confusion about Korean names is further complicated by the fact that Korean women retain their maiden name even after marriage.

A visitor left me her calling card in a celadon bowl. Paper fish, a palm without fingers, an opaque windowpane to be pricked or burned with a cigarette. How far does a burning wall perfume the sky?

Is the visitor my enemy? Why am I teaching her English when she speaks almost as well as I? What a vast land: "almost." From Tokyo, she is half Korean & half Japanese and says to me in her breaking English, "We look so much alike we could almost be sisters!"

Lesson: poets are not qualified to teach Conversational English as a Second, Third, Fourth, Fifth language. My subversive thoughts were running away from our two-way mirror, out the room, under the door.

Legally abandoned
orphan
foster child
eligible for adoption
immigrant
legal resident alien
naturalized citizen
alien registration number A35300104
passing for American-born
passing for Chinese
my maiden name even after marriage

I didn't know Jesus of Nazareth
had siblings. Aramaic is not even
my second language. And so my heart
leapt for Joseph. Our father,
who art in shadow.

The statues of Mary
show one swaddled infant, the first.

Held by her left
arm to protect her
heart or held by her right
arm to protect his?

The family trees of most Koreans have been accurately kept for many centuries with some traced to over 1500 years. Koreans have a pride in their ancestry and the origin of their family name.

One takes pride in a defect
such as poor eyesight. To have been born
in a time of spectacles is a miracle. Had I been
a nobleman's daughter, I would have been good
at ripping the seams out of clothing
to wash the pieces, but not good
at sewing them back
together. What sisters are for. What
mothers are for.

What servants are for.

At the eye doctor I fail to read my ancestral chart, the giant E combs the giant white poster into a blurring rain. The chart reads me and while the doctor turns away it wrinkles into a snicker. The black spoon's concave palm momentarily protects the left eye from the scorn of the right. If eyes could talk and mouths could read…

With their grace and poise the Korean women have much to offer a modern society.

What has a modern society to offer us? Have the world's women formed a government-in-exile and where can I take the civil service test? How many poems shall I write? How quickly shall I pass.

What shall we hide under our Western dress aside from our modesty? What style modernity between millions of pairs of daikon legs?

Many foreigners coming to Korea hear about the Korean "kisaeng" and may even have an opportunity to attend a "kisaeng" party where they are royally entertained by a bevy of attractive girls. For the average Westerner this sudden flood of feminine attention is almost overwhelming. The expense of an evening with "kisaeng" recreation can leave a heavy dent in one's pocketbook, so be prepared.

I was not prepared
when the visitor took back her card
so quickly it nicked me across the cheek. And yet
I turned, and kept turning
the other one. I waited

for a matched set. I practiced

my English in my borrowed face and practiced
pretending to be half-Japanese.

My son says inside when he means outside.
He says close the door when he wants it opened.

The education of women was as impractical during the Yi Dynasty as sending the family cow to learn the Chinese classics.

A young girl could go far in the entertainment world if she showed real promise in creative poetry which was the Korean sijo.

A poet learned in the art
of conversation! Counting syllables
for the sijo. Counting cups
of soju going down my host
father's throat. Though we may be cows
we count, so be prepared for this sudden
flood of feminine attention.

The older kisaeng took great care in finding a ranking nobleman to spend the first night with the newly graduated girl. Throughout her entire life, the kisaeng was proud of her "first night man." The life of the kisaeng is short and they must retire at the age of thirty.

First night
first man
first life
first short
first retire
first age

Women at work. Poetry
not comfort. Classics
or cattle.

Scottish historian James Gale noted that "dancing-girls" and the laboring women were the only groups seen during the day.... not often pretty in feature from the Western point of view, but striking ... with never a shadow across her easy-sitting conscience; happy in the role she is called upon to play, and feeling that she is a very important part of what the east calls society ...

Call upon our visitor with the celadon
bowl stolen from the museum for our first night
of poetry, of women's
work, of half-faced
miracles, of Western doors heavy
lidded as an Asian eye.

"Close your eye slowly, more slowly," the director of the documentary about war crimes against Koreans told me.

Slow like glass as a verb.

From open to close is a distance
of a few millimeters swept away
by a few sparse lashes, turned
down to protect the Mongoloid eye from sudden sandstorms.

Light reflects off my computer
monitor not the glittering
rice paddy, not the sewing
machine's glittering
needle dipping like a cormorant into tomorrow's
Nike shoe and this is
the Culture at work.

From physiognomy to economy, what
does any sky know
of impracticality? What does woman know
of miracles?

6 ADOPTION MYTHS AND RACIAL REALITIES IN THE UNITED STATES

Dorothy Roberts

For several decades there has been a vociferous debate about transracial adoption, concerning primarily the adoption of Black children by white parents. One side shouts that thousands of Black children lingering in foster care are harmed by policies that prevent loving and capable white people from adopting them. The other side shouts that Black children are best raised in Black families and that their adoption by white people threatens to undermine Black culture. The debate often stalls on disagreements about Black cultural distinctiveness and white people's ability to raise Black children. Other more critical questions are often overlooked: Why are there so many children in foster care in the first place, and why are so many of them Black? The answer to these questions lies in the disturbing reality of race and child welfare policy. To me, what is wrong with the dominant arguments supporting transracial adoption has to do with politics, not love and culture. Support for transracial adoption often not only ignores racism in the child welfare system but also reinforces the racial biases and systemic injustices that produce the grossly disproportionate placement of Black children in foster care.[1]

In this chapter, I focus attention on the racial politics that are critical to understanding transracial adoption in the United States and to developing a just approach to it. First, it is important to dispense with several issues that, although they tend to dominate debates on this topic, should not be in dispute. I accept the following propositions relevant to transracial adoption: Adoption is a legitimate means of creating families, forming bonds that can be as loving and socially significant as biological ones; there are too many children in foster care and adoption is one means of creating "permanency" for these children; and white people are capable of being good and loving parents to children of other racialized groups. The argument I make in opposition to transracial adoption is not that it inherently injures Black culture or community or that white people cannot lovingly raise nonwhite children. Too few white people are interested in adopting Black children to cause any significant impact on Black culture or solidarity. Too many white people have cared for Black children to discount the possibility of transracial love. Although I am Black, my own father, who I was very close to and loved tremendously, was white. I never questioned that he loved me or that he was a wonderful father to me. But I know just as deeply that the existence of intimate interracial relationships cannot negate or solve the pervasive and systemic racism that persists in the United States.

The debate over transracial adoption is important not because of cultural difference or transcendent love but because of adoption's role in the politics of racism. This chapter therefore examines how the racialized US child welfare system creates the conditions under which transracial adoption seems a necessary and even benevolent act. Far from healing the wounds of racism, advocacy for transracial adoption often contributes to the racist ideologies and practices that devalue Black family ties. A just approach to transracial adoption must acknowledge and contest the racial reality of foster care and adoption in the United States.

racial reality of adoption in the united states

Adoption often provides to children a loving home and to capable adults a chance to parent. But adoption is also a political institution reflecting social inequities, including race, class, and gender hierarchies, and serving powerful ideologies and interests. Most children awaiting adoption in the nation's foster care system are African American or Latino.[2] Black children's "need" for adoption results from biased decision-making and policies, including adoption policies, that systematically disadvantage Black families.[3]

The racial disparity in adoptable children reflects a general inequity in the US child welfare system. African American and Native American children are overrepresented in the national foster care population.[4] That is, the overall percentage of these groups in the foster care population is greater than their representation in the general youth population. In 2000, Black children made up two-fifths of the nation's foster care population, although they represented less than one-fifth of the nation's children.[5] Taken together, children of color comprised only about 30 percent of the general youth population but about 60 percent of children in foster care.[6] Children of color from all major ethnic groups are also *disproportionately* represented in the foster care system compared to white children. In 2000, African American children were four times as likely as white children to be in foster care.[7]

Poverty is a key contributor to this racial disparity. Most cases of child maltreatment involve parental neglect, which is usually difficult to disentangle from the conditions of poverty. Social work professor Duncan Lindsey concludes, "inadequacy of income, more than any factor, constitutes the reason that children are removed."[8] The very definitions of child neglect and the design of our child welfare system are targeted at the problems of poor families, not middle-class and affluent ones. Black families have a greater risk of involvement in the child welfare system in part because they have lower incomes and are more likely to live in poverty than white families.

There is also considerable evidence that racial disproportionality results from biased practices within the child welfare system itself. Researchers have detected differential treatment at every point in the child welfare decision-making process—reporting, investigation and substantiation, child placement, service provision, and permanency decision-making. A 1999 study of missed cases of abusive head trauma, for example, discovered that doctors failed to detect the abuse twice as often in white children as minority children.[9] Another study of Philadelphia hospital records reported that African American and Latino toddlers hospitalized for fractures between 1994 and 2000 were over five times more likely to be evaluated for child abuse, and over three times more likely to be reported to child protective services, than white children with comparable injuries.[10]

Research has similarly found that Black women are much more likely than white women to be reported by hospital staff for substance abuse during pregnancy and to have their babies removed by child protective services.[11] Child protection decisions are not immune from deeply embedded racial stereotypes about Black female immorality and Black family dysfunction that consciously and subconsciously affect decision-making in other systems. These studies also show that racism leaves many white children unprotected when doctors and caseworkers fail to intervene because they are reluctant to place them in an inferior foster care system that damages children and their families. The public would not tolerate white children being placed in foster care at the rates experienced by Black children; indeed, the answer is not to remove more white children from their homes, but to change the dominant approach to child protection.

State agencies are far more likely to place Black children who come to their attention in foster care instead of offering their families less traumatic assistance at home. According to federal statistics, Black children in the child welfare system are placed in foster care at twice the rate for white children. A national study of child protective services by the US Department of Health and Human Services reported that "[m]inority children, and in particular African American children, are more likely to be in foster care placement than receive in-home services, *even when they have the same problems and characteristics as white children.*"[12] Foster care is the main "service" state agencies provide to Black children brought to their attention. Once removed from their homes, Black children remain in foster care longer, are moved more often, receive fewer services, and are less likely to be either returned home or adopted than any other children.[13] Thus, the overrepresentation of Black children in the adoption market stems largely from the child welfare system's inferior treatment of Black families.

The racial disparity in the child welfare system also reflects a political choice to "address" the startling rates of Black child poverty by punishing parents instead of tackling poverty's societal roots. In the last several decades, the number of children receiving child welfare services has declined dramatically, while the foster care population has skyrocketed.[14] As the child welfare system began to serve fewer white children and more Black children, state and federal governments spent more money on out-of-home care and less on in-home services. This mirrors perfectly the metamorphosis of welfare once the welfare rights movement succeeded in making Aid to Families with Dependent Children (AFDC) available to Black families in the 1960s. As welfare became increasingly associated with Black mothers, it became increasingly burdened with behavior-modification rules and work requirements until the federal entitlement was abolished altogether in 1997. Both systems responded to their growing Black clientele by reducing their services to families while intensifying their punitive functions.

This systemic inequality, in the welfare of children and in the state's approach to it, produces the excessive supply of adoptable Black children in foster care. The overrepresentation of Black children in this population is the result of massive state supervision and dissolution of families. This interference with families helps to maintain the disadvantaged status of Black people in the United States by disrupting family and community ties and by reinforcing the quintessential racist stereotype that Black people need government supervision. Placing large numbers of children in state custody—even if some are ultimately reunited with their families or transferred to adoptive homes—interferes with a community's ability to form healthy connections among its members and to engage in collective action. Foster care often destroys children's ties to their families, friends, and neighbors, and subjects parents to years of intensive state regulation. Moreover, concentrating state supervision of families in Black neighborhoods has damaging community-wide effects on the role of parental and government authority in residents' lives.[15]

adoption myths

Advocacy for transracial adoption is largely premised on several myths. A fundamental myth of contemporary child welfare policy is that adoption can solve the problems with foster care by giving foster children "permanency" and substantially reducing the foster care population. In the last several years, federal and state policy has shifted away from preserving families and toward "freeing" children in foster care for adoption by terminating parental rights. Most notably, the Adoption and Safe Families Act (ASFA), passed by Congress in 1997, promotes adoption through a set of mandates and incentives to state child welfare departments.[16] As a result of ASFA, most state agencies shortened time frames for permanency planning, increased emphasis on adoption, and implemented concurrent planning that prepares adoptive homes for foster children while providing reunification services to parents.[17] ASFA also imposes arbitrary timelines that speed up the time within which agencies should petition for termination of parental rights.

The overlap of ASFA and the 1996 federal welfare adjustment law marked the first time in US history that the federal government mandated that states protect children from abuse and neglect with no corresponding mandate to provide basic economic support to poor families.[18] Like welfare policy's promotion of marriage, the reliance on adoption furthers the neoliberal agenda to replace state support for families with private remedies for social and economic inequality.

This federal policy has increased adoptions of children from foster care, but Black children represent an increasingly smaller percentage of these children. In 1997, 44 percent of all children adopted from foster care were Black, compared with only 35 percent in 2001.[19] More important, ASFA has led to *greater* racial disparity in the best outcome for children in foster care—reunification with their birth families.[20] Many Black children remain in foster care as legal orphans, without official ties to their parents, whose rights were terminated, and without adoptive homes. The new federal policy has increased the overall numbers of adoptions at the expense of Black children's family ties. Moreover, adoptions of children in foster care do nothing to address the underlying needs that place children in the system in the first place.

In addition, there are several myths about transracial adoption's role in furthering this flawed view of adoption as the solution to foster care's problems. Transracial adoption became a particularly popular instrument for this approach based on the mistaken belief that Black children lingered in foster care mainly because of "race-matching" policies and that large numbers of white families would eagerly adopt Black children in foster care if these policies were eliminated. But have federal laws abolishing race matching done more to expand Black children's access to adoption or to expand white adults' adoption options? As law professor Richard Banks argued, federal law still permits child welfare agencies to practice racial discrimination: white adults remain free to reject Black children for adoption and to exercise their preference for white children.[21] Most agencies report no increase in the proportion of domestic transracial adoptions since the enactment of the Multiethnic Placement Act (MEPA); the number of white families adopting older children of color, those most "in need" of adoptive homes, remains very low.[22] These children are most likely to be adopted by single Black women.[23]

If the government's goal is to increase adoptions of Black children, greater emphasis should therefore be placed on recruiting and supporting Black adoptive parents. Yet MEPA's "diligent recruitment" provision is largely ignored; the federal government imposes penalties for race matching but not for failing to recruit adoptive Black families.[24] Indeed, Elizabeth Bartholet, a leading advocate of transracial adoption, even opposes recruitment from Black communities, as well as kinship foster care, on the grounds that they interfere with efforts to increase adoption of Black children by white people.[25] Yet subsidized guardianship programs, which give relative caregivers financial assistance without the need to terminate parental rights, have proven to be a successful alternative to adoption. In short, federal adoption policy has done more to increase the disproportionate disruption and regulation of Black families than to increase adoptions of Black children.

disparaging black family ties

It is bad enough that advocates of transracial adoption largely ignore the policies and systemic inequities that produce so many adoptable Black children. Even more alarming is the way advocacy for transracial adoption often reinforces these policies and inequities. The campaign to increase adoptions in general and transracial adoptions in particular makes the devaluation of foster children's families and the rejection of family preservation efforts its central components. Adoption is no longer presented as a remedy for a minority of unsalvageable families but as a viable option—indeed, the preferred option—for all children in foster care. Black mothers' bonds with their children are especially disparaged as barriers to adoption by white people, and extinguishing them is seen as the critical first step in the adoption process.

Congressional and media discussion of ASFA linked family preservation policies to white middle-class couples' difficulties in adopting Black children in foster care. For example, a 1998 *US News and World Report* article entitled "Adoption Gridlock" began with the story of a white North Carolinian couple who resorted to adopting two Romanian orphans after several American agencies rejected their offer to adopt a Black child.[26] More recently, a *Seattle Times* article, "New Bias in Child Welfare," blamed an office created by the Washington State Children's Administration to preserve Black families for keeping white foster parents from adopting a little boy, Tyrese, who was "half black."[27] "After taking in more than 70 foster children over 40 years, the Nikolaisens fell in love again," the article began. The reporter then painted the foster family as loving saviors thwarted by a misguided caseworker who "wanted to send Tyrese back to his troubled home." These articles imply that the emphasis on reuniting Black children with their birth families unfairly prevents (more suitable) white couples from adopting them. The quicker termination of parental rights and abolition of race-matching policies were linked as a strategy for increasing adoptions of Black children by white families.

The spotlight of transracial adoption discourse fixates on two sympathetic characters—the needy Black child and the giving white adoptive parent. Left out or portrayed in a negative light are Black parents. The media leave the impression that Black parents involved with the foster care system have all abandoned their children or don't deserve to have them. Newspaper stories mistakenly call *all* of the half million children in foster care "orphans of the living"—even though most still have ties to families who care for them. As *The Nation* columnist Katha Pollitt points out, calling children in foster care "orphans" teaches the public to view their parents "as being, in effect, dead."[28] Transracial adoption advocates tend to conveniently silence the poor Black mothers who fight desperately, without resources and without adequate legal representation, to regain custody of their children from a wealthy and powerful bureaucracy.

toward a just adoption policy

A just approach to transracial adoption recognizes the link between the availability of Black children for adoption and systemic inequities. It places transracial adoption within a broader child welfare policy that relies primarily on supports to families—not adoption—to reduce child maltreatment and foster care placement. While permitting white people to adopt Black children, this policy emphasizes recruitment of adoptive parents from children's relatives and communities. And it never promotes adoption by disparaging or devaluing the parents of children in foster care.

Without acknowledging—no, fighting for—Black parents' bonds with their children, advocacy for transracial adoption tends to devolve into an especially pernicious type of white benevolence toward Black people, a benevolence that depends on loss of Black family integrity in favor of white supervision of their children. White compassion for Black children should not depend on Black children "belonging" to white people, to use Bartholet's term. This is a particularly selfish way to approach child welfare that perpetuates rather than challenges America's racial hierarchy. Rather, white people should show their care for Black children by struggling for programs and policies that would improve the welfare of Black children living within their own families and communities.

notes

1 An important exception is Barbara Katz Rothman, *Weaving a Family: Untangling Race and Adoption* (Boston: Beacon Press, 2005).

2 US Department of Health and Human Services (DHHS), Administration for Children and Families, *The AFCARS Reports (TARs)*, http://www.acf.hhs.gov/programs/cb/dis/afcars/publications/afcars.htm

3 Dorothy E. Roberts, *Shattered Bonds: The Color of Child Welfare* (New York: Basic Civitas Books, 2002). In this book, I elaborate the reasons for and impact of racial disparities in the child welfare system.

4 US DHHS, *TARs*.

5 US DHHS, *TARs*.

6 US DHHS, *TARs*.

7 Child Welfare League of America, "Research and Data," *The National Data Analysis System (NDAS)*, http://www.cwla.org/ndas.htm.

8 Duncan Lindsey, *The Welfare of Children* (New York: Oxford University Press, 1994), 155.

9 Carole Jenny and others, "Analysis of Missed Cases of Abusive Head Trauma," *Journal of the American Medical Association* 281 (1999): 621.
10 Wendy G. Lane and others, "Racial Differences in the Evaluation of Pediatric Fractures for Physical Abuse," *Journal of the American Medical Association* 288 (2002): 1603.
11 Ira J. Chasnoff, Harvey J. Landress, and Mark E. Barrett, "The Prevalence of Illicit-Drug or Alcohol Use During Pregnancy and Discrepancies in Mandatory Reporting in Pinellas County, Florida," *New England Journal of Medicine* 322 (1990): 1202; Daniel R. Neuspiel and Terry Martin Zingman, "Custody of Cocaine-Exposed Newborns: Determinants of Discharge Decisions," *American Journal of Public Health* 83 (1993): 1726.
12 US DHHS, *National Study of Protective, Preventive, and Reunification Services Delivered to Children and Their Families* (Washington, DC: US Government Printing Office, 1997).
13 Mark E. Courtney and Vin-Ling I. Wong, "Comparing the Timing Exits from Substitute Care," *Children and Youth Services Review* 18, no. 4–5 (1996): 307–335; Steven L. McMurtry and Gwat-Yong Lie, "Differential Exits of Minority Children in Foster Care," *Social Work Research and Abstract* 28, no. 1 (1992): 42–48.
14 US DHHS, *National Study of Protective.*
15 Roberts, *Shattered Bonds,* 236–254.
16 *The Adoption and Safe Families Act of 1997,* Public Law 105–89, US Statutes at Large 111 (1997): 2115, http://www.acf.hhs.gov/programs/cb/laws/pi/pi9802.htm.
17 US DHHS, *National Survey of Child and Adolescent Well-Being (NSCAW), 1997–2005,* Office of Research, Planning & Evaluation, http://www.acf.hhs.gov/programs/opre/abuse_neglect/nscaw/index.html.
18 Courtney and Wong, "Comparing the Timing Exits," 329.
19 Courtney and Wong, "Comparing the Timing Exits," 326.
20 Courtney and Wong, "Comparing the Timing Exits," 325.
21 R. Richard Banks, "The Color of Desire: Fulfilling Adoptive Parents' Racial Preferences Through Discriminatory State Action," *Yale Law Journal* 107, no. 4 (1998): 875–964.
22 US DHHS, *NSCAW, 1997–2005.*
23 US DHHS, *NSCAW, 1997–2005.*
24 US DHHS, *NSCAW, 1997–2005.*
25 Elizabeth Bartholet, *Nobody's Children: Abuse and Neglect, Foster Drift, and the Adoption Alternative* (Boston: Beacon Press, 1999).
26 Amanda Spake, "Adoption Gridlock," *US News and World Report,* June 22, 1998.
27 Jonathan Martin, "New Bias in Child Welfare," *Seattle Times,* July 11, 2005.
28 Katha Pollitt, "Subject to Debate: Republican Party and Unwed Mothers," *The Nation,* December 12, 1994, 717.

7 THE FINER MEANING

Kimberly R. Fardy

I don't know how it began, because I don't know where I came from. You would think a tree without roots would die, but somehow, through the deliverance of the Almighty's breath into my lungs, I have survived.

When I was younger I had deep conversations within my mind. Maybe they were just fantasies, or maybe just plain lies, but they seem to have stemmed from a deeper understanding of myself, as if I remembered some past existence. I held portraits of both my mother and my father within me—how they resembled me, where they came from, the struggle that ultimately forced them to put me on the social systems' auction block. It rarely crossed my mind that they might have given me up simply because they did not want me. I would claim my laughter, my sadness, and my silence as my father's presence within my soul. My kindness, my loyalty, my unbreakable strength and will came from my mother. What hurt was the truth. I knew no matter what I believed, I would never be their child again, and they would never be my parents.

If I were raised like other people would it have been the same? Would I be where I am today? Would I have lost or would I have gained? At 22 years old I have come to accept the life I've lived, but still, I wonder—in another life, how would the dice have rolled?

Of course, I still asked the wind why I was posted up like a modern-day slave on the block. Did my mother think it better to release me to the auctioneer than keep me in a poor condition? Did she think the system would give me more opportunity than she could provide? Maybe her decision was not even about finances; maybe she was just emotionally unavailable. Unable to provide me with what she thought I deserved.

I believe that some of the best medicine is knowing your history from the words, actions, and prayers of your peoples.

Growing up black with white parents in white suburbia is a brutally silencing reality. There are no resources to help black youth transition into a healthy adulthood in this environment. There are no instructions about how to defend yourself and develop a positive identity under such conditions. Fortunately, I was blessed with two black sisters, and together we fought for our lives. In eighth grade I began associating with the only white kids I could relate to—the poor ones. They had also been cast out of society due to something that was out of their control. These relationships were never deep friendships though, and I knew that. I was well aware that no matter what, I was still the nigger with a pass. After three years of relationships built on convenience, my pass was revoked. I was raped by one of the white boys. When I told the girls in our crew that I had been raped, they told the boys. The sister of the boy who raped me took the lead in verbally degrading me. She spoke publicly about the problems my sisters and I had faced as black girls in white suburbia. She insulted my family. I was lucky to have one of my sisters there with me. Together we defended our roots against a crew of 15 angry white boys and girls. It felt like a lynch mob, and we were the strange fruit. After they'd sent a wave of racist abuse crashing down on us, my sister decided to handle business the way she had learned to in the city. She pulled out a knife and went for the sister of the boy who took my treasures. After that, my sister ran away. I continued to fight with those kids, and the principal soon suggested that I leave. I left the school and, not long after, home.

Sometimes my own reflection surprises me, cause I feel so much older than I look. Folks have said I got a poised demeanor, a wise soul, sometimes I think I was just forced to grow up too fast, like so many other black and brown girls throughout the States. Having to think, hustle, and work like adults, before we were able to play like children.

I have been blessed with loyal friends, whom I consider family. Still, when I join them for their family reunions I am reminded of the missing link on my gold chain. I have learned to fill the void with my own unique outlook. That link has become my perspective as a first-generation Jamaican, third-generation Irish American removed and reclaimed. It is my perspective as a child born to a father in prison facing deportation and a teenage mother on welfare. It is my perspective as a person who was put into the system from birth and later adopted by white Americans to face the cruel world of a black-eyed pea in a bowl of rice. It is my perspective as a queer/stud woman of color growing up with no role models who looked like me, thought like me, acted out like me, and lived like me. It is my perspective as a young black woman, raised by a strong white woman, who taught me about willpower through her four-year battle with breast cancer and demonstrated love through an undying commitment to her adopted children. It is my perspective as a young woman orphaned again by the loss of her second mother. It is my perspective as a survivor of neglect, molestation, rape, survival sex, homelessness, racism, sexism, and hate crimes. It is my perspective as a university student—employed, housed, and engaged to a phenomenal woman. It is my perspective that has made me the warrior, survivor, and advocate I am today.

And it is my perspective that pushes me to breathe another breath, survive, and laugh, knowing—to live is to survive, and to survive, well, that is the finer meaning.

8 PARENTS IN PRISON, CHILDREN IN CRISIS

Ellen M. Barry

Ms. H, an African American mother, served time in state prison for killing her violently abusive husband in self-defense. After her release from prison, she raised her three children, got a nursing degree, became a certified counselor, and has spoken widely on the experiences of battered women and their children. When her adult daughter had a psychotic breakdown and was jailed for being disorderly, the daughter's eight-month-old, Ms. H's granddaughter, was made a dependent of the juvenile court. In spite of the fact that her conviction was twenty-one years old, Ms. H was denied custody of her granddaughter by the court because of her felony conviction.[1]

There is a widespread belief in the United States that parents who go to prison or jail are bad parents. This attitude is informed (or misinformed) in part by the barrage of reality cop shows and crime dramas as well as the deluge of media reporting on violent crime. In fact, recent studies have shown that, while the crime rate in the United States has remained relatively stable, the reporting of violent crime by media has risen dramatically.[2] Unless they themselves have been incarcerated or have a family member or loved one who is incarcerated, very few members of the general public base their negative attitudes toward criminal defendants or prisoners on firsthand experience. Thus, as with any complex human dynamic, the reality about imprisoned parents is far more nuanced: they are extremely diverse in their experiences, as are their actions and their abilities to parent. Just as with parents in the general community, parents in prison have made mistakes, many even serious mistakes, in their parenting. But as with people in the community, most incarcerated parents have also made good choices for their children. They may not have been perfect parents, but in most instances, they have been "good enough" parents.[3]

All parents in this country have rights and obligations with respect to their children that are protected, at least on paper, by a network of laws, regulations, and court decisions that honor the familial bond between parents and children. Children are also protected by laws that prohibit child abuse and mistreatment.[4] Yet despite this effort to codify rights and obligations, the implementation of these laws happens in an environment of pervasive racism and insidious class bias. In fact, current policies and practices show a disregard for the health and well-being of children, particularly low-income children of color. Many advocates for children point out, with great concern, the damaging effects of the current "cradle to prison pipeline."[5] Based on current trends, African American[6] boys born in the past several years have a 1-in-3 chance of going to prison before they reach age 30.

Cutbacks on public spending, including schools, after school programs, and childcare facilities;[7] criminalization of children at younger and younger ages;[8] controversy over the morality of executing children;[9] and continuing tolerance of corporal punishment in schools in some states[10] are just a few of the current indicators of the underlying animosity toward children. Although these trends may be spearheaded by Right-wing politicians, policymakers, and religious leaders, they would not have the momentum to survive and take hold without massive support, or indifference, by mainstream America.

The removal of children from their parents, their siblings, and their extended families based solely on the incarceration of a parent is one important manifestation of this indifference toward the well-being of poor children and children of color. Placing significant numbers of children of color in rotating foster care with little chance of obtaining stable and loving homes during their childhoods is of no benefit to these children and is a source of great damage to their parents, their families, and their communities. And removal of infants from incarcerated parents who have done nothing to injure or abuse their infants and placement of these children with adoptive parents is a crime against these children and against their parents, siblings, relatives, and communities. The devastating impact of this injustice is clear when we consider that as of 2005 over 2.2 million people were incarcerated in US prisons, jails, and detention centers, and that a staggering 65 percent of these individuals were from communities of color, particularly African American and Latino communities. Native American prisoners, though small in number, are nevertheless also dramatically overrepresented in the criminal justice system.[11] It is estimated that upwards of 3 million children currently have a parent in prison. Given that incarceration has become a cross-generational issue in many communities, this figure is only the tip of the iceberg in understanding the full breadth and depth of the impact of mass incarceration on communities of color and low-income communities in the United States.

While all communities of color have suffered from the ravages of racism and its many manifestations, the African American community is arguably the most visibly affected by racism in the criminal justice system at the present time. Over a million African Americans in this country are currently or formerly incarcerated, on parole, on probation, in detention, or otherwise directly affected by the criminal justice system.[12] In most African American communities, almost everyone knows somebody who is or was in jail or prison. If a parent has been incarcerated, the likelihood that his or her children will also be incarcerated greatly increases. Some policymakers have used this reality to justify removal of children from incarcerated parents on a more systematic basis. A few have argued the extreme position that parents who go to prison should automatically lose their parental rights.[13] But most would support a more moderate position: parents who go to prison should be able to "prove themselves" as good parents, and if they meet all of the requirements laid out by the juvenile court and the department of social services,[14] they will be reunited with their child or children. In fact, the juvenile court/social service system in the United States reflects the same pervasive racial and class bias as the correctional system. Just as African Americans are dramatically overrepresented at every stage of the criminal justice system (from arrest to prosecution to conviction to sentencing to mandatory minimum and execution), they are similarly overrepresented in the removal, detention, and separation of their children through state intervention.[15]

This coalescing of two systems, the correctional and the juvenile court/ social service systems, results in the disproportionate removal of infants and children from low-income Latino and African American families, because they are more likely to be incarcerated, poor, and lacking access to resources that might otherwise prevent their involvement with social services. By the same token, a greater percentage of affluent white families are available to adopt these children of color. Put in this context and in the context of race and class in present-day United States, transracial adoption becomes an understandable symbol of institutionalized racism against communities of color.

> *Ms. C was a new immigrant from Nicaragua. After the birth of her second child, she had a postpartum breakdown. The oldest two children were removed from her care and placed in foster care with a middle-class white family that wished to adopt the two girls. Ms. C, whose English was quite limited, was given eight hours a month of visitation with her daughters and little other support or encouragement concerning reunification with her daughters. When her third daughter was born, she was removed from Ms. C's custody based solely on the fact that the previous two children had been removed from her. She was arrested and convicted of child stealing after she took her newborn daughter from the social services office during a regularly scheduled visit. After a long and complicated legal battle, she lost permanent custody of both older girls, although she was found fit to retain custody of her youngest daughter.*[16]

Unlike systems in many other countries, the US legal system allows for the termination of parental rights on a number of grounds, including incarceration, institutionalization, drug or alcohol addiction, and the length of time the child has been in foster care. Due to the racist and class bias in this country, a bias that pervades all institutional systems, including the foster care/dependency system and the criminal justice system, a disproportionate number of people of color, particularly low-income African American and Latino parents, are more likely than white parents to lose temporary and often permanent legal custody of their children.

For the past 35 years, there has been a major political and philosophical conflict in the juvenile court/social service field between those who support "family reunification" and those who support "permanency" and severance of the natural parents' ties with their children. As a result, there is a deep, inherent tension embedded in the federal/state network of laws and regulations governing children in foster care. On the one hand, parents whose children are placed in foster care are entitled to "reunification services," a broad category of supportive services that aim to enable parents to overcome the problems and obstacles that led to the removal of their children in the first place. According to federal law, children should be returned to their parents "wherever possible." However, the Adoption and Safe Families Act (1997) also states that "if, in the judgment of social services and the juvenile court, it is impossible for parents to meet the terms of the reunification agreement, children should be provided with a 'permanent home.'"[17]

This conflict between reunification of families and removal of children for adoption has arisen, in large part, because of the heartfelt and legitimate concerns that children deserve a permanent and loving home and that the past practice of moving children from foster home to foster home throughout their childhoods without a stable, permanent home ("foster care drift") caused untold harm to children.[18] Yet while this concern for permanency for children in foster care is legitimate, terminating parental rights does not guarantee a child a permanent home. And the desire to make adoption a possibility earlier in a child's life must be balanced with the often devastating consequences of depriving that child of any relationship with his or her parents, siblings, grandparents, cousins, and other relatives. In addition to these individual relationships, some of which may have great significance to any given individual, children of color who are placed with white adoptive parents also face the real, and potentially devastating, impact of losing their cultural and racial identity. Mainstream literature tends to minimize the effects of this damage, but as the contributors to this volume demonstrate, children removed from their own communities and placed in white adoptive homes face lifelong emotional repercussions.[19]

Of course, many children of color who are placed with white foster parents or with white adoptive parents have positive experiences with their new families. This essay does not address the question of whether it is ethically appropriate for an individual white parent to adopt a specific child of a different racial background. The debate concerning the ethics of transracial adoption has raged for many decades without resolution. One of the contributing factors toward the acrimonious tone and narrow perspective apparent across many of these discussions is the standpoint of many of those advocating for transracial adoption. The majority of articles and books written about the subject are from the perspective of white adoptive parents who have adopted children of other racial backgrounds and are therefore powerfully invested in defending a system that has given them the opportunity to parent. Very few reflect the perspectives of transracial adoptees or their birth parents who are often silenced by the forceful rhetoric of "rescue," as adoptive parents are silenced by the role of "rescuer"—both camps are supposed to be grateful, not critical. Because of this, it has been very difficult to introduce a discussion about the underlying racial and class-based societal structures that have led to the increase in children of color available for adoption in the United States. The concerns raised in this essay are directed at the cumulative impact of the effects of slavery, racism, poverty, and criminalization of communities of color in this country, and the ways in which this pervasive racial climate has shaped the present-day social services and criminal justice systems.

Given that this broken system cannot, and will not, be fixed overnight, we must acknowledge that on a practical level, many children of color who are now in nonrelative foster care might be better off if they were placed with white adoptive parents who are committed to raising these children lovingly and ethically, with a healthy sense of themselves and their racial identities.

Ultimately, however, we must re-examine and challenge the fundamental causes of the increasing removal of children of color from their parents, their extended families, and their communities. The removal of large numbers of infants and children from their parents and their subsequent placement with white adoptive families damages children, families, and entire communities. We need only to look to US history to identify many egregious examples of children of color who were removed from their families and communities as a method of controlling and destroying those communities. From the kidnapping of Native American children who were then placed in Mission Schools, far from their families, their languages, and their cultures, to the destruction of African families through the brutal separation of children and parents at the slave markets, to the present-day separation of children of incarcerated parents from their parents, relatives, and communities, our society has long used the removal of children as a way of terrorizing, separating, and destabilizing people of color.

In the 1970s, the National Association of Black Social Workers described transracial adoption as a modern form of slavery, in which black children were trafficked from black to white families, a characterization later derided by those on both sides of the political spectrum. However, the ongoing legacy of slavery in the adoption of black children of incarcerated parents becomes evident when we examine the links between transracial adoption and the criminal justice system. A brief historical survey is useful here. After abolition, former plantation owners who became sharecropper "bosses" needed a new way to control black labor. The criminal justice system, and in particular a series of Black Codes targeted at African Americans, served this function. African Americans who were sentenced under these racially discriminatory codes were often returned to the plantations under the Convict Lease system, another system of forced labor.[20] The Black Codes and the Convict Lease system laid the foundation for the racially discrepant criminal justice system that continues to operate as a racialized system of social control today. Just as slavery, in its day, was described by white people as a necessary and justifiable institution, the criminal justice system is today widely viewed as dispensing justice despite its racially discrepant impact. And just as slaves were viewed by Southern white people as inferior and naturally suited to brutal treatment, black people in prison are seen as criminals who are "bad" and worthy of punishment.

It is no coincidence that, as the civil rights movement took root and began to flourish in the early- to mid-1960s, the number of prosecutions and convictions of African Americans and other people of color increased. Many of these convictions were related, directly or indirectly, to civil rights activism.[21] The Black Panther Party grew in strength and popularity in the African American community during this period. Law enforcement, never a legitimate source of justice and protection for black people or Africans during slavery or for former slaves in the postwar South, became an even greater tool of repression during the civil rights era. Yet despite all the efforts of law enforcement, the court system, and many government officials to prevent it, the power of the civil rights movement led to some significant legal victories for African Americans and, ultimately, for many other marginalized and oppressed groups in this country, including other people of color, women, gays, children, and people with disabilities.

However, in spite of the progress, the hard-fought victories of the civil rights movement have been continually undercut by the massive movement to criminalize and demonize African Americans. As the strength and radicalism of the Black Panther Party grew, the US government and law enforcement responded with stronger and more damaging attacks on communities of color. Large numbers of black men and women ended up in jail and prison, and some of the strongest leaders of the movement were killed or set up and incarcerated for life.[22] Increasing numbers of African American youth became victims of police brutality, along with frequent harassment and racial profiling. More and more people of color were criminalized through biased prosecution for welfare fraud, crack cocaine, drug sales, and "gang" activity. As economic conditions worsened in the country, unemployment rose, and incarceration of people of color escalated throughout the 1980s and '90s. The statistic bears repeating: By 2005, the US population in prisons, jails, and detention centers had exceeded 2.2 million, and over 65 percent of those people were men, women, and children of color. Each one of these people has family members and other loved ones, and the vast majority of prisoners are parents of young children. The criminal justice system, a system founded on systematic racism, devastates these children's families. After their parents are incarcerated, the child welfare system, another racially discriminatory system, steps in.

consequences of incarceration on the parent-child bond

Within this context, the separation of African American children and other children of color from their imprisoned parents becomes significant and racially charged for the entire community. It becomes even more problematic when these children are taken from extended families and placed in nonrelative foster care or adopted into white families. One can only conclude from this widespread pattern that race and racism play a role in the operation of the US foster care system. There are many social workers, child welfare workers, and juvenile court judges who are deeply concerned about creating an effective, fair, and just legal system for families in crisis, but it is impossible for these individuals to do anything but temper discrete situations within a racist and class-biased criminal justice system and a heavily enmeshed social services system.

Although the vast majority of prisoners in US prisons and jails are men, the number of women incarcerated over the past twenty years has escalated at a rate that has dramatically outstripped the percentage increase of men in prison. Thus, after two decades of increasing incarceration for poor white women and women of color, women now represent almost 10 percent of the prison population. And while parental incarceration affects the bonds between fathers and their children in significant ways, because of complex social and economic factors, the effect of incarceration on mothers and their children is often far more traumatic and disruptive. When fathers go to prison, their children are most often in the custody and care of their mothers, and a significant percentage of these children maintain some form of contact with their fathers during incarceration.[23] When mothers go to prison, fathers rarely step in to care for their children. The majority of these children are cared for by their maternal grandmothers or aunts, but a significant number, as many as 35 percent, are removed from their mother's custody and placed in foster care. Given the stringent legal requirements of the existing foster care laws and regulations, it is virtually impossible for incarcerated mothers to comply with the time requirements for reunification with their children. Even if mothers are on parole or probation, the obstacles for reunification are still enormous. Formerly incarcerated women have great difficulty getting jobs with adequate wages, obtaining housing, getting job training, arranging for daycare, and meeting the requirements of the juvenile court reunification agreement. They face enormous discrimination based on their status as former prisoners, and women of color face even more difficulties as a result of both personal and institutionalized racism.

Incarcerated women who give birth while in prison or jail are at much greater risk of losing permanent legal custody of their infants, particularly if they are estranged from their extended families. Even if a pregnant woman in prison has a close relationship with her relatives, it is often impossible for these relatives to get to the prison within the very limited window of time that they are given by corrections and the department of social services to pick up the newborn infant. If relatives fail to pick up a newborn, the baby is made a dependent of the juvenile court in the county where the prison is located. Because of the racial and class demographics of the population of women in prison, the majority of babies who are placed in foster care under these circumstances are infants of color and virtually all are from families without financial means. Because the majority of women's prisons are located in predominantly white, rural areas far from more racially diverse urban areas, these infants are most often placed with white foster families in relatively less diverse communities.

Once these mothers are released from prison, they are often unable to maintain contact with their infants, either because they are required by law to return to the community where they were convicted or because their need for housing and other support leaves them little choice but to return to their home and family despite their desire to reunify with their infants. Thus, many women in these circumstances face permanent separation from their infants and termination of their parental rights that is strictly related to their incarceration.

One disturbing trend that has appeared in the past decade or two has been the emergence of fundamentalist religious organizations targeting pregnant women in prisons and jails.[24] Many prison ministry organizations have provided important services to incarcerated mothers and their children. However, there have been a number of documented instances in which religious groups have befriended pregnant women in prison who were receiving little support or few resources from their families, convinced these women not to terminate their pregnancies, and promised to take care of their infants only while these women served their time. But once the infants were placed with one of the group's families, the organization would cut off all contact with the mothers, who would lose all contact with their infants.[25]

> *Ms. L, a fifty-two-year-old African American grandmother with a ten-year-old son and a twenty-three-year-old incarcerated daughter, was denied placement of her infant grandson because social services believed she was "too old."*

> *Ms. G was a fifty-year-old Latina grandmother who had been employed for most of her adult life in an automobile plant, owned her own modest*

home, and had no criminal record. She was denied placement of her granddaughter because social services felt that she had "failed" with her own daughter, who was in prison on drug-related charges.[26]

Another reality for many of these women is that, although they may have support from their extended families, and their mothers, sisters, or other relatives who may be willing to provide a loving and supportive home for their children, the relative caregivers may be treated with the same lack of respect and consideration accorded the imprisoned mother. On the one hand, these relative caregivers are expected to take care of their kin, particularly older, "hard to place" children, with little or no financial compensation or supportive services. On the other hand, when highly adoptable, nondisabled infants are born to mothers in prison, grandparents and other relatives often hear a different story: that they are "too old," "too frail," and "lack sufficient resources," or that they made a mistake with their own children so they cannot be trusted to raise a grandchild.

In virtually all instances, incarcerated mothers and their family members lack sufficient information from social services and the juvenile courts to make informed and effective decisions on behalf of their children and themselves. Families, particularly families of color and non-English-speaking families, are rarely represented in juvenile court proceedings, and though incarcerated parents may have representation, they rarely get to speak with their attorneys or attend juvenile court dependency hearings until very late in the dependency process, when an effective case for parents to maintain custody and contact with their children can rarely be established.

ethical and legal ramifications of parental rights termination

The permanent removal of a child or children rips the heart out of a community and leaves the adult generation without hope. The dramatic overincarceration over the past several decades of greater and greater numbers of women, particularly women of color, and also men of color, has led to an increase in the number of children separated from their parents both temporarily and permanently. In many cases, the children are removed from their communities and placed with families of different racial/ethnic backgrounds, often with devastating results for these adoptees. Black children are significantly more likely to be placed in foster care than white children are, and they remain in foster care for longer periods of time. In addition, research studies have found a clear connection between race and the return of children to foster care rather than to their natural parents: children of color, compared with white children, are substantially less likely to be returned to their parents.[24]

This social phenomenon must be seen for what it is—a manifestation of deeply rooted patterns of racial and economic inequity, not a matter of individual cases of "child neglect"—before irreparable harm is inflicted on future generations of low-income African American, Latino, and other racialized families and communities. Termination of parental rights is a concept that is both artificial (the legally imposed pronouncement that a parent and child are no longer "related" to each other) and inherently immoral. It derives in large part from the deeply flawed but persistent belief that children are commodities that can somehow be transferred from one family to another, and that children cannot tolerate the "insecurity" of having more than one set of parental figures in their lives. In fact, the opposite is true: children respond to, and flourish in, the genuine, unselfish love of more than one (or two) parental figures. Children of incarcerated parents benefit, in most instances, from contact with their original parents; in the few cases where a parent has been so abusive to a child that no future contact with the parent during the child's early life would be advisable, children should, in most instances, be placed with relatives. The loss of the parent is often devastating to the child, but the double loss of separation from siblings and close relatives compounds this trauma. The relationship between the child of an incarcerated parent and that parent *belongs* to that child; no social services system, judge, or legal system has the right to deprive that child of that relationship. Any child of an incarcerated parent will have a wide range of feelings and emotions about his or her parent, including anger, sadness, love, and ambivalence. However, it should be the right of the child to either claim or deny that relationship with the parent, to forgive or refuse to forgive, and to continue the relationship or to end it.

After several decades of a massive escalation in the incarceration of people of color and in the removal of thousands of children of color from their parents and their extended families, the cumulative damage to these communities of color is palpable. At the same time, a grassroots movement of activists and advocates has also grown in response to these repressive trends and is challenging the effects of the continuing expansion of the prison-industrial complex and its many tentacles. This grassroots movement took form in the 1970s on the heels of the civil rights and women's movements.

Throughout the 1960s and early '70s, the prisoners' rights movement in the United States had focused almost exclusively on male prisoners. At the time, with a few notable exceptions, women in prison were virtually invisible to the progressive community and to the general public.[28] In the mid- to late 1970s, however, an increasing number of women activists, both in and out of prison, started to raise questions and concerns about issues that were of specific concern to women in prisons and jails, including the care and custody of children during their mother's incarceration, the treatment of pregnant women in prison, and the sexual harassment of women prisoners by male guards and staff.[29] Prior to the mid-1970s, the majority of class action lawsuits challenging conditions of confinement involved male prisoners, but after this time, women in prison started to protest conditions of confinement as well.[30] A handful of grassroots organizations sprang up around the country, focusing their energies and attention on the unique issues affecting women prisoners and their children.[31] During the 1980s, this handful of organizations became hundreds, and in 1985, the first National Roundtable on Women in Prison, a national gathering of formerly incarcerated women, their advocates, and family members, took place. In 1988, the National Network for Women in Prison was formed at the Fourth National Roundtable for Women in Prison in the San Francisco Bay area. From their inception, the National Roundtables and the National Network for Women in Prison have been led by formerly incarcerated women and focused on imprisoned and formerly imprisoned women's leadership and empowerment.[32]

As the movement grew throughout the 1990s, the leadership and involvement of formerly incarcerated women became an increasingly significant aspect of the grassroots activism. In the late 1990s, activists working with women prisoners and their children played a vital role in the emergence of a new movement challenging the growth of the prison-industrial complex as it affects women, men, and youth; family members and children of prisoners; and entire communities.[33] Most recently, the grassroots movement involving women prisoners and their allies has contributed to two additional emerging movements: one involving children and family members of prisoners,[34] and the other involving formerly incarcerated men, women, and youth speaking out in their own voices about the injustice of mass incarceration and the lifelong collateral consequences of criminalization.[35]

The growth in these grassroots movements has been accompanied by an increasing awareness among policymakers, academics, and media about the real issues confronting incarcerated parents and their children. A number of academic researchers and experts are making thoughtful contributions to the public discourse on the issue of parental incarceration. Activists, researchers, and practitioners are beginning to work in collaboration with each other to document the scope and substance of the impact of mass incarceration and family disruption on low-income communities of color.[36] It is my hope that the effort to document and expose the damage that the two very different but interrelated systems of corrections and social services have inflicted on the very fabric of low-income communities of color in this country will provide activists with the information and tools they need to bring about a complete transformation of both correctional policy and foster care/dependency laws, with respect to incarcerated parents and children of incarcerated parents.

Needless to say, this will be no small task. One fruitful avenue that we should explore is the development of protective legislation similar to the Native American Child Custody Act acknowledging the legitimacy of African American, Latino, and other racial/ethnic heritages.[37] Such legislation would directly and indirectly undercut and contradict existing law concerning race and adoption, and will likely be met with strenuous opposition from pro-adoption lobbies. However, given the ongoing impact of the removal of children from low-income communities of color, it is essential that advocates raise these issues despite the opposition that we will meet. Another area that needs special focus is the reaffirmation of the strength and the validity of the extended family as a source of support for the children of incarcerated parents. We must make a true priority of placing infants and children with extended relatives, and back up that commitment by continuing to advocate for increased benefits and supportive services for grandparents and relative caregivers. Finally, and most importantly, we must press for the proliferation of alternative treatment programs for women who are currently incarcerated that will enable women to serve their time in residential, community-based treatment programs with their infants and children. Several states, such as California and Illinois, have legislatively mandated programs and a number of other states have similar programs that are not statutorily protected.

As we review social services and juvenile court policies that affect incarcerated parents and their children, we must also promote decarceration strategies in order to reverse the rising tide of incarceration and criminalization of low-income people of color in the United States. These may include diverting people with addictions from prison to treatment centers, eliminating mandatory minimum sentences, and removing "truth-in-sentencing" provisions that keep prisoners behind bars for longer. We need to establish alternatives to incarceration for those prisoners who can be released immediately and work to create alternatives that meet the specific needs of as many people as possible, including the very large number of women with infants and young children who could be placed in residential treatment programs in lieu of incarceration.[38]

Those of us who are involved in prison or welfare rights activism need to build alliances with immigrant rights activists in order to defend the parental-child bonds of nonresident and undocumented incarcerated people, whose families are often torn apart by the machinery of not just two, but three, separate bureaucracies. And ultimately, as people who care about creating a better world for all children, we must ask ourselves whether the policies and programs that we put in place "for the good of the children" are really what is best for these children and their communities.

acknowledgments

I want to acknowledge and thank all of the parents in prison, children, and family members with whom I have worked over the past 30 years, who have shared their experiences and their lives with me and with the staff and volunteers of Legal Services for Prisoners with Children.

notes

1 Michaelah D., unpublished transcript, legal archives, Legal Services for Prisoners with Children (LSPC), 1540 Market Street, Suite 490, San Francisco, CA 94102.

2 Janine Jackson and Jim Naureckas, "Crime Contradictions: U.S. News Illustrates Flaws in Crime Coverage," *Fairness and Accuracy in Reporting*, May/June 1994, http://www.fair.org/index.php?page=1501.

3 Phyllis Chesler, *Mothers on Trial: The Battle for Children and Custody* (New York: McGraw Hill, 1986). See "Mothers in Prison."

4 See *Adoption and Safe Families Act* (1997): 105–189. See complying state statutes.

5 Marian Wright Edelman, *Resetting Our Nation's Moral Compass*, May 2005, www.childrensdefense.org. Edelman comments further that, as of 2001, there were 58,000 black males in prison and only 40,000 who were graduating from college.

6 The author uses African American in this essay to signify all US residents of African descent, including immigrants with origins in Africa and the Caribbean who are often targets of over-policing and police brutality.

7 National Education Association, "No Child Left Behind Act of 2001," *Issues in Education*, www.nea.org; "Facing Reality: What Happens When Good Schools Are Labeled 'Failures'?" MassPartners for Public Schools, www.masspartners.com.

8 Amnesty International, "Betraying the Young: Human Rights Violations Against Children in the US Justice System," 1998 Amnesty International Report, *Library*, http://web.amnesty.org/library/engindex; Sue Burrell, "Legal Issues and Liabilities in Juvenile Confinement Facilities" (Youth Law Center: San Francisco, November 2000).

9 American Bar Association, *Juvenile Death Penalty*, http://www.abanet.org/crimjust/juvjus/juvdp.html; in a significant move, the US Supreme Court struck down the use of the death penalty for juveniles (March 1, 2005), *Roper v. Simmons* (03–633) 112 S. W. 3d 397, affirmed.

10 For information on corporal punishment in schools, contact Parents and Teachers Against Violence in Education (PTAVE). PTAVE is a 501(c)(3) nonprofit organization: PO Box 1033, Alamo, CA 94507-7033, phone: 925-831-1661, fax: 925-838-8914, email: ptave@silcon.com. Over 20 states still allow children to be hit, paddled, and physically disciplined in other ways.

11 Particular mention must be made of the impact of incarceration on Native American communities. While the number of Native Americans in US prisons today is small in comparison with the number of other prisoners, a recent review conducted by the Foundation for National Progress (FNP), an umbrella organization for the magazine *Mother Jones*, found that 709 per 100,000 Native Americans and Alaska Natives were incarcerated in state prisons in 2000. The rate was surpassed only by African Americans, whose jail rate was a startling 1815 per 100,000. In 1980 there were 145 per 100,000 Native Americans in California's prisons, a rate that jumped to 767 per 100,000 in 2000. FNP, July, 2001.

12 Dorothy E. Roberts, "The Social and Moral Cost of Mass Incarceration in African American Communities," *Stanford Law Review* 56, no. 5 (April 1, 2004): 1271–1305; see Vincent Schiraldi and others, "Young African Americans and the Criminal Justice System in California: Five Years Later," *Publications and Library* (Report, Center on Juvenile and Criminal Justice, February 1996), http://www.lindesmith.org/library/schiraldi2.cfm.

13 Conversation between the author and a senior legislative analyst regarding drafting California statutory language concerning recently enacted federal foster care regulations (Sacramento, 1980).

14 Jurisdictions have a variety of different names and structures for the agencies that have authority over families and their children.

15 Susan Kellam, "The Color of Care," *Connect for Kids*, July 26, 1999, http://www.connectforkids.org/node/118?tn=lc/ra; Child Welfare League of America, "Children of Color in the Child Welfare System," *National Data Analysis System* (January 2004).

16 Jennifer C., unpublished transcript, legal archives, LSPC.

17 See *Adoption and Safe Families Act* (1997): 105–189.

18 Pew Commission on Children in Foster Care, "PEW Commission Report on 'Foster Care Drift,'" Press Office reprint of article from *Fostering Families Today Magazine* (May/June 2004): 18–19, http://pewfostercare.org/press/files/FosterArticle3.pdf.

19 See chapters by Raible, Harris, and Lo in this volume.

20 See Milfred C. Fierce, *Slavery Revisited: Blacks and the Convict Lease System, 1865–1933* (New York: African Studies Research Centre, 1994); Angela Y. Davis, *Are Prisons Obsolete?* (New York: Seven Stories Press, 2003).

21 See Ward Churchill and Jim Vander Wall, *The COINTELPRO Papers: Documents from the FBI's Secret Wars Against Domestic Dissent* (Boston: South End Press, 1991); Paul Wolf and others, "COINTELPRO:

The Untold American Story Compilation" (paper, World. Conference Against Racism, Durban, South Africa, September 1, 2001).

22 Churchill and Vander Wall, *The COINTELPRO Papers*; Wolf and others, "COINTELPRO."

23 Ellen Barry, River Ginchild, and Doreen Lee, "Termination of Parental Rights Among Prisoners: A National Perspective," in *Children of Incarcerated Parents*, ed. Katherine Gabel and Denise Johnston (New York: Lexington Books, 1995), 149. The percentage of children removed from incarcerated fathers is considerably lower.

24 One such organization, Babies Out of Bondage, has been operating in southern California for the past decade. The organization has actively solicited pregnant women in California state prisons (legal archives, LSPC).

25 Conversation with staff attorney Cassie Pierson of Legal Services for Prisoners with Children, who has documentation concerning eight different instances of this occurrence from 1998–2006.

26 Legal archives, LSPC.

27 Mark E. Courtney and others, "Race and Child Welfare Services: Past Research and Future Directions," *Child Welfare* 79, no. 4 (1996): 339–369; Westat Chapin Hall Center for Children, "The Role of Race in Parental Reunification," in *Assessing the Context of Permanency and Reunification in the Foster Care System* (December 2001), http://aspe.hhs.gov/hsp/fostercare-reunif01/chapter6.htm; Child Welfare League of America, "CWLA Fact Sheet and Relevant Research," *National Data Analysis System*, http://ndas.cwla.org/research_info/specialtopic1a.asp. For every 1000 African American or Black children in the US population in 2002, there were 17 in foster care, compared to only 5 per 1000 white children in the US population.

28 A few of these notable women continue to challenge the prison-industrial complex: Angela Davis was not only a visible and respected leader in the early movement, but also continues to play a significant role in the present-day movement; Assata Shakur, an active member of the Black Panther Party in the early 1970s, remains an active and visible leader even as she lives in exile in Cuba.

29 Early support for this work came from a few university-based clinics, most notably the original Women's Prison Clinic at NYU Law School, under the direction of Barbara Swartz (1976–1985), and the Women's Prison Project at UC Santa Cruz.

30 Deliberate indifference to medical needs: New York, see *Todaro v. Ward*, 565 F.2d 48, 52 (2nd Cir. 1977); custodial sexual abuses and misconduct: New York, see *Fort v. Ward*, 621 F.2d 1210 (2nd Cir. 1980); discriminatory denial of vocational training: Michigan, see *Glover v. Johnson*, 138 F.3d 229, 245 (6th Cir. 1998); medical treatment for pregnant and postpartum women: California, see *Harris v. McCarthy*, No. 85-6002-WMB (MCx) (C.D. Cal. filed Sept. 11, 1985) (settlement agreement Oct. 1987).

31 Some of these early organizations included Aid to Incarcerated Mothers (AIM), Boston, MA (f. 1975); Prison Mothers and Their Children (MATCH), Pleasanton, CA (f. 1977); Legal Services for Prisoners with Children (LSPC), San Francisco, CA (f. 1978); Aid to Children of Incarcerated Mothers (AIM) Atlanta, GA (f. 1982); Chicago Legal Advocacy to Incarcerated Mothers) (CLAIM), Chicago, IL (f. 1983).

32 The National Network for Women in Prison (c/o Legal Services for Prisoners with Children, 1540 Market Street, Suite 490, San Francisco, CA 94102). According to its bylaws, the membership of the board of directors must be at least 50 percent formerly incarcerated women and 50 percent women of color. At all National Roundtables, keynote speakers and conference panelists have included a high percentage of formerly incarcerated women and women of color and a diverse audience of participants.

33 In the late 1990s, a small group of activists from the San Francisco–Oakland area proposed a gathering to examine and organize around the dramatic expansion of the prison system in all of its manifestations. Adopting Mike Davis's phrase, "the prison-industrial complex," this group hosted a conference of over 3500 people from every state in the United States and 11 other countries in September 1998 at UC Berkeley, launching the "Critical Resistance" (CR) movement. CR now has 10 chapters in the United States and many contacts worldwide (Davis, "Hell Factories in the Field: A Prison-Industrial Complex," *The Nation*, February 20, 1995, 229).

34 Contact Legal Services for Prisoners with Children regarding resources concerning children and families of prisoners and the "Children of Incarcerated Parents Bill of Rights" (San Francisco Partnership for Incarcerated Parents, September 2003). Other groups working with children and family members of prisoners include Aid to Incarcerated Mothers, Boston, MA; the Osborne Association, New York, NY, nominated for the "Children's Nobel Prize" in 2004; Families and Loved Ones of Louisiana's Incarcerated Children (FLIC), New Orleans, LA; and Aid to Children of Incarcerated Mothers, Atlanta, GA, among many others.

35 In early 2000, a diverse group of formerly incarcerated women and men met at LSPC to discuss the urgent need to create a movement of people who have been imprisoned. This group wanted to speak out in their own voices about the inequities and obstacles that they faced as former prisoners "criminalized" by the past four decades of rampant incarceration. The group, now known as All of Us or None, has sparked a nascent nationwide movement.

36 For example, the Family Rights Project is a collaborative effort between the Brennan Center at NYU Law School and three grassroots organizations around the United States—Legal Services for Prisoners with Children (San Francisco), Chicago Legal Advocacy to Incarcerated Mothers (Chicago), and MECCA's Place (Baltimore)—as well as academic researchers Beth Richie and Marty Guggenheim, that is documenting the experiences of incarcerated mothers and their children with the juvenile court dependency system.

37 Minnesota Legislative Reference Library, "Minnesota Minority Child Heritage Protection Act," *Resources on Minnesota Issues* (September 2004), www.leg.state.mn.us/lrl/issues/mmchpa.asp. See, for example, the history of the act.

38 The Community Prisoner Mother-Infant Care Program (CPMP), for example, is a community-based alternative to incarceration that provides for a woman sentenced to state prison in California being placed with her infant or young child in a residential treatment program in lieu of incarceration. While the program has its limitations, it also provides an invaluable opportunity for incarcerated mothers to be with their young children instead of being separated. See CA Penal Code Sec. 3401, et seq.; see also recent legislation passed in Illinois creating similar alternative programs. Future models should be community-based and -run, as opposed to being correctionally based.

Minneapolis **Tribune** | **Family**

Nurse helps troubled waifs in Vietnam

Staff Photo by Pete Hohn

Rosemary Taylor, with children who have been adopted by families in Minnesota.

By Jacquelyn K. Jones

Rosemary Taylor was sent to Vietnam in 1967 by the Australian Council of Churches to help care for the elderly and handicapped people at Phu My refuge. But there she saw that there was more to be done for children.

Thousands of them had been abandoned because their families couldn't afford to care for them or they had become separated from their families during evacuations. Many of the children were fathered by American servicemen.

"I saw that there was a need to work with the abandoned children. I didn't ask anybody. I saw the need and so I started an orphanage," Miss Taylor said.

One orphanage led to another. Now Miss Taylor is the supervisor of four orphanages in Saigon. One child also led to another. Since 1967 Miss Taylor has arranged for the adoption of more than 2,000 children by families in Europe, Canada and the United States.

Minnesota families have adopted 34 Vietnamese children, many of them through the arrangements of Miss Taylor and her staff of 12 people. Some of these parents and children recently attended a reception for her in Minneapolis.

They watched her slides of the orphanages and they heard her talk of how things are getting worse for the children now that the Vietnam war is over.

"Adoption is the only answer for many of the abandoned children," she said. "If they remained in Vietnam they would die from disease or starvation. My biggest problem is trying to keep the children alive until they can be adopted."

Miss Taylor, 34, a former high-school teacher from a family of five children in Adelaide, Australia, seems reluctant to talk about her motivation or her work.

"My starting an orphanage had nothing to do with my childhood," she said. "I had a very happy childhood."

Other persons acquainted with her work tell more about what she has done.

Barbara Baden, a nurse who has worked with her in Vietnam, tells about the opening of the first nursery for 15 children, of how Miss Taylor brings very sick young children from other orphanages to her facilities to give them medical care.

"She provides care for the children until she can arrange for them to be adopted," said Miss Baden. "I don't like to call Rosemary's homes orphanages; they are more like waiting stations."

Doris Schenaue, social worker at Children's Home Society in the Twin Cities, tells

Children
continued on page 7E

Original caption reads: "Rosemary Taylor, with children who have been adopted by families in Minnesota."
Staff photo by Pete Hohn, *Minneapolis Tribune,* Sunday, December 2, 1973.

9

ORPHANING THE CHILDREN OF WELFARE

"Crack Babies," Race, and Adoption Reform

Laura Briggs

In 1994, at the height of the neoconservative effort to put an end to AFDC (Aid to Families with Dependent Children, or "welfare"), Speaker of the House Newt Gingrich suggested a policy alternative: put the children of welfare mothers in orphanages. His comment to this effect was widely reported, and liberals professed shock. Then-President Bill Clinton, child of a sometimes-single mother himself, denounced it; his weekly radio address called it a plan to take children out of "loving homes." But a few days later, something much less publicized happened: Gingrich amended "orphanages" to "group homes." The furor abated. Liberal *Washington Post* columnist Mary McGrory argued that the plan was humane and well-grounded in much liberal sentiment.[1] Sadly, she was right about the latter, if not the former. A version of Gingrich's vision of poverty policy became law, with support from liberals, expanding both the size and significance of the child welfare system.

Although the Dickensian quality of the word "orphanages" brought down a firestorm of criticism, to neoconservatives—and many liberals—removing children from impoverished families was a natural outgrowth of where antipoverty programs had long been heading. In the 1960s, liberal concepts like the "culture of poverty" and Democratic policy papers like the Moynihan Report identified the cause of poverty as family and childrearing, rather than unemployment or wages. As the Moynihan Report had it, "Black matriarchs" emasculated their sons, making them unable to compete for jobs, while the "culture of poverty" inculcated habits of being poor in one generation after the next. In the 1970s child welfare workers were given vast new powers to remove children from families if they suspected abuse or neglect—with neglect definable as poverty—without a legal case or even having to offer evidence for their suspicions.[2] In the 1980s the War on Drugs identified (implicitly Black) "crack babies" as a new "bio-underclass," destined from birth to be uneducable and unemployable; liberals endeavored to put the children in foster care, while conservatives worked to put their mothers in jail. In the 1990s, identifying AFDC with a host of ills, conservatives and centrist Democrats worked simultaneously to end income supports for impoverished mothers and to move their children not just into foster care but out again, into adoptive families. In 1996 and 1997, the adoption tax credit and the Interethnic Placement Provisions (an amendment to the Multiethnic Placement Act, hence known as MEPA-IEP) did just that.[3]

In recent years, the foster/adopt system has replaced AFDC as the primary government policy affecting impoverished mothers and their children. While the system is not cost-effective, it continues to be the bedrock of federal poverty policy. We don't know exactly how many people it affects because the trappings of confidentiality, the voluntary and hence incomplete nature of national statistics-keeping, and its decentralized nature (there is not *a* foster care system, but more than fifty, since each state and territory has its own) make it extremely hard to track. It is nevertheless clear that since 1996, the foster care system has expanded. We cannot show that it has been good for children to be taken from their families, although proponents justify the foster and child welfare system in these terms. While there are no comprehensive statistics about what happens to children who are in foster care (states treat that information as confidential and aggregate it in diverse and sometimes incomplete ways), we know from smaller studies that fostered children are overrepresented in the populations of prisons and psychiatric institutions, as are their grown counterparts.[4] Why this infatuation with a system that is massively expensive and doesn't work?[5] The answer is a deep-rooted belief that impoverished families, mothers in particular, are toxic to their children. Grounded in a liberal savior complex and a centuries-old English history of viewing the poor as "vicious," the system relies on the theory that poor people are poor because they have bad character and imagines that the right kind of family—mothering really—can redeem these children.

In this chapter, I explore some of this history, beginning with the elaboration of the "culture of poverty" by Oscar Lewis and other social scientists in the 1950s and '60s; continuing on to the "crack baby" crisis of the late 1980s; and, finally, looking at the adoption tax credit and MEPA-IEP, which, alongside welfare reform, were supposed to transform poor people into productive citizens by taking away their children and putting them in (implicitly white) middle-class homes. At each of these times, there were significant realignments in the forms of public policy and the meanings of race. The "culture of poverty" concept worked to signal the end of the era of governmental support for Black civil rights, while the "crack baby" epidemic marked the height of the Reagan-Bush era's criminalization of poverty through the War on Drugs. The adoption tax credit of 1996 was initially part of the welfare reform bill. Taken together, these two pieces of legislation serve to mark the bad faith of state relationships to working-class women, children, and families.

the culture of poverty

The concept of a culture of poverty began its career as a social science paradigm elaborated by anthropologists, sociologists, and journalists who associated themselves with the Left, yet by the 1980s it was firmly the property of neoconservatives. Whether it ever really was a progressive concept is not so clear. In the hands of its originator, Oscar Lewis, it focused on behaviors and beliefs learned in childhood, including a looseness about sexuality, multiple partners, the conception of children outside of nuclear families, and carelessness about children's upbringing, including both neglect and violence. In 1961, Lewis summarized his understanding of the culture of poverty:

> In anthropological usage, [culture] implies, essentially, a design for living which is passed down from generation to generation. In applying this concept of culture to the understanding of poverty, I want to draw attention to the fact that poverty in modern nations is not only a state of economic deprivation, of disorganization, or the absence of something. It is also something positive in the sense that it has a structure, a rationale, and defense mechanisms without which the poor could hardly carry on. In short, it is a way of life, remarkably stable and persistent, passed down from generation to generation along family lines.[6]

This is a striking definition; in three sentences, Lewis mentions that this culture is "passed down from generation to generation" twice. This way of understanding poverty is fundamentally about children and child-rearing. Later, in his 1966 book, *La Vida,* Lewis put an age to it: By the time children were six or seven, he argued, they were so damaged by the effects of the "culture of poverty" that they were essentially doomed to repeat the impoverished lives of their parents. In the hands of those like political scientist Edward Banfield in 1970, the "culture of poverty" served to make a very familiar distinction in US culture—what historian Michael Katz calls the Anglo-American tradition of distinguishing between the "worthy" and "unworthy" poor.[7] Although Lewis never meant his theory to have this effect, it presented a profoundly hopeless prognosis for the inhabitants of this cultural category.

Oscar Lewis was careful in his original articulation of the culture of poverty thesis to assert that "modern" poverty was different in its psychological effects from "traditional" poverty. Traditional poverty was consistent with social cohesion, strong family units, and healthy sexuality and gender norms. Children coming from such contexts, then, might have suffered from a lack of health care or nutrition, perhaps might have some learning problems, but would not have been deeply psychologically damaged by their own families.[8] It is striking how neatly this maps onto contemporary beliefs about adoption: While children from US foster care are often "bad seeds," with problematic families whose members or characteristics might reappear in frightening ways, children from overseas—even Eastern European children with long histories of institutionalization, who are older, who in fact are pretty much like US foster children in most ways—are a safer bet.

In 2002 a researcher looking for endocrine markers of early childhood stress and trauma indirectly made this very point. He compared two groups: postinstitutionalized Romanian children and post–foster care children adopted by US families. By virtually any measure—age at adoption, aggressiveness toward peers and family, trouble getting along with other children, school problems, and delinquency—these two groups of children offered the same (considerable) behavioral and emotional challenges to their adoptive families.[9] Finding these children so similar in so many dimensions raises the question: Why did Americans rush to Romania in 1991 (when 2594 state department visas were issued for Romanian "orphans," with only 100 each in 1990 and 1992),[10] to adopt deeply troubled kids at considerable expense and with very little formal support for raising them, when they could have adopted substantially similar children in the United States, with institutionalized support and government subsidy? While the motives and beliefs of adopters are as heterogeneous as the children they adopt, I think part of the answer is that these would-be adopters saw these two groups of children as having very different prospects in life, even if they had the same troubles.

the mythical crack baby

But let us return to our chronology. In the 1980s pessimism about the inherited culture of poor children turned into a concern about their biology. By 1989 "crack babies" were the news story of the year. Major newspapers ran huge, multipage features,[11] and network news shows bombarded their audiences with images of women using crack cocaine during their pregnancies, characterizing these offspring as likely to be born early; to experience exceptionally high rates of perinatal mortality; to be born addicted and quivering; to experience a host of neurological, digestive, respiratory, and cardiac problems; and to be headed toward a childhood of learning difficulties, hyperactivity, and, ultimately, delinquency and jail.[12] This was also an intensely racialized moral panic. Although the typical user of both cocaine and crack was a young white male, by 1985 television and print media were portraying crack as a drug used by African Americans, and, to a lesser extent, Latinos. From 1988 to 1990, the nightly news engaged in a war against crack mothers, who were almost by definition Black. In that period, 55 percent of the women portrayed in network TV news stories were Black; in later years, from 1991 to 1994, it was 84 percent.[13] The newspapers were, if anything, worse.[14]

At the urging of federal drug czar William Bennett, many hospitals—especially those serving mostly Black patients—introduced routine screening for cocaine into delivery rooms, and mothers who tested positive lost their newborns on the spot; a number went to jail, still bleeding from labor.[15] Even before delivery, some crack-using pregnant women were persuaded to say that jail was the best place for them.[16] Between 1985 and 2000, more than 200 women faced criminal prosecution for using cocaine and other drugs during pregnancy, and tens of thousands lost their children to foster care.[17] Black women, in particular, went to jail for cocaine use out of any proportion to their representation among drug-using pregnant women.[18]

The "crack baby" epidemic produced the contemporary foster care and child welfare system. Between 1985 and 1988, the number of children in out-of-home placement—foster care, psychiatric institutions, and the juvenile justice system—increased by 25 percent.[19] In the post–Reagan social service landscape, these policies initially taxed foster care systems to the breaking point, but "essay" quickly became a rallying point for agencies to lobby for—and get—massive new funding. Congressional reports, hearings, and funding appropriations reflected the new urgency about caring for the "littlest victims" of crack, and built a much larger institutional capacity (at the same time that a massive prison system was also being built, in no small measure for these same children's parents). Foster parents of these so-called crack babies were canonized by the popular press; they were caring for "babies in pain," who disrupted families and would never be normal.[20]

There was also profound popular opposition to "crack mothers" getting their children back. The most fully developed and dramatic account of why crack mothers could not parent their children came from Hollywood in the popular film *Losing Isaiah,* as Sandra Patton has argued in her important book, *Birthmarks.*[21] In *Losing Isaiah,* the child's Black birthmother (played by Hollywood's only Black sweetheart, Halle Berry) is living in a crack house and abandons him in a pile of garbage so that she can go get high. A heroic white social worker (Jessica Lange) takes in the quivering infant after he suffers a brain hemorrhage and raises him despite incessant crying, hypersensitivity to stimuli, and hyperactivity. The child bonds with the new family, but birthmom reappears, having gotten clean. A race-conscious family court voids the adoption and awards custody to the birthmother. Isaiah fails to bond with his birthmother (at the Black Power daycare), and the white social worker has to step in to save the day again.[22]

Neoconservative commentators were among the most vociferous in promoting the notion that there was a crack baby crisis. Douglas Besharov of the conservative American Enterprise Institute referred to the birth of a "bio-underclass" that Head Start could not help. This analysis was quoted by syndicated columnist Charles Krauthammer, who, in high eugenicist mode, referred to a '"generation of physically damaged cocaine babies whose biological inferiority is stamped at birth,"' claiming this group comprised 5 to 15 percent of all Black children.[23] Even liberal African American commentators like Derrick Z. Jackson of the *Boston Globe* and William Raspberry of the *Washington Post* joined in, arguing that crack caused the high rates of Black infant mortality and that efforts to decriminalize drugs should be opposed because of the effects of cocaine on babies.[24]

The bitter irony of all of this rhetoric is that none of it was true. Physicians and researchers now believe that crack has very little, if any, effect on pregnancies or fetuses. In March 2001 medical researcher Deborah Frank and her colleagues did a meta-analysis of all research on the effects of prenatal cocaine exposure published in English between 1984 and 2000 that met certain minimum criteria: they had a control group, subjects were prospectively recruited, examiners were masked as to which children had been exposed to cocaine, and children with exposure to more than one risk factor in utero (opiates, amphetamines, phencyclodine, or HIV) were excluded. Their conclusions, published in the prestigious *Journal of the American Medical Association (JAMA)* are literally incredible to most lay people; the researchers found virtually no evidence that cocaine use during pregnancy had any negative effects on offspring. They wrote:

> After controlling for cofounders, there was no consistent negative association between prenatal cocaine exposure and physical growth, developmental test scores, or receptive or expressive language. Less optimal motor scores have been found up to age 7 months but not thereafter, and may reflect heavy tobacco exposure. No independent cocaine effects have been shown on standardized parent and teacher reports of child behavior scored by accepted criteria.[25]

While the study showed debatable evidence for attention problems, that was it. Most of the effects once attributed to cocaine turn out to be the effect of things like alcohol, tobacco, marijuana, or environment—including homelessness or domestic violence. Other researchers and analysts have largely confirmed this account in the medical literature. The most recent peer-reviewed, adequately controlled, large-scale prospective longitudinal studies have shown no effect or questionable effect of in-utero cocaine exposure.[26] But this assessment has had little effect on social scientists, popular culture, or policymaking. As suggested in Wendy Chavkin's commentary on the research by Frank and her colleagues in the same issue of *JAMA,* the entire "hullabaloo" about "crack babies" seems to have had much more to do with politics than it ever did with medical effects on fetuses.[27]

While in one sense the hysteria *was* about politics, medical researchers were among those who had led the charge against "crack mothers." It was their work that provided the foundation for the media, child welfare, and public policy assault on cocaine-using pregnant women. There was a strong bias within the peer-review system among researchers on this issue for work that confirmed that cocaine had terrible effects on pregnancy; plenty of articles (that we now know were wrong) were published that insisted on links between crack exposure and elevated rates of premature labor, placenta previa, neural and digestive system abnormalities, kidney malformations, Sudden Infant Death Syndrome (SIDS), excessive crying, hypersensitivity to touch, attentiveness problems, and hyperactivity. At the height of the anticrack campaign in the media in 1989, one researcher noted that the likelihood that a study of cocaine effects on pregnancy outcomes would be accepted for the annual meeting of the Society of Pediatric Research was significantly affected by whether or not it found adverse effects. Studies that showed no effect on a pregnancy had an 11 percent acceptance rate, while those that found undesirable effects on fetuses had a 57 percent acceptance rate, despite the fact that negative studies tended to be better designed, more likely to have control groups, and more likely to compare polydrug exposure with and without cocaine.[28]

There is a haunting question about how the most vulnerable, most impoverished people in the United States—pregnant women, often prostitutes, sometimes using multiple drugs (prominently alcohol and tobacco), often homeless, more often than not facing violence during their pregnancies, frequently dealing with long-term illhealth and often mental illness—became a symbol of everything that was wrong with the country. For all these reasons, it often seemed plausible that the children of "crack mothers" weren't doing well. Of course, these infants were not doing well, but crack was merely a marker of their mother's distress, not the cause of the children's. The entire edifice of the moral panic about "crack babies" rested on two statistics, both of which ultimately proved to be wrong. The evidence for a growing "epidemic" of cocaine use, rooted in the newly available, cheap form of the drug, crack, was a slight increase in a daily and weekly usage statistic provided by the General Accounting Office. These statistics were notoriously unreliable because they were based on very small samples. Even the slight increase reported proved wrong: The percentage of the US population using crack remained absolutely stable between 1988 and 1994.[29] A second statistic showed a sharp rise in the mortality rate of African American infants in Washington, DC, in the first half of 1989; officials later realized that a large number of these deaths had really occurred in 1988, and infant mortality rates had stayed, in fact, relatively stable.[30]

While the knowledge that the case for the crack "epidemic" wreaking havoc in inner cities and blighting a generation of babies was extraordinarily shaky was available for those who cared to find it even in the late 1980s, few people did. "Crack babies" were poster children for the War on Drugs and an allegory for debates about abortion. They became Exhibit A for the mostly conservative policymakers and prosecutors who wanted to show why small-time drug users were a danger to society as a whole and deserving of jail time (since what were being called "boarder babies" were putting incredible strain on hospital finances, and, once out, the children were entitled to expensive special education classes at public expense), and why fetuses needed to be protected from dangerous mothers who would kill them if they were lucky, to paraphrase the columnist Krauthammer.[31]

At the precise moment when the Reagan and (first) Bush administrations had all but succeeded in disallowing race as a legitimate term of political grievance through their attacks on supports such as affirmative action, and following decades of deindustrialization and the flight of jobs from cities that disproportionately affected communities of color, race re-emerged sharply as a term by which to characterize pathology, indeed, a specifically biologized pathology. The terms of this discourse explained away a multitude of problems caused by Reagan-era economic policies, such as homelessness and increasing infant mortality rates, especially among African Americans. The "crack baby" crisis invited people not to think about the economic causes that led communities of color and urban youth of whatever race to be disproportionately involved in the low-level retail side of the drug trade, or the ways that cuts to social services and government transfer payments left working-class families scrambling. It also discounted another story one could have told about impoverished children in this era: the effects on youth of the steadily expanding work days that working-class parents had to put in to make ends meet. In its place, the "crack baby" epidemic offered bad parenting, moral failure, and a criminal recklessness about fetuses. Once again, we find a redefinition of poverty at a critical policy juncture that rests on an account of children and childhood. Where the concept of the culture of poverty intervened in the War on Poverty to produce an anomalously pessimistic view of the childhood of the working class, the narrative of crack babies produced a biologized account of the growing impoverishment of urban communities of color.

welfare reform and adoption reform

It was the narrative of heroic white adoptive families, à la *Losing Isaiah,* that provided the opening for a neoconservative redemption story in the 1990s. Following the "crack baby" epidemic, would-be adopters turned in significant numbers to overseas adoption. At the same time, there were various efforts to expand the pool of potential adoptees to include US foster children in a serious way. In part, this effort mapped onto changes in the way race was being defined, and also, as always, a shift in poverty policy. Not incidentally, welfare reform and adoption reform were coupled; indeed, both were initially part of congressional conservatives' "Contract with America."[32]

By the early 1990s, neoconservatives were engaged in a full-court push to end AFDC, based on their particular reading of the "culture of poverty" and the theory's apparent assertion that it was impossible to end poverty through income supports without ending the culture of poverty. Indeed, they argued, AFDC *caused* fatherlessness by providing support only to single mothers, hence effectively introducing a major disincentive to marry. Fatherlessness, in turn, caused every horror and moral failing known to humans. So welfare causes social pathology. The following passage by William Niskanen in the journal of the conservative think tank, the Cato Institute, is a personal favorite because he lists abortion among the social pathologies caused by AFDC.

> Analysis of the state data for 1992 yields the following estimates of the effects of an increase in Aid to Families with Dependent Children (AFDC) benefits by 1 percent of the average personal income in the state: the number of AFDC recipients would increase by about 3 percent; the number of people in poverty would increase by about 0.8 percent; the number of births to single mothers would increase by about 2.1 percent; the number of adults who are not employed would increase by about 0.5 percent; the number of abortions would increase by about 1.2 percent; and the violent crime rate would increase by about 1.1 percent.[33]

With antipoverty programs like this, poverty—moneylessness—looked like a preferable alternative.

This conservative loathing of AFDC was met by centrist-liberal acquiescence and even agreement. Sylvia Ann Hewlett and Cornel West, would-be champions of feminism and racial justice for African Americans, respectively, titled their effort to counter the Right's welfare reform efforts, *The War Against Parents.* The book proposed the expected liberal response—championing governmental income supports for families—but also indicated how dominant the Right's account of the horrors of unmarried motherhood had become. Hewlett and West agreed that fatherlessness was a great injury to children, contributing to problems as varied as youth violence, substance abuse, lowered SAT scores, and childhood obesity, arguing that female-headed households were a huge public policy problem that government action ought to solve.[34] Following as it did the 1995 Million Man March's mobilization in part to demonstrate support for Black fatherhood, this book suggests how few people were willing to defend working-class women's mothering in the mid-1990s. Without fathers to balance it, working-class motherhood had become the root of most social evils.

The legislation that ultimately came to embody Newt Gingrich's goal of putting the children of welfare mothers in orphanages was the adoption tax credit and a major subsequent piece of legislation (originally also contained in the welfare reform bill) calling for the "Removal of Barriers to Interethnic Adoption."[35] It was framed primarily in terms of race or, rather, the assertion that the reason so many children "languish" in foster care was race-matching policies that supposedly discriminated against white would-be adoptive parents. As Patton has shown, what ultimately became the adoption tax credit was originally part of the same bill as the welfare reform act of 1996.[36] This linkage made explicit what had been implicit in much of the previous debate; notwithstanding who actually received AFDC, "welfare mother" referred to

Black, Latino, and Indian (less often, Asian) women, and the placements being sought (after their children were moved to orphanages or group homes) were with white families.

This neoconservative policy proposal was a twist from previous political alignments. In the 1960s and '70s, it was liberal civil rights advocates who argued that adoption could make racially heterogeneous families.[37] Although interracial adoption in that era was primarily a gloss for adoption of biracial babies by white families—which under a different regime of racial meanings would not have been transracial at all—it was nevertheless a complicated thing for white families to do under the reigning segregationist paradigm.[38] It requires some work to untwist these strands, to understand how, after decades of transracial adoption as a liberal project, the journal of the Right-wing American Enterprise Institute could run an article denouncing "Adoption and the Color Barrier" and liberal Barbara Kingsolver could write a novel that sensitively and movingly portrays the Indian Child Welfare Act as a necessary bulwark to ensure Native American cultural survival.[39]

As many have argued, the 1990s saw a realignment of mainstream racial meanings that began to imagine the possibility of a multicultural ruling class.[40] New sciences of race insisted on our common genetic heritage,[41] while computer software, popular magazines, and television advertisements for shaving cream invited us to imagine races morphing into each other through visual technologies that juxtaposed different faces onto each other. As Donna Haraway argues, Michael Jackson, the child symbol of Black pride that medical treatment made into a "white" adult, became the perfect symbol of the way race was supposed to (not) signify.[42] At the same time, as the Census Bureau recorded, this was purely (or precisely) a cosmetic realignment. Poverty rates for those who understood themselves as Latinos, American Indians, Alaskan Natives, and African Americans remained more than three times the rate for whites, while for Asian and Pacific Islanders it remained one and a half times higher.[43]

The 1996 legislation prohibiting race matching in adoption continued this pattern, masking the racial bad faith of neoconservative and liberal colorblindness through a superficial multiculturalism, while gutting affirmative action in employment and education and dismantling the federal safety net for poor women and children. Perhaps more than at any time in the three decades of arguments about childhood that preceded it, there was no attempt to hide the contempt that was embedded in the adoption tax credit's pity of the poor. Even as welfare reform all but eliminated federal transfer payments to help working-class women raise their own children, the 1996 adoption reform provided a $6000 tax break to (implicitly white) middle-class families who adopted "special needs" children—with nonwhite a subcategory of the definition of special needs. Combined with the 1980 federal Adoption Assistance and Child Welfare Act that provided subsidies to middle- and upper-class families adopting from foster care, the adoption tax credit meant that the federal government would provide upwards of a $13,000 bonus for middle-class white people to raise the same children taken from families for poverty-related neglect that it wouldn't pay to alleviate. If the problem with foster care, as critic Elizabeth Bartholet complains, is that working-class people can do it for the money,[44] now middle-class people can do adoption for far more.

Nevertheless, efforts to provide massive monetary incentives to persuade potential US adopters to reconsider domestic poor children have been accompanied by only token efforts to depathologize these children. At the same time, the private adoption system in this country has grown steadily larger and more expensive. A few decades ago, there was effectively only one system; now, there are decidedly two. The public system deals with working-class, traumatized kids, and the private system provides ($30,000) white infants, with both the private adoption system and the increasingly commodified reproductive technology market (with eggs and sperm for sale) presumed to be the source for higher-quality, lower-risk reproductive products.

Nor does it seem likely that public child welfare agencies are going to be inundated with requests to adopt children out of foster care any time soon. Whether promulgated by the Left or Right, white people or people of color, the belief that racially heterogeneous families are a good thing has never been tremendously popular in the United States, particularly among white people, despite the reality of how many people live in "mixed" families and, indeed, the rarity of racial purity (here or anywhere in the Americas). The fight over transracial adoption has always been a bit of a red herring in public policy within the United States. Since the 1960s, there have never been that many white families anxious to adopt African American children, nor have there been barriers for white families otherwise meeting agency criteria (i.e., not gay or lesbian, with sufficient income, and so on) to adopt 10-year-old diabetic Black children with trauma histories. There has been, in some states, an unseemly scramble by white families to get Black infants, in which white families have felt that Black families had an "unfair" advantage.[45]

But the argument that so many children "languish" in foster care due to there are barriers to transracial adoption was always a distraction from the fact that the state is putting overwhelming numbers of impoverished children, particularly children of color, in foster care in the first place, not because of abuse or actual neglect, but as a matter of policy, as a replacement for giving "welfare" to their mothers. Indeed, since the 1996 "removal of barriers to inter-ethnic placement," in the language of the act, the number of Black children in foster care has increased.[46] At the risk of being an economic reductionist, I would submit that fights over transracial adoption—while tremendously important in individual lives—were never much more, at the policy level, than a highly engaging controversy that served to cover up the far wider question. That is why so many children whose birthparents have been accused of little more than poverty are in foster care to begin with—40 percent of whom are white, and most of whom never become "free" for adoption anyway. In a policy that has been developing since the 1960s, we have—through the myths of a culture of poverty, crack babies, and now adoption reform—replaced a relatively cheap program, AFDC, that never served its recipients very well, with an ever-growing foster care system and a poverty policy that is far more expensive but brutally punishes women—and their children—for being poor by taking their children away.

acknowledgments

An earlier version of this essay was coauthored with Ana Teresa Ortiz and published in *Social Text* 75 (September 2003). Thanks to both for permission to rework it here. I also wish to thank Maribel Briggs Ortiz, Dana Nelson, and Amy Kaplan for their comments and help with this piece, as well as our audience at the American Studies conference.

notes

1 Mary McGrory, "Orphanage Idea Has Many Parents," *Washington Post,* December 13, 1994.

2 Barbara J. Nelson, *Making an Issue of Child Abuse: Political Agenda Setting for Social Problems* (Chicago: University of Chicago Press, 1984), 88–90.

3 Originally part of the welfare reform bill, the Interethnic Placement Provisions were passed under the Small Business Job Protection Act of 1996 (PL 104–188), sections 1807 and 1808. See http://naic.acf.hhs.gov/general/legal/federal/pl104_188.cfm.

4 Dorothy E. Roberts, *Shattered Bond: The Color of Child Welfare* (New York: Basic Civitas Books, 2002), 202–207.

5 Administration for Children with Families, US Department of Health and Human Services, *Characteristics and Financial Circumstances of AFDC Recipients* (Washington, DC: Government Printing Office, 1997); Shelly Waters Boots and Rob Green, *Kinship Care or Foster Care? How State Policies Affect Kinship Caregivers* (Urban Institute, 1999), http://www.urban.org/url.cfm?ID=309166. It is massively more expensive for states to keep children in out-of-home care than AFDC ever was. According to federal government sources, the average AFDC payment in 1996 to families with one child was $3444 a year, while the average cost of a foster-care placement in 1996 was $6000 a year.

6 Oscar Lewis, *Children of Sanchez: Autobiography of a Mexican Family* (New York: Random House, 1961).

7 Edward C. Banfield, *The Unheavenly City: The Nature and Future of Our Urban Crisis* (Boston: Little Brown, 1970); Michael B. Katz, *The Undeserving Poor: From the War on Poverty to the War on Welfare* (New York: Pantheon Books, 1989).

8 Oscar Lewis, *La Vida: A Puerto Rican Family in the Culture of Poverty—San Juan and New York* (New York: Random House, 1966).

9 Victor Groza and Scott D. Ryan, "Pre-Adoption Stress and Its Association with Child Behaviour in Domestic Special Needs and International Adoptions," *Pyschoneuralendocrinology* 27, no. 1–2 (2002). Many other researchers have confirmed this similarity; see Thais Tepper, Lois Hannon, and Dorothy Sandstrom, eds., *International Adoption: Challenges and Opportunities* (Meadowlands, PA: Parents Network for the Post Institutional Child, 1999).

10 US Department of State, Bureau of Consular Affairs, *Immigrant Visas Issued to Orphans Coming to US,* http://travel.state.gov/family/adoption/stats/stats_451.html.

11 See Lynn Duke, "Crack Abuser's Baby Is Born, Doctors Don't Yet Know Cocaine's Effect on Infant," *Washington Post,* December 29, 1989; Lynn Duke, "For Pregnant Addict, Crack Comes First / Drug Use Blamed for DC Infant Deaths," *Washington Post,* December 18, 1989.

12 For a detailed review of the news programming of 1989, see Drew Humphries, *Crack Mothers: Pregnancy, Drugs, and the Media, Women and Health* (Columbus: Ohio State University Press, 1999). Some characteristic newspaper articles include Delores Long, "Bennett: Take Infant If Mother Is on Drugs," *Boston Globe,* December 1989; "Pregnant Drug User Glad for Jail," *Chicago Tribune*, December 16, 1989; William Raspberry, "Addicts and Babies," *Washington Post,* December 20, 1989; Abe M. Rosenthal, "How Much Is a Baby Worth?" *New York Times,* December 15, 1989.

13 Humphries, *Crack Mothers,* 21, 42–47.

14 See, for example, Duke, "For Pregnant Addict"; Derrick Z. Jackson, "America's Shameful Little Secret," *Boston Globe,* December 24, 1989.

15 Humphries, *Crack Mothers.*

16 "Pregnant Drug User Glad for Jail," *Chicago Tribune.*

17 Lynn M. Paltrow, David S. Cohen, and Corrine A. Carey, *Year 2000 Overview: Governmental Responses to Pregnant Women Who Use Alcohol or Other Drugs* (Philadelphia: National Advocates for Pregnant Women of the Women's Law Project, 2000); Humphries, *Crack Mothers.*

18 Paltrow, *Year 2000 Overviews;* Dorothy Roberts, *Killing the Black Body* (New York: Random House, 1997), 150–201.

19 "More US Children Using Foster Care," *Boston Globe,* December 12, 1989.

20 See, for example, Martha Shirk, "Foster Parents Struggle with Babies in Pain," *St. Louis Post-Dispatch,* November 19, 1989.

21 Sandra Patton, *Birthmarks: Transracial Adoption in Contemporary America* (New York: New York University Press, 2001).

22 *Losing Isaiah,* film, directed by Stephen Gyllenhall (Paramount Pictures, 1995).

23 Charles Krauthammer, "Crack Babies Forming Biological Underclass," *St. Louis Post-Dispatch,* July 30, 1989.

24 Jackson, "America's Shameful Little Secret"; Raspberry, "Addicts and Babies."

25 Deborah Frank and others, "Growth, Development and Behavior in Early Childhood Following Prenatal Cocaine Exposure: A Systematic Review," *Journal of the American Medical Association* 285, no. 12 (2001): 1613.

26 Veronica H. Accornero and others, "Behavioral Outcome of Preschoolers Exposed Prenatally to Cocaine: Role of Maternal Behavioral Health," *Journal of Pediatric Psychology* 27, no. 3 (2002); Gideon Koren and others, "Estimation of Fetal Exposure to Drugs of Abuse, Environmental Tobacco Smoke, and Ethanol," *Therapeutic Drug Monitoring* 1, no. 1 (2002). The one study to show negative effects was Lynn T. Singer and others, "Cognitive and Motor Outcomes of Cocaine-Exposed Infants," *Journal of the American Medical Association* 287, no. 15 (2002).

27 Wendy Chavkin, "Cocaine and Pregnancy—Time to Look at the Evidence," *Journal of the American Medical Association* 285, no. 12 (2001): 1626. The conclusions of Frank and others have not gone entirely unchallenged; Singer and others, "Cognitive and Motor Outcomes," offer contrary evidence, though an attendant commentary suggests that it might have something to do with the kind of drug that was available in Cleveland, in particular, where the Singer study took place. See Barry Zuckerman, Deborah A. Frank, and Linda Mayes, "Cocaine-Exposed Infants and Developmental Outcomes: 'Crack Kids' Revisited [Editorials]," *Journal of the American Medical Association* 287, no. 15 (2002).

28 Gideon Koren and others, "Bias against the Null Hypotheses: The Reproductive Hazards of Cocaine," *Lancet* 2, no. 8677 (1989).

29 Humphries, *Crack Mothers,* 44–45.

30 Lynn Duke, "DC Revises Infant Death Figures: Rate for 6 Months Remains More Than Twice National Average," *Washington Post,* December 16, 1989.

31 Krauthammer, "Crack Babies Forming Biological Underclass."

32 *Welfare Reform Reconciliation Act of 1996,* HR 3829, 104th Cong., 2nd sess., Sec. 4723 (July 17, 1996). See http://frwebgate.access.gpo.gov/cgi-bin/getdoc.cgi?dbname=104_cong_bills&docid=f:h3829ih.txt.pdf. See also n. 37, below.

33 William Niskanen, "Welfare and the Culture of Poverty," *The Cato Journal* 16, no. 1 (1996).

34 Sylvia Ann Hewlett and Cornel West, *The War against Parents: What We Can Do for America's Beleaguered Moms and Dads* (Boston: Houghton Mifflin, 1998).

35 Attached to a number of different bills along the way, these provisions were ultimately enacted in the *Small Business Job Protection Act of 1996,* Public Law 104–188, 104th Cong., 2nd sess., Sects. 1807 and 1808, (August 20, 1996). See http://naic.acf.hhs.gov/general/legal/federal/pl104_188.cfm.

36 Patton, *Birthmarks,* 138; see also *Personal Responsibility and Work Opportunity Reconciliation Act of 1996,* HR 3734, 104th Cong., 2nd sess., *Congressional Record* 142, no. 114, daily ed. (July 30, 1996):

H8829–H8958, http://frwebgate.access.gpo.gov/cgi-bin/getdoc.cgi?dbname=104_cong_bills&docid=f:h3734enr.txt.pdf.

37 "Adopting Black Babies," *Newsweek,* November 3, 1969; Dawn Day, *The Adoption of Black Children: Counteracting Institutional Discrimination* (Lexington, MA: Lexington Books, 1979); Christine Ward Gailey, "Ideologies of Motherhood and Kinship in US Adoption," in *Ideologies and Technologies of Motherhood: Race, Class, Sexuality, Nationalism,* ed. Heléna and France Winddance Twine Ragoné (New York: Routledge, 2000), 11–55; Patton, *Birthmarks*; Elisabeth Shepherd, "Adopting Negro Children: White Families Find It Can Be Done," *New Republic,* 1964.

38 The clearest evidence of this I know of is the story of a white California minister who gave up on his family's effort to adopt a biracial toddler following a year of cross-burnings, trash on the lawn, and hateful acts by members of his community. See "Drip, Drip, Drip: Adopted Mulatto Infant," *Newsweek,* April 4, 1966.

39 "Adoption and the Color Barrier," *The American Enterprise,* May/June 1996; Barbara Kingsolver, *Pigs in Heaven* (New York: HarperCollins, 1993).

40 See Michael Omi and Howard Winant, *Racial Formation in the United States: From the 1960s to the 1990s,* 2nd ed. (New York: Routledge, 1994).

41 Evelynn Maxine Hammonds, "New Technologies of Race," in *Processed Lives: Gender and Technology in Everyday Life,* ed. Jennifer Terry and Melodie Calvert (New York: Routledge, 1997), 107–122.

42 Donna Haraway, "Race Universal Donors in a Vampire Culture," in *Modest_Witness@Second_Millennium.Femaleman™_Meetsoncomouse©: Feminism and Technoscience* (New York: Routledge, 1997), 213–266.

43 Joseph Dalaker, *Poverty in the United States: 2000* (Washington, DC: US Census Bureau, 2001), 10.

44 Elizabeth Bartholet, *Nobody's Children: Abuse and Neglect, Foster Drift, and the Adoption Alternative* (Boston: Beacon Press, 1999).

45 Patton, *Birthmarks.*

46 Carla Bradley and Cynthia Hawkins-León, "The Transracial Adoption Debate: Counseling and Legal Implications," *Journal of Counseling and Development* 80, no. 4 (2002): 437.

SHOPPING FOR CHILDREN IN THE INTERNATIONAL MARKETPLACE

Kim Park Nelson

Adoption has ... become big business. Go to any adoption conference for the first time, and you'll be surprised by the numbers of "advertisers"—agencies, facilitators, magazine publishers, insurance companies, greeting card vendors, and toy manufacturers—seeking to sell you their services.[1]

the industry of transnational adoption

The growing practice of transnational adoption can be understood through a simple supply and demand equation. This equation operates on a global scale, where individuals (usually white) from rich nations adopt individuals (usually not white) from poorer nations. While the equation might be simple, this is a complicated exchange, where children, the governments of the two nations, both sets of parents (birth and adoptive), (usually) two adoption agencies, adoption workers, social workers, childcare providers, attorneys, and a host of other intermediaries may be involved. Typically, everyone is compensated, either monetarily, materially, or socially, creating a complex economic relationship.

Adoptive parents pay for the services associated with the adoption they are completing and are willing to do so because it gives them the opportunity to build a family and because of the tremendous demand for children in rich nations. This demand is created by the enormous cultural pressure to complete one's life with family (which includes children), the relative shortage of "healthy" white infants in rich nations, social anxiety about domestic transracial adoption, and, I argue, white parents' desire to enrich their lives by parenting a child from a foreign culture. The demand is met with supply from poorer nations around the world, where the potential to procure healthy infants is great and the possibilities for realizing a healthy profit are just as great. Regrettably, the demand is so great that illegal baby markets have developed as child trafficking, and even in many legal transnational adoptions, child procurement and adoption payments border on (or cross the border to) the unethical.

This chapter uses transnational adoption guides as a primary source for understanding how parents navigate the maze of the adoption marketplace. The adoption guides represent material publicly available to parents who seek practical advice on a complicated and expensive undertaking. Because these guides are such a valuable resource to prospective adoptive parents, I see them as playing a key instructional role. My intent is to analyze the messages that are sent to parents through these guides and critique these messages and their limitations, especially in light of the failure to consult adult transnational adoptees, who remain an untapped source of knowledge.

I am in a unique position for researching transnational adoption, as I am a transnational and transracial adoptee myself.[2] I was adopted from South Korea in 1971 at the age of seven months. My interest in the history and practice of transnational and transracial adoption stems from my own life experiences, including the sense that my experience has been largely represented through the filtered views of adoptive parents, adoption workers, and other researchers. I have also had the good fortune to connect with several other adult adoptees in the last ten years. We have our own perspectives about our experiences, and I intend to counter the misrepresentation we have encountered when other researchers inject their interests and agendas into their work about us. I cannot claim impartiality (nor, I would argue, could most adoption researchers), but I do have as great an interest in uncovering truths about adoption practices and adoptee experiences as any researcher. Because I am critical of researchers who do not reveal their personal stake in their research, I feel compelled to reveal mine. I neither support nor condemn the practice of transracial and transnational adoption but believe strongly that power differentials between parents and children, institutions and individuals, white people and people of color, and rich and poor nations are great enough that the potential for abuse is enormous. I also believe that adult adoptees have an important role to play in challenging these abuses and that an unsentimental critique of the current practice of transnational adoption is a critical first step.

created demand in international adoption

For many Americans, childlessness is not an option, and being a parent has become an essential part of an adult's identity. Young adults, if childless, are constantly queried about when (not if) children are planned. While they still experience some discrimination, "nontraditional parents," such as single people and gay and lesbian couples, who in previous times would not have been expected (or allowed) to parent, receive more support (culturally and technologically) than ever before to become parents. Many of these parents cite having children as a way to become "normal."

In her book *Barren in the Promised Land,* Elaine Tyler May outlines the history of childlessness in America and identifies the post–World War II baby boom of the 1950s and '60s[3] and the "new pronatalism" of the 1980s and '90s[4] as two times when the pressure to become a parent has been particularly potent. These two time periods are demographically related in that the "second baby boom" of the 1980s and '90s is a response to the childbearing activity of the unusually large generation of the first baby boom of the postwar era. May also documents the cultural creation of anxiety during the 1980s and '90s about having (and not being able to have) children, where "advertisements suddenly began to link children to consumerism and the good life ... [and] parenthood began to permeate the nation's popular culture. Plots of movies and television shows and even popular songs revolved around the baby quest."[5] The solutions for the unfortunate infertile person (including single parents and gay and lesbian parents, for whom finding a reproductive partner is a barrier) are surrogacy, artificial insemination, fertility treatments, or adoption. At the time of the new pronatalism (the 1980s and '90s), when there was more cultural pressure than ever to have children, prospective parents were also realizing the trials and hazards of domestic in-race and transracial adoption.

There is also a sizable population of fertile parents who choose adoption because they believe that adoption, rather than reproduction, helps to solve population problems or helps to give children without families or means of support loving homes. Often, these children are infants of color or foreign infants.

why transnational adoption?

Transnational adoption has been a viable option for parents in the United States (as well as Canada and Western European nations) since the mid-1950s. When adoptable infants became less available domestically as a result of access to new family planning technologies and the diminished numbers of unwed mothers who chose to relinquish their children,[6] the swelling baby boom population was just reaching the age of parenthood, creating high demand for adoptable children. The civil rights movement may have also contributed to the increase in the practice of these adoptions as activists successfully desegregated more arenas of American life and whites became more comfortable sharing their lives with people of other races. At the same time, adoption agencies became more selective in their placement with adoptive parents, with the result that parents were often required to pass certain standards of income and age and be infertile.[7] These criteria may have made it more difficult for African American parents to adopt waiting African American children and indirectly encouraged further transracial adoption of nonwhite people by white people.

Much criticism has been directed at the practice of transracial adoption of American children, mainly against those involving African American and Native American children and white adults, with less criticism thus far for transnational adoption. Opposition to the practice of transracial adoption galvanized in the early 1970s and led to implementation of same-race adoption policies at most adoption agencies by 1975. At its conference in 1971, the National Association of Black Social Workers (NABSW) resoundingly rejected the practice of transracial adoption (predicting that transracial adoptees would have poor psychological adjustment and racial identity and be unable to cope with episodes of racism and discrimination without the guidance of a parent of the same color). They led efforts to end the procedure to protect children and prevent "cultural genocide." The same year, a meeting of American Indian leadership issued a statement that identified transracial adoption as "cultural genocide."[8] In 1978, as a response to activists who pointed to gross abuses of child welfare policy, in which children were routinely and forcibly removed from Native American homes, and the lasting damage to the children and their communities, Congress passed the Indian Child Welfare Act, which practically forbade the adoption of Indian children by non-Indians. Likely as a result of these actions, from 1974 to 1976 the rate of domestic transracial adoption decreased greatly.[9]

By the 1980s, restrictions on transracial adoption were being challenged in court by white adoptive parents and the American Civil Liberties Union. Courts were unanimous in ruling that race could not be the chief consideration in adoption. Many states maintained laws to limit transracial adoptions, but in the 1990s a coalition of forces from the right and middle successfully pushed for federal legislation regulating the role of race in adoption.[10] The Multiethnic Placement Act of 1994 and the Adoption and Safe Families Act of 1997 mandated that transracial adoptions be handled the same way as all other adoptions and forbade the consideration of race as the sole factor to delay adoption placement. The Interethnic Placement Provisions, enacted in 1997, prohibited the consideration of race in adoption placement entirely. Yet many prospective parents still do not undertake domestic adoptions because the supply of children does not match parents' demands. Most prospective adoptive parents seek to adopt healthy infants, while two-thirds of American children in foster care are over age five and many have health problems or disabilities.[11]

By the end of this decade of adoption legislation, the adopting public was aware of the possible pitfalls and complications of domestic transracial adoption. In addition to the NABSW position (renewed in 1991), which portrayed domestic transracial adoptions as controversial and possibly unethical, a few highly publicized court cases where children of color were returned to birthmothers after adoption contributed to the idea that these adoptions were potentially reversible and emotionally wrenching. Thus, ever since legal barriers have been removed, prospective adoptive parents seem reluctant to complete domestic transracial adoptions. In contrast, very little public criticism has been voiced about international transracial adoption. Instead, according to adoption advocates Rita Simon and Howard Alstein, parents see the practice as "achiev[ing] instant sainthood"[12] because "in adopting foreign children, the parents feel that they are cooperating in their children's efforts to burn their bridges. The children have no option but to adapt to the new world. There is no going back."[13]

foreign babies as a cultural commodity

Prospective parents are also motivated to adopt foreign children for reasons other than the difficulties of adopting domestically. While most parents want to adopt to address childlessness or to give a child in need a home, many also voice an interest in the cultural enrichment they feel will result from the adoption. This is perceived as a "bonus" in adopting transnationally among liberal white parents.

Theorist bell hooks, in her essay "Eating the Other," explains why white people were drawn to commodify the cultures of the "other" (nonwhite people) in the early '90s, arguing that whites believe that they are enriched through their consumption of the "exotic."

> The commodification of Otherness has been so successful because it is offered as a new delight, more intense, more satisfying than normal ways of doing and feeling.… [E]thnicity becomes spice, seasoning that can liven up the dull dish of mainstream white culture.[14]

The commodification, hooks also points out, is made possible by white privilege, and while racial boundaries are transgressed (by white people), they are not left behind. She specifies that "when race and ethnicity become commodified as resources for pleasure, the culture of specific groups … can be seen as constituting an alternative playground where members of dominating races … affirm their power-over … with the Other."[15] She goes on to give a number of examples from film and television where white people benefit from the consumption of the culture of nonwhite people. In *Cannibal Culture: Art, Appropriation, and the Commodification of Difference*, Deborah Root describes the Western historical depiction of Eastern and indigenous cultures as at once violent, primitive, savage, sublime, and erotic, but above all, as authentic.[16] This authenticity is what is desirable and becomes marketable. Root points to the link between luxury and colonialism in the contemporary Western psyche, suggesting that the colonial mindset provides power and freedom, affording imperial Western whites the luxury to do or have anything they desire.[17] Reminders of the colonial past appear frequently in advertisements, prompted by its association with luxury and the "exotic."[18]

This creation of desire for authentic objects of culture is extended to foreign children in transnational adoption, where the object of culture is an Asian, Latin American, or Eastern European baby. According to hooks and Root, parents as consumers are already conditioned to want the authentically exotic, and what better way to meet this desire than to adopt an authentically exotic child? Parents' ideals of the authentic exotic are met by trips to foreign nations to pick up their foreign children, with ample opportunities to shop for authentic, exotic merchandise while there.

When parents describe their attitudes about adopting transnationally, many express their appreciation of the "enrichment" they will receive as a result of having someone foreign-born in the family. I can't help thinking that these expectations by parents are somewhat misguided. Most of their children will grow up totally assimilated in American culture, without the ability to bring the cultural enrichment from their birth countries that these parents say they will so appreciate. Nonetheless, this is a belief shared by all the adoptive parent authors of the adoption guides I consulted for this essay.[19]

supply-side market forces

In 1988 there were 3.3 families seeking to adopt for every successful placement. By 1995, this number had increased to 6 families.[20] In the year 2000, 500,000 Americans were on the market to adopt a child, up 150 percent from 5 years earlier. Transnational adoptions in the United States now occur at the rate of 18,000 per year, fueling the change in adoption services "from the tightly self-regulated realm of social-service agencies and unwed mothers' homes to the free market." The heightened demand for adoptable babies has sent adoption fees, which should theoretically be untouched by laws of supply and demand, soaring, and desire for the children is so high, prospective parents are willing to pay the price. The huge demand for adoptable babies in the United States, Canada, and the rich nations of Europe has prompted nations with adoptable populations to react, and intermediaries in both the birth and host countries to step into the profitable middleman role. In 2000 the adoption industry generated $1.5 billion in adoption spending, with costs for transnational adoptions ranging from $15,000 to $50,000, up from around $1000 in the early 1970s (my own adoption cost my parents $1097.50 in 1971). One US adoption agency reported revenues of $4.1 million with a profit of $937,515 in 1998.

the adoption market

The high returns the adoption industry currently enjoys as a result of high demand from the adopting public have led to heightened competition in the international adoption marketplace. In her 2000 book *Adoption and Ethics: The Market Forces in Adoption*, Madelyn Freundlich details this phenomenon, where dozens of agencies are in place in each adoptive birth country, each promising to deliver the best quality child from that country most expeditiously for progressively higher fees.[21]

Unfortunately, another result of heightened demand in Western nations has been the kidnapping and selling of children from Latin American nations. In her 1995 documentary film *Baby Business*, Judy Jackson remarks, "Even in the Third World, demand outstrips supply."[22] The US State Department reports that the largest number of kidnapped children adopted in the United States are from Mexico.[23] Madelyn Freundlich lists a number of incidents worldwide where children were bought from parents for $5–70 per child and sold abroad at great profit.[24] Mary Ellen Fieweger, in her article "Stolen Children and International Adoptions," reports of women in Ecuador whose children were kidnapped, or who were coerced or threatened to give up their children for adoption.[25]

Fieweger conveys her surprise when she found that lawyers are the key organizers and profiteers from these illegal adoptions.[26] Jackson also reported this finding, documenting individual lawyers who each arrange dozens to hundreds of transnational adoptions yearly. The system of illegal adoption from Ecuador to the United States or European nations is stimulated by demand from adopting nations and made possible because the lawyers are "beyond the reach of the law of either the sending or receiving country."[27]

Illegal adoptions are profitable because of the great demand for children. In Guatemala, the agency cost of producing a child for adoption is about $1000, including $25 for a falsified birth certificate, Guatemalan court filing fees, and time in a "fattening house," an illegal nursery where traders keep kidnapped children before their adoptions abroad and "fatten them up" so adoptive parents will receive a healthy looking baby. The total fee paid for such a baby in the United States is $15,000, for a difference of $14,000 per child that goes to lawyers and other intermediaries.[28] Other reports state that some birthmothers are given $100 for healthy babies, or $50 to become pregnant with children to be used in adoptions abroad, in a transnational surrogate motherhood that is much less expensive than a surrogacy in the United States or Europe. These reports reveal that fees for the adoptions of these babies are between $3000 and $30,000.[29] This money may also go toward bribes, "donations" to orphanages, or unknown recipients. Often, prospective parents are instructed not to ask where the money is going. Freundlich differentiates between black (illegal) and gray (legal but unethically profitable) market adoptions, specifying that while gray market adoptions are legal, the chain of custody of monies paid for services related to adoption is often purposely obscured, implying that great profits may be realized by individuals in the trade.

Commenting on children's vulnerability to illegal adoptions in war-torn nations, Jackson offers two examples: El Salvador, where thousands of children were taken from parents by the Salvadoran army, declared "displaced," then adopted out to the United States and other rich nations; and Sarajevo, where 50,000 children went missing during the recent war that fragmented Yugoslavia. (See Ch. 11.)

Transnational adoptions have become so common that they have resulted in measurable income streams to some birth countries, to the annual tune of $15–20 million in South Korea (estimated 2001 GDP of $865 billion), $5 million in Guatemala (estimated 2001 GDP of $48.3 billion), and $2 million in Honduras (estimated 2001 GDP of $17 billion).[30] Although this income is desperately needed in many poor birth nations, there is plentiful evidence that the money does not support the economies of these nations, but has instead "promoted corruption and fraudulent practices."[31]

Fieweger notes that in the late 1980s, a shift occurred from Asian to Latin American countries as main sources of children for adoption, because high birthrates and poor economic conditions continued in Latin America, while in Asia, birthrates stabilized and living conditions improved.[32] Although the focus soon returned to Asia, Latin American countries had begun and continue to be motivated to participate in exporting their children.[33] Fieweger links the practice of illegal adoption in Ecuador with colonialism:

> Since the Spanish Conquest, the relationship between Latin American countries and those of the developed world has not been one of equality. Traditionally, these third-world republics have been providers of natural resources, purchased at bargain prices by the developed world, first Spain, then England, and today, the United States. Many Latin Americans object to international adoption because, as they see it, Latin American children have become another natural resource in demand in the developed world.[34]

Jackson also makes this connection, remarking that Mexico has long been used as a source of cheap labor and that the use of its children as a commodity is consistent with this exploitation. In a pattern reminiscent of colonial economic practices, US and European prospective parents seek to find and adopt the best (attractive, healthy, and intelligent) babies foreign countries have to offer, from orphanages or otherwise, leaving the children with the least assets for survival to languish.[35]

international adoption guides: how to acquire the right child for you

Whatever the country of origin, the process of adopting a child transnationally is an enormous logistical undertaking. Once prospective parents have made the decision to adopt from abroad, they must decide whether they want to complete a private or agency-assisted adoption, find an agency or intermediary, complete a home state approval (which will assess the prospective parents as appropriate for parenting), get authorization from the Bureau of Citizenship and Immigration Services (BCIS), secure the endorsement of the birth nation and its adoption agency, wait for and be referred to a child, petition for the adoption, pick up the child (often in the child's birth country), complete the adoption, obtain traveling papers for the child, and finalize at home by completing the adoption paperwork.

Because this is a complex process, there are many possible obstacles along the way. Each potential obstacle can translate into lost time and money for prospective parents. With the great potential cost of transnational adoption, and the large number of prospective parents, there is a demonstrated market for informational materials about how (or how not) to complete these transactions. A *US News and World Report* article, "The Adoption Maze," has a consumer protection "buyer beware" slant about the hazards of transracial adoption, like consumer exposé articles on products or services.[36] Many "how-to" materials for transnational adoption are available in print and online and constitute a set of instructions that tell parents how to safely navigate and, sometimes, how to act and think, about their adoptions.

With this in mind, I have chosen to examine three transnational adoption "how-to" guides. They are *International Adoption: Sensitive Advice for Prospective Parents* by Jean Knoll and Mary-Kate Murphy, *How to Adopt Internationally: A Guide for Agency-Directed and Independent Adoptions* by Jean Nelson-Erichsen and Heino R. Erichsen, and *The International Adoption Handbook: How to Make Foreign Adoption Work for You* by Myra Alperson.[37] Knoll and Murphy are both adoptive mothers, one married (Murphy) and one single (Knoll). The two met in a hotel where both were staying when they adopted their children. The book combines journal-style descriptions of the adoption experience from Knoll's point of view with commentary from Murphy and brief stories from several other unnamed parents. Nelson-Erichsen and Erichsen are a married couple who are adoptive parents and the founders and operators of an adoption agency that specializes in international adoptions. They offer a nuts-and-bolts approach to transnational adoption, including step-by-step adoption advice and information given with a high level of detail, with some additional personal advice. The style of Alperson's book is a blend of the other two, containing how-to information interspersed with personal anecdotes. Currently, all three books are widely available for sale and are presently the only such guidebooks specifically geared toward prospective parents of foreign children in print. Prospective parents who wanted a printed resource or "how-to" manual today would probably purchase one or more of these three books. All were written by transnational adoptive parents, presumably because they themselves had wished for such a guide as they went through their adoption processes.

Most materials about international adoption for prospective parents emphasize the positive aspects of building a family through the adoption experience. With respect to the almost sacred institution of family and parenting, these materials only briefly question parents' motives in adopting internationally or ask parents to do so themselves. Instead, these books empathize with people who must endure the humiliation of judgment about whether they would be good parents and other hardships of the adoption journey. All three books focus on the adoption process, not parenting, though all give some "starter" advice on parenting the newly adopted child. All offer a chronological treatment of the adoption process from the idea of adoption to beginning parenting.

the adoption process

The three books describe, in more or less detail, the stages of the transnational adoption process. The first stage is the decision to adopt a foreign child. Alperson states that many people can adopt internationally, even if age, marital status, or some other barrier would bar a domestic adoption (11–12). She is especially encouraging to single women in their 40s. Her message is that anyone can have a family through international adoption.

Obviously, for prospective parents wanting to start a family, this is a good thing because transnational adoption solves the problem of the domestic baby shortage. This highlights the existence of a hierarchy of parents and children in the adoption market; just as white infants are most in demand in the domestic market, middle-class heterosexual married couples in their mid-20s to mid-30s are most favored in the domestic adoption process. Because in-race adoptions are most desired and white prospective parents are most populous, individuals or couples without these most-favored characteristics are forced to look for children to adopt out-of-race and/or out-of-country. On the other hand, many parents choose to adopt transnationally because they feel unprepared to raise African American children but think they can be successful raising Latin Americans or Asians (Knoll and Murphy, 32). This draws attention to a racial hierarchy of babies available for adoption, with European Americans on top, followed by foreign Asians and Latinos, and African Americans on the bottom. These examples emphasize both the high value of white babies and white "middle American" parents within adoption circles (and within society), and the consequently lower value of foreign children or children of color and single, older, poor, or gay/lesbian parents.

Alperson encourages parents to gather information about transnational adoption by reading magazines, newsletters, and papers; to find out more from other parents by joining parents' groups, talking to successful parents, and going to adoption conferences; and to access online resources, contact adoption agencies, and get in touch with state agencies (12–17). This process of educating oneself about the transnational adoption process is very similar to that of gathering information to make a large purchase—a new car for instance (which costs about the same amount as a transnational adoption).

Parents must also decide from which country to adopt. Alperson suggests parents assess their own attitudes to help answer this question (17–19). This would include their assessment of community, especially what parents have in terms of "support for children of color." Alperson uses veiled language such as this to encourage parents to think about race. The implication is that if parents are not comfortable with children of color, they should seek to adopt from Eastern Europe or Russia instead of Latin America or Asia. Knoll and Murphy add that the country can often be determined according to parents' criteria, such as length of wait to adopt, length of visit for child pickup, cost, and other factors (22).

All three books address the choice to use an adoption agency, use a facilitator, or go independent (where the parent finds a baby from the birthparents), and all offer pros and cons for each alternative. The three also have lengthy sections on the voluminous paperwork involved, no matter what method is used. Parents must open a BCIS file, schedule a home study, file for child abuse clearance, and collect documentation needed in the birth country. Nelson-Erichsen and Erichsen specify dozens of forms to file or obtain, questions to ask, and decisions to make. All the guides discuss how to cope with waiting. This seems to be a common experience among the parents who wait for paperwork to be cleared, for decisions to be made, and for a child to be found.

Alperson remarks that adoptive parents do not have to wait in line at the BCIS to get forms (with the immigrants) but can call to get forms mailed (39). This implies that Alperson does not think of her own or other transnationally adopted children as immigrants and alludes to the elevated status potential parents have (and perceive they have) over immigrants themselves as facilitators of immigration. This is one of many examples that show how adoptive parents place themselves at the top of a national hierarchy, with their children below them and immigrants or nationals of the "Third World" on the bottom. Since the publication of Alperson's guide Congress has enacted legislation that sidesteps the immigration queue altogether; the Child Citizenship Act, passed in 2000 and enacted in 2001, states that foreign-born adopted children with at least one adoptive parent with US citizenship become citizens as soon as they emigrate.[38] This places transnationally adopted children among the most privileged immigrants in the United States with regard to access to citizenship.

The next step in adopting is completing a home study, a daunting process that includes a parenting evaluation, child abuse clearance, references, and background checks. The home study is designed to ferret out any information indicating fitness (or lack of fitness) for parenting. Prospective parents must disclose personal information including attitudes and beliefs about parenting and adoption, past mental/physical health, finances, a personal history, and environmental conditions of their home. Of course, parents must also submit several more government forms at this time (including a set of fingerprints) and comply with an FBI criminal record check. I support the extensive evaluation of parents before a transnational adoption takes place, but the current process overemphasizes ruling out the possibility of criminal activity and greatly minimizes the need for cross-cultural and US race literacy. Yet the latter is essential for successful transracial (which the majority of transnational adoptions are) placements.

Once all the paperwork is completed and parents are approved, they wait for a "referral" or a child whom they can choose to accept for adoption. After this has occurred, many parents go abroad to pick up the adoptees. Both Alperson and Nelson-Erichsen and Erichsen provide traveling tips and packing lists for parents traveling to pick up their adoptees. Nelson-Erichsen and Erichsen also offer health advice for traveling, including that travelers should be wary of all dining establishments except first-class restaurants or homes of upper-class nationals in order to avoid unsanitary food and food poisoning (116). This is another example of parents' class placement of themselves above most Third World nationals.

Alperson and Nelson-Erichsen and Erichsen also give health advice for adopted children once they are in the adoptive parents' custody. Alperson suggests health checks for children new to the United States and gives a list of tests and vaccinations (88). Nelson-Erichsen and Erichsen write a lengthy chapter on health problems of foreign orphans, with a large emphasis on First World versus Third World health standards, where the Third World is portrayed as dirty, poor, and abusive and its children are portrayed as malnourished, sickly, and diseased. Their advice for how to care for new babies includes a warning against treating adoptees like "First World kids" at first, with an explanation that these children will be overwhelmed and possibly unappreciative of too many choices and toys. They also give advice on feeding, explaining that the children have generally had small portions of low quality food in the past, so overeating or food hoarding is common, but that these tendencies usually go away the longer the child has been in the United States (129).

costs

The complicated transnational adoption process encourages the marketplace behavior of parents and the treatment of children like merchandise. Parents must shop for children to choose their national origin, their race, and their gender. Because the decisions to be made are so large and difficult, the adoption industry is full of companies or individuals offering services to help parents through the process. Knoll and Murphy offer commentary from a frustrated parent who said, "I would have done anything. We had waited long enough" (70), implying that parents are willing to pay a large price to have the adoption process end with a successful placement.

Like any other good consumer guide, Alperson's and Nelson-Erichsen and Erichsen's books both include itemized price lists for all the services adopting parents require, along with tax credits and other financial assistance available. Alperson includes information on resources like credit cards, bank loans, and mortgage refinances to pay for adoptions. Nelson-Erichsen and Erichsen's book estimates the cost for transnational adoption in 1999 to be $12–25,000, not including foster care, travel, and medical care (37). Knoll points out hidden costs as well, giving the example that she had trouble getting maternity leave because her employer usually takes it out of women's disability funds, and as she would have no physical disability (from giving birth), her leave was compromised (86).

Nelson-Erichsen and Erichsen warn *against* offering gifts or support to birthmothers or families, arguing that adoptive parents' responsibilities are to the child and not to his or her parents and relatives, with an additional caution that if adoptive parents give the birthmother anything, she will be back to solicit them again (136). This is another good example of the privileged, white adoptive parents further separating themselves from and stigmatizing lower-class birthmothers of color by representing them as greedy or grasping and thus morally inferior to the adopters. It is clear that the parents in this transaction want the woman's child but nothing else. Somewhat ironically, Nelson-Erichsen and Erichsen also warn that gifts or support of any kind to birthmothers could be seen as baby buying and strongly advise against it.

Alperson more honestly acknowledges parent consumerism in transnational adoption, saying:

> It's true that as adoptive parents, we are indeed consumers looking for the right adoption service to … meet our goal … [but in] choosing an international adoption … it is important to respect the culture and the traditions of the people in whose country we are guests. (86)

Alperson discourages parents from commodifying other cultures and advises parents not to be "ugly Americans" abroad. While acknowledging the reality that services leading to adoption are paid for, she also emphasizes that the ultimate goal is to build a family.

dealing with race

The primary way these authors handle race and the racial differences between themselves and their children is by highlighting only the positive aspects of having a child from another race and country in the family. Alperson states:

> Intrigued by the challenge of bringing a child from another culture into their lives … some people adopt internationally because they want their family experience to be a multicultural one … Once I began to considering international adoption, and then when I actually started the process, I realized it was a gift—to me. (10)

Nelson-Erichsen and Erichsen echo this remark.

> Immigrant orphans are doubly magic. They evoke social change. Infants and children bridge American social divisions of color, culture, and nationality.... Our family has extended far beyond the confines of a white middle-class community. We benefited from the companionship of children and adults of other ethnicities and nationalities we otherwise might not have met. (10)

Knoll and Murphy make similar comments about personally benefiting by incorporating another culture into the family (32).

These remarks illustrate parents' denial of the complexity and difficulties people of color face in the United States because the authors only see how diversity benefits them, explicitly ignoring how it might disadvantage others. Nelson-Erichsen and Erichsen take this one step further by assigning the responsibility of social change to these children, ignoring the fact that adoptee assimilation does not solve the problems of disenfranchisement, lack of access, and racial elitism that underlie racial inequality.

The parents referred to in these books use the strategies of racializing themselves or deracializing their children to minimize differences between their children and themselves. In Alperson's book, she describes a process by which parents become racialized when they attempt to take on the racial and ethnic identities of their adopted children. She quotes one mother who says, "My daughter was born in China and is an adopted American. I was born in America and I'm an adopted Chinese" (106). Alperson describes this as an ideal attitude. Other parents deracialize their children and de-emphasize the child's race by practicing "colorblindness" in the family and stressing the child's "American-ness" (105). This is a confusing phenomenon until it is understood that there is tremendous desire within families that become racially mixed through adoption for everyone in the family to be "the same." Imagined homogeneity helps these families cope with their outward differences and be more like a "normal" family.

The authors of all three books minimize incidents of racial discrimination and teasing against children and offer superficial advice on how to cope with it. Alperson contributes one page on racial incidents, suggests ignoring them or deflecting them with humor (112–113), and stresses that a mother's love can put things right (110). Nelson-Erichsen and Erichsen advise that parents find friends from the child's minority group and think about possible consequences of racial prejudice, which are not discussed in much detail (185). They lament continued racial prejudice but state, "Nevertheless, our lives were enriched by transracial adoption" (185), without realizing that parents' enrichment will not compensate for the discrimination and racism faced by their children. These books do nothing to explain the complexities and difficulties of not being white in the United States, and to the contrary, suggest that racism toward their children is a superficial problem easily remedied. None of the parents who write these books seem to realize that racism in the context of transracial adoption is not about them but about their transracially adopted children.

conclusion

Transnational adoption has become widespread in the United States. There is tremendous social pressure for Americans to become parents. Since there are more prospective parents seeking to adopt than healthy white infants waiting to be adopted domestically, the market has become transnational. The exchange of children for adoption fees across national borders can be described in terms of market supply and demand. Nations with orphan populations have responded to this demand and are now the sending countries of transnational adoptees.

The transnational adoption marketplace is difficult, complicated, and expensive enough to warrant "how-to" literature for prospective parents. These materials inform prospective parents on how to reach their goal of becoming parents. Because these guides are often written by successful adoptive parents, they are also an account of parents' experiences and attitudes.

This chapter highlights the power differences between white people and people of color, the rich and the poor, the more and less empowered in the adoption circle. Parents are willing to support the growing and expensive transnational adoption industry to acquire children with whom to build family. Children are adopted from abroad instead of domestically because of hierarchical differences between domestic-white, international-of-color, and domestic-of-color babies. Parents in the United States view themselves as superior to parents in poor countries, further easing their decision to adopt transnationally. They simultaneously see their foreign-adopted children as enriching, authentically exotic, and yet part of the family, therefore no different from the parents themselves. These views enable these parents to reproduce their own white privilege through the act of transnational adoption. Transnational adoption "how-to" guides for parents show that many prospective parents are aware of how to take advantage of the adoption market and, more pointedly, see themselves as more deserving of the parenting experience than parents in poor countries. Racial and cultural literacy is not viewed as a prerequisite for parenting children of color, to the detriment of the children who are exchanged as commodities in the international adoption marketplace.

notes

1 Myra Alperson, *The International Adoption Handbook: How to Make an Overseas Adoption Work for You* (New York: Henry Holt, 1997), 5.

2 I have completed reviews of transracial adoptee narrative accounts and social work and social policy research on transracial adoption. I plan to complete my dissertation on adult transracial adoptee experiences using the collected life stories of adult adoptees.

3 Elaine Tyler May, *Barren in the Promised Land: Childless Americans and the Pursuit of Happiness*

(Cambridge, MA: Harvard University Press, 1995), 129.

4 May, *Barren in the Promised Land,* 213.

5 May, *Barren in the Promised Land,* 214.

6 Constance Pohl and Kathy Harris, *Transracial Adoption: Children and Parents Speak* (New York: Franklin Watts, 1992), 29.

7 Pohl and Harris, *Transracial Adoption,* 30.

8 Charles E. Jones and John F. Else, "Racial and Cultural Issues in Adoption," *Child Welfare United States* 58, no. 6 (1979): 373-82.

9 Jones and Else, "Racial and Cultural Issues," 374.

10 Pohl and Harris, *Transracial Adoption*, 33.

11 Kim Clark and Nancy Shute, "The Adoption Maze," *US News and World Report* 130, no. 10 (2001): 60–66, 69.

12 Rita J. Simon and Howard Altstein, *Transracial Adoption: A Follow-Up* (Lexington, MA: Lexington Books, D. C. Heath and Company, 1981), 106.

13 Simon and Alstein, *Transracial Adoption*, 105.

14 bell hooks, *Black Looks: Race and Representation* (Boston: South End Press, 1992), 21.

15 hooks, *Black Looks,* 23.

16 Deborah Root, *Cannibal Culture: Art, Appropriation, and the Commodification of Difference* (Boulder: Westview Press, 1996), 40.

17 Root, *Cannibal Culture,* 122.

18 Root provides many examples of "exotic" and colonial-themed luxury products and services, ranging from travel/tourism to perfume, clothing, and art.

19 These are *International Adoption: Sensitive Advice for Prospective Parents* by Jean Knoll and Mary-Kate Murphy (Chicago: Chicago Review Press, 1994); *How to Adopt Internationally: A Guide for Agency-Directed and Independent Adoptions* by Jean Nelson-Erichsen and Heino R. Erichsen (Fort Worth, TX: Mesa House Publishers, 2000); and *The International Adoption Handbook: How to Make Foreign Adoption Work for You* by Myra Alperson (New York: Henry Holt and Company, 1997). All subsequent references to these guidebooks appear in text.

20 Clark and Shute, "The Adoption Maze," 60–66. All statistics in the paragraph come from this source.

21 Madelyn Freundlich, *Adoption and Ethics: The Market Forces in Adoption*, Adoption and Ethics Series (Washington, DC: Child Welfare League of America Press, 2000), 43.

22 *Baby Business,* VHS, directed by Judy Jackson (Montreal: National Film Board of Canada, 1995).

23 Francis T. Miko, *Trafficking in Women and Children: The US and International Response* (US Department of State, 2000), http://usinfo.state.gov/topical/global/traffic/crs.0510.html), 8.

24 Freundlich, *Adoption and Ethics*, 46–47.

25 Mary Ellen Fieweger, "Stolen Children and International Adoptions," *Child Welfare* 7 (1991): 285–291.

26 Fieweger, "Stolen Children."

27 Fieweger, "Stolen Children."

28 Jackson, *Baby Business.*

29 Freundlich, *Adoption and Ethics*, 49.

30 Freundlich, *Adoption and Ethics*, 63; GDP information from *CIA World Fact Book.*

31 Freundlich, *Adoption and Ethics,* 63.

32 Fieweger, "Stolen Children."

33 US Department of State, "Immigrant Visas Issued to Orphans Coming to the US," http://travel.state.gov/family/adoption/stats/stats_451.html.

34 Fieweger, "Stolen Children," 290.

35 Freundlich, *Adoption and Ethics*, 40.

36 Clark and Shute, "The Adoption Maze," 60–66, 69.

37 See note 19. All subsequent references to these guidebooks appear in text.

38 "The Child Citizenship Act of 2000" (US Citizenship and Immigration Services, 2000), http://uscis.gov/graphics/publicaffairs/factsheets/adopted.htm.

11 DISAPPEARED CHILDREN AND THE ADOPTEE AS IMMIGRANT

Patrick McDermott

Migration has always been a part of my life. My father, Orest Meykar, was a Ukrainian immigrant, an engineer who had lived and worked in the United States before retiring to Central America where his pension would stretch further. My mother's migration was much shorter. Lucia Cruz is from Morazán, a rural department in eastern El Salvador. At 16 she migrated to the capital looking for work, like so many young campesina women, because there is little money in el campo. Lucia found a job as a domestic in Orest's house in the wealthy Colonia Escalon section of San Salvador. She worked there from the mid-1970s into the early 1980s. I was born in November of 1980.

El Salvador is a poor country and at the time I was born it was also on the brink of war. These factors gave rise not only to migration but also to crime. In my case, those two social phenomena collided. A woman stole me from my mother when I was three months old and sold me. When I was eight months old I embarked on my own migration. A couple in the United States adopted me and from August 1981 on I lived there, in Massachusetts. While the circumstances of my migration were somewhat different from those of other Salvadorans, I was far from alone in my migration. By 1984 war had pushed half a million Salvadorans to flee to the United States.

The Salvadorans who arrived in the United States through international adoption during the war are as much a part of the story of El Salvador as we are a part of the story of the United States. In the States Salvadoran adoptees are usually only seen as adoptees and not recognized as the Salvadoran immigrants that we are. The same social factors that drove thousands of Salvadorans to leave their homeland to emigrate to the United States caused many of us Salvadoran adoptees to become available for adoption. These same factors continue to affect the lives of Salvadorans in El Salvador, of Salvadoran adoptees in the United States and all over the world, and of other Salvadoran emigrants to the United States. Adoption to the United States doesn't separate Salvadoran adoptees from the realities of El Salvador, but rather out-country adoption is part of those realities.

control of the country's wealth and power. In the 1970s a disgruntled group of politicians and activists that had been pushing for reforms began to form guerrilla armies. They financed these armies through kidnapping wealthy Salvadorans for ransom.[6] On October 10, 1980, one month before I was born, four of these guerrilla armies came together to form the Frente Farabundo Martí para la Liberación Nacional, known as the FMLN.[7]

Four months later, on January 10, 1981, when I was three months old and still in El Salvador, the FMLN launched a general offensive known as their "Final Offensive." The Final Offensive was a multi-elemental attempt at toppling the oppressive Salvadoran government through simultaneous military attacks, mass defection by government troops to the guerilla forces, and a general strike aimed at disrupting the country's infrastructure. Yet the military attacks were less than simultaneous, the defection on the part of government soldiers was minimal, and the general strike did not materialize; the Final Offensive failed to overthrow the Salvadoran government. Meanwhile the United States, now under the Reagan administration, began heavily funding the Salvadoran government forces. The FMLN responded with a new strategy: attempting to wear down the government forces over time. This strategy—known as Prolonged Popular War—was used by the North Vietnamese who eventually forced the United States to withdraw from Vietnam.[8] The Prolonged Popular War and government counterattacks lasted until 1992 and drove many Salvadorans into refugee camps and to the United States. The conflict would also be responsible for making many Salvadoran children available for adoption.

Part of the government's counterinsurgency plan was to wipe out popular support for the guerrillas by attacking the civilian population. Because the mountainous departments of Chalentenango and Morazán were guerrilla strongholds, the government focused its effort in these two departments.[9] As a result the civilians in those areas suffered greatly. These counterinsurgency missions were conducted by battalions such as the Belloso and the Atlactl, both of which received instruction in the United States.[10]

One counterinsurgency mission carried out by these two battalions occurred in May 1982 in the department of Chaletenango in the cantón (hamlet) of Los Amates. Los Amates was located in northern Chaletenango near the Sumpul River. As the army approached Los Amates, the villagers began fleeing the area. Among the villagers were a woman named Francisca Romero, her husband Marcelino, and their children. As the Ramirez family ran from Los Amates, Francisca was separated from Marcelino and their daughter, Elsy. Francisca hid in the cornfields with her two other children and some other villagers. From where she was hiding she saw the soldiers pass by with a group of children that they had seized from the escaping villagers. Francisca saw Elsy among them but was powerless to reclaim her; the soldiers would have killed her, and she had her other children to take care of.[11]

Magdalena Ramos, known as Mayda, was another woman who lived in Los Amates. She had a son, Nelson Aníbal. Nelson's father, Geovanni, had joined the guerillas but was killed in combat before Nelson's birth. Mayda and Nelson were originally from Chichilco and had fled to Los Amates when soldiers arrived in Chichilco. When the soldiers arrived in Los Amates, Mayda and Nelson attempted to flee across the Sumpul river and were captured. The soldiers brought them, along with a group of others, mostly women, children, and elderly, to Loma Pacha. There the soldiers demanded that all the women give them their children, who they loaded onto a helicopter.

Children like Elsy and Nelson, taken from their parents or other relatives, are known in El Salvador as niños desaparecidos (disappeared children). The systematic disappearing of children by the military is not a phenomenon specific to El Salvador. It is also known to have occurred in Argentina and probably has happened many other places during war. In El Salvador, many of these children were disappeared, like Nelson Aníbal Ramos, when the Salvadoran military forcibly took them from their parents. Other children the soldiers seized were survivors of massacres or were left behind after the population had fled their villages during military incursions.

The cases of Salvadoran adoptees adopted during the Salvadoran armed conflict (1980–1992) can be divided into two categories. The first category comprises those cases for which the adoption was directly related to war. These children, as discussed above, were disappeared by soldiers either on the battlefield or as part of counterinsurgency missions. The second category comprises those cases that, despite not being directly related to the war, are still very much directly related to the social dynamics of El Salvador of which the war was a part, including dynamics of poverty and social inequality. The exact circumstances under which adoptees in this second category became available for adoption vary. In my case, I was stolen by a woman my mother had hired to care for me. In other cases biological mothers voluntarily relinquished custody of their children or were coerced into relinquishing custody of their children by corrupt lawyers and their underlings.

In the United States, Salvadoran adoptees are seen mostly as success stories. Anglo Americans generally view adoptees as having barely escaped growing up in poverty and not as having been separated from their birth families and birth countries. Often when people find out that someone was adopted from El Salvador as an infant, they say "Oh, so then you don't remember it." Unfortunately, in many cases this statement implies that not remembering it means it doesn't matter. Our pasts do not exist. Any pondering of the reasons such children as we may have ended up available for adoption is quickly written off through comments such as, "Your mother probably wanted the best for you," or some other similar, thoughtless platitude. Such platitudes have become institutionalized and have even been used by the adoption agencies. My whole life people have asked me, "Don't you feel lucky to have been able to grow up in the United States?" But what people mean by this question is more "Aren't you glad you got to be an American?" than "Aren't you glad to be a Salvadoran living in the United States?"

According to Ralph Sprenkels, editor of a book on El Salvador's disappeared children (*El Día Más Esperado* or *The Much Hoped For Day),* because of the high price that American couples paid to Salvadoran lawyers when adopting a child, many such lawyers started proactively searching orphanages for adoptable children.[12] They usually brought toys, clothes, and food on these adoptable-baby finding missions to gain the confidence of the orphanage personnel. Some corrupt lawyers and their underlings lured biological mothers, usually in poor or refugee communities, to surrender their babies with false promises that they'd see their children again in a few years or receive money from the adoptive family in the United States. Most of these mothers would never again see their children. Those who would see their children again would have to wait many years.

Nelson and Elsy remained in El Salvador after they had been disappeared but many other niños desaparecidos were adopted to the United States. Most Anglo Americans adopting children from El Salvador—and most of the Salvadoran adoptees themselves—have never even heard the term "niños desaparecidos." Lea Marenn, who went to El Salvador to adopt her six-year-old daughter, tells the story of her journey in her book, *Salvador's Children.* She places adoption in the context of the US relationship with El Salvador by posing a rhetorical question. "Oh, the dull fingers and savage bellies of El Norte," she writes. "If North Americans were childless, did El Salvador have to make up for that too?"[13] Marenn's question suggests a disturbing role assigned to El Salvador, making it a source not only for cheap labor and goods for North America but also a source for children as well.

Just as many North American consumers are unaware of the origins of their (inanimate) products, so many adoptive parents are oblivious to the origins (like those described by Sprenkels) of their Salvadoran children. Other than knowing that there was a conflict going on, adoptive parents and Salvadoran adoptees are often unconscious of the ways Salvadoran adoption fits into the relationship between the United States and El Salvador. My adoptive parents were particularly protected from knowledge of my pre-adoptive life because they did not travel to El Salvador to get me. What adoptees and their adoptive parents were told about the situation in El Salvador at the time of their adoption varied. The parents of one Salvadoran adoptee I know were simply told that their son was "found by the side of the road." This well-meaning adoptive parent assumed that the child must have been simply abandoned. However, if we consider the context of the war, it is entirely possible that this child was left behind as the villagers fled a military incursion. Certainly the adoption agency didn't mention this scenario to the adoptive parent. To do so would have suggested the very real possibility that the child's biological family in El Salvador may have still been (and is still) looking for the child.

The adoption agency my parents dealt with told them that due to the war in El Salvador they (whomever "they" might be) were "trying to get all the kids out." My parents took this to mean that because of the danger posed by the war, the children were essentially being evacuated for their own safety. This is the idea the adoption agency was probably trying to convey, although their exact intention is unknown. I am sure that my adoptive parents were not the only ones told such a story by adoption agencies. Therefore it would also be safe to say that I was not the only adoptee who grew up believing that the reason I was available for adoption was this humanitarian mass evacuation of children. Ironically, the profit-driven, proactive searching for adoptable children that Sprenkels describes is a disturbing manifestation of the concept of "trying to get all the kids out."

The Salvadoran armed conflict ended on January 16, 1992, when the government of El Salvador and the FMLN signed the peace accords at the Castle of Chapultepec, Mexico. Through the peace accords, the FMLN became a legitimate political party. Other components included the reduction of the army by half. Atlactl, Belloso, and other rapid response battalions were disbanded. A new civilian police force called the Policía Nacional Civil was created. The Chapultepec accords also spawned a United Nations Truth Commission to investigate the allegations of human rights violations that occurred during the war.[14]

Ten months after the signing of the Chapultepec accords, the UN Truth Commission sent a delegation to Guarjila in the department of Chaletenango. Jon Cortina, a Jesuit from Spain who had been working in El Salvador for a number of years, negotiated with representatives of the delegation to ensure that the people of the region would be able to testify before the delegation. When the delegation arrived in Guarjila, a very long line of people formed. Among those in line were Francisca Romero and Magdalena Ramos. Cortina had met Francisca shortly after the end of the war and was familiar with her case. With his support, both she and Magdalena testified before the Truth Commission regarding the disappearance of their children.

The Truth Commission's report, entitled "From Madness to Hope," was published on March 23, 1993. While the report did denounce many of the other human rights abuses that occurred during the war, "From Madness to Hope" did not address the issue of the disappeared children. The only mention of Francisca Romero's disappeared daughter Elsy was through her name appearing in a list of more than 18,000 victims that was appended to the report.

After the report was published, Cortina formed a small human rights group in Chaletenango to disseminate the report and the previously repressed truths it contained. Cortina's group also began investigating the cases of disappeared children. The group came into contact with other mothers who had lost their children during the same military operation in which Francisca and Magdalena's children had disappeared. Francisca, Magdalena, and three other families formed a group to begin searching for their missing children. In April 1993 they held a press conference in San Salvador to make their search initiative known. The group tried to bring the cases of the disappeared children before the attorney general but they were turned away.

It was chance that eventually led to the reunion of Francisca, Magdalena, and the other families from Guarjila with their children. Francisca Ramirez's cousin Santos had heard of an orphanage in Santa Tecla called Aldeas Infantiles SOS (Children's Village SOS) that was supposedly full of children who were originally from Chaletenango. Passing by Aldeas Infantiles SOS in January of 1994, Santos saw a little girl who had only one arm. He knew that Francisca's daughter Elsy had lost an arm to a bomb before she was disappeared.

The Aldeas Infantiles SOS in Santa Tecla is part of a global network of Children's Villages operated by an Austrian Organization called SOS-Kinderdorf International. There is insufficient evidence to draw any conclusions about the level of knowledge the SOS in Santa Tecla had about where the children were coming from and what, if any, action they took based on what they knew.

When Santos returned to Chalatenango with the news of the girl at Aldeas Infantiles SOS, more than 25 families in Guarjila wanted to go there to look for their disappeared children. A group of these families went and found that the children there were in fact the disappeared children of the families from Guarjila. The director of the facility only knew that the children had been brought there by the Damas Voluntarias de La Cruz Roja Salvadoreña (Volunteer Women of the Salvadoran Red Cross). A reunion was arranged to take place 10 days later on January 16. Jon Cortina was present. In total 11 families were reunited with their children that day. In only one of those cases was the daughter old enough at the time of her disappearance to be able to recognize her family before they recognized her. Francisca and Elsy, who was by then about sixteen years old, would not be reunited until the following month because Elsy was six months pregnant at the time and not able to travel to Guarjila.

Due to the success of those 12 reunions many families began to come to Jon Cortina looking for help in searching for their disappeared children. On August 20, 1994, Cortina and others formed La Asociación Pro-Búsqueda de Niñas y Niños Desaparecidos (Association in Search of Disappeared Children).[15]

Although I was unaware of the events that transpired in El Salvador after I left, they would later come to affect me greatly. I was 13 years old when Pro-Búsqueda was formed. At the time I was living the life of a typical American teenager in suburban Massachusetts and knew nothing about the creation of Pro-Búsqueda or any other events in El Salvador. By 1994 the other Salvadorans I knew who had been adopted to the United States as infants around the same time I was had long since forgotten about El Salvador and the war. Salvadoran adoptees and their adoptive parents had the luxury of forgetting about the war. Of course this is a luxury that people in El Salvador did not have.

Migration is a fact of life for Salvadorans. Remittances sent home from those who have immigrated (usually without papers) to the United States are the most important source of income for the tiny Central American country. And whether the migration is in the form of fleeing the horrors of war, as it was during the 1980s, fleeing poverty, as it has been since the war concluded, or being adopted out of the country, family separation is always a part of migration.

Sometimes the separation isn't permanent. In my case I was able, through Pro-Búsqueda, to finally reunite with my family. The reunion took place on May 9, 2002. Of course, 22 years prior, when we were separated, I was just an infant, so at the reunion I had to be told which of the women was my mother and who my sisters were. In the four years that have passed since reuniting with my family, I have had almost daily phone contact with them and have visited them in El Salvador five times. The situation for my family no longer resembles the typical family separation that occurs in international adoption. Instead, my family's situation now fits into a pattern shared by many Salvadoran families whose relatives have emigrated to the United States.

Usually, where one goes, more follow. This raises the question of whether I would like to bring other family members to the United States. This is not a question of simply wanting to visit with them or wanting them to see where I grew up. Nor would it be a question of my sisters or my mother improving their lives by coming here and assimilating into American society. Beyond whether this would even be desirable, it is simply not realistic. My sister, like most Salvadorans who are not wealthy, could not get a tourist visa to come here. Nor would she want one. If she came to the United States, it would be to work for a few years, save some money, and return to El Salvador. But obtaining an immigrant visa for my sister would take at least 12 years due to immigration backlogs, and even then the US government would quite probably deny her entry.

So for now, I am the only member of my immediate family who has come to Los Yunai (the United States) and gained access to US wages. And while I didn't come here illegally across the Arizona desert as so many of my compatriots have, I nevertheless play the same role that those undocumented migrant workers play for their families: I help out my sister financially when I can. Of course, the fact that I am a college student means that my life also has a dimension different than that of many other Central American immigrants. Eventually, a college education means I might be able to spare both the 200 some dollars for an iPod *and* the 200 dollars that will get nephews in El Salvador their books, clothes, and shoes. For now, though, I have to balance wiring money to El Salvador and buying phone cards to call my family there with buying my own books and paying tuition.

The armed conflict in El Salvador has been over for more than a decade. Out-migration continues at a high rate, but international adoption is no longer a significant part of the movement of people from El Salvador to the United States. Today, most migrants from Central America make the journey illegally across Mexico and over the southern US border. During the journey one runs the risk of being robbed, raped, or deported, or falling from the moving trains that some migrants hop to come north. And you can add to those dangers simply not knowing where you are or if you will make it to your final destination, or whether you will eat or sleep that week. Although these experiences are most likely unknown to the adoptees who have lived a relatively privileged life in the United States, "voluntary" immigrants and involuntary adoptees were driven from Central America by the same social forces. This should be reason enough for us to acknowledge and foster the connections between us.

notes

1 Open Door Society of Massachusetts, "Welcome Home," *ODS News* 34 (1981): 3.
2 Myrna L. Friedlander, "Ethnic Identity Development of Internationally Adopted Children and Adolescents: Implications for Family Therapists," *Journal of Marital and Family Therapy* 25 (1999): 43–60.
3 Adam Pertman, *Adoption Nation: How the Adoption Revolution is Transforming America* (New York: Basic Books, 2000), 73.
4 Ralph Sprenkels, ed., *El Día Más Esperado* (San Salvador: UCA Editores, 2001), 246.
5 Tina Rosenberg, *Children of Cain: Violence and the Violent in Latin America* (New York: William Morrow and Company, 1991), 248.
6 Rosenberg, 240–243.
7 Comisión Nacional de Educación Política, FMLN, *Origen Del FMLN* (September 2002) [FMLN document online]; available from http://www.fmln.org.sv/.
8 José Angel Moroni Bracamonte and David E. Spencer, *Strategy and Tactics of the Salvadoran FMLN Guerrillas: Last Battle of the Cold War, Blueprint for Future Conflicts* (Westport, CT: Praeger, 1995), 15–23.
9 Sprenkels, 61–62.
10 Mark Danner, *The Massacre at El Mozote: A Parable of the Cold War* (New York: Vintage, 1994), 43–52.
11 Sprenkels, 63–82.
12 Sprenkels, 246–247.
13 Lea Marenn, *Salvador's Children: A Song for Survival* (Columbus: Ohio State University Press, 1993), 62.
14 Danner, 158.
15 Sprenkels, 82–96.

PART THREE

COLONIAL IMAGINATIONS, GLOBAL MIGRATIONS

Mary R Hyde, matron, and students at Carlisle Indian Training School

12 IF I PULL AWAY

Shandra Spears

There is no future and no past, only a long, isolated now
I am not connected to past relations
I am not connected to future generations
I am pulled from the flow of time.
When two robins build a nest together,
Lay eggs and incubate them,
And the eggs hatch, and the babies grow,
And the young birds mature and fly away,
I am not part of that.

> *My baby face contains a secret: I am thirty-six years old*
> *Unmarried, childless, I am single maybe because I am fat,*
> *Or because I am damaged in some way*
> *that is discernible to the men who date me*
> *Or because I've settled for friendship too often*
> *Or because I lack self-esteem*
> *and don't believe I deserve good love*
> *At thirty-six, it is time to grow up*
> *Not in all the ways I've grown up already*
> *But by choosing a partner and raising children*
> *That is how the adults of all species reach maturity*[1]

There is no future and no past, only a long, isolated now
I am not connected to past relations
I am not connected to future generations
I am pulled from the flow of time.
In the story of my life, I am meant to be a pet, or a companion,
To fill in missing pieces in people's lives,
To be a bandage over the wound in adoptive parents' hearts

> *My parents come to see me.*
> *They do this because they know it's important to me*
> *that they make the trip, that they come to me.*
> *We have lunch in the market, and walk along the boardwalk.*
> *Stopping at the beach, my mother smiles her most loving smile.*

You still look like my little girl, she says.
It's true; I do. My inner child is not so deep inside.
I put on the extra cuteness as I smile back.
It feels good when she feels good about me,
But inside, I feel queasy.
In this endless now, our moment at the beach
is all the moments.
They take turns going to the water's edge with me.
Mom and I collect rocks;
Dad and I skip stones across the water.
My heart breaks as I smile,
Because this is the only way we can be together
Me as a baby girl child, and
them loving the child they remember.

There is no future and no past, only a long, isolated now
I am not connected to past relations
I am not connected to future generations
I am pulled from the flow of time.
As if all the human beings who live out their human stories
Are somehow not like me; in my specialness as a chosen child
there is a secret.
The sense that the world is not as I expected it to be,
And I am not who I expected to be.
The unvoiced relationships of power and mastery
The ghoulish half-life of truths not told

This is a moment within the endless now
The summer of 2005, when I awoke,
like Sleeping Shanderella
From a long, lonely time, to rediscover my womanhood.
Slowly discovering that the only way I know love,
The only consistent love I know,
The only long-term relationship in my life,
The only proof that I can *love,*
is the love I feel for my parents
At thirty-six, the only Valentine I received was from my dad.
He always sends a Valentine to his girls, my mom said.
I felt loved, and blessed,
But it was the first clue that something is wrong
with still being my mom and dad's little girl.

There is no future and no past, only a long, isolated now
I am not connected to past relations
I am not connected to future generations

I am pulled from the flow of time.
Into a myth-creation story that conceals
Instead of revealing.
It is all disconnection, disconnection
The way I grew up to be white
The way I learned to date white men
The way I was intended to be white
Somehow, in pulling away from that whiteness,
I have been locked into a perpetual state of childhood
Forgetting or never knowing that I was Native
And, rediscovering my Nativeness, remaining a girl child;
Learning so late, or never connecting
to the things that would position me as Woman.
I am an auntie, a friend, an artist, and a teacher,
Wondering how I've never also become a mother.

But I talk to my parents of adult things; dating and children.
I talk to them about the legislation
that sets a two-generation cutoff rule for "Indians,"
So that if I do not have children
with the right kind of Native man,
My children will be erased as "Indians,"
Though they may live as Canadians.
I make the connections:
The way my grandparents were removed,
The way my father was removed,
The way that I was removed;
That these are all connected to the way
My children could be removed
If I can get past the cultural infertility
That sets me apart from the flow of life
To bear those children,
As a Native ancestor and a Native descendant.
I talk to them outside of the myths
About the reality of my present moment.

There is no future and no past, only a long, isolated now
I am not connected to past relations
I am not connected to future generations
I am pulled from the flow of time.
Into a life of story, in which I am not born, but chosen
In which I sprang into existence in the moment
when my father's eyes met my big brown baby eyes
and I looked up to him and smiled

All is disconnected and grey
Except for that moment, which has colour and life.
All is constructed reality, an identity woven in adulthood
        from reunions
        from teachings and political awakening
        from contextualizing my life.
But that moment of myth, when my parents chose me,
Has a resonance for me that feels real.

It is the baby story that makes me feel real.
Not the birth story that I learned as an adult,
But the adoption story that I learned as a child.
It is the baby love and baby smile
        that feel like real love,
Not the theoretical Native family
        with myself as a wife and mother
        to a Native husband and Native children.
It is the mythology about Indians in which I was steeped,
The fantasy Indian who is not quite real.
I live within a myth about adoption
        that conceals the truth of my birth
And I live within a myth about Indians
        that conceals the truth of my future
            and my past.

There is no future and no past, only a long, isolated now
I am not connected to past relations
I am not connected to future generations
I am pulled from the flow of time.
The myth of loving, white adoptive parents
Somehow overpowers any other kind of love.
To keep this love is to trade in all other possible loves.
If I pull out of this story, what will happen?
If I pull away, will I leave a jagged, bleeding hole
        in my heart's ability to love?
Will I leave a jagged, bleeding hole
        in the family that has always supported me?
Or will I find wholeness in a life that is truer
        and more real?

This is what it means to be in an identity crisis,
When people take in babies and keep them alive,
With social position, with food, with shelter and love.
The babies are consumed, or purchased.
They grow into young children who live and thrive.

They grow into young adults who struggle with half-truths.
They grow into adults who struggle to mature.
We were loved, many of us, by loving people
Who had no idea how to help us survive
In a way that touches the future
Or connects with the past.

There is no future and no past, only a long, isolated now
I am not connected to past relations
I am not connected to future generations
I am pulled from the flow of time.
This is not what is written
    on my Mother's and Father's Day cards.
This is the dark, deep poetry of
    what is personal and political.
This is the sharp blade that slices away love
    to reveal dark sores of truth.
These are the teeth I use to chew the trap off my leg.
This is not the whole of my life, but a turning point.

This is the half-life of adoption stories:
Half-in and half-out of identities,
Half-in and half-out of careers,
Half-in and half-out of relationships,
We swim on top of a pool of stories
While others build adult lives on solid ground.

There is no future and no past, only a long, isolated now
I am not connected to past relations
I am not connected to future generations
I am pulled from the flow of time.
To live within pretty stories of love and middle-class tidiness
    that conceal the meaning of our realities.
Parents are married, white and middle-class.
Families live in suburbs.
White, middle-class parents love better.
Loving people deserve children more.
Wealthier people deserve children more.
Children are special and chosen.
Birth parents just couldn't do for us.
We are white if they say we are white.
We live whatever story they tell us to live.

But underneath these stories,
Birth parents struggle in on- and off-again relationships,

Give us up in a moment of panic or anger,
Or we are stolen, or we are sold.
Birth parents live all their lives with pain, shame, and grief.
Adoptive parents are not entitled to babies,
but get to have us because they fit a profile.
They struggle and hurt with their own dysfunction and grief.
Adoptees are not entitled to parents, and we would die
if someone didn't take care of us.
Abandoned children are dead children without this help.
Racism and classism and international systems of oppression
create situations in which babies are moved around.
And it all gets covered up under the myth
of loving, white, middle-class North American
adoptive parents,
who are themselves struggling,
And we are all supposed to be very grateful
While we struggle to make sense of our lives.

There is no future and no past, only a long, isolated now
I am not connected to past relations
I am not connected to future generations
I am pulled from the flow of time.
When I began to write, the robins were building their nest.
I saw them caring for the eggs, and then the babies.
I saw the baby birds mature and fly away.
I saw the nest fall to the ground.
Whatever struggles this small family endured,
They were able, at least, to accomplish that mundane miracle.
I hold tight to the belief that I, too, can be part of the miracle of life,
Not as a special character in a special story,
But as an adult woman, a Native woman, slogging away,
Wrenching my life back from the white direction
imposed by three generations of cultural genocide,
Struggling to date a kind of man I was never taught to date,
Struggling to become the wife and mother I was never raised to become,
Struggling to be the grandmother and great-grandmother
Of a Native family that was supposed to fade away.

I see and recognize the flow of life
I slip in and start to swim.

note

1 The distinction between human and animal can vary based upon cultural positioning. As a First Nations person, I view myself as part of a community that also includes four-legged, winged, and other types of relations. To be human is to be an animal like the rest of my relations, but one who walks on two legs. I learn from those "older brothers and sisters," not as someone who is separate or superior, but as someone who is dependent upon them and as someone who learns from their examples. Every individual within other species does not give birth. Some, like nondominant wolves, do not give birth but serve the children of the alpha female instead. This piece questions my nondominant or "lone wolf" position—what is it that places me outside of the "alpha wolf" child-bearing process? This is not only a biological question but also a question of social position. Why have I been socially positioned as more of a daughter than mother? What is it about my adoption/reunion experience that has created this lasting childhood? Is there a connection? As well, cultural and historical positioning can cause theorists to view maturity and parenthood in different ways. Some feminist theory separates our biological ability to give birth from our value as human beings, and as women, in order to protect us from systemic oppression. The First Nations cultural perspective toward interconnectedness does not always match other value systems that depend on making distinctions and separations. From my cultural position, a number of strengths are attributed to women based upon our ability to give life—an identity connected with, rather than disconnected from, motherhood, even as we also relate on an extended-family level. This can create an uncomfortable tension with non-Native theorists. This poem is intended to express a specific moment in time, a new awareness of maturity beyond the ways that I have already matured, and a new awareness of myself apart from my life roles as auntie, friend, cousin, granddaughter, artist, and teacher.

Top: Apache children on arrival at Carlisle Indian School in Pennsylvania
Bottom: Same children four months later (photos taken by the US Army Signal Corps)

13 FLYING THE COOP

ICWA AND THE WELFARE OF INDIAN CHILDREN

Heidi Kiiwetinepinesiik Stark & Kekek Jason Todd Stark

the eagle who thought he was a chicken

James Waldram, in *The Way of the Pipe*, recounts the story of an eagle who thought he was a chicken. As the story goes, one day a farmer found a wounded eagle and placed him out in the chickens' coop to recover. This eagle began mimicking the chickens to survive in his new environment. He ate like the chickens, slept like the chickens, and adopted the behavior of the chickens. Then one day an Indian man came by the farm and saw this eagle who thought he was a chicken.

> So he said, "What's that eagle doing there in the chicken coop?" The farmer said, "Well, I found it in the ditch, mended its wing and put him in there.... The eagle can fly out any time. Its wing is healed.... He just thinks he's a chicken I guess."[1]

The farmer agreed to let this Indian man take the eagle out of the coop, but the eagle remained docile. He just kept bobbing his head like a chicken. The eagle no longer understood who he was, no longer identified as an eagle and appreciated the gifts that came with that identity.

> So the Indian took the bird to the mountain and said, "You have to know who you are and what you stand for..." The eagle started to flex his wings. His keen eyesight started to return, and the strength in him started to come back. The eagle flew and soared and everything came back to him, who he was and that he wasn't a chicken. He gained everything he'd lost because of where he was placed.[2]

Many American Indian children are in a situation that parallels this story. Their removal from their homes and placement outside their tribal communities has led to a loss of identity. They often risk becoming eagles that behave like chickens. Tribal nations have struggled against state, county, and local agencies' attempts to remove their children and place them in non-

Indian homes, the symbolic chicken coop. Their fight to limit the destructive results of this mass removal led to the Indian Child Welfare Act (ICWA).

building the chicken coop: the making of policy relating to american indians

Making up less than 1 percent of the United States' population, American Indians are often classified as racial minorities. However, American Indians possess a status that none of the other racial minorities can claim; they are indigenous to North America, and Indian tribes have a government-to-government relationship with the United States, formalized through treaty-making. Lumbee scholar David Wilkins, in his study of American Indian politics, found that

> the pre-existence of well over six hundred independent tribal nations, bands, pueblos, etc., well in advance of the formation of the United States, each having a number of integral attributes, including a bounded land base, an appropriate economic system, a governmental system, and sociocultural distinctiveness, necessitated the practice of aboriginal sovereigns negotiating political compacts, treaties, and alliances with European nations and later the United States.[3]

When the formal treaty-making process was ended in 1871,[4] US policymakers invoked the commerce clause of the US Constitution to redefine the political relationship between Indian tribes and the United States, acknowledging that direct power for dealing with Indians affairs rests ultimately with Congress, instead of the individual states.[5] This unique legal relationship has allowed tribal nations to petition the federal government for protection from state and individual interests. This relationship, according to Wilkins,

> broadly entails the unique legal and moral duty of the federal government to assist Indian tribes in the protection of their lands, resources, and cultural heritage. The federal government ... is to be held to the highest standards of good faith and honesty in its dealings with Indian peoples and their rights and resources.[6]

Yet Congress has often utilized this power to create and implement policy that has proved detrimental in the lives of American Indians.

entering the chicken coop: the removal of american indian children from their homes

In the 1880s the United States first imposed a federal boarding school policy intended to force American Indians to assimilate into American society, rather than segregating them by removing them from their lands and confining them on reservations, as was previous policy. The federal government had realized that these reservation policies were proving too costly and ineffective as a means for solving their so-called Indian problem. Policy reformers began to see compulsory residential vocational education as a means of alleviating the US federal government of its trust responsibility to tribal nations and as a vehicle for integrating American Indians into American society. Then-President Chester A. Arthur, in his first annual message to Congress in 1881, preached this new national policy, asserting that the solution was "to introduce among the Indians the customs and pursuits of civilized life and gradually to absorb them into the mass of our citizens."[7] Congress followed suit, passing a law in 1882 that authorized the use of vacant army posts and barracks for Indian industrial training schools.[8] Ojibwe historian Brenda Child, in her study of early-20th-century boarding schools, explains, "The idea was conceived ... that boarding school education, which removed young children from their tribal environment, would 'civilize' and prepare Indians for citizenship while providing them with a practical, vocational education."[9]

But by the mid-1920s, boarding schools were being closed, perhaps indicating that the assimilation policy had been a "miscalculation of major proportions."[10] This massive "miscalculation" was highlighted in 1928, when the Institute for Government Research published "The Problem of Indian Administration," commonly referred to as the Meriam Report.[11] This report detailed the devastating effects federal Indian policies of land allotment and assimilation had had on tribal nations, calling for a reformation in Indian policy. In addition, the Meriam Report outlined the deplorable conditions of boarding school life for American Indian children, which were further publicized by a series of articles in *Good Housekeeping*. These articles urged the "American woman to recognize the many past and present injustices against Indians, one of the worst of which was removing children from their families to live and be reared in overcrowded, disease infested boarding schools where callous government officials overworked and starved their pupils."[12] The Meriam Report, coupled with this public attention on the failures in Indian education, led policymakers to shift away from their goal of assimilation and reconfigure their approach to Indian education.

Furthermore, by the 1940s, institutional living was recognized by social welfare agencies as detrimental to young children's development.[13] Adoption was considered to be better, since it provided children a permanent placement in the more "natural" familial arrangement. Unfortunately, many adoption agencies viewed minority (as well as handicapped and older) children as "hard to place." Various programs were created in the 1940s and '50s to promote the placement of these children. By the mid-1950s, the public had a growing interest in adopting American Indian children and both the Area and Central offices of the Bureau of Indian Affairs (BIA) began receiving many more letters inquiring into the possibility of doing so.[14] David Fanshel, who had an extensive background in adoption research, argued that this increased desire in adopting American Indian children could likely be attributed to recent experiences of families adopting internationally being viewed as successful, as well as to a 1957 National Council of Protestant Churches study of the American Indian (37). This study resulted in increased attention to the children's general welfare—thought to be deplorable; Indian children's adoption into Caucasian families was seen as the suitable solution.

Out of a desire to promote the external placement of American Indian children, in 1958 the BIA and the Child Welfare League of America (CWLA) established the Indian Adoption Project.[15] A nationwide survey conducted in 1957 showed that "there were approximately 1,000 Indian children legally free for adoption who were forced to live in foster homes and institutions because adoptive resources had not been found for them" (Fanshel, 35). The Indian Adoption Project placed approximately 395 Native children with Caucasian families during the course of 9 short years.[16]

In 1960 CWLA asked Fanshel to conduct a study of 97 of the children placed through the Indian Adoption Project to determine how they had adjusted to their adoptions and to establish the characteristics and backgrounds of families who adopted outside their racial background. Prior to their adoption, the children "had been identified by social workers as being likely to spend their childhood years in intermediate living arrangements; a succession of foster homes or boarding schools seemed to be their fate" (Fanshel, iii). To be eligible for the project, the child had to be established as one-fourth or more Indian; the child had to be considered adoptable both physically and emotionally; and either the parent(s) had to release the child for adoption after careful casework counseling or, if the child was "abandoned" or "neglected" and was seen by social welfare agencies as needing permanent removal, the court had to assure the child's "adoptability." Any child meeting these criteria was referred for adoption by the program director, who worked as a liaison between the agency responsible for the child and the adoption agency until the child was adopted (Fanshel, 40).

Fanshel's study involved a series of interviews with adoptive parents and was structured with two goals in mind.

> One goal was to develop systematic knowledge about the characteristics of the couples who adopted the children. It was hoped thereby to gain increased understanding of the phenomenon of adoption across racial and ethnic lines. A second objective was to develop a picture of the experiences encountered by the families and children for a five-year period after the children were placed. (iii)

If the interviewed parents felt positively about their decision to adopt transracially, and if this practice resulted in permanent placement with minimal developmental difficulties for the children, "agencies might thereby be encouraged to become increasingly venturesome in their placement policies" (iii). However, because the children were all under the age of two when they were placed and thus less than seven years old at the time of the study, they were not interviewed for this study. It is, therefore, limited in its ability to discern the effects of transracial adoption on the children involved. Nevertheless, the study does lend insight into the transracial placement of American Indian children prior to the passage of the Indian Child Welfare Act.

the farmer's perception of the eagle: adoptive parents on transracial adoption

Fanshel's study sought information on the background and social attitudes of the families who adopted American Indian children. The parents in this study were in various stages of parenting when they sought to adopt an American Indian child. For some this would be their first child, while others had biological children already, and some parents had previously adopted either Caucasian or non-Indian minority children. The study found that the parents primarily chose to adopt American Indian children, instead of non-Indian children, at the encouragement of their adoption agencies. Parents expressed a range of emotion regarding their decisions. One father acknowledged his decision was too hasty, stating:

> When they asked us if we would accept an Indian child, we were ready to discuss the possibility although we had never seen an Indian child. As I look back upon it, we did not really think through the situation sufficiently. When I saw Tina, I felt troubled and continued to feel troubled even after taking her. When I am really being honest with myself, I have to recognize that I am essentially a prejudiced person. (89)

While most of the parents involved in the study had put a great deal of thought into their decision to adopt, many admitted they had put little thought into the larger implications of adopting American Indian children. Their transracial adoptions forced many parents to recognize their own and/or others' underlying feelings about race and skin color. One mother discussed the discomfort she felt.

> The agency from which we had adopted our first child could not offer us another baby other than a handicapped child or a child from a racial minority. We mulled it over, and with reservations, approached the agency.... I realized I found it very painful to have people stare at me when I went out with the baby.... The caseworker never appreciated the side of me that was so frightened of difference. (103)

This mother eventually sought psychiatric help in coping with the discomfort she felt regarding her child.

Although some parents were troubled by the racial make-up of their children, others were glad for the opportunity to adopt an American Indian child. Fanshel recognized the varied and complex opinions parents maintained about American Indians. Some of the parents he interviewed claimed to embrace the chance to adopt an Indian child immediately because they perceived of Indians as the "real" Americans, while others expressed feelings of compassion for Native peoples. One father said he was comfortable with the idea of adopting a Native child because he felt "Indians in this country had a tough break," asserting further that as a child he always rooted for the Indians instead of the cowboys (85). Other parents were willing to adopt Indian children only if they had light complexions, many explicitly expressing their unwillingness to adopt African American children. One father argued:

> The agency had asked us if we would consider an Indian child and we thought about it and decided it would be okay as long as the child would be light-skinned. Since I come from the South, I would have hesitated to consider a dark-skinned child because people might jump to the wrong conclusions. We did not want the child to be taken for part-Negro. The agency said we would have a better chance of being accepted [for a child] if we took an Indian. (84)

Parents were asked a series of questions to ascertain what qualities they attributed to "acceptable" children. Only 15 percent of mothers were willing to adopt a child characterized as "obviously Negro" and 22 percent were open to children characterized as "not obviously Negro in appearance, while 71 percent of the parents claimed they would easily adopt an 'Oriental' child" (119). Most parents qualified their responses, claiming that while they personally had no emotional aversion to adopting an African American child, their communities would prove hostile to the child and thus adoption was not in the child's best interest. The responses demonstrated that many parents expressed attitudes toward Indian children similar to those held about Asian children, with some stating that "they were often stopped on the street by people who inquired as to whether the Indian child was Korean" (119).

Fanshel's study provides a window into adoptive parents' complicated and differing views on the practice of transracial adoption in the late 1950s and early '60s. Yet Fanshel also acknowledged that the answer to whether the transracial adoption of Indian children was sound could not be ascertained through a series of interviews with white adoptive parents. He warned:

> Whether Indian children are to be placed in any significant numbers in white homes in the future will depend on the attitudes of the Indian tribal organizations.... The climate of transracial adoption has changed in that minority groups tend to see this as the ultimate indignity that has been inflicted upon them. It seems clear that the fate of most Indians is tied to the struggle of Indian people in the United States for survival and social justice. Their ultimate salvation rests upon the success of that struggle.... Only the Indian people have the right to determine whether their children can be placed in white homes. (341)

By the time Fanshel published his study in the 1970s, many tribal leaders had long been protesting the tremendous rate of removal of Indian children from their homes, which had increased when CWLA and the BIA initiated the Indian Adoption Project.

when eagles are made to peck: removal rates and effects

American Indian children accounted for 3.1 percent of the total population of children cared for out of their homes, even though they were less than 1 percent of the total child population in the 1950s and '60s. Therefore, American Indian children were in out-of-home placement at a rate 3.6 times greater than the rate for non-Indian children.[17]

Doubts about the capacity of American Indian families to raise their children continued long after the boarding school era. State agencies argued that removal was in the best interest of many American Indian children, which resulted in "as many as 25 to 35 percent of the Indian children in some states [who] were removed from their homes and placed in non-Indian homes by state-courts, welfare agencies, and private adoption agencies" before the passage of the Indian Child Welfare Act in 1978.[18] Congress also found that countrywide, Indian children were placed in foster care or in adoptive homes at 5 times the rate of non-Indian children, while in Montana, foster care placement for Indian children was at least 13 times greater than for non-Indian children; in South Dakota, adoptions of American Indian children accounted for 40 percent of all adoptions made by the state's Department of Public Welfare between 1967 and 1978, even though they were only 7 percent of the juvenile population; in Washington, the Indian adoption rate was 19 times greater and the foster care rate was 10 times greater; and in Wisconsin Indian children ran the risk of being separated from their parents at a rate nearly 1600 percent greater than non-Indian children.[19]

During the congressional hearings that led to the Indian Child Welfare Act, information was presented from the 1971 BIA school census that showed 34,538 children were living in institutional facilities instead of their homes, which translated into more than 17 percent of the Indian school age population and 60 percent of children enrolled in BIA schools. According to the census, "On the Navajo reservation, about 20,000 children, or 90 percent of the BIA school population [were living] at boarding schools."[20]

The removal of Native children would lead to far more serious problems than adoptive agencies and local/state agencies anticipated. Local and state agencies removed Indian children applying determinants that ignored the traumatic effects this forceful removal was having. Congress recognized the concerns raised by American Indian activists and leaders during a 1978 hearing. The Subcommittee on Indian Affairs declared that:

> The separation of Indian children from their natural parents, especially their placement in institutions or homes, which do not meet their special

> needs, is socially and culturally undesirable. For the child, such separation can cause a loss of identity and self-esteem, and contributes directly to the unreasonable high rates among Indian children for dropouts, alcoholism and drug abuse, suicides, and crime.[21]

Congress also argued that the removal of American Indian children aggravated the conditions that initially gave rise to the break-up of the family, finding that this perpetuates the continuing cycle of poverty and despair.[22]

These issues have been a concern of Indian child-welfare advocates working to decrease depression, suicide, and alcoholism. At a 1990 conference on the ICWA, presenters Evelyn Blanchard and Irving Berlin discussed the long-term effects of out-of-home placement, presenting findings from a study of 100,000 Indian children in foster placement. The study, conducted by Tom Halverson of the University of Utah, found alarmingly high suicide rate among those 18 to 20 years of age—"six to ten times greater than it was for the national average."[23] Halverson also found that "the rate of depression in both the young men and the young women who have been in foster care in Anglo homes has been in the range of about 40 percent of those who have been studied—an enormous rate of depression."[24] Transracial placements were proving to have detrimental effects on American Indian children.

the eagle flexes its wings: passage of the icwa

The accumulation of assimilation policies, state involvement, and the soaring out-of-home placement of Indian children led to concern among many American Indians. Tribal leaders became alarmed that their children and communities were being decimated by mainstream child welfare practices, and many people became concerned these practices at the state and local level were impeding the sovereignty of the tribes. State and local agencies, while claiming to determine the best interests of American Indian children, often neglected their cultural needs. The need for remedy pushed Native activists to approach the federal government for reprieve from state and local agencies, leading eventually to the passage of the ICWA.

In 1968 members of the Devil's Lake Sioux Tribe of North Dakota, concerned with the level of cultural decimation they were facing, approached the Association of American Indian Affairs (AAIA), established in 1923 to "defend the rights of American Indians and Alaskan Natives and to promote social, economic, and civic equality for their communities."[25] The AAIA began work on the issue, bringing awareness and information to public and professional channels while collecting data and testimonials to present to the federal government.[26] Senate oversight hearings on the placement of Indian children finally began during the second session of the 93rd Congress on April 8–9, 1974. Senator James Abourezk, chairman of the Subcommittee on Indian Affairs, ran the hearings as well as presenting testimony. During further hearings on the matter in the Senate in 1977, Abourezk stated, "up to now … public and private welfare agencies seem to have operated on the premise that most Indian children would really be better off growing up non-Indian."[27]

In an examination of child welfare practices for American Indian children, the Committee on Interior and Insular Affairs in the House of Representatives found that the separation of the children from their families generally occurred when:

1. The natural parent does not understand the nature of the documents or proceedings involved;
2. Neither the child nor the natural parents are represented by counsel or otherwise advised of their rights;
3. The agency officials involved are unfamiliar with, and often disdainful of, Indian culture and society;
4. The conditions that led to the separation are not demonstrably harmful or are remediable or transitory in character; and
5. Responsible tribal authorities are not consulted about or even informed of the nontribal government actions.[28]

In addition to these concerns, Congress recognized that Tribes were being denied their right to govern their children and be notified of the conditions facing their own people. Thus, a Declaration of Policy was established during hearings for the ICWA stating:

> The Congress hereby declares that it is the policy of this nation, in its fulfillment of its special responsibilities and legal obligations to the American Indian people, to establish standards for the placement of Indian children in foster or adoptive homes which will reflect the unique values of Indian culture, discourage unnecessary placement of Indian children in boarding schools for social rather than educational reasons, assist Indian tribes in the operation of tribal family development programs, and generally promote the stability and security of Indian families.[29]

The ICWA became law on November 8, 1978. In the act, Congress clearly defined "the relationship of the federal government to the tribes, determining that the Federal government has assumed the responsibility for the protection and preservation of Indian tribes and their resources," including their children. Congress found:

1. There is no resource that is more vital to the continued existence and integrity of Indian tribes than their children and that the United States has a direct interest, as trustee, in protecting Indian children who are members of or are eligible for membership in an Indian tribe.
2. That an alarmingly high percentage of Indian families are broken up by the removal, often unwarranted, of their children from them by non-tribal public and private agencies and that

an alarmingly high percentage of such children are placed in non-Indian foster and adoptive homes and institutions.

3. That the States, exercising their recognized jurisdiction over Indian child custody proceedings through administrative and judicial bodies, have often failed to recognize the essential tribal relations of Indian people and the cultural and social standards prevailing in Indian communities and families.[30]

The act was passed with two specific goals: It intended to protect individual Indian children and the maintenance of their families while protecting the future existence of the tribe as a sovereign entity[31] because "removal of Indian children from their cultural setting seriously impacts long-term tribal survival and has damaging social and psychological impact on many individual Indian children."[32] In large part the concerns that emerged during the congressional hearings on the ICWA were based on studies showing recurring developmental problems encountered during adolescence by Indian children raised in a Caucasian environment.[33] Therefore, it is clear that Congress's concern over the placement of Indian children in non-Indian homes was based in part on evidence of the direct detrimental impact of such placements outside their culture on the children themselves (as opposed to on the tribes that lost them).[34] More generally, placements in non-Indian homes were seen as "depriving the child of his or her tribal and cultural heritage."[35]

The Senate Report on the ICWA incorporated the testimony of Louis La Rose, chairman of the Winnebago tribe, before the American Indian Policy Review Commission:

> I think the cruelest trick that the white man has ever done to Indian children is to take them into adoption courts, erase all of their records and send them off to some nebulous family that has a contrary value system and that child reaches 16 or 17, he is a little brown child residing in a white community and he goes back to the reservation and he has absolutely no idea who his relatives are, and they effectively make him a non-person and I think … they destroy him.[36]

The underlying rationale of the act is to prevent decisions about the welfare of Indian children from being based on a "white, middle-class standard."[37] The ICWA congressional findings demonstrate that Congress perceived the states and their courts as employing just such a "white, middle-class standard" in their determinations for child placement.[38]

Congress recognized that "the survival of tribal nations is significantly jeopardized if the children, the only real means for the transmission of the tribal heritage, are raised in non-Indian homes and denied exposure to the ways of their people."[39] Furthermore, state removal of Indian children "seriously undercuts the tribes' ability to exercise their rights as self-governing communities" because without their children tribes are stripped of the core that composes their political future. "In no area is it more important that tribal sovereignty be respected than in an area as socially and culturally determinative as family relationships."[40] With the ICWA, Congress recognized this aspect of sovereignty and established a policy that would at least attempt to place Indian children in homes that reflect the unique values of their Indian cultures.[41] Congress's actions were monumental because the culture of a tribe embodies the nucleus of tribal existence, so it is imperative that Indian children have an opportunity to learn their culture for tribal existence to continue.

the eagle soars: procedural elements of the icwa

Jurisdictional provisions are the core of the Indian Child Welfare Act, because the ICWA was written with the acknowledgment that "tribal court judges are more knowledgeable than state court judges about Indian childrearing customs and traditions."[42] The ICWA thus gives exclusive jurisdiction to the tribal court if the child lives on the reservation or is a ward of the court. When the child resides off the reservation, then the child's tribe and the state court have concurrent jurisdiction. Exceptions to tribal jurisdiction are made when either parent objects, the tribal court declines participation in the proceeding, or the local or state court finds good cause not to transfer the proceeding.[43] Furthermore, the court is also required to apply the highest applicable legal standard of protection, either state or federal, to the rights of the parent or Indian custodian. Therefore, the ICWA preempts conflicting state law.[44]

The ICWA entails four significant procedural components: notice, the right to counsel, requirement for the testimony of an expert witness, and active efforts. First, the ICWA requires notice of the proceeding to be sent by registered mail with return receipt requested to the parents or Indian custodian and the children's tribe.[45] The act also stipulates that "no foster care placement or termination of parental rights proceeding shall be held until at least ten days after the notice is received by the parents" or the Indian custodian and the children's tribe.[46] The notice requirement of the ICWA is in place so that the state, county, or other social service agency cannot proceed with a child custody hearing without contacting the parents and the tribe, an essential component for the protection of the Indian family.

In typical child custody proceedings, if the parents' whereabouts are unknown, notice is served by publication. Usually the publication of the notice does not occur in the local newspaper or the various Indian newspapers, but is placed in the state's finance and commerce journal. Congress recognized the absurdity of the involved parents receiving notice in this manner, so required notice by registered mail. Furthermore, the state, county, or local social service agency must make diligent efforts to locate and notify the parents by actively contacting the last known address, family members, neighbors, and the tribe to find the whereabouts of the parents in order to advance the child custody proceeding.

The ICWA, additionally, gives parents the right to counsel in child custody proceedings.[47] This element is important because generally state courts do not appoint counsel to parents in child custody proceedings.[48] Furthermore, the ICWA requires the testimony of a qualified expert witness to support an out-of-home placement.[49] The purpose of this requirement is "to provide the court with knowledge of the social and cultural aspects of Indian life and diminish the risk of any cultural bias" from state, county, and local social service agencies.[50] The term "qualified expert witness" encompasses "any people who are, because of their knowledge of Indian culture and traditions, capable of opining on the question of whether an Indian child is suffering emotional or physical harm."[51] However, some states have enacted stricter laws defining a "qualified expert witness." In Minnesota, for example, qualified expert witnesses are tribally designated and their qualifications as experts are not subject to challenge by the state, county, or other social service agencies.[52]

This requirement for qualified, expert testimony provides a mechanism for an individual with knowledge of Indian culture and traditions to testify that the components of the families' child-rearing practices in question either meet the social and cultural standards of the child's tribe or are against tribal values. Therefore, expert testimony must be provided within 90 days after an emergency removal occurs and is also required before the court can order the rights of a parent to be terminated.[53] This testimony is required because the court must be persuaded "by clear and convincing evidence that continued custody with the parent or Indian custodian will result in serious emotional or physical damage to the child."[54]

An example of the necessity of this clause can be seen regarding cultural practices in child rearing. For instance, many Indian tribes perform rite-of-passage ceremonies by taking their young children out to secluded locations where they fast and pray for understanding of their lives' purpose and future. Typically if a non-Indian social worker discovered that parents placed their children in secluded locations by themselves for one or more days and nights without food and water, the social worker might argue that child abuse or neglect had occurred. What the expert testimony requirement provides is that the testimony of an individual with knowledge of Indian culture and traditions inform the court, in this case that the fasting is not any form of abuse or neglect, but rather a valid Indian child-rearing practice and ceremony. On the other hand, if a parent leaves his or her child alone in the home for a lengthy period of time to go out drinking, the qualified expert witness would be present to testify that such a practice is not an acceptable Indian child-rearing practice, allowing the court to determine that the child should be removed.

Finally, the ICWA requires county agencies to use "active efforts to provide remedial services and programs designed to prevent the breakup of the family."[55] Active efforts have been defined as "active, thorough, culturally appropriate actions by the local social service agency to fulfill its obligations to prevent the out-of-home placement of an Indian child and to return an Indian child to their family at the earliest possible time once out-of-home placement has occurred."[56] The active effort requirement of the ICWA ensures that agencies take into account the prevailing social and cultural traditions of the pertinent Indian tribe, while involving and using the available resources of the extended family, the tribe, Indian social service agencies, and individual Indian caregivers.[57]

the eagle regains his identity

Even though the federal government has a responsibility to uphold the general welfare of Indian tribes, this responsibility has not always been fulfilled. Many historical policies, including the assimilation policies of the late 19th century, had detrimental effects on American Indian communities. These effects, coupled with public perceptions that discounted the complex, kinship-based social structures in American Indian families, led to high rates of removal of American Indian children by the 1950s. These high removal rates raised concern and brought Native activists to approach the federal government for a reprieve from the state and local agencies that were removing their children, leading to the passage of the Indian Child Welfare Act of 1978.

Today, tribes are flexing their wings, reclaiming and reasserting jurisdiction over American Indian child welfare, and partnering with local, county, and state social welfare systems on behalf of their children. As this history is understood and the procedural elements of the ICWA are implemented, Indian children will begin to "fly the coop," remembering that they are "eagles," not "chickens," and recovering what has been lost for generations.

notes

1 James B. Waldram, *The Way of the Pipe: Aboriginal Spirituality and Symbolic Healing in Canadian Prisons* (Orchard Park NY: Broadview Press, 1997), 2.
2 Waldram, *Way of the Pipe,* 3.
3 David E. Wilkins, *American Indian Politics and the American Politics System* (New York: Rowman and Littlefield, 2002), 42.
4 16 US Stat 566.
5 Vine Deloria, Jr., *Behind the Trail of Broken Treaties, An Indian Declaration of Independence* (Austin: University of Texas Press, 1985), 142. The commerce clause is at Art. 1, sect. 8, clause 3.
6 Wilkins, *American Indian Politics,* 47.
7 Vine Deloria, Jr., and Clifford M. Lytle, *American Indians: American Justice* (Austin: University of Texas Press, 1983), 8.
8 Deloria and Lytle, *American Indians: American Justice,* 11.
9 Brenda Child, *Boarding School Seasons: American Indian Families, 1900–1940* (Lincoln: University of Nebraska Press, 1998), 13.
10 Deloria and Lytle, *American Indians: American Justice,* 12.
11 Frederick E. Hoxie, *A Final Promise: The Campaign to Assimilate the Indians, 1880–1920* (New York: Cambridge University Press, 1989), 242.
12 Child, *Boarding School Seasons,* 33.
13 David Fanshel, *Far from the Reservation: The Transracial Adoption of American Indian Children* (Metuchen, NJ: The Scarecrow Press, 1972).

14 Fanshel, *Far from the Reservation,* 37. All subsequent citations appear in the text.

15 Marc Mannes, "Factors and Events Leading to the Passage of the Indian Child Welfare Act," *Child Welfare* 74, no. 1 (1995): 266–267.

16 Marc Mannes, "Factors and Events," 267.

17 Marc Mannes, "Seeking the Balance Between Child Protection and Family Preservation in Indian Child Welfare," *Child Welfare* 72, no. 2 (1993): 144.

18 B. J. Jones, "The Indian Child Welfare Act: Protecting the Integrity of Indian Tribes and Ensuring Future," *ABA [American Bar Association] News,* October 1995, 1.

19 House Committee on Interior and Insular Affairs, *Indian Child Welfare Act of 1978 [ICWA]: Hearings on S. 1214,* 95th Cong., 2d sess. (February 9, March 9, 1978). (Hereinafter House Hearings on ICWA.)

20 House Hearings on ICWA, 30.

21 House Hearings on ICWA, 4.

22 House Hearings on ICWA, 4.

23 Irving Berlin and Evelyn Blanchard, "Long-Term Effects of Out-of-Home Placement of Indian Children," (paper, "The Indian Child Welfare Act: Indian Homes for Indian Children Conference," University of California, Los Angeles, CA, August 22–24, 1990).

24 Berlin and Blanchard, "Long-Term Effects."

25 Marc Mannes, "Factors and Events," 265.

26 Marc Mannes, "Factors and Events," 269.

27 Senate Select Committee on Indian Affairs, *Indian Child Welfare Act of 1977: Hearings on S. 1214,* 95th Cong., 2d sess. (August 4, 1977).

28 House Committee on Interior and Insular Affairs, *Indian Child Welfare Act of 1978,* 95th Cong., 2d sess., 1978, H. Rep. 96–42. (Hereinafter House Report.)

29 ICWA, US Code 25 § 1902.

30 ICWA, US Code 25 § 1901, 3–5.

31 *Mississippi Band of Choctaw Indians v. Holyfield,* 490 US 30, (1988).

32 Senate Select Committee on Indian Affairs, *Indian Child Welfare Act of 1977,* 95th Cong., 2d sess., 1977, S. Rep. 95–597, 52. (Hereinafter Senate Report.)

33 Senate Report, 43.

34 *Holyfield,* 490 US at 30.

35 *Holyfield,* 490 US at 45.

36 Senate Report, 43.

37 *Holyfield,* 490 US at 37.

38 *Holyfield,* 490 US at 44–45.

39 House Hearings on ICWA, 193.

40 *Holyfield,* 490 US at 45.

41 ICWA, US Code 25 § 1902.

42 B. J. Jones, *The Indian Child Welfare Handbook: A Legal Guide to the Custody and Adoption of Native American Children,* (Chicago: American Bar Association, 1995), 29. See also: *Holyfield,* 490 US at 30.

43 ICWA, US Code 25 § 1911, b.

44 ICWA, US Code 25 § 1921.

45 ICWA, US Code 25 § 1912, a.

46 ICWA, US Code 25 § 1912, a.

47 ICWA, US Code 25 § 1912, b.

48 Jones, *Indian Child Welfare Handbook,* 55–56.

49 ICWA, US Code 25 § 1912, e–f.

50 Jones, *Indian Child Welfare Handbook,* 55–56.

51 Jones, *Indian Child Welfare Handbook,* 59.

52 *Minnesota Indian Child Welfare Tribal-State Agreement,* sec. Part II.G & Part I.E.32 (1998).

53 Jones, *Indian Child Welfare Handbook,* 59. See also: ICWA, US Code 25 § 1912, e.

54 Jones, *Indian Child Welfare Handbook,* 59. See also: ICWA, US Code 25 § 1912, e.

55 ICWA, US Code 25 § 1912, d.

56 Mary Jo Brooks Hunter, "Active Efforts, or Reasonable Efforts Disguised as Active Efforts," (paper, Indian Law Conference, University of North Dakota School of Law, April 2005), 2.

57 Hunter, "Active Efforts," 2–3.

14 FROM ORPHAN TRAINS TO BABYLIFTS

Colonial Trafficking, Empire Building, and Social Engineering

Tobias Hübinette

International adoption, sometimes known as intercountry or transnational adoption, the movement of mainly nonwhite children from the postcolonial so-called Third World to predominantly white adopters in North America, Northern and Western Europe, Australia, and New Zealand, was born in the mid-1950s in the aftermath of the Korean War.[1] This huge child migration, today involving close to 30,000 children annually, has transferred an estimated half a million children, of whom almost one third come from Korea.

The practice was initiated in the receiving countries as a rescue mission with strong Christian undertones, while during the 1960s and '70s it came to be perceived as a progressive act of solidarity. Today, in the leading adopting regions of North America, Western Europe, and Oceania, international adoption has developed into the last resort for many suffering from infertility, while a discourse of multiculturalism celebrates international adoptees as bridges between cultures, symbols of interethnic harmony, and embodiments of global and postmodern cosmopolitanism. At the other end, in the sending countries, the governments conceive of international adoption as part family-planning method and part child welfare practice. Despite regular outbursts of criticism regarding international adoption coming from domestic oppositional circles in the countries of origin, most governments treat international adoption as a necessary evil, even though they consider it a degrading and humiliating business, well aware that the practice saves social welfare expenditure and generates huge amounts of money for a profitable adoption industry.

Academically, studies of international adoption are usually limited to the fields of medicine and psychiatry or to social work and psychology. Instead of following in the footsteps of these dominant ways of looking at international adoption and merely reproducing mainstream adoption research, I examine and analyze the practice from a different perspective, employing the lenses of anthropology and migration history, American empire building and international relations, and Korean military authoritarianism and patriarchal modernity. I use international adoption from Korea as the principal case study, as Korea has by far provided the most internationally adopted children, and since the practice itself was initiated in connection with the Korean War. At the one end, international adoption is put in relation to a particular Western mode of adopting and to other previous and contemporary child and forced migrations, and set within the context of emerging American world dominance after World War II. At the other end, international adoption is connected to Korea's modernization process and seen as a disciplining method of regulating and controlling women's bodies and reproduction in the name of social engineering and development. Lastly, I argue that to fully understand international adoption's history and current articulation, it is necessary to study it from many different angles and perspectives.

the western mode of adoption

International adoption reflects a particular method of Western adoption, going back to the first American adoption law in Massachusetts in 1851, and, through international cooperation (however coerced), this specific way of adopting is rapidly spreading across the globe, destroying and replacing non-Western traditions of fostering children among extended kinship networks. Adoption as social practice or legal institution has existed in every culture in the world at some time. However, modern Western adoption practice deviates from most practices worldwide because it is overwhelmingly extra-familial, meaning that no biological or other relationship exists between the birth and adoptive families prior to adoption, and above all that the link between the birth family and the adoptee is generally totally severed so that they will remain unknown to each other, and the adoptive family gives the child a completely new identity by law.

American feminist Mary Kathleen Benet proposes that this unique and peculiar Western mode of adoption can be seen as a compensation for the breakdown of the extended family as a result of modernization and the corresponding elevation of the nuclear family in Western countries.[2] A parallel to this, pointed out by several adoption researchers, is how middle-class, Western concepts of abandonment and abandoned children diverge from those in non-Western societies, where fostering and circulation of children among relatives are much more common than adoption itself. Yet the divergent concepts are made hegemonic by way of conventions like the Hague Conference on Intercountry Adoption.[3] It should be noted that the Western mode of adoption is changing slowly; in many Western countries birthmothers whose children were adopted away before the revolution of 1968 have begun to come out and raise their voices. They are writing books about their experiences and speaking out about how all too often they were pressured and coerced into giving up their children by family, social workers, adoption agencies, and religious groups, and they are challenging sealed records, trying to reconnect with their children, and advocating open adoption practices where the link between the birth families, the adoptee, and the adoptive family is not completely broken off.

comparative child and forced migrations

International adoption, the movement of children from non-Western countries to adoptive parents in the West, was initiated on a large scale in connection with the Korean War, even if Western missionaries, settlers, and tradesmen occasionally had previously adopted "indigenous" or "native" children at the time of the classical colonial era. Such examples of transracial adoptions precede as well as parallel the Korean case: the kidnapping of 18,000 Roma children in 18th-century imperial Austria, who were put into Catholic foster homes to dilute Romani bloodlines; the 50,000 "lost birds" of Native American children in Canada and the United States who were placed in white families up until as late as the mid-1990s; and the "stolen generations" of 25,000 Aboriginal children in Australia who between 1900 and 1970 were forcibly separated from their parents and transferred to the custody of Anglo families as a civilizing project.[4] However, unlike international adoption, these examples of domestic transracial adoptions of children from indigenous and minority groups to white families have been highly charged and contested and sometimes even branded ethnocide or cultural genocide.

The closest parallels to international adoption in the history of global child migration would be the 130,000 children shipped from the British Isles to populate the Empire between 1618 and 1967, and the 100,000 American children transported by the "orphan train" from the East Coast and placed out to substitute parents in need of labor in the Midwest between 1854 and 1929.[5] Linda Gordon describes an intriguing incident where ethnicity played a major role during the orphan train program.[6] In 1904, a group of 40 New York Irish orphans was sent to live with Catholic families in Arizona. However, the Catholics turned out to be Mexican Americans, and the local Anglos were so outraged at this transgression of race boundaries that they instigated a mass abduction of the children, carried out at gunpoint. The irony is the sudden "whitening" of the Irish orphans, widely despised by the Protestant majority as "paddies" of a decaying and uncivilized "Celtic race." Through this direct action, transracial adoption as a white privilege was resolutely reinstated, and this privilege continues in the contemporary era. One can only imagine the reactions if Korean middle-class couples, whether in Korea or living overseas, suddenly started to adopt white children, or if Korean children were to be sent to Latin American or African countries for international adoption, for that matter.

In the pre–civil rights United States, a handful of states went so far as to legislate against interracial adoption or even fostering of white children by nonwhite people, and in the late 1990s a widely publicized controversy erupted when a black woman in Detroit wanted to adopt a white girl.[7]

In their magisterial study of children as refugees, Everett Ressler, Neil Boothby, and Daniel Steinbock trace international adoption's modern precursors back to World War I, when Armenian children who had survived the massacres in the Ottoman Empire were moved to Greece and Russia.[8] Hundreds of thousands of children of war *(Kriegskinder)* from the disintegrating empires of Austria-Hungary, Russia, and Germany were also transferred temporarily as foster children to Great Britain, Switzerland, the Netherlands, and the Nordic countries under the supervision of the Red Cross and Save the Children.[9] During the Spanish Civil War between the two world wars, 20,000 Spanish children *(niños de la guerra)* were relocated to institutions and substitute parents in France, Latin America, Scandinavia, and the Soviet Union, of whom 2000 to 3000 stayed permanently.

The same process was repeated before and during World War II when 20,000 Jewish children from Nazi-dominated Central Europe were brought to England and other Western European countries (the *Kindertransport)*, and when 70,000 Finnish children of war *(sotalapset)* were moved temporarily to Sweden, 10,000 staying as adopted or foster children.[10] In addition, the Nazi German *Lebensborn* program transferred at least 200,000 Eastern European children who, based on their appearances, were deemed racially acceptable and thus worthy of being Germanized and adopted into German families.[11] Finally, from the end of the war and up to 1953, around 5000 children from China, Taiwan, Eastern Europe, Greece, Germany, Italy, and Japan, many fathered by American soldiers, were transferred as unaccompanied refugees to the United States for adoption, while more than 2500 Japanese children in Manchuria abandoned by the retreating imperial army were taken into Chinese families.[12]

Other cases of forced migration preceding the contemporary international adoption boom include the six Taino Indians—four of whom died almost immediately upon arrival—who Columbus brought back as gifts to the Spanish king with his first voyage of 1492–1493; the Algonquian "Indian princess" Pocahontas who passed away in England in 1617; the Inuit boy Minik who Admiral Robert Peary brought back from Greenland in 1897; and the "Court Negroes" once popular among Europe's monarchs, one of them being Hannibal, the great-grandfather of Russia's national poet Aleksandr Pushkin, who was adopted by Czar Peter the Great himself.

Contemporary international adoption, having flown in almost half a million children to Western countries during a period of 50 years, has parallels to the Atlantic slave trade—which between 1510 and 1870 shipped 11 million Africans to the New World, to the dispatching of 12 million Indians and Chinese as indentured labor to the vast European empires between 1834 and 1941, and to the present day's massive trafficking of women and children for international marriage and sexual exploitation. A comparative study of these four subsequent forced migrations, conceptualized as a long Western tradition of transporting nonwhite populations intercontinentally, would make a welcome addition to the literature on both migration and international adoption.

While clearly there are widely divergent purposes for which the enslaved and the adopted have been forcibly made migrants, some striking similarities come to mind when we compare the Atlantic slave trade and international adoption. Both practices are driven by insatiable consumer demand, private market interests, and cynical profit making, and both utilize a highly advanced system of pricing where the young, the healthy, and the light-skinned are the most valued. Both are dependent on the existence of native intermediaries in the form of slave hunters and adoption agencies as well as a reliable and efficient global transportation system of shipping routes. Both the enslaved and the adopted are separated from their parents, siblings, relatives, and significant others at an early age; stripped of their original cultures and languages; reborn at harbors and airports; Christianized, rebaptized, and bestowed with the names of their masters; and in the end only retaining racialized nonwhite bodies that have been branded or given case numbers. The so-called house or servant slaves must have been the closest parallels to international adoptees as both live permanently together with their masters and are legally defined as belonging to their household and their family. Furthermore, both practices have been legitimized by the same shallow argument that when moved to their new homes, the material situations of the slaves and the adoptees are unquestionably greatly bettered as both are benefiting from the wealth and civilization of the West. Finally, both groups are brought over only to satisfy the needs and desires of their well-to-do acquirers.

The anthropologist Igor Kopytoff has also commented on the unsettling parallels between the commodification of slaves and adoptees in his study of the cultural biography of commodities.[13] A crucial difference is, of course, that slave and indentured labor, at least in its classical versions, belong to history, and contemporary trafficking in women is illegal and universally condemned. Only international adoption remains largely uncontested, made legal through various "international" conventions that in reality privilege Western concepts of adoption. In fact, international adoption has even increased since the end of the Cold War as a result of the globalization of predatory neoliberal capitalism, recent transformations in the international division of labor, the mass popularization of the discourse of multiculturalism, and a middle-class birthrate rapidly falling to far below replacement level in practically every Western country.[14]

u.s. empire building

International adoption originated as a rescue mission immediately after the Korean War. Organized by Western individuals and voluntary agencies, the intent was to transfer children fathered by American and other UN soldiers, often the products of large-scale sexual exploitation and military prostitution, to adoptive homes in the United States and Western Europe. The issue of mixed children and war orphans and their difficult conditions in Korea was openly discussed in Western media in the early 1950s, and their numbers were often widely exaggerated.[15] This public interest in and obsession with the mixed children of postwar Korea is strongly reminiscent of how Eurasian children in the French and Dutch colonies of Southeast Asia, products of informal concubinary relations or rape and prostitution, were viewed and treated during the classical imperialist age. According to Ann Laura Stoler, who has studied the "mixed question" and the subject of intimate relations in a colonial setting, these children were objects of rescue fantasies and relief projects for the European homeland populations, especially among Christian philanthropist, humanist, and women's groups. They were represented as abandoned orphans when in reality they often were physically and forcibly separated from their native mothers and assembled and brought together at special orphanages and boarding schools to uphold white prestige and protect their perceived European-ness from being culturally, linguistically, and morally indigenized, but also from becoming politically dangerous as anti-Western father-haters or even father-murderers as adults.[16]

These mixed-race children epitomized the bodily boundary markers between the colonizers and the colonized as well as a kind of a buffer class, by their very presence challenging Western concepts of child rearing. The same is the case with the stolen generations of mixed Aboriginal children in Australia who were legally taken by force from their indigenous mothers to be uplifted and domesticated, raised and educated as white Australians, again showing how Western ideas of adoption came to rule over and destroy non-Western concepts of fostering and circulation of children among extended family members. Nevertheless, it is important to remember that the mostly American concern for and adoption of mixed Asian children in the 1950s differs fundamentally in one important respect from the way the French, Dutch, and British empires in Asia dealt with the problem of mixed children fathered by European settlers before World War II: Few if any of these were ever adopted and moved to metropolitan Europe. Instead they were left behind even after decolonization, as in the case of the Anglo-Indians or Eurasians of India.

The Korean War marked the beginning of the Cold War and the initial stage in global American hegemony. The author Pearl S. Buck, winner of the Nobel Prize in literature and adoptive mother of at least seven mixed children from China, Japan, and Germany, spoke out forcefully to encourage Americans and Western Europeans to adopt Korean children in the 1950s and 1960s. Laura Briggs writes about how Buck used tropes of child rescuing, anticommunism, and American paternalist responsibility to argue for the adoption of Asian children.[17] Buck would eventually engage her own adoption agency, Welcome House—founded in 1949 to adopt mixed children from China and Japan—in the adoption of Korean children. This heavy US involvement in the origin of international adoption and early interest in Asian children is interpreted by Christina Klein as an expression of a Cold War mentality and a discourse on familial love, with America acting the benevolent "white mother" to create familial ties to Asian people through the sponsoring or adopting of Asian children, while Asians were infantilized, feminized, and portrayed as unable to take care of their own children.[18] In this way, argues Klein, international adoption became an integral part of American foreign policy, used to facilitate political relations and to legitimate anticommunist interventions in the region.

The same pattern followed in country after country. Especially in East Asia, from the beginning the dominating supply base of international adoption, the Korean situation was the precedent. American invasions in countries such as Vietnam and Thailand resulted in international adoption from those countries. Thus, it is no coincidence that the countries supplying the most children for international adoption to the West, and primarily to the United States, almost all fall under the American sphere of influence and have been exposed to American military intervention, presence, or occupation, even if civil wars, ethnic cleansing of minorities, and corrupt dictatorships also must be added to explain why these supplying countries became involved with the practice in the first place. Even if African and Muslim countries like the Sudan, Sierra Leone, Afghanistan, and Iraq are missing from the list of sending countries in the US sphere of influence, the list is still long: Korea, Vietnam, Thailand, Cambodia, the Philippines, Taiwan, Indonesia, India, and Sri Lanka in Asia; and Colombia, Chile, Brazil, Peru, Honduras, Haiti, Mexico, El Salvador, and Guatemala in the Americas. The fact that Asia dominates as a continent further underscores the orientalist bias at work, where Asian children in many Western countries are widely perceived as being docile and submissive, clever, hardworking, kind, quiet, and undemanding, besides being cute, childlike, and petite.

the korean modernity project

In 1960 a student uprising ended Korea's first president Syngman Rhee's increasingly autocratic rule, which was followed by a short period of democratization. Park Chung Hee's military revolution of 1961 abruptly curtailed the short experiment with democracy and installed a dictatorial military regime that harshly oppressed its students and workers, guided by fierce anticommunism, developmentalism, and modernization theory.[19] At the time of the military takeover, Korea was still an agrarian society suffering from symptoms of mass poverty, typical for a developing country. Eliminating these symptoms became a major focus. Within a period of 30 years after the start of the first 5-year economic plan in 1962, the authoritarian developmental state of Korea transformed itself from an agricultural society to a modern industrial nation with astonishing speed and horrifying efficiency. The two principal measures implemented to decrease a perceived overpopulation were family planning and emigration; international adoption can be seen as a combination of both. Hence, the era of authoritarian regimes with presidents Park Chung Hee (1961–1979) and Chun Doo Hwan (1981–1987) was to become the time when international adoption witnessed its heyday; three out of four of all placements occurred during those periods.

One of the earliest actions of Park's military government, on September 30, 1961, was to pass the Orphan Adoption Special Law, Korea's first modern adoption law, followed by the Child Welfare Act, both meant to facilitate international adoption as an alternative to costly institutional care.[20] The decree created a legal basis for international adoption of Korean children and established a framework for the most effective adoption industry in the world, characterized by efficient agencies, speedy procedures, and secure logistics.[21] After an amendment in 1967, the law stipulated that every adoption take place according to Korean law and through a government-licensed agency working closely with a Western counterpart, both of which charged fees to adoptive parents.[22] The agencies mandated for international adoption were expected to employ professional social workers, doctors, and nurses to run the orphanages as well as provide both short- and long-term foster care and domestic adoption. The passing of the adoption law and the setting up of an institutional framework for international adoption marked the professionalization of social work and the bureaucratization of social welfare in Korea. From then on, Korea would embark on a rocky road from tradition to modernity; international adoption was to become one of its most successful self-regulating and self-disciplining practices of control and purification in the reproductive field.

In 1979 President Park Chung Hee was killed by one of his closest aides and after a short democratization period, the new military strongman president, Chun Doo Hwan, came to power through a coup d'état. In 1980 the new government outlined a new approach to international adoption, integrated in the so-called nongovernmental foreign policy to expand the emigration program and further develop friendship ties with Western allies.[23] Through a process of government deregulation, the quota system was abolished and the four agencies were allowed to compete with each other in tracking down unrestricted numbers of adoptable children. Consequently, a thriving adoption industry was created and resulted in the largest numbers ever sent abroad in a decade, with almost 70,000 international placements. The agencies engaged themselves in profit-making business activities and real estate investments, and were running their own delivery clinics, foster homes, and temporary institutions, and most importantly, administering a growing number of maternity homes for young and unwed mothers to secure a continuous supply of healthy newborns.

The number of international adoptions has gone down since the 1980s, although it still involves around 2000 Korean children every year. At the same time, the relinquishing mothers are now almost all teenagers or at least under the age of 25 years, and often spend their pregnancies behind the secluded walls of the agencies' own maternity homes; the majority come from middle-class backgrounds where the stigma of premarital sexual activity has the potential to ruin future social advancement for both parents and children. So in Korea for more than half a century, international adoption has been an economically rewarding business for the adoption agencies, an easy way out of avoiding social welfare expenditures for the Korean government, and, most importantly, a brutal method of upholding a rigid patriarchal system for Korean society as a whole. International adoption is, in other words, one of the Korean modernity project's most long-lived mechanisms of power, used to cleanse the country of "impure" and "disposable" outcasts in the name of social engineering and eugenics.

between colonialism and modernity

It is through this understanding of the intimate and indivisible relationship between colonial and modernist modes and manners that I conceptualize international adoption as a mixed project of colonial uplifting, civilizing, and assimilating non-Western children and modernist service professionalization and institutionalization of family intervention so as to regulate, control, and discipline women's reproduction, ultimately upholding a patriarchal system in the countries of origin. In this way, international adoption allows us to understand the contradictory complexities of power not only on the Western side, but also from the Koreans, with their decision to act as intermediaries in tracking down and delivering adoptable children. I am consciously distancing myself both from those nationalists in the supplying countries who blame everything on Western racism, and from critics of international adoption in Western receiving countries who blame everything on traditional values. Instead, I am trying to understand how international adoption has developed and exists between a complex dynamics of the twin projects and double bind of colonialism and modernity.

notes

1 It is important to note that so-called domestic adoptions of First Nations children in North America can also be considered international adoptions, since they involve nation-to-nation transfers.

2 Mary Kathleen Benet, *The Politics of Adoption* (New York: The Free Press, 1976), 14.

3 Claudia Fonseca, "The Politics of Adoption: Child Rights in the Brazilian Setting," *Law & Policy* 24, no. 3 (2002): 199–227; Catherine Panter-Brick, "Nobody's Children? A Reconsideration of Child Abandonment," in *Abandoned Children*, ed. Catherine Panter-Brick and Malcolm T. Smith (Cambridge: Cambridge University Press, 2000), 1–26.

4 Zoltan Barany, *The East European Gypsies: Regime Change, Marginality, and Ethnopolitics* (Cambridge: Cambridge University Press, 2002), 93; Wesley Crichlow, "Western Colonization as Disease: Native Adoption and Cultural Genocide," *Critical Social Work* 2, no. 2 (2002): 104–127; Robert Van Krieken, "The 'Stolen Generations' and Cultural Genocide: The Forced Removal of Australian Indigenous Children from Their Families and Its Implications for the Sociology of Childhood," *Childhood* 6, no. 3 (1999): 297–312; Pauline Turner Strong, "To Forget Their Tongue, Their Name, and Their Whole Relation: Captivity, Extra-Tribal Adoption, and the Indian Child Welfare Act," in *Relative Values: Reconfiguring Kinship Studies*, ed. Sarah Franklin and Susan McKinnon (Durham, NC: Duke University Press, 2001), 468–493.

5 Philip Bean and Joy Melville, *Lost Children of the Empire: The Untold Story of Britain's Child Migrants* (London: Unwin, 1989); Marilyn Irvin Holt, *The Orphan Trains: Placing Out in America* (Lincoln: University of Nebraska Press, 1992).

6 Linda Gordon, *The Great Arizona Orphan Abduction* (Cambridge: Harvard University Press, 1999).

7 Randall Kennedy, *Interracial Intimacies: Sex, Marriage, Identity, and Adoption* (New York: Vintage Books, 2003), 389–392. Two famous but nonetheless extremely rare examples of such reversed, switched, and almost counterfactual adoption cases are the white orphans in Rudyard Kipling's famous novel *Kim* from 1901 and in the Nobel Prize–winner Rabindranath Tagore's equally well-known novel *Gora* from 1924, both raised as natives in British India.

8 Everett M. Ressler, Neil Boothby, and Daniel J. Steinbock, *Unaccompanied Children: Care and Protection in Wars, Natural Disasters, and Refugee Movements* (Oxford: Oxford University Press, 1988), 9–12.

9 Monika Janfelt, *Stormakter i människokärlek: Svensk och dansk krigsbarnshjälp 1917–1924* [Great Powers in Human Love: Swedish and Danish Support to Children of War 1917–1924] (Åbo: Åbo Akademi University Press, 1988).

10 Pertti Kavén, *70.000 små öden* [70,000 Small Destinies] (Otalampi: Sahlgren, 1994); Ingrid Lomfors, *Förlorad barndom, återvunnet liv: De judiska flyktingbarnen från Nazityskland* [Lost Childhood, Regained Life: The Jewish Refugee Children From Nazi Germany] (Gothenburg University, Department of History, 1996).

11 Catrine Clay and Michael Leapman, *Master Race: The Lebensborn Experiment in Nazi Germany* (London: Hodder & Stoughton, 1995).

12 Yara-Colette Lemke Muniz de Faria, "'Germany's "Brown Babies" Must Be Helped! Will You' US Adoption Plans for Afro-German Children, 1950–1955" *Callaloo* 26, no. 2 (2003): 342–362; Daniel P. Quinn, "The Placement of Refugee Children in the United States," *Catholic Charities Review* 45, no. 7 (1961): 13–18; Wen-Shing Tseng and others, "Transethnic Adoption and Personality Traits: A Lesson from Japanese Orphans Returned from China to Japan," *American Journal of Psychiatry* 147, no. 3 (1990): 330–335.

13 Igor Kopytoff, "The Cultural Biography of Things: Commoditization as Process," in *The Social Life of Things: Commodities in Cultural Perspective*, ed. Arjun Appadurai (Cambridge: Cambridge University Press, 1986), 64–91.

14 Susan Bibler Coutin, Bill Maurer, and Barbara Yngvesson, "In the Mirror: The Legitimation Work of Globalisation," *Law & Social Inquiry* 27, no. 4 (2002): 801–843; Esben Leifsen, "Person, Relation and Value: The Economy of Circulating Ecuadorian Children in International Adoption," in *Cross-Cultural Approaches to Adoption*, ed. Fiona Bowie (London: Routledge, 2004), 182–196; Steven L. Varnis, "Regulating the Global Adoption of Children," *Society* 38, no. 2 (2001): 39–46.

15 Charles G. Chakerian, *Concerns, Responsibility, Opportunity: First Report on Korea* (New York: Church World Service, 1962); Helen Miller, "Korea's International Children," *Lutheran Social Welfare* 13 (Summer 1971): 12–23.

16 Ann Laura Stoler, *Carnal Knowledge and Imperial Power: Race and the Intimate in Colonial Rule* (Berkeley: University of California Press, 2002).

17 Laura Briggs, "Mother, Child, Race, Nation: The Visual Iconography of Rescue and the Politics of Transnational and Transracial Adoption," *Gender & History* 15, no. 2 (2003): 179–199.

18 Christina Klein, *Cold War Orientalism: Asia in the Middlebrow Imagination, 1945–1961* (Berkeley: University of California Press, 2003), 143–190.

19 Chungmoo Choi, "Transnational Capitalism, National Imaginary, and the Protest Theater in South Korea," *Boundary 2* 33, no. 1 (1995): 235–261; Gi-Wook Shin, "Nation, History and Politics: South Korea," in *Nationalism and the Construction of Korean Identity*, ed. Hyung Il Pai and Timothy R. Tangherlini (Berkeley: University of California, Center for Korean Studies, 1998), 148–165.

20 Pilwha Chang, "A Feminist View of Social Policy in Some East Asian Countries," *Asian Journal of Women's Studies* 2, no. 1 (1996): 7–37; Chin Kim and Timothy G. Carroll, "Intercountry Adoption of South Korean Orphans: A Lawyer's Guide," *Journal of Family Law* 14, no. 2 (1975): 223–253.

21 Erica E. Penner, *Comparative Analysis of International Child Adoption Practices and Policies in Korea and China* (Toronto: McGill University, School of Social Work, 1996), 35–36.

22 Youn-Taek Tahk, "Intercountry Adoption Program in Korea: Policy, Law and Service" in *Adoption in Worldwide Perspective: A Review of Programs, Policies and Legislation in 14 Countries*, ed. R. A. C. Hoksbergen (Lisse: Swets & Zeitlinger, 1986), 79–91.

23 Rosemary C. Sarri, Yeonoak Baik, and Marti Bombyk, "Goal Displacement and Dependency in South Korean–United States Intercountry Adoption," *Children and Youth Services Review* 20, no. 1–2 (1998): 87–114.

Mihee-Nathalie Lemoine, *50-53,* Seoul 1995, acrylic on paper

15 SCATTERED SEEDS

THE CHRISTIAN INFLUENCE ON KOREAN ADOPTION

Jae Ran Kim

Jesus loves the little children,
All the children of the world
Red and yellow, black and white
They are precious in his sight
Jesus loves the little children of the world.
—C. Herbert Woolston

I will bring thy seed from the east, and gather thee from the west; I will say to the north, give up; and to the south, keep not back; bring my sons from afar, and my daughters from the ends of the earth.
—Isaiah 43:5–6

The statue of Mary rises from the ground, her arms stretched out, palms upward in prayer. The deep folds of her long gray robes melt into the foliage of a half-dead winter garden. It is nearly the end of March and still jacket chilly. The whole landscape before me seems washed in sepia; the sky and Mary are cold and gray; the brittle fallen leaves from last autumn gather at Mary's feet and parched brown grass licks up to the garden's stone border. The church buildings surround me in a half circle. Directly behind Mary is the daycare that used to be Baek Paek Hap, White Lily. Once it was an orphanage, my orphanage. Under the blank gaze of Mary, I arrived as a 14-month-old infant, one of six kids found abandoned that day, passed from a city official at Daegu City Hall into the waiting arms of a nun. Once I was Catholic, and like all of the babies and children of Daegu who came through the doors of White Lily, I baptized myself with holy tears and became a sacrificial lamb of God and an American family.

Daegu is a large urban center in the middle of the country, bereft of the southern coastal charm of Pusan and the cosmopolitan energy of Seoul. This third largest city in South Korea spreads into suburbs. The night before, I had traveled through the city over hills, and I saw the mountains past the horizon line of modern office buildings and apartments. Still, to me, Daegu seems flat and industrial.

I have come to this garden and this statue to exhale. I have just asked a nun for my file. She looks me up in her computer and prints out a document. It is the same one I already possess, nearly blank. *Sorry, there is no more information*, she tells me. *Nothing else I can do*. We pass by the rows of little red sneakers and black Mary Janes; walk past the drawings on the wall. I picture the garden in bloom and wonder if white lilies are among those flowers that ornament Mary's robes throughout the spring and summer.

han 한/恨

There is a word—han—that is at the very essence of the Korean experience. Han is an emotion, a state of consciousness, and a physiological state. Defining han is equivalent to grasping at a kite string just inches out of my reach; it's as if I can see it and know its shape and size but it is always twisting away, just at the moment I think it's in my hand. Han is the soil and mountains and vegetation of a country ravaged by war. Han is the collective consciousness of a people colonized, occupied, divided, raped, and beaten. Han is in the blood and breath and dreams of Korean individuals. And han is inherently embedded in the experiences of the thousands of Korean children cross-culturally adopted to North America, Europe, and Australia.

Andrew Sung Park defines han as "the collapsed pain of the heart due to psychosomatic, interpersonal, social, political, economic, and cultural oppression and repression."[1] In terms of Christianity, han is the individual or collective consequence of being sinned against. Park identifies global capitalism, patriarchy, and racial and cultural discrimination as the root causes of collective han; all play an integral role in the phenomenon of the adoption of Korean children by foreigners.[2]

To understand how adopted Korean children experience han, we must take a critical look at the factors that created the international adoption phenomenon, including the Korean War; Christianity, in both the United States and South Korea; global capitalism; the devalued status of women and patriarchy as it relates both to cultures and Christianity; combined with racialized discrimination against Asian and Amerasian children. Each of these factors contributed to the overall backdrop for South Korea's emergence as an international adoption leader. Yet there was one additional factor no one could have predicted—a farmer from Oregon named Harry Holt.

harry holt

In many ways Harry Holt embodied the American ideal. Adoption literature presents Harry, together with his wife Bertha, as the archetype of the 1950s. Harry is usually portrayed as paternal, hardworking, and masculine—a man of the earth and the unquestioned spiritual and authoritative head of the household. Due to his many health problems, he often dictated orders from bed. Bertha is described as the ideal caretaker, mothering their six biological children and eight adopted children and often administering medical treatments to Harry. While Harry was making his endless trips to Korea, it was Bertha who ran the household as well as the ever-increasing administrative details of the Holt Adoption Agency.

Holt has long been mythologized as "just a plain, humble farmer" by the media and the Holt organization, in an attempt to disguise the ambitious and dogmatic nature of his mission to promote Christianity. Bertha Holt writes in their biography *Bring My Sons from Afar*,

> It must surely be true that in the beginning God created a plan to rescue the Amerasian children of the Korean conflict.... They were the backwash of war, the outcasts of society ... but God did not forsake them.... He chose a fifty-year-old weakened by a long scar on his heart.[3]

In fact, Harry Holt was a businessman—and a successful one. In addition to his sawmill business in Oregon, Holt had been proceeding with plans to expand his business in South America. Instead, after a heart attack in 1950, Holt sold his business and purchased farmland. It was also during this time that his approach to Christianity grew to a zealous fervor.

In the summer of 1955, Harry Holt was on his way to Korea to look into adopting the Korean orphans the Holt family had been sponsoring under the ministrations of a Christian relief organization, World Vision. Experiencing insomnia during a layover in a Tokyo hotel room, Harry reached over to the hotel nightstand, pulled out the Gideon Bible, and, according to Bertha,

> In the darkness he thumbed through it and put in his finger and turned on the light. His thumb was on Isaiah 43:5. Fear not for I am with thee. At that moment he was assured that it was not Harry Holt, it was the Lord Himself who was doing this. He wept for joy, then he read two more verses:
>
> I will bring thy seed from the east, and gather thee from the west; I will say to the north, give up; and to the south, keep not back: bring my sons from afar, and my daughters from the ends of the earth.[4]

It was a calling, he believed, to facilitate adoptions between all the orphaned children and American parents. Holt redirected his former enthusiasm for business toward a new horizon—to bring Korean war orphans from the "cold and misery and darkness of Korea into the warmth and love of your homes."[5] At the time Holt was making plans to adopt his sponsored Korean orphans, the United States allowed only a limited number of foreign children to immigrate under the Refugee Relief Act, and further limited the number per US family to two. Holt wanted to adopt six more. With the help of Senator Richard Neuberger, HR 7043 was passed on July 31, 1955; on October 14, 1955, Holt brought eight Korean children to Oregon. Shortly after, the Holt Adoption Agency was born.[6]

From the beginning, established social welfare agencies based in the United States opposed Holt on two factors. First, the agencies believed that children adopted internationally should be placed in same-race homes, and second, the Holts had used a legislative loophole to adopt, thereby circumventing state and federal agency procedures, including home study assessments. In fact, social workers from the American Social Agency actively lobbied against Holt, but according to Bertha, "The Lord managed to legally bypass [the American Social Agency's] roadblock."[7]

Buoyed by his success at evading the social welfare agencies and encouraged by the media attention and subsequent requests by others wishing to adopt, Harry became increasingly messianic. The Holts purchased land in Tecate, Mexico, and began building facilities for an orphanage. Harry writes in the Holt *Newsletter*:

> The Mexican government does not allow resident missionaries; however, the Lord has opened the door to the orphan work in Mexico and we hope to preach the gospel "with our hands and feet," ... to show the love of God through the care of their children.... It is our desire to place these children in good, well-adjusted, born-again Christian homes.... We want these children to grow up to credit their families and communities.[8]

One of the biggest complaints of the social welfare agencies was that the Holts relied on proxy adoptions, which meant that adoptive parents adopted their children sight unseen and all the legal work of obtaining visas was handled by the proxy, which in this case was Harry Holt. Proxy adoptions were the easy way to bypass the laws and statutes regarding adoption in the United States. Even parents deemed unfit for adoption by US agencies were able to adopt through proxy. Holt felt the only qualification necessary was the statement of faith; the agencies accused Holt of disregarding home study assessments and endangering the welfare of the children.

Joseph Rod, the director of the Child Welfare League of America at the time, accused Holt of paying Korean officials "$50 a head" for the custody of each child, and testified that Holt children were being abused and prospective parents should be approved by the Department of Health, Education, and Welfare.[9] In June 1957 the Holts learned that one of their adoptive mothers was being investigated for the murder of her adopted Korean child; because the mother was a Christian, they believed the American Social Agency was attempting to use this murder investigation as a means to stop their program. "I remembered Harry's warning that the American Social Agency would make trouble for us," wrote Bertha, "as the false accusation was planned to ruin our program."[10]

The mother was eventually acquitted. Bertha wrote, "The Lord brought victory so the enemy forces had to think up a new way to attack. 'With us is the Lord our God to help us and fight our battles.' II Chronicles 32:8." Two and a half months later, Harry assigned that mother one-month-old twins.[11]

One of the other criticisms the Holts faced involved their sending sick children to the United States for adoption. Newspaper and magazine articles from the time accused the Holts of purposely transporting sick children, many of them with active-tuberculosis, to the United States. In 1958 "[It was] broadcast on TV that we imported nine dead babies, one with TB, and three who were seriously sick, and that we should be investigated," wrote Bertha.[12] The charitable arms of evangelical Christians in the United States reached far and wide, as nurses and clinics opened their doors to administer care to the active tuberculosis-infected children sent to America. The Holts continued to send children who were so sick that many died in transport on the airplanes; others died in cars en route to their new adoptive homes.

Holt disagreed with Joseph Rod's recommendations that the Department of Health, Education, and Welfare oversee his program. Holt's animosity toward social welfare agencies was so deeply felt that it was only after his death in 1964—nine years after Holt first began adoptions out of Korea—that the agency succumbed to all of the Oregon Welfare Department's requirements for licensing, which included parent home studies conducted by licensed social workers.

economics and christianity

Just over half of all South Koreans today practice Protestant Christianity or Catholicism.[13] The largest period of growth in Protestant Christianity occurred from the early 1960s through the late 1980s.[14] This growth correlates with South Korea's postwar economic and industrial reconstruction and is also the period in which adoptions out of the country occurred in its greatest numbers. From the 1960s to the end of 1989, adoptions out of South Korea increased dramatically, with just under 3000 children sent out in the 1950s and over 6100 by the end of the 1960s. By the end of the 1970s, those numbers had risen to over 46,000 children and by 1989 South Korea had sent over 66,500 children overseas.[15]

The practice of Christianity rose dramatically, writes Andrew E. Kim in his article "Korean Religious Culture and Its Affinity to Christianity," partly because of the ability of Western Christian missionaries to synthesize Korea's shamanistic-based beliefs into Christian ones, one of which is the concept of material rewards for spiritual work.[16] Christianity has often been touted as being against the accumulation of wealth, since "the love of money is the root of all evil," but according to Max Weber, the Protestant view that fruitful rewards result from heeding God's will justifies the pursuit of wealth.[17] As Park notes, "the Protestant ethic ironically twists the reality of the Christian gospel.... It underpins the pursuit of wealth by Christians through capitalism, claiming such wealth as the outcome of God's blessing."[18] For a country in postwar reconstruction, the idea of divine reward, prosperity, and national pride and strength would be extremely desirable. South Korean Christians today are so concerned with prosperity and wealth that they give their churches names such as the Church of Plenty.[19]

The Korean Christian emphasis on monetary abundance provides yet another rationale for the continuation of foreign adoption placements. Adopting a child from Korea can cost an American couple over $10,000. The adoption industry benefits South Korea to the tune of over $15 million a year.[20] In addition, it resolves the problem of what to do with all those abandoned children and unwed mothers, so South Korea does not have to spend millions of dollars (trillions of won) on costly social programs.

adoption as business

Park describes several ways in which global capitalism in the United States creates han, all of which correlate to the adoption business. Park states that free trade between developed countries and less developed countries never benefits the latter. Park also writes, "The products of these ... corporations are imported back to the advanced capitalist countries and are used to undersell the competition, resulting in the additional destruction of the local entrepreneurship."[21]

Holt was well aware of this practice and took special pride that his agency wasn't "selling" children as domestic agencies were. In a letter to Erv Raetz, director of World Vision, Harry writes:

> The root of the trouble seems to be money. I have been told that anyone in California can buy a healthy American baby for $3000. If we bring in more children we weaken the monopoly which will cut the price of babies. I think God has a special place in hell for those who sell little ones.[22]

Holt recognized the tug between supply and demand in which his adoption program was involved. Holt would later find that his ambition to provide children for American couples would influence his former position on charging fees for adopting, but whatever his position on cost, it was secondary to his desire to fill the demand for children.

adoption as proselytization

I have at times believed my parents adopted me for the purpose of adding bonus points to their heavenly tally. It is no secret that many of the first agencies to actively recruit families for the adoption of South Korean children were faith-based organizations like Holt's. "It is our personal desire that these children go into Christian homes. We want to let these children we serve come to know Jesus," states Holt's adoption handbook.[23]

The Holts believed that the only qualification prospective adoptive parents had to have was a personal belief in Jesus Christ. According to Ellen Herman, author of the *Adoption History Project,* "[the Holts] were happy to accept couples who had been rejected, for a variety of reasons, by conventional adoption agencies."[24] The form letter Holt sent to prospective parents read, "In the enclosed application you are asked to state in your own words what your faith is and what Jesus Christ means to you personally."[25] Close friend Senator Richard Neuberger referred to the Holts as modern-day "Good Samaritans" in Congress.[26]

Many in the adoption field are uneasy with the relationship of agencies like Holt and their Korean affiliates because of their emphasis on Christianity. Robert Ackerman, the Immigration and Naturalization Service officer in charge of adoptions at the US embassy in Seoul during the 1980s, worried that the more extreme religious adoption agencies viewed adoptions as "a quick means of spreading the gospel, a head start on proselytizing."[27]

Ackerman had reason to be concerned. Following Holt's example, adoption agencies with unabashed religious agendas flourished and continue to operate today. An Internet search for "adoption" and "Christian" brings up thousands of web pages by organizations with names like "Christian World Adoption Agency"[28] and "All God's Children Adoption Agency."[29] The Holt Adoption Agency, now called Holt International, still operates with an evangelical aim. Its mission statement: "Holt International Children's Services is dedicated to carrying out God's plan for every child to have a permanent, loving family."[30]

Because private adoption agencies do not have to follow the same strict governmental regulations as public adoption agencies, they are just as susceptible to unethical practices as the Holt Agency in the early days. Organizations like these profess, as did Holt, that the mission of the agency is humanitarian in nature—in other words, *in the best welfare of the child.* Closer inspections, however, prove otherwise. These agencies are not in the business of finding parents for children, but finding children for parents. Brian Luwis, the founder of America World Adoption Association, writes:

> We knew virtually nothing about adoption or of orphans. We just wanted a child fast and within our limited resources.... Our belief [is] that God entrusts one mother and one father with total responsibility for any child ... hence, the open adoption option ruled out some domestic adoptions and our time and cost parameters eliminated the rest. We also wanted a newborn for our first child but an equitable domestic adoption was unaffordable and the wait for an infant was at least two years. [We were] open to any nationality, we researched all countries that met our cost and time criteria.[31]

Statements like Luwis's eerily reinforce the fact that the adoption industry often uses Christianity as a guise for fulfilling American parental needs. The Holts believed that their mission to adopt "Amerasian" children had succeeded so well that their supply fell short of the demand back in the States. Bertha wrote, "Since the number of families wanting children increased far beyond the number of Amerasian children available, Harry told Mr. Foreman to assign full Korean children to families."[32]

racism disguised as altruism

The underlying theme of Protestant Christian philosophy in the welfare of children of color was often that of "saving the heathen" from the "dark or savage" ways of their native cultures. It was the way to justify the removal of Native American children from their homes and force them into boarding schools[33] in order to "kill the Indian, save the Man."[34] As Holt wrote in his "Dear Friends" letter, "We would ask all of you who are Christians to pray to God that he will give us the wisdom and strength and the power to deliver his little children from the cold and misery and darkness of Korea."[35]

Holt's letter reveals much about the beliefs Americans held about people of color: Korea is a country of "misery and darkness" and people of color are not willing or able to take care of their own. Holt's letter lends credence to Park's assessment that the religion is inherently racist. Writes Park, "The church has often promoted the perception among its (usually white) members that they are superior to adherents of other religions, and this has in turn often been extended to perceptions of racial superiority as well."[36]

We must not forget that at the core of transracial adoption, children of color are being adopted by white parents. White parents may feel that they are exempt from being racist; after all, they adopted a child of another race. Yet through promoting the "we are all God's children" mentality, Christianity breeds a sort of colorblindness that is often as dangerous to a child of color as overt racism. This mentality often leads to statements such as, "I don't see [child's name] as Korean, she's just my daughter."

Collectively, Korean Christian churches have not taken a stand on the issue of adoption, and if adoptees are mentioned at all, it is often in the context similar to that dreamed up by Pastor Jin S. Kim, a Korean American minister who writes in his sermon "Jesus the Adoptee": "I am convinced that adoptees have a unique and natural insight into the heart of Jesus Christ who is the adoptee par excellence, the archetype of all adoptees in the world ever born."[37]

Kim advises adoptees to "understand from the earliest age that their only true father is their Father in Heaven" and suggests that Jesus as a son of God adopted by humans was the first "cross-cultural" adoption. Kim advises empathy from the Korean American congregation, but nowhere in the sermon does Kim encourage Korean Americans or Koreans to adopt. Instead, his answer is Korean Adoptees Ministry (KAM), a support group for Korean adoptees at a Korean Presbyterian church in Minnesota, which advertises its services to adoptees and adoptive families with the catch phrase, "Blood is thicker than water! Jesus' love is thicker than Blood!" The paradox is that KAM claims the only way to "heal" the pain of adoption is to figuratively become adopted yet again, that is, "to become a child of God."[38]

Mission to Promote Adoption in Korea (MPAK), on the other hand, has been actively promoting adoption by Koreans. MPAK's founder and president, Stephen C. Morrison, was adopted at the age of 14. Morrison travels to Korean churches spreading the gospel of adoption, relying heavily on the Bible. The organization has facilitated several adoptions of Korean children, most to Korean American families living in the United States.

"My conviction is that the time has come for Koreans to open up their hearts to adopt homeless Korean children," writes Morrison on his website. "As a Christian, I have especially tried to reach out to the Korean Christians to look at such children with the compassion that Christ felt for them.... I really believe the day will come when Korean families will adopt all the Korean orphans."[39]

⊡ ⊡ ⊡

The last part of the long drive to Ae Ran Wan is up a narrow, curvy, hill-cut road. Our driver parks on a steep slope and I enter the building that houses pregnant women, most of whom will place their child for adoption. The director greets us warmly and leads us into her small office. We talk about the program; Ae Ran Wan is a Christian organization that provides shelter and training to young pregnant women. Kim Yongsook, the director, reports that only 10 percent of the 250-plus women who came through Ae Ran Won in the year 2000 kept their babies. According to Adoptee Solidarity Korea, of the young women who now enter Ae Ran Wan in any given year, 70 percent intend to keep their children but after "counseling," only 30 percent decide not to relinquish their child.[40]

"We suggest that it's not a good idea to keep the baby without the biological father," Kim Yongsook explains, "and if the unwed mother and biological father are too young or too weak financially, we suggest that they give the baby up for adoption. We can't push, we can suggest."[41] Part of the mother's stay at Ae Ran Won includes writing a letter to her child. Some of these letters have been compiled in a book, *I Wish for You a Beautiful Life: Letters from the Korean Birth Mothers of Ae Ran Won to Their Children*.[42] Most emphasize the hope that these abandoned children end up in Christian homes.

Korean society, like most societies (including those thought of as equitable or progressive, such as the United States), values women for their potential fertility as wives. In other words, a woman's value is dependent not on her ability to produce monetary income, her intelligence, or her skills, but on her ability to bear children *for her husband.* It is one of the reasons unmarried women abandon their children to white couples in the United States, Europe, or Australia—to have a chance to marry a future husband as a childless/virginal woman and provide him biological children. It is also one of the reasons white Christian couples who are infertile adopt—to comply with God's commandment to "go forth and multiply." Intercountry adoption provides relief for two sets of parents.

It is also easier for the Korean government to send children overseas than it is to construct a government-funded social safety net for divorced or abused women and their children, male substance abusers, the mentally ill, or even the poor and unemployed. According to Park, Korean women experience han when they are abandoned or abused by men. "Patriarchy breaks their broken hearts yet further," writes Park, "thus producing han, the deep wound of the heart and soul."[43] Missing from Park's analysis, however, is the han passed down from women to their children, many of whom women in Korea abandon due to the difficulties of raising fatherless children there.

I wasn't allowed to meet any of the young women currently at Ae Ran Won, although meeting the birthmothers there has now become a standard part of many Motherland tours for adoptees and their families. These Motherland tours, set up through partnerships of adoption agencies in the United States and South Korea, typically involve some limited amount of contact between birthmothers, adoptees (often aged from 10 to young adulthood), and adoptive parents.

These visits are often difficult for the adoptees, many of whom are "the same age as the birthmothers" said one South Korean interpreter about a visit to a mothers' home in Korea in 2005. "The girls are young, 14, 15 years old. Some adoptees do not want to see the birthmothers. The birthmothers cry a lot, but they are happy that their [future] children will have such good lives."[44] Although these meetings are often quite poignant, one has to wonder for whose benefit these meetings are made. Do adoption agencies arrange these visits for the benefit of the adopted children and their parents as a way to understand their own relinquishments and adoptions, which may or may not have stemmed from the same circumstances? Are these visits for the adoptive parents, so they can feel good about having "saved" both a child and a birthmother? Are they for the birthmothers, who need their guilt assuaged, or to encourage their relinquishment of their unborn child? How much is this choreographed meeting with a vanload of robust, milk-fed teenagers with their American designer clothes, electronic gadgets, and affectations a justification for a birthmother's plans to hand over her own child to a family that can afford to take her relinquished children on family vacations halfway around the world?

As we stuff ourselves back into the agency's van and snake down the steep hill toward the congestion of Seoul, I cannot make myself turn around and look. Like many others, I have turned my back on the women and girls housed here, who believe that giving up their child is the Christian thing to do. In a way, I hope they truly believe that, for it will be their only comfort in the months and years to come.

I have never been a good sleeper. My father used to joke that I was still on Korea time because even as a child I was up at night, unable to sleep. The plane ride home from Korea is no exception. Korean Air is much more comfortable than any US airline I've ever traveled on. The meals are tastier and the flight attendants don't look down their noses at you. Yet I am almost in shock—a combination of time differences, dry cabin air, and a body completely fatigued but unable to shut down. I am unable to read, something that usually relaxes me. I'd barely slept the previous night. My eyes are closed but sleeping is not an option. Through the low-level background noise of the airplane, the conversations and flight attendants whooshing past, I hear a baby crying, and I twist my neck to see where the sound is coming from. A woman is walking up and down the aisle, bouncing a 6-month-old girl at her shoulder. A white woman. A Korean baby.

She lives 20 miles away from me in Minnesota. This is her second child from Korea. My friend eagerly fusses over the plump little girl and asks to hold her.

She's lucky to have you, my friend tells the mother, whose eyes moisten. *God has been good to us,* the mother responds. *We're lucky to have her.*

notes

1 Andrew Sung Park, *The Wounded Heart of God: The Asian Concept of Han and the Christian Doctrine of Sing* (Nashville: Abingdon Press, 1993), 16.
2 Park, *Wounded Heart of God*, 45.
3 Bertha Holt, *Bring My Sons from Afar* (Eugene, OR: Holt International Children's Services, 1986), 1.
4 Holt, *Bring My Sons*, 4.
5 Harry Holt, "Harry Holt's Dear Friends Letter, 1955," *Adoption History Project*, http://darkwing.uoregon.edu/~adoption/archive/HoltDearFriendsltr.htm.
6 The Holt Adoption Agency (now Holt International) incorporated in 1956, according to Holt International. Holt did not comply with all of the United States' licensing requirements until 1962.
7 Holt, *Bring My Sons*, 9.
8 Holt, *Bring My Sons*, 3.
9 Holt, *Bring My Sons*, 68.
10 Holt, *Bring My Sons*, 44.
11 Holt, *Bring My Sons*, 49, 57.
12 Holt, *Bring My Sons*, 66.
13 Korean National Statistical Office (KNSO), International Statistical Cooperation Division, "Table: Participation of Religions Action," 2003, http://www.nso.go.kr/eng/qna/data/participation%20of%20religious%20action.xls. According to the KNSO, 36.8 percent of South Koreans practice Protestant Christianity and 13.7 percent practice Catholicism.
14 Andrew E. Kim, "Korean Religious Culture and Its Affinity to Christianity: The Rise of Protestant

Christianity in South Korea," *Sociology of Religion* 61, no. 2 (2000): 117.

15 South Korean Ministry of Health and Welfare, Global Adoption Information and Post Service Center, "Statistics, 1953–2004," http://www.gaips.or.kr/adoption/adoption.php.

16 Kim, "Korean Religious Culture."

17 Max Weber, "Asceticism and the Spirit of Capitalism," in *The Protestant Ethic and the Spirit of Capitalism*, trans. Talcott Parsons and Anthony Giddens (London: G. Allen & Unwin Hyman, 1930), 102–125.

18 Park, *Wounded Heart of God*, 50.

19 Kim, "Korean Religious Culture," 120.

20 Mathew Rothschild, "Babies for Sale: South Koreans Make Them, Americans Buy Them," *The Progressive* 52, no. 1 (1988), available at "Babies for Sale," *ModelMinority.com: A Guide to Asian American Empowerment*, July 30, 2005, http://modelminority.com/modules.php?name=News&file=article&sid=478.

21 Park, *Wounded Heart of God*, 46–47.

22 Holt, *Bring My Sons*, 10.

23 Rothschild, "Babies for Sale."

24 Ellen Herman, "Bertha and Harry Holt," *Adoption History Project* at http://darkwing.uoregon.edu/~adoption/people/holt.htm.

25 Herman, "Bertha and Harry Holt."

26 Herman, "Bertha and Harry Holt."

27 Rothschild, "Babies for Sale."

28 "A Christian International Adoption Agency," Christian World Adoption, http://www.cwa.org.

29 "Adoption and Relief Services," All God's Children International, http://www.allgodschildren.org.

30 Holt International Children's Services, "Introduction to Holt," Holt International, http://www.holt-intl.org/intro.shtml.

31 Brian Luwis, "The Spirit of Adoption," America World Adoption Association, http://awaa.org/stories/spiritofadoption.aspx. (Slightly different version of text now on site.)

32 Holt, *Bring My Sons*, 33.

33 David Wallace Adams, *Education for Extinction: American Indians and the Boarding School Experience 1875–1928* (Lawrence: University of Kansas Press, 1995); Andrea Smith, "Soul Wound: The Legacy of Native American Schools," *Amnesty Magazine*, Amnesty International USA, http://www.amnestyusa.org/amnestynow/soulwound.html.

34 Official Report of the Nineteenth Annual Conference of Charities and Correction (1892), 46–59. Reprinted in Richard H. Pratt, "The Advantages of Mingling Indians with Whites," *Americanizing the American Indians: Writings by the "Friends of the Indian" 1880–1900* (Cambridge, MA: Harvard University Press, 1973), 260–271, http://socrates.bmcc.cuny.edu/bfriedheim/pratt.htm.

35 Herman, "Harry Holt's Dear Friends Letter."

36 Park, *Wounded Heart of God*, 65.

37 Jin S. Kim, "Jesus the Adoptee: A Contextual Theology of Liberation for the Adoptive Community," Church of All Nations Discipling for Outreach (Cando.org), January 16, 2003, http://www.cando.org/resources/sermon.asp?contentid=61.

38 Korean Adoptees Ministry home page, http://www.kam3000.org.

39 Stephen C. Morrison, "Adoption... Isn't It Our Responsibility?" Mission to Promote Adoption in Korea (MPAK), http://www.mpak.com/HomeEnglish.htm.

40 Adoptee Solidarity Korea (ASK), "News," http://www.adopteesolidarity.org/. ASK is an organization of adults who were adopted from Korea as children and who have become repatriated. Their goal is to advocate for women and children in South Korea and to promote domestic adoption.

41 Rothschild, "Babies for Sale."

42 Sara Dorow, ed. *I Wish for You a Beautiful Life: Letters from the Korean Birth Mothers of Ae Ran Won to Their Children* (St. Paul, MN: Yeong and Yeong Book Company, 1999).

43 Park, *Wounded Heart of God*, 20.

44 Interview with K. S. on August 14, 2005.

PART FOUR

GROWING THROUGH THE PAIN

Birth Certificate, 1962 During the fight, her mother threw her birth certificate at her. This is how she found out her real father's name.

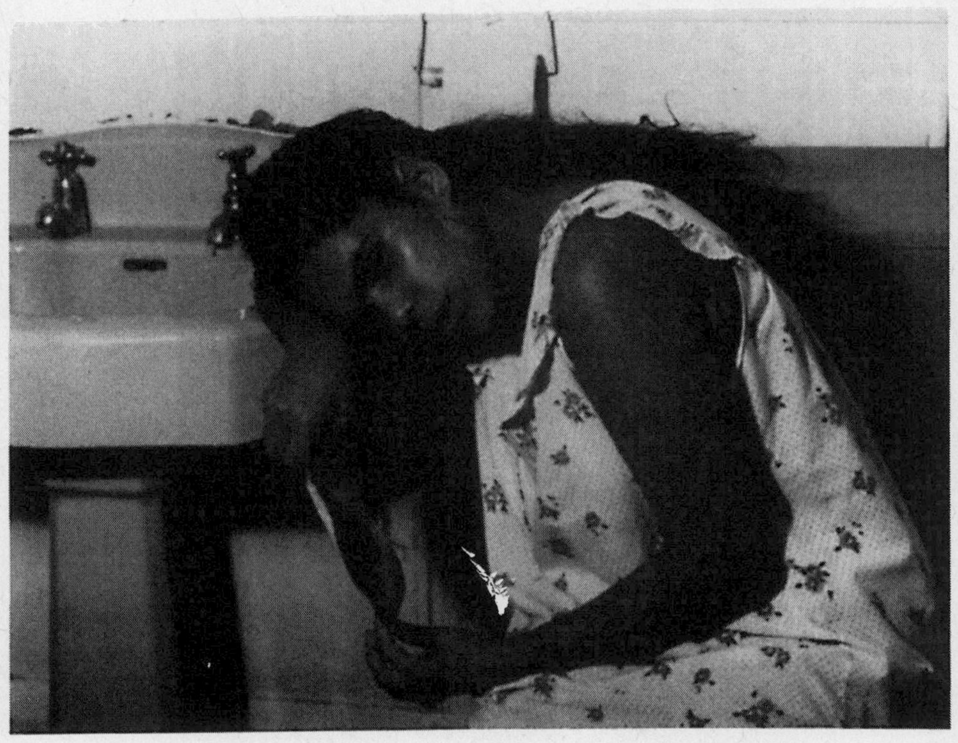

Tracey Moffatt, *Birth Certificate,* 1962, 1994, from a series of 9 images
Offset print, 80 x 60cm

16 HUNGER

Shannon Gibney

My brother Ben was fighting. He was white and he was fighting to eat his steamed asparagus and garlic mashed potatoes. There was something in his throat, there was something no one could see that was growing in his larynx. He sat at the dinner table and bowed his head while everyone else prayed. He couldn't eat because there was something in the way and he was my little brother who was white when I was black, who had once kicked in a wall because I wouldn't shut up.

Lately, I have been lying awake mornings, imagining the meaty red contours of Ben's throat, the way it must swell from all those things he never said. I have watched him gag when he swallowed, I have seen him turn away from me after I told him I could no longer stay at my parents' house.

This is the whole secret I am telling: my parents are white and they locked me in my room because I'm black and crazy and that's not changing. My little brother sat outside the door that night, shaking, because nothing had changed. When he heard me scream, he swallowed but he was still hungry.

You have to decide to be in this family, my father told me, his stolid hips blocking the doorway. *You can't just stop speaking to your brother because of words.* He was talking about my other brother, Jon, the one who can eat whatever he wants, the one who has married a white woman and has a white baby and a white five-year-old. The one who makes $120,000 a year and told me to stop telling his white five-year-old about how I was black and how I was adopted.

When I was six, Jon would read me any book I wanted, and then sit patiently while my brow furrowed and I tried to make some kind of sense out of the characters on the page. *No, that's "hunger,"* he would tell me. *Listen to how it sounds. Hear it in your mouth before you say it.* I wanted to tell my father that Jon was the one who had taught me the weight of words in the first place, how they can corrupt silence and therefore change the landscape of the intangible.

Instead, I said, *Get the fuck out of my room.* My father's face reddened, and he charged toward me. I had chosen the wrong words, but I hadn't been thinking about the silence, the way it had been about to burst anyway, holding on for 28 years. *Silence wants the words, too,* I thought. *Silence wants them to come.* But as usual, my father wasn't hearing the silence—he was too concerned with what had been said.

Outside the door, Ben's larynx was spreading across his throat. Soon, he hoped, the throbbing would stop and he could eat again. My mother had made him a milkshake, but now she was in my room, telling me that she was scared, had always been scared that I would leave the family one day. I hadn't spoken to Jon for five months by that time.

But that night, my parents would not let me go. I told them to get out, I began throwing things into my bag, saying I would drive the ten hours back to Minneapolis that minute. My father grabbed my arm and would not let go. My mother braced her body against the door and said that we had to talk. They forgot that I was 28 and had a job in editing and ran three miles every afternoon. They forgot that I knew how my hair caught in my pick when I combed it, but eventually, always gave.

My stomach started to shake and I sat in a corner, sniffing. There was a crack in the wall, and I realized that it was fighting too, that all it had ever done was last and that itself was a lesson. My parents were talking around me, saying how they needed to break through, bridge the distance I had created between us. *When I was born,* I was thinking, *I was already far from you, and since then you have only walked further, faster.* I wanted to tell them I would always be this way. I wanted them to take a good look at me. One day soon, I hoped, they would see me when they saw themselves.

On the other side of the door, Ben could not drink the milkshake. It choked him, and he ran to the bathroom and spit it out.

Hours later, after my parents had finished with me, they let me go. They marched out of my room, heads down, eyes full. They knew what they had done; they had done what they had to do. I lay in my bed on my stomach, sleep spreading through my joints like malaria, and I couldn't move. *This is love,* I thought.

Except for the laboring furnace, the house was finally quiet, and I could see my brother on the other side of my door, knuckles poised to rap. His stomach was still screaming, though mine had quieted, and he wanted to tell me that he had heard everything. He was trying to say that he still couldn't eat, and didn't know when he would be able to.

I watched him there, and I knew what hunger was.

17 KOREAN PSYCH 101

CONCEPTS OF HWA-BYUNG (화병/火病) IN RELATION TO KOREAN ADOPTION

Beth Kyong Lo

photographs and documents

I am an immigrant. I am first generation with no heavy accent, no accent. I do not speak my native tongue. I am an immigrant like my husband, who came to America once the Vietnam conflict ended; being Hmong, known as American helpers fighting against communism, his family fleeing the mountains of Laos only seemed reasonable. But I do not retell stories of the old days when I was a little kid liking American songs but not understanding a word of them or learning English from *Sesame Street* and TV commercials. I do not tell stories about white kids who tried to bully me for being Asian and me beating them up because I could not fight with my words. I have no stories about the times I rode water buffalos with my brother and he had to bite the balls of his to get him moving, or when I skipped school to go to the fish pond and my mother found out and greeted me with a huge smile and a switch behind her back. I have never crawled beneath a schoolhouse and gotten stung by a scorpion, all for a pencil that had fallen through the floorboards. I have never lived through war. My immigration was quiet and Anglo-sized. First generation turned third.

The very first picture of myself is when I was Korean. Not Korean American, not Korean adopted, just plain Korean. I sit, in white pajamas, on a woman's lap. She has no identity. Her face is not there, only a chin and wisps of short hair stare down at me. This woman, this mystery woman, seems petite with her thin arms holding me on her lap. I look up at her. No smile. No emotion. Lips slightly agape, like I am in awe, like I am surprised by her motherliness. It is strange to think that my first exposure to language was Korean, that I sat on her lap listening to her talk to me in smooth flowing tongue. To this day, I love listening to Korean people speak with one another. I eavesdrop, closing my eyes and pretending I understand every word and am at home.

The Child—this baby with an elongated face, medium nose, black eyes (a little big).
Good shaped ears, black hair, smooth forehead, and fine skin looks.
Lovely, enjoying good health with healthy digestion and appetite.
Eats more than other babies her age, sleeps all day, frets when diaper is dirty or wet. Loves to be bathed.
She is growing quite well without any troubles, so claims her foster mother.

According to my social history report, my caseworker visited my foster mother for information about me and to take pictures for my new parents on August 27, 1975. One month old. The caseworker saw me as cute and loveable and hoped that I would be placed in a suitable home where I could look forward to a bright and happy future. Resentment rises inside me as I look at these documents of my early existence:

Sacred Heart. Sacred Medicine. Sacred Hospital.
Beautiful and healthy, elongated with olive skin tone
and big black watermelon eyes.
Normal, normal, good, normal, negative, normal.
One month and healthy, healthier than most her age.
Han Gang. Sung Sim.
9.9 pounds, August 19, 1975.

mythology

My parents had me in therapy by the time I was nine. I started out with a psychologist but was on the psychiatrist's couch by twelve. My list of "symptoms" was long and varied: panic attacks, fear of dying, stomachaches, and migraines. I chronically missed school, I was unable to sleep over at friends' houses, I had a tortured relationship with food, and I chased my mom and dad around the house with a dull kitchen knife because they weren't my "real parents." All of this landed me in therapy that would last until my first year in college. The labels piled up in my charts—Oppositional Defiant Disorder, Separation Anxiety, Major Depressive Disorder, Bipolar I, restrictive eating behaviors, Attention-Deficit Hyperactive Disorder. All those labels seemed to scream what a freak I was; they also screamed that no one could figure out what was wrong with me.

But I knew what was wrong.

My name was Kim Hei Kyong. I was born on July 23, 1975, but of course that is just a guess. I was handed to policemen that day by a "neighborhood woman" who found me, wrapped in a yellow quilt, on her doorstep. Because I was found in the Itaewon neighborhood of the Yongsan district in Seoul, where the American military base is located, I assume that I am from mixed blood. My physical features seem to confirm this assumption. Korean exchange students' eyes widen when I tell them where I was found and they say, "That's a really bad neighborhood. No good girl get caught there at night." Korean Americans, first to fourth generation, and other Korean adoptees tell me I cannot possibly be full Korean, that I do not look full Korean. I can accept it when Korean people tell me this, for I expect it, but to hear the same from another adoptee—that is when I feel truly alienated. To belong nowhere is to be invisible and to be invisible induces a deep rage. Asian Americans protest their invisibility in this country, so it is ironic that the many I have encountered have seemingly done their best to exclude me as well.

A rage runs through my bones, aching to be released from the pit of my stomach. I have worn so many masks over the years that my skin feels gray and my features have faded. Like a ghost, I feel doomed to wander the earth forever, invisible and disconnected from the world of the living.

I trick myself into believing I do know who I am by over-intellectualizing my history and status as a Korean adoptee. But I really do not know a thing about myself, not when I imagine *Her* letting me slip from her arms. How easy it is for me to hate.

hwa-byung 화병/火病

Hwa-byung is a culture-bound syndrome of a Korean folk illness that translates as "fire disease" and is recognized in the Diagnostic and Statistical Manual of Mental Disorders–IV. In Eastern medical philosophy, fire represents one of five universal elements that keep the mind and body well. If fire is excessive, it disrupts the balance of bodily elements and causes physical and mental disease. Hwa-byung is experienced by the patients as a physical and psychological phenomenon caused by interpersonal conflicts and repressed anger, or anger turned inward and against the self as a defense against loss. It is understood as being caused by han.[1]

Han 한/恨 contains grudges, lamenting, regret, resentment, grief, and angst. It is conceived of as an ailment of the mind and heart, an inconsolable state of mind. Yong Hoon Hwang writes about collective han as being a group emotion that arose because of sociocultural oppression (e.g., patriarchy, colonialism, classism) and individual han as centering around psychological suffering with a personal component. She writes, "Han-full experiences are inherited and remain at the bottom of Korean psyche as a collective unconscious, which can easily be triggered by another han-full experience."[2] She also describes han in terms of meaninglessness, separation anxiety, and existential anxiety, all inflicted by an individual or a damaging structure, and indicates that it may extend outside of Korea.

Han can be transformed into positive energy and used for actions such as countering repressive regimes, but it can also develop into mental illness, especially when feelings of hopelessness and powerlessness are present.[3] Thus enters hwa-byung, exhibited in the form of panic attacks, fear of impending death, gastrointestinal problems, loss of appetite, phantom epigastric pain (upper-mid abdomen), insomnia, headaches, nervousness, sad moods, fatigue, short-lived outbursts of anger, and hypervigilence—all symptoms of depression, somatization (disorders containing physical ailments and sensations due to psychological distress), and anxiety disorders. Sometimes it has been compared to post-traumatic stress disorder, though not as frequently as to depression.

Hwa-byung or *wool hwa* 울화/鬱火 (pent-up anger) is the accumulation of stressful life events with poor social support, and thus limited opportunities to express anger. Korean psychiatrists view hwa-byung as a mix of cultural, psychological, and biological factors. Some feel that hwa-byung is purely Korean culture–bound and others believe that it is a major, universally known depression that is culturally expressed. Others suggest hwa-byung is a way to identify and communicate emotional difficulties with living situations and interpersonal relationships.[4]

Hwa-byung is thought to exist most commonly in Korea among middle-aged, poorly educated women in low economic brackets who live amid family discord, particularly marital discord. These women are committed to traditional patriarchal beliefs, may have quick temperaments, and have hard and unhappy lives in general.[5]

However, traditional assumptions about who lives with hwa-byung do not account for people in the United States. An even higher rate of incidence occurs for Korean Americans (11.9 percent)—across gender, class, and education—than for Korean nationals living in Korea (4.3 percent). Granted, there has only been one study of hwa-byung among Korean Americans and another Korean study claims the prevalence rate of hwa-byung in Korea is 7.3 percent.[6] The latter study attempted to identify if hwa-byung accounts for adjustment factors, such as ways to identify and communicate emotional frustrations over living situations and interpersonal relationships, or if it truly is related to psychopathology.[7] The study supports the latter. Researchers found that hwa-byung often exists simultaneously with psychiatric disorders, particularly with major depressive disorder, and therefore should be seen as a cultural expression of psychiatric disorders.

Whereas anxiety is thought to arise from experiences of danger, depression is said to be due to loss, particularly a loss interfering with a life goal. Such devastating losses may undermine a person's sense of self and way of life. Depending on the intensity of the emotional reaction of the person, individuals who have experienced loss and/or danger are at risk of developing depressed and anxious states of being, depending on the impact of the event(s) and factors that render the person vulnerable (early negative experiences; negative schemata; genetics that affect sadness, fear, and personality disposition; stressful life events; culture; and social support). Accordingly, life stressors and vulnerability factors have a major impact on who becomes ill with hwa-byung. After all, not all Korean people who suffer from han develop hwa-byung.

the trouble with dichotomous thinking

Because of the 15,000 Korean adoptees residing in Minnesota alone and the recent boom of literature expressing our experiences—*Seeds from a Silent Tree, The Language of Blood, A Single Square Picture,* and *Dust of the Streets: The Unforgotten War*—our mental health issues have become of national interest.

Korean orphans were originally placed in predominately white, Christian, rural or suburban families, and were seen as assimilating successfully within their families. Assimilation was a way in which Korean adopted children could avoid being sent back to the foster care system. White families insisted on "colorblindness" and enacted guilt mechanisms if their Korean children rebelled or hinted at wanting to rediscover their cultural heritage—they should be grateful they had been saved. A study published in 2003 revealed that, nearly half a century after Korean international adoption began, white adoptive parents continue to downplay their Korean children's heritage and consider their family identity to be "Caucasian with Korean children rather than a multiracial or multicultural family unit."[8]

The assumption in American society is that Korean adoptees are well-adjusted, but many of us have not verbalized our plights until the past ten years or so, possibly because we have grown up and suddenly possess credible thoughts and emotions, or maybe because we feel freer to speak up now that we have created our own stability and no longer live with our parents. Then again, many of us adoptees have mastered suppressing depression and anxiety about being abandoned and then raised in a white world, since our assimilation was necessary for our survival in an environment that we hoped would not re-abandon us.

We must, therefore, be cautious about terms such as "well-adjusted," lest we internalize them in an arrogant and self-destructive manner. Studies have shown that the social adjustment of intercountry adoptees in early childhood tends to be smooth.[9] Once placed, children demonstrate positive adjustment to their families and generally good well-being. However, adolescence and young adulthood is not as smooth. Adolescent adoptees have demonstrated high levels of depressive disorders, substance abuse, suicidal tendencies, and other adaptation problems.[10]

The "well-adjusted" concept can also be dismissive and potentially shaming, pitting adoptees against each other with the stereotypical *good* and *bad* labels, the favored story being, of course, the successful adaptors. I believe the adjustment concept is used by naïve white parents who want to make themselves feel better or protect themselves from certain hardships that arise in adoptions. Denial is a human condition that protects us from feeling overwhelmed by negative and unbearable experiences. Denial helps us reassure ourselves that our lives are going as we have imagined. Parents in denial tend to gloat about how well their child is doing (yes, when they are still young) as they watch other couples run into chaos and rage-induced problems, thinking, *that's never going to happen to us.*

But children grow into adults who encounter racial discrimination without the protection of their families. Unable to seek Korean support systems because they were "totally cut off from their Asian cultures"[11] and, without the presence of their white families no longer recognizable as American by the white mainstream, Korean adoptees may harbor frustrations and psychological difficulties.

I do not intend to blame adoptive parents for the personal difficulties of adoptees, but I believe that parents' attitudes of superiority and faith in a hierarchy (that places the experiences and perceptions of adoptive parents over adoptees) do not benefit their children. Many of the Korean adoptees I've known have experienced depressive and anxious states sometime during their lives—some more quietly than others—and repressing grief does not make one "well-adjusted." Denial of anger, sadness, and loss festers and—as seen in hwa-byung—causes great distress.

six is enough—
a father (54), a mother (44), two sons and two daughters.
The perfect family living harmoniously, warm and courteous,
Healthy strong people.
  Mother
Mother so diligent and kind holds me all day till my head flattens
From laying against her arm, and my voice disappears
'cause I never have to cry.
Oh, how they love me so so much.

hwa-byung and adoptees

I have not diagnosed myself with hwa-byung. I am suggesting clinicians recognize that our symptoms run deeper than Western diagnostic criteria and labels. There are fundamental emotions that humans across cultures share—happiness, sadness, fear, anger—but all societies develop their own standards of what is acceptable and unacceptable to express. For example, Asian cultures generally discourage the expression of negative emotions due to the belief that they equal weakness (lack of control) and are socially inappropriate (ego-centered and lacking group unity). In other words, Asians tend to be concerned with how their emotional expressions may impact other people.[12] Collectivist groups experience emotions as "relational phenomena, embedded in relations with others and perceived to reflect the state of those relationships," and individualist (Western system) emotions are centered on the subjective experience.[13]

This is not to say that people in collectivist societies do not get sick from emotional buildup. Depression may be experienced in psychosomatic terms (chronic headaches, body aches, and other symptoms that do not have a medical explanation). Eastern and Middle Eastern cultures tend to project psychological issues onto the body.[14] This raises the question of whether the culture shapes expression of emotions, as well as psychiatric states. Patients suffering from hwa-byung recognize that they suffer both physical and psychological ailments. Traditional Asian medicines have considerable influence on health beliefs in relation to balance (yin/yang), fundamental in matters of health and sickness. Since hwa-byung is seen as an element that disrupts the body's balance to a severe degree, traditionally the Korean people sought answers and advice about their psychological and physical conditions from herbal doctors. More recently, physicians who practice Western medicine are more commonly sought because Koreans have begun to pay more attention to their physical symptoms and disregard the psychological ones.

Western treatment tends to place emphasis on using symptoms to diagnose disease rather than considering the context.[15] It is important to identify and understand cultural patterns, identities, and relationships as they relate to grieving and adjusting to trauma.[16] As young as the research is in the area of culture and trauma, most of the literature agrees that an individual's culture is helpful in protecting against psychopathology because it is seen as a support system that helps diminish feelings of alienation. While some white adoptive parents think that emphasizing only "American" culture is substantial in helping Korean adoptees adjust and assimilate to their new lives, it is actually alienating them further by denying the importance of where they came from. This can cause disruption in the self and may manifest in the form of mental health difficulties later in life.

Transcultural child psychiatry (a blend of clinical skills, developmental studies, and cultural/social studies) provides an effective intervention in reworking notions of culture, child development, and family systems.[17] Researchers have also noted that the Cultural Family Model has been helpful for transnational adoptees, using the therapist as a cultural translator who acknowledges cultural differences yet bridges gaps and dispels myths and stereotypes in order to explore perceptions. These models and others that use culturally sensitive frameworks have been found effective both in treating patients and in recognizing how traditional psychiatric approaches are ethnocentric and biased.[18]

a possible treatment option

A seemingly growing trend among adult Korean adoptees is to reclaim their Korean identities, although I must note this is speculation. In speaking with other Korean adoptees, I have noticed that many have changed their names back to those given them at birth or have returned to Korea to live. There they learn to speak, eat, and breathe Korean culture. They search for their birth families or reach out for Korean lovers; some reach for anything and everything—literature, movies, music, cookbooks—that has the word Korean in it. They gather as a group, creating a community where they can compare stories and sometimes wounds.

So it seems plausible that Korean psychology could satisfy our loss, which might stem from maladaptive bereavement of culture, land, family, and identity. My interest in hwa-byung is an attempt to find additional treatment alternatives in working with Korean adoptees and their multitude of Western diagnoses. Korean adopted individuals may suppress anger about their fate, their adoptive homes, their birth families, and Korean people (for not accepting and adopting them), and thus tend to encounter episodes of depression, anxiety, interpersonal relationship difficulties, eating disorders, and other psychiatric problems. Even though Korean adoptees have been raised in the United States, we are still immigrants from a different land and have acculturation issues—often similar to but also distinct from non-adopted Koreans.

It is my belief that while adopted Koreans may or may not experience hwa-byung, processing depression and anxiety in a cultural context could help dispel feelings of alienation and build a sense of inclusion. Therefore, there are two reasons concepts of hwa-byung should not be easily dismissed within Korean adopted communities:

1. Instead of simply treating the disorder with medications and Westernized understandings of disorders, treating an adoptee's history and beliefs according to his or her loss of culture, home, and family might be more productive. These losses cause a sense of social alienation, which in turn amplifies depression and other emotional disorders related to repressed emotions. As one can see through my personal experience, as well as those of many frustrated adoptive families, too many psychologists do not deal with issues of adoption, particularly transracial/transcultural adoption. This deficiency puzzles me since there is such an emphasis on attachment and psychodynamic theories in the psychology field.
2. Hwa-byung integrates many Western diagnoses in one syndrome, and so can eliminate the practice of labeling people with an array of diagnoses. Rather than compartmentalizing symptoms into a Western-style diagnosis, it may be more helpful for adoptees struggling with rage, depression, and anxiety to relieve shame-based beliefs by understanding their experiences in terms of attachment and bereavement gone astray.

Hwa-byung is a fascinating concept that advances the idea that psychiatric diagnoses, particularly major depression and anxiety, can be culturally expressed. The somatization of life stress and psychiatric vulnerabilities, identity, and wounded fate is important to consider when working with Korean Americans, as well as adopted Koreans. In essence, hwa-byung can be understood in terms of suffering, trauma, bereavement, and anger toward fate and life. Korean adoptees tend to be forgotten in Korean immigrant stories, yet we are also immigrants and need to be recognized as people who also have adjustment problems well into our adult years. And although it is Koreans who are specifically naming this concept of suffering at the hands of oppression and displacement, as well as the resultant emotions oppression and displacement produce, this concept does appear in other cultures and may be useful in treating other transcultural/transracial adoptees.

wheezing

The dust from the basement settles in my lungs as I flip through my baby book my mother has saved for me. I cannot breathe and I know it is not due to my allergies. I laugh bitterly at every comment, every lie; was the system corrupt or were these caseworkers in denial? Who was benefiting from these grossly inaccurate—by any country's standards—assessments of an infant's "health"? How could I be healthy when I only gained 6 ounces within 4 months? I weighed 10 pounds at 5 months. How could they write about my bright and happy future? The neglect I experienced as a vulnerable infant seems to have condemned me to rage and attachment issues. The American doctors told my adoptive mother I was pre-autistic. And what of my chronic stomachaches and headaches? And what of my lifetime battle with food—a love and hate relationship that keeps me underweight?

These pages stir resentment, rage, violence—all those emotions need to be felt and recognized before individual forgiveness and forward movement become possible. Unfortunately, not one of my therapists has ever addressed my loss of Korean land, culture, and people, nor my experience of being abandoned and then neglected because of assumptions I was "mixed race." None of those clinicians addressed my being transracially adopted and considered how I might adjust. I still have a hard time sleeping because of nightmares of being stalked and killed, or because my stomach aches with homesickness for *Her* even though I've never known her outside of the womb. I have had child after child (six children, two miscarriages) in search of fulfillment but still cannot identify what is missing. I speak childish Hmong when in the presence of Koreans just so they will not know I am part Korean, so they will not tell me the usual—"You can't possibly be full Korean." And I constantly search to replace my roots with my Hmong family, only to be reminded that there, too, I am not truly one of them.

However, through writing, acknowledging my past and accepting fate (or that I'm here for many reasons), attempting not to alienate myself from other Korean adoptees (no matter how insecure and paranoid I get around them), and flinging myself into the abyss of motherhood and family, I have found a somewhat progressive peace of mind.

It is hard to speculate whether certain adoptees will truly recover from their trauma. I have had Korean adoptees tell me that we will always struggle with depression and anxiety, but our victory is in being able to cope with them every time they arrive; it is in accepting our past and maintaining our present state of being. Pessimistic? Maybe. But a great start in acknowledging and understanding a highly complex position.

notes

1 Chang Hee Son, *Haan of Minjung Theology and Han of Han Philosophy* (Lanham, MD: University Press of America, 2000).
2 Yong Hoon Hwang, "A Study of Hwa-Byung in Korean Society," *Dissertation Abstracts International: Humanistic and Social Sciences* (1995): 11.
3 Hwang, "A Study of Hwa-Byung."
4 Keh-Ming Lin, "Hwa-Byung: A Culture Bound Syndrome?" *American Journal of Psychiatry* 140, no. 1 (1983): 105–107.
5 Young-Joo Park and others, "The Conceptual Structure of Hwa-Byung in Middle-Aged Women," *Health Care for Women International* 23, no. 4 (2002): 389–397.
6 Keh-Ming Lin and others, "Hwa-Byung: A Community Study," *The Journal of Nervous and Mental Disease* 180, no. 6 (1992): 386–391.
7 Lin and others, "Hwa-Byung."
8 Kathleen Ja Sook Bergquist and others, "Caucasian Parents and Korean Adoptees: A Survey of Parents' Perceptions," *Adoption Quarterly* 6, no. 1 (2003): 56.
9 Herma J. Versluis-den Bieman and Frank C. Verhulst, "Self-Reported and Parent Reported Problems in Adolescent International Adoptees," *Journal of Child Psychology and Psychiatry* 36 (1995): 1411–1428.
10 Anders Hjern and others, "Suicide, Psychiatric Illness, and Social Maladjustment in Intercountry Adoptees in Sweden: A Cohort Study," *Lancet* 360 (2002): 443–448.
11 Luke Kim, "Psychiatric Care of Korean Americans," in *Culture, Ethnicity, and Mental Illness* ed. Albert C. Gaw (Washington, DC: American Psychiatric Press, 1993), 347–375.
12 Jeanne Tsai and others, "Emotional Expression and Physiology in European Americans and Hmong Americans," *Emotion* 2, no. 4 (2002): 380–397; Hwang, "A Study of Hwa-Byung."
13 Batja Mesquita, "Emotions in Collectivist and Individualist Contexts," *Journal of Personality and Social Psychology* 80, no. 1 (2001): 68–74.
14 Keith Oatley and Jennifer M. Jenkins, *Understanding Emotions* (Cambridge, MA: Blackwell Publishers, 1996).
15 Judith Zur. "From PTSD to Voices in Context: From an Experience-Far to an Experience-Near Understanding of Responses to War and Atrocity Across Cultures," *The International Journal of Social Psychiatry* 42, no. 4 (1996): 305–317.
16 Marten DeVries, "Trauma in Cultural Perspective," in *Traumatic Stress: The Effects of Overwhelming Experience on Mind, Body, and Society,* ed. Bessel A. van der Kolk, Lars Weisaeth, and Alexander C. McFarlane (New York: Guilford Press, 1996), 398–413.
17 Vincenzo DiNicola, "Ethnocultural Aspects of PTSD and Related Disorders Among Children and Adolescents," in *Ethnocultural Aspects of Post-Traumatic Stress Disorder: Issues, Research, and Clinical Applications,* ed. Anthony J. Marsella and others (Washington, DC: American Psychological Association, 1996), 389–414.
18 Fred Gusman and others, "A Multicultural Developmental Approach for Treating Trauma," in *Ethnocultural Aspects*, 439–457.

18 EVOLVE

Bryan Thao Worra

Father, you will be pleased to know the guillotine
stopped falling on heads in France
in the year I was born,

after just one last
fellow, whose name I cannot find,
nor his crime.

I admit
I have not looked
very hard into the matter—
Curiosity is one thing,
Morbidity is another.

Father, I saw you in the shadow of my mirrors:
an elusive memory, known only through my mother,
described as "widow of _______" after signing
those papers releasing me for adoption by the
Americans
like a paper bird.

And I know you by features *widow of* and I do not
share.
Those jungles are distant assassins of my identity.

I cannot lift the leaves of that last tree that held you to
curse their poor arboreal
nursing. It would change nothing.

Accusations are futile.
Your last words are lost, my father,
and I would never have understood them anyway.

I cannot put you to rest. I cannot pronounce our family
name.

You are just bones among bones that cannot get up.

You are a smile gleaming, white
as wax melting,

scattered and dusting
the mountains of our ancestors.

In your wake, I rise with the most
delicate of freedoms…

19 LIFELONG IMPACT, ENDURING NEED

John Raible

I often refer to myself as one of the guinea pigs of the ongoing social experiment known as transracial adoption. I was adopted during the early 1960s, well before transracial adoption, which reached its peak in the United States around 1970, was popularized. As one of the first biracial adoptees of black and white parentage to be placed with a white family, I have frequently found myself in the position of spokesperson for—and, for a time, against—transracial adoption. Over the years, parents and social workers have expressed to me, in a variety of ways, their curiosity about how we guinea pigs turned out. I have always tried to answer as sincerely as I can, speaking for myself only, as one adoptee among many.

Ever since I was a teenager in the mid-1970s, I have been invited to talk publicly about my experiences. Since then, I have found myself positioned on various sides of the transracial adoption controversy and debate. For a time, I was the darling of white adoptive parent groups, when I entertained adoption conference audiences with poignant tales of overcoming the prejudice of narrow-minded bigots in the virtually all-white environment in which I grew up. In my 20s, I gravitated intellectually and emotionally to the perspective of the National Association of Black Social Workers and their militant stance denouncing the racism rampant in child welfare practice. I appreciated that there existed an organized group of adoption professionals who understood implicitly some of what I was going through as a young, transracial adoptee trying to make sense of race.

As the transracial adoption controversy heated up again in the 1980s, I allowed myself to be exploited by television producers, who liked to portray me as the "ungrateful angry young adoptee" on talk shows. In between these public spectacles, I was interviewed and written about by numerous journalists, all with their own particular slants on the controversy. I even appeared in a film about transracial adoption. Sometimes, strangers at adoption conferences recognize me from *Struggle for Identity: Issues in Transracial Adoption,* a documentary featuring six adult adoptees of various backgrounds. In that film, I am the oldest of the half-dozen adoptees, and I speak both as an adopted person and as an adoptive parent. In addition to public speaking, I am active in the virtual adoption community online. I host my own website about transracial adoption, and I respond to questions posted by parents, students, and others interested in transracial adoption at the website of the New York State Citizens' Coalition for Children. All of this is to demonstrate that I have been publicly involved with the controversy, one way or another, for the past quarter-century.

Now, 40 odd years into my own journey through transracial adoption, I have reached a point where I no longer choose to debate whether white parents should adopt transracially, or how well they are able to raise children of color. Instead, I recognize that transracial adoption is a reality for many families. Regardless of what I, or black social workers, or Native American activists, other adult adoptees, or even candid, seasoned adoptive parents report about the pros and cons of the experience, there will always be adults who are eager to become adoptive parents of children of other races. This phenomenon is likely to continue unless public consensus finally shifts away from viewing adoption simply as a benign or politically neutral intervention into the lives of less fortunate children. I believe public perceptions of adoption are likely to shift, and quite soon. I foresee a backlash, for instance, to the global roundup of children from impoverished and war-torn nations, and the attendant abuses by unscrupulous adoption marketers. Their more outrageous activities make headlines from time to time, revealing the motivations of those who are more interested in profiting from the sale of babies than in the welfare of children and families in crisis.

Until such a shift occurs, many would-be parents will travel thousands of miles and spend easily as many dollars to visit impoverished communities around the globe in search of children to take home and call their own. Moreover, most of those children will be brown, while most of the adopters will be white. Other parents will open their homes to children in the overpopulated foster care system, a disproportionate number of whom are children of color who come from impoverished backgrounds within the United States.

the limits of transracial adoption research

Despite a plethora of reports and research into transracial adoption, a number of questions continue to elude researchers. While most researchers have focused on children and young people, I am concerned about the impact of transracial adoption on *mature* adoptive families. I have spent my adult life attempting to understand the transracial adoption experience as an adoptee, as an adoptive parent, and, most recently, as a researcher.

My questions are framed by the history of transracial adoption as I have come to understand it as an educational researcher with interests in multicultural education. Unanswered questions include the following:

- What are the long-term implications of transracial adoption for adopted individuals and for mature adoptive families over time?
- Do long-term transracial adoptions disrupt (break down) more often than other adoptions?
- What kinds of support and education do families need in order to prevent disruptions?
- Do transracial family members automatically develop multicultural awareness when they take in children of another race?
- How important is such awareness to the quality of open communication about tough race and adoption issues in adoptive families?
- Is there a link between heightened awareness and a deeper sensitivity to the core adoption issues?

At the heart of such questions, which attempt to address issues that may make some people uncomfortable, is a recognition of the origins of transracial adoption in the social engineering schemes of bygone eras. I suspect that the practice of transracial adoption remains problematic precisely because its origins were not as benign as parents, in particular, have been led to believe. As an outgrowth of child welfare policy in this country, transracial adoption is a relatively recent innovation in the field of social work. Partly for this reason, the lifelong cumulative impact of the practice on adult adoptees and mature adoptive families has yet to be documented. While researchers have studied transracially adopted children and adolescents, few scholars have yet investigated the ways race and adoption combine to influence, for example, evolving family dynamics, shifting racial identities, or the life choices—and chances—of adoptees as they progress through their 30s, 40s, 50s, and beyond.[1]

Those who have closely followed the controversy over transracial adoption know that much of the existing research into its effects on individuals and families has been undertaken primarily with adoptive parents and, importantly, while their adopted family members were still children or adolescents. For example, some researchers have chosen to interview or survey adoptive parents about their children's social adjustment and self-esteem.[2] Others have questioned adoptees' teachers and parents and sometimes the young people themselves in attempts to investigate their racial identities and their feelings about being adopted.[3] All of these studies tend to focus on "outcomes," as if the effects of transracial adoption can be known, measured, and summarized once adoptees have, if only just barely, passed through childhood. Finite, outcome-oriented research ignores the ongoing, lifelong impact of the adoption experience itself on adoptees and their families. In addition, most of the existing research has failed to capture the continual negotiation and performance of fluid racial identities over the course of the life span. This becomes an important area for investigation, particularly as adoptees move through different social contexts, far beyond the protective buffers of the nuclear adoptive family of their childhood.

This state of affairs in transracial adoption research is a result of the apparent newness of the field. Transracial adoption is commonly assumed to be a relatively recent invention. For example, many people consider the adoption of Korean War orphans by white American parents in the 1950s to be the earliest transracial placements. From this perspective, it seems logical that 20th-century transracial adoption researchers would focus exclusively on adoptive parents and their immature children, beginning in the 1960s. In fact, the bulk of studies of transracial adoption has been carried out since the 1960s.[4] Since few transracial adoptees from the 1950s and '60s had grown to maturity, it made sense for the research undertaken during the 1970s to focus on young children and maturing families with teenagers and preteens. Before they could more completely assess the impact of transracial adoption on individuals over the entire life span, researchers would have to wait for the first generation of post–World War II transracial adoptees to establish their own lives and households and face their own life challenges as autonomous adults.

In my view, the literature on transracial adoption will remain incomplete and inadequate until the voices of mature adoptees and family members are included. At present, during the opening decade of the 21st century, the children adopted during the early days of the social experiment of the 1950s, '60s, and '70s have reached maturity. I anticipate that we will be hearing more from these adoptees—and their white siblings—as they find their voices and begin to articulate their experiences as mature adults, with a more distanced perspective on the days of their childhood and youth. I welcome the chance to hear their adult voices, which I trust will go a long way toward challenging the infantilization to which adoptees as a group continue to be subjected. That is, I hope that our collective adult voices will demonstrate tangibly that transracial adoptees are not perpetual children, as we often appear to be in research and in public discussions about transracial adoption.

The following example demonstrates how adoptees are positioned as perpetual children. I frequently hear the film *Struggle for Identity* described as featuring six "young people." Yet the six of us were adults, not "young people" (read "children"); I myself was 35 at the time of filming! Hopefully, the growing chorus of mature voices will serve as a reminder that adoptees do indeed grow up and spend most of our lives as adoptees *in adulthood.* Moreover, the voices of what have come to be called the "invisible children" in transracial families, namely, the nonadopted white siblings who grew up with a brother or sister adopted from another race, will add another rich layer to the growing scholarly literature on the ongoing social experiment. [See Chapter 21 for one such voice.—Ed.]

supporting transracial families in the 21st century

As a multicultural educator and transracial adoption researcher, I have come to believe that there are steps white parents can (and must be encouraged to) take if they choose to adopt transracially. Adoptive parents who are genuinely committed to raising emotionally healthy, multiculturally competent, and self-confident black, brown, and biracial children can be helped and prepared better by adoption professionals. I am not opposed to transracial adoption *per se*; I simply believe these adoptions need to be done in a responsible and ethical manner, by the appropriate, carefully selected families, and for the right reasons. Foremost of these reasons are the lifelong needs of adoptees, which should be the focus of discussion.

In my work with adoptive families, I find that effective transracial parenting takes on an added sense of urgency once parents recognize and come to terms with the obvious (but often overlooked) fact that adoptees will not be children forever. Usually, this awareness begins to develop once their children reach school age. By this time, many adoptive parents have grown attached to their adopted children and sincerely love them as if they were their own biological offspring. As their children progress through school, conscientious parents who develop a sophisticated multicultural analysis learn to accept the fact that, for the most part, transracial adoptees will live adult lives self-identifying as people of color in a race-conscious, sometimes hostile society.

Parents are not the only family members who must sooner or later come to grips with the primacy of race and the durability of racism. My interviews with a number of nonadopted siblings who grew up with a brother or sister of another race reflected the complex feelings and issues that arise as a result of their parents' decision to adopt transracially. As one might expect, the comments of white siblings from transracial families ran the gamut from wholehearted endorsement of transracial adoption as an ideal on the one hand to adamant opposition to it on the other, based largely on the difficult and sometimes tragic circumstances some of the siblings reported in their families. Chief among their complaints were the lack of understanding of race dynamics, the poor to nonexistent preparation their parents received, and the discomfort they themselves frequently felt as racially marked individuals whenever they appeared in public as an interracial family. While several of these siblings have gone on to adopt children as adults, few have chosen the transracial option; others candidly stated the reasons they would never adopt a child of another race. As unwitting participants in the transracial adoption experiment, many siblings now in adulthood have become all too aware of the pitfalls of racism and public ambivalence, if not outright hostility, directed at their families as they have been forced to deal with racism and the reactions of others to the interracial nature of their families.

Fortunately, a few siblings reported more positive experiences, mainly due to their parents' investment in educating themselves and their children—adopted and nonadopted alike—about cultural differences, making a commitment to antiracism, and the importance of understanding adoption issues. These savvy parents come to understand that, on top of their ongoing personal struggles with racism in school and elsewhere, transracial adoptees must also untangle complex feelings related to being adopted. Given the complexity of these intertwined issues, and the potential psychological and emotional harm that can ensue if they are not attended to, learning to navigate safe passage as a transracial family is risky business.

Adoption, by itself, is a dramatic, life-altering event, which incurs lifelong consequences for families. Adoptions that cross race lines add a complicating overlay of issues pertaining to difference and discrimination on top of the core adoption issues, making the ongoing support and education of transracial families crucial to their well-being and happiness. For this reason, I contend that parents, adoptees, and their siblings need and deserve ongoing and long-term postadoption support.

Fortunately, increasing numbers of agencies offer postadoption services to families. Some agencies automatically provide counseling to adoptees and their families on an as-needed basis. Others facilitate ongoing communication between adoptive families and the adoptee's birthparents or siblings, through "open adoption" arrangements. Still other service providers assist adoptees in the search process, should they choose to seek information about their origins as adults. A few agencies even provide multicultural education classes for parents and culture camps for children, along with other experiences designed to help families embrace a multicultural lifestyle.

In my view, these are hopeful signs indicative of the changes that need to take place in the way transracial adoption is practiced. Yet the agencies providing these kinds of postadoption supports are the exception rather than the rule. Moreover, with the rise of independent adoption facilitators and private (nonagency) arrangements between birthmothers or orphanages and adopters, there are fewer organized structures in place to support families through the lifelong journey of adoption. Far too many parents remain unprepared to address issues such as racial identity development, antiracism advocacy skills, or cultural awareness with their children. Far too few receive any sort of guidance about the special considerations of raising children of color in a race-conscious society. Furthermore, too many parents never receive training in the core issues basic to adoption or how to address them in their families. In my view, when parents are poorly served and woefully unprepared, adopted children—and adopted adults—suffer unnecessarily.

I will close this chapter by offering the following case as an example of the complexity of the intertwined issues of race and adoption that will confront increasing numbers of mature transracial families. Without professional support and education, many families will be left to struggle on their own to find ways to cope, as the following example illustrates.

the need to address race and adoption in the family

A few months ago, I received an email from a complete stranger who found me online. Emily (not her real name) wrote to me after she had read a transcript of a speech I gave back in 1990.[5] In those remarks, I attempted to convey to adoptive parents why I identified so strongly with African Americans and black culture, even though I am, in the eyes of some, "only half black." Emily had written to me to say that the speech resonated with her own situation, in spite of our being of different generations and nationalities and having different family circumstances.

While Emily and I have never met, I sensed a connection immediately as I read her heartfelt expression of the confusion and longing she is experiencing as an adult adoptee. In her email, she described herself as a mixed-race woman of Asian and European descent. Now in her late 20s, Emily reported feeling estranged from her well-intentioned white adoptive parents. I was saddened to read that Emily feels that her family situation, in her words, has "deteriorated." I interpreted this to mean that communication lines have broken down, leaving Emily—and I imagined her parents and siblings as well—feeling discouraged, hurt, and confused.

Emily went on to write about how tired she feels after years and years of living as the only person of color in an otherwise all-white community. I could certainly empathize with her desire to move to an integrated, cosmopolitan environment, and with her wish to finally find a place where she might fit in. I empathized also with the frustration and heartache she articulated, feeling more and more distanced from her adoptive parents, who simply don't understand her adult reality or her adult needs as a woman of color and as an adoptee. I noticed that, interestingly, Emily made no mention of her connection to her birth family, something I, too, have downplayed in my own life.

I felt dismayed reading Emily's email for a number of reasons. To begin with, I was frustrated because it sounded like Emily was going through many of the same struggles I went through in my teens and twenties, yet we are of different generations; we were born more than 20 years apart. Even though more than half a century has passed since the contemporary transracial adoption experiment began, here was yet another family that found itself unprepared to deal effectively with the complex issues of race and adoption. It angers me that too many adoptees, like Emily, are left to struggle by themselves through the quagmire of race politics and with the undercurrent of adoption issues, which can create challenging obstacles to attaining an inner life of satisfaction and contentment.

Although adoption professionals and educators know so much more now about adoption issues and about multiculturalism, many white parents still have few opportunities to learn about life from people who are culturally different, namely, adult people of color. For white parents, this results in a general lack of exposure to diverse perspectives, not to mention a concomitant lack of firsthand experience with racism. For adoptees, this means that transracially adopted children of color may reach adulthood psychologically and emotionally unprepared to handle the harsh realities they will inevitably face. Once they grow beyond the cute and cuddly early childhood stage, transracial adoptees predictably will experience racism from various individuals and institutions they encounter. Unprepared adopted children of color may grow up feeling alone, like Emily, emotionally abandoned, misunderstood, and failing to belong or fit in comfortably in any community, either of color or white.

Emily's example, and untold countless others, has led me to conclude that the professionals who promote transracial adoption, especially if they charge for their services, have an ethical obligation to prepare their clients—parents and children alike—for a lifetime of navigating the potholes and hills, cracks and crevices of rough terrain. This terrain is particularly challenging because it is simultaneously racial, cultural, and emotional. For this reason, I maintain that agencies and adoption professionals would serve their clients well by providing lifetime counseling, multicultural education opportunities, and other forms of postadoption support to families long after the initial adoptive placement has been made.

Re-reading Emily's email calls forth my own ambivalent feelings about my journey through transracial adoption. While it may not be popular or politically correct to admit this, I realize that fundamentally, *I regret that adoption had to happen to us in the first place.* Please don't misunderstand: admitting genuine feelings surrounding the fact that my birthmother relinquished me takes nothing from the love and gratitude I feel for my adoptive parents and family. But the paradox that is the inheritance of all adoptees, who arguably have been given a fresh start in life, is rooted in the opposite experience of profound loss. Emily's email reminds me that I am not done grieving my own early multiple losses, specifically, lost connections with my birthparents and siblings, and with the foster family who cared for me for nearly three years during a crucial time in my development.

For those of us who do make it through the tumultuous years of adolescence and early adulthood (and I encounter too many stories of self-destruction, including suicide, among transracial adoptees), there can be the added developmental task of finding the emotional wherewithal to "adopt" our parents as adults. Family members should understand that this part of the emotional journey of adoption can take decades.

Finally, re-reading Emily's email leaves me with the uneasy reminder that there are countless transracial adoptees out there living and struggling in isolation, who feel unable to share their feelings about their adoption losses or their experiences with racism. Breaking through this isolation remains challenging, partly because in our society we get very little practice in how to dialogue openly and honestly about uncomfortable topics. Often, it is simply easier to remain silent. Compounding this difficulty is the vast experiential gulf between individuals who occupy a different racial status or designation, even if we do share loving family ties. I suspect that this inability to bridge the experiential gulf between parents and adoptees contributes significantly to adoption disruptions.

In my travels throughout the adoption community, I still meet far too many family members who remain unprepared to respond appropriately to the unique needs of transracial adoptees. At the same time, I find that adoptees—and increasing numbers of parents—are yearning to talk about race and adoption. More and more parents are reaching the understanding that whether adoptees are still children living as dependents, or whether they have left home and are living on their own, transracial adoptees *need* to talk, and parents need to be prepared to talk, even if at times people feel uneasy.

I believe that dialogue can assist in preventing adoption disruptions. Following Marie Adams,[6] I define disruption as the emotional estrangement between adoptees and their parents, even if legal ties of adoption are not severed, as in the case of adoption dissolutions. For parents and adoptees, an emotional disruption is traumatic, even if the adoptee apparently "caused" the estrangement. Beginning adopters can be encouraged to make a comprehensive adoption plan for their family, to head off foreseeable problems. Such a plan would include counseling as needed and ongoing education at different life stages in core issues of adoption and loss, as well as in race dynamics and racism. Adoption professionals have an obligation to help adoptive parents anticipate their adopted children's needs well into adulthood. Such long-range planning becomes especially urgent in the case of transracial adoption.

My reply to Emily included encouragement to somehow keep the lines of communication open with her parents. After all, dialogue is a two-way street, regardless of the races or status of the parties involved. If I've learned anything along my journey, it is that blaming others helps no one find healing or happiness. I also know that reinforcing strained, broken, or missing family ties—adoptive, foster, and biological—is a worthwhile and necessary endeavor. At some point, Emily, like other adult adoptees, will have to find a way to emotionally recommit to her family, by adopting them psychologically, on her own terms.

I offer this chapter in the spirit of the ideals of multicultural education and genuine communication, which I believe can serve as antidotes to the painful historical and emotional legacy of transracial adoption. As I continue to voice my maturing perspective, I hope that another adoptee somewhere may find solace and affirmation in these written words. I hope, too, that adoption professionals will be motivated to rethink their ongoing responsibilities to adoptees and their families. I hope the white siblings of transracial adoptees will feel empowered to express their own truth. I hope that transracial adoption researchers will endeavor to ask the right questions and maintain a spirit of open-minded inquiry, and not simply use their own studies to bolster an already formed opinion on the controversy. Finally, I hope that adoptive parents will be moved to take one further, admittedly difficult—but not impossible—step on a precarious, but ultimately rewarding, lifelong sojourn. My secret desire is for all family members to become effectively "transracialized,"[7] a term I discuss elsewhere to describe the ways individuals can learn to live antiracist lives based on genuine relationships of caring among individuals from a variety of racial and cultural backgrounds, both within and outside the family. I hope parents will use their experiences of transracial parenting as the departure point to embark upon a multicultural journey filled with excitement, purpose, and dedication to the unfinished project of finally integrating a still-divided society.

notes

1 A notable recent exception is the work of Marie Adams, the author of *Our Son, A Stranger: Adoption Breakdown and Its Effects on Parents* (Montreal: McGill–Queen's University Press, 2002), who documented the effects of adoption disruptions on white adoptive parents.

2 Joyce Ladner, *Mixed Families,* (Garden City, NY: Anchor Press/Doubleday, 1977); R. McRoy, L. Zurcher, M. Lauderdale, and R. Anderson, "Self-Esteem and Racial Identity in Transracial and Inracial Adoptees," *Social Work* 27, no. 6 (1982): 522–526; Rita Simon and Howard Altstein, *Adoption, Race, and Identity: From Infancy Through Adolescence* (New York: Praeger, 1992); K. M. DeBerry, S. Scarr, and R. Weinberg, "Family Racial Socialization and Ecological Competence: Longitudinal Assessments of African American Transracial Adoptees," *Child Development* 67, no. 5 (1996): 2375–2399.

3 Helen Noh Ahn, *Identity Development in Korean Adolescent Adoptees: Eriksonian Ego Identity and Racially Ethnic Identity* (Berkeley: University of California School of Social Welfare, 1989); Lucille J. Grow and Deborah Shapiro, *Transracial Adoption Today* (New York: Child Welfare League of America, 1974); Ruth G. McRoy and Louis A. Zurcher, Jr., *Transracial and Inracial Adoptees* (Springfield, IL: Charles C. Thomas, 1983); Rita Simon, Howard Alstein, and Marygold Melli, *The Case for Transracial Adoption* (Washington, DC: American University Press, 1994).

4 M. Sellers, "Transracial Adoption," *Child Welfare* 58, no. 6 (1969): 355–356; E. Shepherd, "Adopting Negro Children: White Families Find It Can Be Done," *New Republic*, June 1964; Rita Simon and Howard Alstein, *Transracial Adoptees and Their Families: A Study of Identity and Commitment* (New York: Praeger, 1987); Ahn, *Identity Development*; DeBerry, Scarr, and Weinberg, "Family Racial Socialization"; Ladner, *Mixed Families.*

5 John Raible, "The Significance of Racial Identity in Transracially Adopted Young Adults" (Conference of the North American Council on Adoptable Children, Washington, DC, 1990, http://www.nysccc.org).

6 Marie Adams makes a distinction between adoption disruptions and dissolutions. Disruptions are emotional, rather than legal, breaks between adoptees and parents due to the child moving out suddenly, running away, becoming incarcerated, and so on. See Adams, *Our Son.*

7 See John Raible, "Sharing the Spotlight: The Non-Adopted Siblings of Transracial Adoptees," (doctoral dissertation, University of Massachusetts at Amherst, 2005).

FROM VICTIM TO SURVIVOR

Ron McLay

the beginning of my journey

I was born at 10:40 AM on December 9, 1961, at Ross Hospital in Paisley, Scotland. My white Scottish mother was married and already had one son by her husband when she arrived at the hospital to give birth to me. She was 19 years old. My appearance as a coloured child was a shock to her husband. The social worker's notes from that time in the "Statement of Case" read:

> *Apparently the mother had allegedly been assaulted by a Pakistani who had been staying in the same lodging house. This had never been reported to police, and Mr. T. had only been informed when it was discovered that the baby was coloured. Due to the fact that the child is coloured the husband is prepared to allow his wife to return only on the condition that the baby does not accompany her.*

There was also a note: "Maybe the baby won't be so dark as his skin doesn't seem so dark today." And thus began my painful journey.

Named after my father and given my mother's surname, I was sent to Crosslet Residential Nursery, an orphanage, at five days old. When I was six months old, I was adopted by white, Scottish parents. My adoptive mother had been a nurse at the orphanage. She would often tell me that she had had a choice of me and a little girl and she chose me because I was so beautiful. She told me that all the nurses loved me and that I was special. When I was 18 months old, she gave birth to her first biological child, a son. When I was a few weeks short of nine, we emigrated to Australia. On my very first day at Gordon Public School, racism found me.

Kids called me names; after a few days this included bashings. I told my parents that kids were calling me names, and I remember my dad telling me, "Sticks and stones will break your bones but names will never hurt you." He repeated this mantra many times over the years. When I ran away from school, my adoptive father caught me. I cried and cried and pleaded with him not to send me back, because the other kids hated me and were fighting with me, but my adoptive father forced me to go back.

My schooling over the next few years usually found me the only dark-skinned person or one of very few. I cannot remember periods of time when I was not racially discriminated against in my Australian school experience. Many, many times I cried bitter tears alone at night, wishing that I could have blonde hair, fair skin, and blue eyes, and be like everyone else. I wet the bed until I was 12. The doctor told my mother it was due to anxiety from being adopted.

People were curious about my appearance, but because I am of mixed race, my honest responses were sometimes contradictory. I always longed to know where I had come from. However, when anyone asked me about it, I would say that it wasn't important, that I wasn't interested. I said this so often that I think I believed it myself for a long time. Yet at every meeting with new people, I relived shame and pain, telling them that I was actually Scottish. I would always get a look of disbelief so I would feel obligated to explain my origins as I knew them.

To add to the pain of adoption, my mother's brother (my uncle) sexually assaulted me on two occasions. When I told my adoptive parents about this, they brushed it off—it was like the racism. They didn't have the ability to cope with it.

I ran away just before my 15th birthday. When I returned after my birthday, my family had eaten my cake, thrown my birthday card away, and given my presents to my brothers. It was also at age 15 that I first tasted alcohol, and I got very drunk the first time. I drank brandy straight out of the bottle and with only one intention—to get "out of it." I was to use alcohol and drugs for the next 25 years for that express purpose—to escape my own mind.

Throughout my teens, I was lonely and rebellious, and I acted out toward my mother in particular. At one stage, she had a mental breakdown from the stress of the fights. She broke a large wooden spoon across my face and told me, "You are demon possessed and I wish that I had never adopted you." My father often tried to keep the peace; he displayed a great deal of love for me all my life. He and my mother argued about me frequently. I wonder what I would have been like without his constant love.

intimate relationships

During my first physical relationship with a woman, I started a pattern. I would begin a relationship and then begin acting crazy, deliberately saying or doing terrible things to provoke my partner. And I was obsessive about being touched. I wanted my partners to cuddle me, stroke my hair, scratch my back, and so on, constantly. For me, sex has been an affirmation of love, and refusal, a rejection.

After a series of relationships, I got married. I think I knew it was a mistake but at the time, I believed it was my last chance to be with someone.

The honeymoon was a nightmare. On our wedding night, my wife told me she didn't want to sleep with me, so I drank everything in the hotel room fridge and slept on the carpet. I had to beg her to sleep with me throughout the relationship. I felt totally rejected. Our marriage lasted four and a half months and I was drinking heavily by the end of it. I told myself I had no reason to live, that I hated myself; I wished I'd never been born. I wished that I had been aborted.

Back at my parents' place I took a packet of tranquillisers and drank a lot of alcohol. In the bush at the back of their place, I used my scuba knife to cut my wrists. I woke up in hospital. They pumped my stomach out and put more than 30 stitches in my wrists. After some time in a psychiatric ward I was released and my dad, whom I always loved a lot and who treated me as his favourite, nursed me back to health. It took a few months.

same racism, new start

Sometime later, after studying to become a stationmaster, I began working on the railways at a North Shore station. One day, I took over selling tickets for a clerk who needed a break. An elderly, well-dressed woman came up to the ticket window and asked for a return ticket. I had to search for it, as I wasn't familiar with the layout of the counter. She looked past me to the woman sitting behind me and said, referring to me, "I think that it's a disgrace that they let these Indonesians into the country when they can't even speak the language. They give them jobs and the worst thing is that my husband fought against people like him." Another time, one of my bosses on the railways called me the "black pearl" in front of the other staff. I never complained but inside I was hurting. Racism was never far away.

I met a really nice woman and married again, but after my daughter was born I felt isolated and useless. I began to have affairs. I would start an affair and then while I was seeing one woman, I would see another. My wife and I separated for 18 months, and then we started again. We were together for more than six years but there were always fights. She told me that I was very controlling and threatening. Birthdays were always difficult times for me, and I would always behave badly. My behaviour has often been very odd, even bizarre at times, and even I would wonder why I said and did things.

I didn't want the marriage to fail, and I wanted to be good, but I felt destined to follow the hard road. My wife and I officially separated, and I moved out to live by myself.

hitting bottom and recovering

My consumption of alcohol continued to increase. Soon, I was drinking every day and binging all weekend. My moods and personality began to get worse and I started fighting with my boss. One day, I had a particularly difficult situation and instead of fighting with her, I just put my hands in the air and said, "I can't take this anymore —please just sack me," and I walked out. I went on a five-day binge.

I gambled more than $3000 on poker machines. I drank bourbon straight from the bottle and flagons of sherry until I had no money left. I picked up the kitchen knife and dragged it across my wrists, wishing I had the courage to kill myself. All I thought of was destroying myself. My life seemed like a total disaster. I felt like I had no friends, no reason to live. I told people I knew they could have my possessions. I told myself that as everyone else had rejected me, I should reject myself, too.

On the fifth day I woke up with empty bottles all around me on the floor. And the kitchen knife. For some reason I cried out to God that I needed help. Then I went to the phone and called a friend. The friend took me to hospital and they in turn sent me to a private hospital to be treated for alcoholism.

I was pacing in the hospital garden when from nowhere I heard a voice saying, "You have chosen to be a victim all your life. If you hand your life over to me it will all change." I believed that it was the voice of God. I felt an intense sense of well-being and a feeling of love, like a feeling of ecstasy. I knew that I would tell the truth about where I'd been when I went back to work, and I didn't care if I lost my job or not. I believed that God would care for me. Having "alcohol dependency" written on my medical certificate would be like looking into a true mirror for the first time in my life.

In hospital we were required to "ID," which means tell our story: "Hello, I'm Ron and I'm an alcoholic…" The first few times I ID'd, I mentioned the circumstances and people in my life I believed had "caused me to drink." After reading a small book called *Alcoholism and the Family* by Dr. George Wilson, I realised I'd been deceiving myself. I was powerless over alcohol and my life was truly unmanageable. Once I realised this, my heart slowly began to change.

My IDs after this were different. I no longer spoke at length about reasons I drank. Rather, I spoke of my experiences as an alcoholic. I have wondered since which came first—the problems and circumstances or the alcohol problem. Obviously, I was adopted before I drank, but what caused the problems? I decided that for me, it was best to accept that I was an alcoholic by heritage—that is, that I was born an alcoholic. Of course, being adopted has had a devastating impact on my life, but to believe I was born an alcoholic means that I'll never be able to convince myself that I'm cured of my drinking problems.

I was pacing in the hospital garden when from nowhere I heard a voice saying, "You have chosen to be a victim all your life. If you hand your life over to me it will all change." I believed that it was the voice of God. I felt an intense sense of well-being and a feeling of love, like a feeling of ecstasy.

I knew that I would tell the truth about where I'd been when I went back to work, and I didn't care if I lost my job or not. I believed that God would care for me. Having "alcohol dependency" written on my medical certificate would be like looking into a true mirror for the first time in my life.

During the time I completed my first Fourth Step, I attended eight or so Twelve-Step meetings a week, as well as a wonderful church with real people. I also started reading books about adoption. While reading, I began to explore my feelings about being adopted and to express some very painful emotions. I even cried while explaining some of the adoption issues to my ex-wife. That was probably the first time that I had cried while sober in many, many years. I still struggled with low self-esteem and self-doubts, wondering if anyone really liked me.

When I discovered the book *Primal Wound* by Nancy Verrier, I found myself in its pages again and again. One statement I particularly identified with was that the adopted child has an identity like "Swiss cheese." My personality was a front that I had created to protect myself from further hurt; always the class clown, I had developed a very strong sense of humour. But while I laughed a lot publicly, I cried bitterly privately. I often felt that when I cried out for help, no one believed me. People couldn't tell that I was in pain because I had been hiding.

meeting my birthmother

I had wondered about my birthmother and my birthfather all my life. However, I often told people who enquired that I wasn't interested in finding them. I alternated between hating my birthmother and fantasizing about her. I am sure that I transferred my hatred of my birthmother onto my adoptive mother and that all my relationships with women have been distorted as a result.

From time to time, I wondered about my father, and I have said many times in my life that I'd like to find out about the "dark side of me." I used to call myself "the dark sheep of the family"—an intended pun on my father's racial background.

When I was 30 years old (before I began treatment for my alcoholism), I was staying for a few days in Bearsden, Glasgow, with my father's sister, whom I liked a great deal. I was about to return to Australia when I told her that I wanted to find my mother. I knew my mother's name, and that I was given the name Lal S. T. at birth. So I caught the train to Edinburgh and went to the General Registry House. I paid the fee and began my search. I felt a great deal of excitement as I searched and my head was spinning with many thoughts.

I found my mother's birth certificate and traced the beginning of a family tree. Then I discovered a cousin's marriage certificate. I found his number in the telephone book and in a state of high excitement, I called.

My cousin's wife answered. I explained who I was and that I wanted information so I could contact my mother. She said that she had the number for my older half brother, and that she would have him phone me. A few minutes later, he called. He was very emotional; he obviously knew about me. I remember feeling very strange when I asked him about "our mother." He was guarded. He told me that no one in the family had spoken to her for four years because she was an alcoholic, and briefly described the difficult and abusive life he and my other half siblings had had—a half sister and two other half brothers, one now dead.

I asked him if there was any information that he could give me that would help me find my mother. He told me that she liked drinking at a particular pub in Glasgow and that she was hanging around with a friend called John M. At around 6:30, I caught a taxi into Glasgow and went straight to the pub. I asked many people but no one had ever heard of her or John. I spent the evening going from pub to pub asking about them, getting many suspicious reactions.

The evening wore on. I started to get very despondent. I had to catch a train back to England the next day to make my flight back to Australia. I decided to give up and jumped into another cab. The taxi driver said, in a conversational way, "You're not from around here—what are you doing?" At that time I thought to be smart and say that yes, I was from around there, but instead I said I was from Australia and I was trying to find my mother. He asked me what my mother's name was and I told him. He said, "I'm sorry, I don't know her."

Almost as an afterthought, I asked him, "Do you know John M?" And he did. I said, "Can you please take me to John—I've got to go back to Australia tomorrow, and I won't have another chance." He took me to John's place, which was a tenement flat, and I knocked on the door several times. It was about 1:30 AM. John eventually came to the door, and it was obvious that he had had a big night drinking. I told him my name and started to explain my story.

He stopped me, saying, "I know all about you—your mother has talked about nothing else for 20 years. If I don't take you to your mother's place and she finds out, she'll kill me." So we walked to another tenement flat. By then it was about 2:00.

The landlord let us in and we knocked on my mother's door. She came out in a nightgown. I held my hand out and said, "Hello, I'm Ron, but you probably know me better as Lal S." She started trembling and shaking, and she fell down at my feet. She held my feet and began to cry bitterly.

She said, "Please forgive me," over and over again, her tears falling onto my shoes. I remember feeling like it was a dream—that I was having an out-of-body experience and that I was looking on.

She held me very tightly and started to talk, saying that I had been stolen from her, and that the matron at the hospital had forced her to give me up. She told me that she had never stopped thinking about me, and that she once saw a boy that she thought was me and she had followed him.

I asked her questions such as how she met my father, what he was like, and so on. I deliberately asked her about the adoption papers (which I had), which said that she had been assaulted. She said that it was not an assault but a one-night stand. She told me that she had hoped the baby was her husband's. She was shocked when I was born, and she was beaten up by two of her brothers a few days after she came home from the hospital. Even thirty years after my birth, only one uncle out of five uncles and an aunt would meet with me.

Two years later, I returned to see my mother with my wife and my daughter. My birthmother was very friendly with my wife and especially my daughter, for whom she had bought an expensive present. Unfortunately, on the third day of visiting, she had been drinking and she became very abusive to my wife. My wife and daughter left. I remained and she calmed down. I stayed in touch for a few years but then stopped writing.

finding emotional sobriety and a community of adoptees

Once I was on the path of sobriety, I began to chase emotional sobriety. I realized that I had never truly loved anyone in my life. At the time, I was incapable of love and trust. What I thought was love was me reaching out for someone to replace my missing mother—it was a very childish and immature concept of love.

While working toward emotional sobriety, I looked at my life and decided I wanted to work through all my issues—I wanted to be whole. I was very enthusiastic about this because I saw that it was possible that I could be well, that life could be wonderful and fulfilling. I wanted to explore my adoption and the sexual abuse. It turned out that my experience with psychotherapists, psychologists, and counselors was often disappointing. Yet, through one counselor, I was given the contact number of a woman who was to become a dear friend. This woman had founded the organisation ICASN (Inter Country Adoption Support Network) and she had organised a meeting of adoptees at a restaurant. I turned up at the restaurant and the journey of recovery from the wilderness of adoption and aloneness began in earnest.

Perhaps the hardest part of this adopted life has been the loneliness that it induces and the lack of people who have understood or given credence to my experience. I tried several times in my life to explain my pain and had not found an understanding person. Yet, when I joined ICASN and listened to the founder's story and talked with and observed the other adoptees, I could see that I was no longer alone. I was 39 years old and had never spoken with a group of adoptees about adoption. Suddenly I was surrounded by adoptees interested in my story! Through this woman I was able to begin a journey of healing that I had not thought possible.

healing my personal relationships

For many months in early sobriety, I was perplexed about why I still became involved in various arguments with other staff at my work. I had always struggled with needing to be right. It was a lifelong obsession about justifying my existence; losing an argument or being bettered by another person was equivalent to extinction. I also behaved in one of two ways—either being overly nice or overly aggressive and defensive. There was no middle ground. There was no normality in my relations with other people.

a new way of loving

During my second year of sobriety I read *The Road Less Traveled*. The author believes that real love is working for the spiritual growth of another person and commitment to that goal. I decided that this would be my definition of love, and it has transformed my attitude toward love. I recall that my second wife often spoke to me about love being about commitment but I just could not understand that at the time. I heard her say the words but was not able to understand her. I now practice love in my life.

Last year I returned to Scotland and England to search for my birthfather, to stay with my birthmother, and to meet some of my maternal relations for the first time. When I arrived at my mother's place, we began a process of getting to know each other. I can't say that it was easy; it was strained at times and we often became confrontational when discussing issues. My birthmother and I spent six days together without much of a break. On the seventh day she accused me of various "crimes," including leaving hair in the bath, not putting my plate away quickly enough after a meal, being a racist, and various other things. The stay with her came to an abrupt halt. At the time I felt a very intense feeling of pain—the thought that I was experiencing a second rejection flashed through my mind.

My birthmother visited my work and left a note for me that said it in part, "Don't ever come near us again in your life." Since she left me this letter, she has emailed me three times. The emails were reasonably innocuous. So what do I make of all this? I see in her behaviour the pain of her own response to the primal wound. I also see the reactive behaviour of someone who grew up in a violent, alcoholic home and was a practicing alcoholic for most of her life. She and I are so similar. I have used the same instincts in defending myself in an alien world. Yet, I choose to continue the relationship; I accept that she is not capable of change. She is my birthmother; no other can replace her. She has had a very hard life and perhaps it was the relinquishment that caused most of the pain.

I saw that my birthmother wanted to change when we both went to a postadoption service in the United Kingdom to start the search for my father and she was told that she could have counselling if she wished. She became very emotional and said that no one had ever given her a chance to talk over the events of the past.

In many respects I had overwhelmed my birthmother with my eagerness. I was trying to drag her along my path of recovery. I tried this with my adoptive mother as well, and I failed in both cases. I wouldn't say that my adoptive mother and I are the best of friends yet but I have it on my agenda to try the love thing on her; I am committed to staying in touch more often. But I have let go of trying to force my recovery on others.

integration and acceptance

One of the stranger aspects of my experience is that my upbringing had given me a "white man's mind." I thought like a white man even though I am not. I spent much of my life, from the age of nine when I first experienced racism at an Australian school, feeling shame at being half Pakistani. I am very sensitive to racism of any kind for obvious reasons, but I have had the mind-bending experience of looking at people I know to have features similar to mine and having racist thoughts about them. I had often joked to people that I'd always wished I could be a white supremacist but was the wrong colour to be one.

However, on a recent trip to the United Kingdom, I went to a Twelve-Step meeting in the midlands and was sitting in the meeting when two Indians/Pakistanis walked in. The most amazing thing happened—I felt like I was no longer the only one! As I walked in parts of Birmingham and Wolverhampton, I walked in areas where Indians and Pakistanis predominated, and I felt that I was just one of many. Another very interesting thing happened—I began to see how beautiful Indian and Pakistani women are. I have also undertaken to eat Indian or Pakistani food when I have a chance, and I wear my korta pyjamas when I eat at these restaurants.

I guess it will seem like a contradiction but I also felt shame that I was half Scottish. I would particularly feel this when asked to explain my origins. I would say that I was born in Scotland and watch the look of disbelief appear on the face of the person I was speaking with. But one of my natural uncles helped me to feel proud of my Scottish ancestry. I went on a tour of the highlands, including the home of my Scottish clan on the Isle of Skye. I found out that my ancestors, on the Scottish side, were from Viking stock. My teenaged daughter was quite happy to be a Viking, as was I!

I have taken various actions along the way to further my recovery. These include embracing my origins by wearing a bracelet bearing my Pakistani birth name, my Scottish Clan name, the name the nurses used in the orphanage for me, and my adoptive name. I have recently completed a photo shoot of myself dressed in different ways—in Pakistani korta pyjamas, Scottish trews, casual clothes, leather clothes, and without a shirt. The different dress styles represent my racial origins, my Australianness, my expressiveness, my exploratory nature, and my natural state. These five pictures will be framed in one picture frame, and I will include the words "integration" and "acceptance" at the bottom. I am also considering how I might integrate my original name and taking more pride in how I dress—to please myself. Before I stopped drinking, I couldn't even stand to look in the mirror.

My attempts to bring to light and empower the real Ron include reaching out to help others. I have joined a committee that assists adoptees and adoptive parents; I participate in service work and work for a Twelve-Step program, visiting and talking with those still suffering from active alcoholism. Of course, there are many adoptees in the program, and I have always shared very frankly when I've had a chance. At a recent meeting, three adoptees approached me after I'd shared my story. We adoptees are mostly anonymously carrying the huge burden of the "primal wound" with no relief, and if I can help in any way, I do. A friend in the program says that true humility is not to think less of yourself but to think about yourself less.

Recently, I began a process to track my birthfather down. I had wanted to find him a long time ago but I had been told that chances were very slim. However, I felt that I needed to try. At the very least, if I could definitely confirm my racial background, then I could investigate it and try to absorb some of the culture—a process I think is absolutely essential for my personal growth and future well-being. I received a letter from the West Midland Post Adoption Service a couple of days ago. Apparently they may have found my father. But that's a story for next time...

So what do I want from life, now that I have discovered it? I want to be at peace in my heart. I want to accept and love myself so that I might be capable of loving others. Onwards to life! I embrace all it has to offer.

TENDING DENIAL

Heidi Lynn Adelsman

My brother's name was Jerome and then Joemie. Mom wrote in his baby book that when she and my father adopted him they changed his name to Michael. My parents hoped to have him home by Christmas but it took four months more, until he was 18 months old. Mom says she was warned that the first month would be difficult. Although Mike was a good eater, all his food went right through him and many mornings they'd wake to the result of his nerves undone, his diaper full to overflowing. Since she couldn't nurse him, Mom rocked him to sleep nightly, singing *Michael Row the Boat Ashore, Hallelujah.* We were his fifth home and he wasn't yet two years old. I was five.

"Why did your parents adopt (transracially)?" people ask. As an employee of St. Paul Court Services in the mid-1960s, Mom saw a disproportionate number of Black children on the county adoption list. She and my dad talked it over and decided to adopt. Less than three years later they divorced.

In 1969 the Minneapolis Public School Board was debating desegregation and busing. They proposed that two schools in our neighborhood "pair," equally dividing the grades and busing the children between the two schools. Due to segregated housing patterns in Minneapolis, our nearly all white school was just 15 blocks away from another school that was 54 percent Black, when less than 10 percent of the children in the Minneapolis Public Schools were children of color. There was great resistance to the proposed busing in our neighborhood. Mom supported it publicly and that was when the harassment began.

At the podium at Hale School Mom spoke out for Minnesota's first attempt at busing. Adults in the audience jeered, "She's the one with the little nigger baby." When my two younger brothers and I left for school in the morning more than one stalker called to say, "I see your little nigger baby at the bus stop." When Mom arrived home, another caller noted where she had been and with whom. She reported it to the police, she tells me today, but they never discovered who the callers were. I remember little but there was one call I never forgot. Mom tried to protect us.

⁂

The foul ringing of the phone wakes me at 4 AM. Mom rises and I hear her king-size bed groan from her departure. The narrow floorboards creak as she walks to where the rotary-dial phone sits on the ledge above the stairs. I hear her say a muffled hello. I lie in my lower bunk, in my bedroom alone, wrapped up and warm in my bedding. A dim light glows from the bathroom further down the hall. I hold my breath. She does not scream "Leave me alone!" into the phone. She responds so quietly I can't hear her, then hangs up the phone and sighs discreetly. I lie in my bed hoping to drift off, reassured, into the safe place of sleep, hoping to hear her lie back down in her bed.

Instead the closet door hinges give as she reaches in and takes out her bathrobe in the darkness. I hear it brush against the belts and scarves hanging neatly on the door. Her hushed feet pass by my room, and I can see her grab hold of the wrought iron handrail and lean onto it for support as she goes downstairs for a cigarette, a cloudy reprieve.

ꟾ ꟾ ꟾ

I remembered the phone call as if it were a nightmare, a nightmare we wouldn't normally discuss. But that one call we did talk about when I was a kid. It was from a man who threatened to break into our home in the middle of the night. Mom only had to tell me once for me to remember forever what he said: "I'm coming in your basement window."

She had hung up on him, but not without saying, "The hell you are, bastard." She told me this boldly, as if to convince us both that she wasn't worried, that she had it under control. But even at eight there was no misinterpreting her lucid fear, no matter how tough my Mom tried to be. Listening for a noise from the basement, I could imagine her lying in her bed trying to silence the pounding explosion within her chest. The next morning, as if it were just another day, we all left for school or work, relieved for the routine events of our lives.

The man Mom was dating was called, too. He was told, "Go to the hospital right now, your girlfriend has had a terrible accident." Lies. Another time the phone rang immediately after he'd walked into his apartment. After one dinner with Mom, someone called him to say, "Look out the window at your car in the parking lot." His car was on fire—it had been fire-bombed, torched.

ꟾ ꟾ ꟾ

My brother's birthfather was African American and his mother was white, and that's what my parents wanted. Mom tried to support Mike's racial identity, affirm that it included both races, that he was white too, that he was biracial. She had his birth record that showed that his mother was Irish and Scottish. Mike's birthmother said she didn't know his father's name but she loved him.

We fully recognize the phenomenon of transracial adoption as an expedient for white folk, not as an altruistic humane concern for black children. The supply of white children for adoption has all but vanished and adoption agencies, having always catered to middle class whites developed an answer to their desire for parenthood by motivating them to consider black children. This has brought about a re-definition of some black children. Those born of black-white alliances are no longer black as decreed by immutable law and social custom for centuries. They are now black-white, inter-racial, bi-racial, emphasizing the whiteness as the adoptable quality; a further subtle, but vicious design to further diminish black and accentuate white. We resent this high-handed arrogance and are insulted by this further assignment of chattel status to black people.

—The National Association of Black Social Workers, 1972

No doubt we talked about race when Mike was first adopted. Children speak their curiosity. But I don't remember conversations on racism. My parents grew up in rural Minnesota and admit they were naïve about race and racism. As little children we had no consistent adults of color in our life to help define our world.

In our society, the developmental needs of Black children are significantly different from those of white children. Black children are taught, from an early age, highly sophisticated coping techniques to deal with racist practices perpetrated by individuals and institutions. These coping techniques become successfully integrated into ego functions and can be incorporated only through the process of developing positive identification with significant black others.

—The National Association of Black Social Workers, 1972

When my parents bought their first home in 1964 it had a racially restrictive covenant in the deed saying no one other than members of the "Caucasian race" could own the home. Such covenants were federally banned in 1948, yet our neighborhood remained largely segregated. Our family had no words to name our everyday emotional struggles connected with race privilege and discrimination, both blatant and subtle. Within our family, in our neighborhood, and institutionally, Mike lived the kind of racism many white people puzzle over in hindsight—"we just didn't know."

In school, our textbooks presented history with no reference to the achievements made by people of color; at stores, what was available were white-race-only greeting cards and bandages in "flesh tone." White privilege maintained access to good schools, job referral networks, and inherited property values—in part the legacy of racially restrictive covenants and the Homestead Act.

Mike garnered a good deal of attention for being "different" and "cute." And while we knew some other adopted biracial children, there were no adults of color consistently in our life, no Black men. Mike had no reference for his racial identity. And any good intentions our family had were countered by the systemic racism that surrounded us and that we still live with.

ᘏ ᘏ ᘏ

As kids, my brothers were best buddies. They scared Mom by sleeping in the tub where she couldn't find them. They fought in the third bench seat of our Country Squire station wagon while I reported the events to Mom from the middle. For a time she could keep track of us all. By adopting she hoped to make a difference in the life of a child. That was what she wanted. But it worked out so badly that today Mom says, "For much of your childhood, I remember little of the life of two out of three of my children."

Our playground, a length along the Minnehaha creek in Minneapolis, was all ours before the asphalt trails brought the public in on bike and walking paths. We played kick-the-can in alleys and came for dinner when Mom called. Until Mike didn't come home one day. Dinners went bad. I ate after school and when it was time for dinner I wasn't hungry. After all the harassment, after he'd started skipping school, it felt like our family was falling apart. I couldn't blame Mike. He said he felt out of place. He didn't fit in our mostly white neighborhood anymore. But I sure missed my little brother. I wanted us to grow up together, to ride our bikes and swim again at Lake Nokomis, to play at the creek.

After the divorce Dad would take us on Saturdays to the old St. Paul Science Museum or Mariucchi Arena at the University of Minnesota. The music echoed in the high-ceilinged sports arena. Skating in the old rink we could imagine the fans in the bleachers cheering wildly. We laced our rented skates on the sticky benches in the warming area. A guardrail that came up to our shoulders gave us the support on the ice that we needed at the beginning of the season, when we might fall.

Mike made friends with a college student looking to "help out." Round and round they went, holding hands and laughing. I sat in the bleachers watching them. He knew how to skate but she helped him anyway. Was he helping her or was she helping him?

The attention Mike got from strangers was unnatural and confusing. Mike had an ominous tendency to make friends quickly—too quickly. He was known throughout our neighborhood. One neighbor said he didn't even know I had another brother. Before he was five Mike would run so far from home our parents panicked. They tied him in the backyard, my dad tells me.

Mike tested well in school but he couldn't focus. He was labeled with diagnoses that stacked up against him—ADD, EBD, FAS, and RAD (Attention

Deficit Disorder, Emotional Behavior Disorder, Fetal Alcohol Syndrome, Reactive Attachment Disorder). At 12 years old, Mike began running away from home for days at a time. It was the beginning of the end of our living together. Mom never knew when she would have to travel in the middle of the night to pick him up. Police, hospitals, and individuals called to report on how he had stolen, wounded, or acted in such a way that he was a threat to himself and others. He lied to Mom. Aging into a young man, Mike had few skills for negotiating his identity; his foundation was shaky.

There were times before bed when Mom would drink. I tried not to talk about what mattered. "We went to counseling if Mike didn't run away before we got there," she recalls. Always waiting for the next call or knock at the door. One counselor told her, "Keep him out; we know he's been violent with women—he hates women from hating his birthmother." Another psychiatrist said, "He never adopted you so get on with your life."

At school, in treatment programs, and in jail, he was famous for being charming—at first. Then the switchblades, the erratic behavior, the abuse came out. "I need to come home, I need money," he called over and over to say. Then he ran, with cash from Mom's purse, with her credit cards. He stole Mom's car and broke into our house when we weren't home, pinching personal items, knives, and more. And so it went for the better part of his young adult life, the calls and the not knowing where he was or even if he was alive.

⊓ ⊓ ⊓

In 1987 Dr. Keith Henry called from Regions Hospital to tell Mom Mike had AIDS. He had contracted pneumonia in prison and was hospitalized. That's where they discovered it. When Mom went to see him there was no guard on duty, so Mike was in a locked hospital unit. Mom couldn't get to him to comfort him or talk with him. But there was a window. She stood outside looking at him looking at her, both crying. It seemed familiar, the window, the wall. It was a metaphor for our lives together.

Growing up with Mike, I witnessed his life of slow death. I saw how he was harmed and went harming. How he was robbed and went robbing. He said this himself, when we sat together on the couch one night watching music videos, shortly before he died: "I've never really let anyone love me."

⊓ ⊓ ⊓

At 28 years old, Mike can no longer inhale from the cigarette he holds in his slim fingers with long nails. His distorted lips won't form a seal tight enough around it. A tumor grows around his mouth, an AIDS-related lymphoma. Trying to hold onto a little pleasure he takes a drag, inhaling more air than smoke.

Together we sit in the dim haze of the smoking room. It's sleeting and dark outside, which helps. This way I can't see the smoke magnified by the sun. The green vinyl chairs we sit in have generous armrests. They're the kind of chair that can be wiped down easily. The wall tile is intentionally yellow. Veterans, the mentally ill, the terminally ill are housed in this nursing home where everyone seems yellow. Sitting in chairs around us others smoke, staring into space. Past crises or poor health have led them to this dying place, too.

"What are you listening to these days?" my brother asks. We like some of the same music. When I came tonight I found him in the smoking room, listening to his Walkman. He took off the headphones as I walked in. "I made this for you," he says and hands me a cassette tape he made from the radio.

"Thanks sweetie," I say, kissing him on the cheek.

The tumor consumes his face from the left side of his lips, up and over his nose. It creeps insidiously toward his eye, again. Not for the first or even second time.

Trying to maintain some semblance of normal life, we had gone to buy shoes at the Foot Locker downtown. It was a bad idea. "I hate going out in public. Everyone stares," he said that day. I saw it. We saw it together. The tumor was gruesome enough to compel stares. "I know," I said holding his hand, "But you're still handsome to me."

Being with him in public jolted my memory. I can still see the many relatives and nameless adults in the late 1960s who towered over us kids, commenting, "Oh, isn't he cute." I thought we got so much attention from the white people around us because Mike's skin was darker than mine, because we were a different kind of family, and maybe because my mom was single. I got sick of the attention. Maybe I felt some of the pity adults express still today regarding "those poor children from broken and/or racially mixed homes."

Now Mike had had so much radiation his jawbone and teeth were beginning to melt. The doctor said no more. It was late October 1993.

Mike held on through Christmas and New Year's. Mom and I took turns visiting Mike in the nursing home. "Here you go," I said, sitting on his bed and showing him the Tevin Campbell CD he had no strength to open. We tried to smile.

A week later he couldn't or wouldn't open his eyes. Holding his hand I told him, "It's okay to go." He didn't open his eyes, but he cried. We cried together. Within a day he passed. But the night before he died he appeared to me in a dream, the tumor gone from his sweet lovely face.

Tracey Moffatt, *Night Cries—A Rural Tragedy,* 1989, 17 minute short film (still). 35mm film, Dolby sound, screening format DVD

22 PERFORMING CHILDHOOD

Rachel Quy Collier

I write this chapter as a response to an ethnographic work published in 1978 by anthropologist Myra Bluebond-Langner. *The Private Worlds of Dying Children* explores the last months of children dying of leukemia and highlights a particularly poignant facet of their relationships with their parents, which resonates with my own experience of adoption.

> Mutual pretense ... was the dominant mode of interaction between the terminally ill and those that attended them, because it offered individuals a way to do what society expected of them. It enabled them to fulfill various social roles and responsibilities necessary for maintaining membership in the society in the face of a threat to continued membership.... The practice of mutual pretense allowed [the children] to act as if they had a future, to act like children. By following the rules necessary for maintaining mutual pretense, they showed themselves responsive to the needs of others. The rewards for such behavior were great. They gained a sense of achievement, satisfaction, and worth in their own eyes and in the eyes of their caretakers (parents and medical staff). By reinforcing the adults' hopes, the children thereby guaranteed their continued presence. They were not left alone.
>
> The children's practice of mutual pretense allowed the caretakers to play their reciprocal roles....
>
> In essence, mutual pretense is the individual's attempt to maintain the social order.... The social order is a moral order. Individuals will go to great lengths to maintain it. For to violate it, to break the rules necessary for maintenance, is to risk exclusion and abandonment, "a fate worse than death itself." The practice of mutual pretense reflects a human dilemma far more fundamental than the fear of "breaking a taboo"—the existential dilemma.[1]

Bluebond-Langner's work illustrates a tragedy that is particularly compelling for me: children caught in an invisible yet strong net of denial and nonacceptance, dying, yet forced to play out a fictive role in order to enable those upon whom they depend for life, however brief, to enjoy their self-appointed roles as caregivers. The primal fear of abandonment imprisons the children; their fear of rejection prevents them from expressing what they know to be true: they are dying. The sacrificial nature of childhood is terribly evident: children exist so that parents, doctors, and other caregivers can act and identify themselves as nurturers, protectors, benefactors. The paradox is that once the children recognize their importance to their parents and other caregivers and decide to maintain the pretense, they become protectors themselves and an ironic role reversal is effected. Who is needy, who gives? The parents and doctors in Bluebond-Langner's study are depicted as caring, or attempting to care, for the children in primarily physical terms, while they are less aware and even neglectful of the children's psychic and emotional well-being; conversely, the children are uncannily aware of their parents' and doctors' emotional and psychological needs. Children's fear of physical abandonment by adults on whom they vitally depend binds them to the implicit agreement not to admit the truth of their mortality. Adults' fragility and neediness can imprison their dependent children.

Children are "willful, purposeful individuals capable of creating their own world," but they are forced by their status as dependents to act "in the world others create for them" (7). This is particularly true for those who never live to become adults and therefore never gain autonomy or independence, like the terminally ill in Bluebond-Langner's study; however, it applies to all children. For children adopted out of one context and into another, the fact that children are by definition made to enter into, survive, and thrive in worlds created by others has a unique relevance. A child born into the "Third World," war, poverty, or some other socially undesirable situation and "relinquished" by an individual or individuals upon whom she originally depends—birthparents, grandparents, neighbors—into a context in which she is available for adoption is cast into the precarious situation described by Bluebond-Langner whereby fear of abandonment, which has in this case actually occurred, could bind the child to act toward whomever takes the place of the original caregivers in order to avoid suffering a second rejection. (Later, the older adoptee may intellectually accept that myriad factors contributed to her "relinquishment" and it is impossible to judge the letting go as a deliberate rejection, but this will be understood psychically and emotionally only with great difficulty.)

> One of the dualities of adoption is the declaration that love means letting go. Women considering adoption are told that if they really love their child, they will release them for adoption. Adoptees are told that their birthmothers loved them so much that they gave them up for adoption. Logically, it does not make sense to believe that if you really love someone, you will stop having a relationship with them. Emotionally, it is what people need to participate in adoption. It becomes clear why love and abandonment can be so closely tied for triad members [adoptees, birthparents, and adoptive parents].[2]

No individual has control over her conception, birth, and subsequent socialization. For an adoptee, this lack of control is intensified by the fact that biological destination (or destiny) differs radically—especially in the case of international adoption—from adopted destination (or destiny). Inherent in what I call the adoption myth is the notion that the adopted life is superior to the original life, whether from an economic, health, educational, cultural, spiritual, religious, or other perspective. Because of this assumption on the part of caregivers (who would not involve themselves in the process of adoption if they did not believe in this crucial tenet) at every stage in the adoption, the adoptee is often bound into a kind of mutual pretense, a denial of the importance of what was lost or taken away. The adoptee, like the children in Bluebond-Langner's study, depends critically on her acceptance by the adoptive parents and society; because of her original abandonment, she does not enjoy the security of guaranteed and everlasting acceptance, no matter how loving and reassuring her adoptive parents. She may feel that behavior perceived as negative by her adopted caregivers will result in permanent banishment. In rearing children, parents often punish "bad" behavior with temporary removal, physical or verbal rebukes, or denial of privileges, all of which could combine to feed the fear of the worst: permanent abandonment. After all, the child may have been told that she was "chosen" by her adoptive parents for a variety of reasons that she cannot comprehend; she could deduce from the positive rewards she receives for good behavior that she was "rejected" by her original family for some original or inherent "badness" and chosen by her adopted family for some opposing, and equally mysterious, "goodness" (or for more superficial qualities over which she has had no control such as gender, age at time of availability for adoption, physical appearance, health). She may not understand that her relinquishment and adoption are not based on anything she is or has done, but rather reflect the needs of her original and adopted families and their social contexts.

Bluebond-Langner's study highlights the various ways families deal with their dying children's illnesses. "Mary's" family denied her the name of her disease, the company of other children suffering from the same sickness, and the truth that she would die. Other families allowed their children to say "leukemia" and socialize with other leukemic children, but none fully accepted the children's mortality. Likewise, adoptive families may to varying degrees admit or deny the pain—of the adoptee primarily, and of the parents who had to give up their child secondarily—hidden beneath the joy of adoption.

Adoption is generally viewed by those in the industry and by adoptive parents as a positive solution to dire circumstances for everyone: the parent or parents who could not support a child because of poverty, war, and so on, find a physically safe, economically secure, and loving home for their child; parents who have the physical and emotional resources to raise a child now

A child must be a child; a parent must be a parent; a doctor, a doctor. Furthermore, an adult member of society must also be "successful," profit from and contribute to the world in ways that are materially, financially measured. Many adoptees feel the double burden of becoming successful adults as a way to "make good on" the investments their parents, caregivers, and society in general have made on their behalf. The challenge I have felt as an adult is to shed the burden of obligation to my past and to realize that those who have helped me have done so out of motives that were never purely altruistic or unselfish. As a former humanitarian aid worker, I recognize that my work with orphaned and poor children did more for me than I perhaps gave to them—at least, what I gave them and what they gave me cannot be properly compared. Both parties gave and received, but the gifts were vastly different.

Society has its obligations from which, perhaps, we can never truly be free. As Bluebond-Langner says, "The funeral is for the living, and so is the dying. The way we are permitted to die, and the way that we permit others to die, is to enable the living to continue the process of their lives" (233); "one dies as a member of society, linked to other individuals [parents, caregivers, medical staff]. Often these individuals' needs are conflicting" (235). Society demands that its members engage in rituals. I believe that the funeral rite permits the grieving to comprehend that the loved one has died and that it is not in itself beneficial to the dead. Likewise, the marriage rite often permits communities to comprehend the bonds of love and commitment made by two of their members. I have deeply ambivalent and anxious feelings when I am required to engage in public rituals, such as my upcoming wedding, that make public what to me are profoundly private experiences, perhaps because I was denied the opportunity to enact the role of grieving child of my biological parents, who are dead to me, and whom I still mourn;[4] perhaps because I have only begun to perceive myself as an autonomous individual who does not exist primarily to fulfill the needs of others. I suppose that this last sentiment is not limited to adoptees. However, adoptees, like all people, begin their lives in a world in which they are malleable, controllable, and utterly dependent.

In literature, the Orphan (who is implicitly a child) is often someone upon whom anyone can inscribe or project what he will, an undefined space where there exist no solid definitions or boundaries such as those derived from biological origin, which often is seen to determine identity and fate. The Orphan is the unknown Other, a blank page. An adopted child can be appropriated, assimilated, made into the image and likeness of her parents and society. She is given a (new) name, language, religion, cosmology, worldview; she is, in a sense, colonized—for her own good, out of love. The demands of living in a society that requires so much can be tiring.

> Some adoptees describe being alone as a safe place for them. When adoptees are alone, they feel there are no expectations or demands on them. For adoptees who feel they have to act or be a certain way to receive love or approval, being alone can feel like a safe haven where they can truly be themselves.[5]

Perhaps since the time of Bluebond-Langner's study there has been a change in the way dying children are treated by medical professionals and parents. I imagine an ideal parent who can tell his child, "Your *body* is ill, it will not heal, it will stop working, but when it finally ceases to function, *you* will transform into something else—a cloud, a butterfly, a drop of rain—to experience another life free from the pain of your present body. I am sad because I love you and want you to remain on earth with me, as my child, but it is not in my control, and I must accept that. Now let us prepare you to leave your body and become something else." My ideal parent differentiates between the fragile and temporary human body and the Self; he asks his ill child, "How does your body feel? And how do *you* feel?" He does not demand that his child perform an act of denial in order to feel better himself; he does not feel denied of his rights as a parent to enjoy the satisfaction that comes from nurturing, protecting, and caring for a dependent being. His love is not self-serving; he knows that the child does not exist to please or glorify him, but to experience the world for however brief a time. He does not demand a living child in return for his investment of love. He can let go.

Ultimately, as Russell says, "An adoptive family should not try to be what it is not—a biological family. This is not to say that an adoptive family is less than a biological family. It is just different."[6] The difference is that someone, something, is missing. I feel that a biological family, in all its imperfections, is whole in a way that an adoptive family is not. For me, having had to pretend that all was well and that the love of my adoptive family could erase or render less significant the missing people and culture is similar to the dying child being forced to pretend he is not dying.

notes

1 Myra Bluebond-Langner, *The Private Worlds of Dying Children* (Princeton, NJ: Princeton University Press, 1978), 228–230. Subsequent citations appear in the text.

2 Marlou Russell, *Adoption Wisdom: A Guide to the Issues and Feelings of Adoption* (Santa Monica, CA: Broken Branch Productions, 1996), 62.

3 Russell, *Adoption Wisdom,* 46.

4 Russell writes, "Grieving in adoption is different in some distinct ways from mourning the death of someone who has died. When someone dies, there is a definite ending that allows grieving to begin. In adoption, there is no death, no ending. In adoption, a state of limbo exists that is similar to the dynamics of mourning someone who is missing in action." *Adoption Wisdom,* 46.

5 Russell, *Adoption Wisdom,* 71.

6 Russell, *Adoption Wisdom,* 50.

PART FIVE

JOURNEYS HOME?

An image can be a destination.

Case No. KL-2869

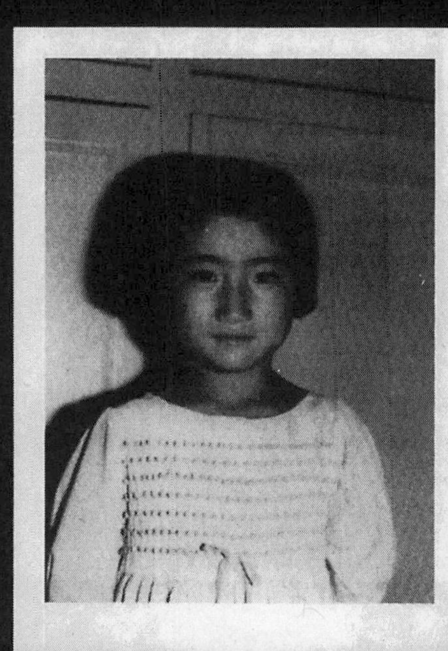

Every journey leads somewhere. Sometimes that place is an image. In its details, we can find answers we seek, even if they weren't the ones we expected.

This year, my journey took me to Korea, where I spent the first nine years of my life. I had questions — a lot of them. While I found no story that could explain everything, I found two images, the *only* images from that time.

In these pictures the messages said "Ahn-nyeong" (hello), goodbye, and all the words that couldn't be spoken.

Design: Laura Gannarelli

23 WHAT LIES BENEATH

Reframing Daughter from Danang

Gregory Paul Choy & Catherine Ceniza Choy

The original premise of the critically acclaimed documentary film *Daughter from Danang* is that complex layers of identity, family, and history lie beneath the surface of an "all-American" identity.[1] One would be hard-pressed to guess that seemingly all-American girl Heidi Bub, who hails from small-town Pulaski, Tennessee, and speaks with a thick southern accent, was born Mai Thi Hiep in Danang, Vietnam, in 1968. At that time, Amerasian children like Hiep, who was born to a US serviceman and a Vietnamese woman, encountered social ostracism and the threat of physical violence because of their mixed-race origins. Fearing for her daughter's safety, Mai Thi Kim sent seven-year-old Hiep overseas in 1975 through "Operation Babylift," a Ford administration plan that relocated Vietnamese children to the United States, Canada, Europe, and Australia for adoption. [See Chapter 27 for more on Operation Babylift—Ed.]

Upon Hiep's arrival in the United States, Ann Neville, a single white woman, adopted her and renamed her Heidi. Back home in Pulaski, Tennessee—birthplace of the Ku Klux Klan—Ann warned Heidi not to tell anyone that she was from Vietnam. Heidi became increasingly estranged from her adoptive mother and started searching for her birth family. On the other side of the Pacific Ocean in Vietnam, her birthmother was also trying to locate and make contact with Heidi. With help from the Internet and journalist Tran Truong Nhu, Heidi and Kim found one another in 1996. The following year, Heidi returned to Vietnam for the first time since her adoption in order to reunite with her birthmother and siblings.[2]

Their emotionally laden reunion is the main subject of *Daughter from Danang*. The documentary film takes viewers on a journey that begins with the expectation of a happy family reunion but continues with tension-filled cultural clashes replacing the joyful initial encounters. Heidi seeks the unconditional love and acceptance of her birthmother but feels increasingly stifled by Kim's constant displays of affection. Heidi's half-siblings and Kim express their expectation that Heidi start helping her Vietnamese family financially and are surprised when Heidi is overwhelmed, uncomfortable, and disappointed by their requests for monetary support. In a highly emotional scene, Heidi claims that she wishes this trip had never happened, that she had never returned to Vietnam. Upon her return to the United States, Heidi expresses ambivalence about her reunion and the Vietnamese side of her family. At the film's end, she concludes that, for the time being, though she has "closed the door" on that part of her family life, she has not locked it.

Since its release in 2002 *Daughter from Danang* has received much critical acclaim. It has earned eight awards and honors from film festivals throughout the United States. It was an Academy Award–nominee for Best Documentary Feature. On the film's official website, the featured reviews and blurbs discuss the film's significance in terms of its engagement of the broad topics of culture clash, family drama, and war casualties. The film has since garnered an even wider audience through its broadcast on the PBS program *American Experience.* And it is the impressive PBS educational website related to the film that begins to reframe *Daughter from Danang* as an important film about adoption.[3] For example, the website features a timeline on the history of adoption and links to online adoption resources.

While the notion that *Daughter from Danang* is a film about adoption might seem obvious, filmmakers Dolgin and Franco have confessed to having, then and now, virtually no knowledge about international, transracial adoption or familiarity with the growing body of published adoptee narratives.[4] After the screening of *Daughter from Danang* as a featured selection of the New Directors/New Films series in New York City in 2002, Dolgin and Franco emphasized the film's message about the persistence of the wounds of war in Vietnam as well as in the United States but did not mention the important role that Asian international adoption plays in that unequal geopolitical and social reality.

Our research about the film has revealed that many film reviews also overlook the relationship of *Daughter from Danang* to adoption studies.[5] Thus, the major objective of this critique is to situate *Daughter from Danang* within the emergent interdisciplinary and multidisciplinary field of adoption studies and evaluate the film according to the theoretical underpinnings of the newest branch of that field—that of adoptee-generated research and cultural production.[6] What contributions does the film make to this growing area of study? How might knowledge and inclusion of the collective experiences of international and transracial adoptees have transformed the film?

We argue that though the beginning of the film underscores the unequal political, social, and economic contexts of international adoption, challenging the popular conceptualization of this phenomenon as primarily humanitarian rescue and colorblind love, these critical interventions become lost as the film continues. Its narrative shifts away from discussions of the *collective* history of international adoption (a history greatly informed by US military interests but popularly framed as humanitarian rescue) and instead foregrounds an *individual* West-meets-East story of culture clash, facilitated by Heidi Bub's "ugly American" naïveté. As a result, the long-term effects of war become overshadowed by Heidi's emotional breakdown at the climax of the film, a breakdown that can be and has been interpreted as indicative of her individual immaturity and ignorance. Thus, despite their good intentions, the filmmakers' success comes at the expense of Heidi's integrity.

Finally, we argue that while the filmmakers intended to critique the ongoing impact of the Vietnam War in both Vietnam and the United States, *Daughter from Danang* inadvertently perpetuates the violence of war through the exclusion and silencing of adoptees' agency and subjectivity. By "adoptees' agency and subjectivity," we mean the ability of adoptees to act and to impact the world around them as well as the ways that adoptees' experiences and their interpretations of these experiences *should* matter to all of us connected to this phenomenon (even those of us who may be connected solely by the viewing of a film about adoption). Rather than pay close and more humane attention to the reasons behind Heidi's highly emotional desires to return to Vietnam and reunite with her birth family, the filmmakers script Heidi as a simpleton who is not a historical agent of her own life, but rather someone who is acted upon. Furthermore everyone around Heidi (including the viewers of the film) seems more knowledgeable than she does about the climactic cultural clash. Thus, we conclude that the film accomplishes the opposite of what the filmmakers intended it to do. Although they intended to illuminate and critique how the politics of the Vietnam War continue in more contemporary times, they inadvertently perpetuate a key aspect of the violence of war—specifically, the objectification, infantilization, and dehumanization of Asian adoptees in the United States—through the film.

the unforeseeable problems of outsiders within

Near the beginning of Dolgin and Franco's Oscar-nominated documentary, a newspaper clipping from *The Columbus Record* in South Carolina is shown briefly, announcing the adoption of six-year-old Mai Thi Hiep, renamed Heidi, by Ann Neville.

> Ann Neville, single, has just adopted a beautiful six-year old Vietnamese orphan. It may seem like an unlikely combination and, at first, it was almost an impossible one. But now they are together and Ann doesn't foresee any problems for the two of them.

The profile reflects one popular understanding of Asian international adoption as a story of humanitarian rescue (i.e., American mother saves an orphaned Amerasian child from a life of dire poverty and physical abuse through the act of adoption). The profile's appearance is preceded in the documentary by film footage of Operation Babylift, a US governmental plan that involved American aid workers coaxing Vietnamese mothers to give up their children so that Americans could make "good homes" for them. The footage of one US aid worker's shameless solicitations for Vietnamese children ("I can take your children and send them to America and it's better for everyone") is especially discomforting and directly counters the representation of Operation Babylift as solely or even primarily humanitarian. The film critically notes that the Ford administration initiative was used to garner American public sympathy for an increasingly unpopular war as well as more funding for the war effort. The history of the US government's subversive military involvement in foreign countries, particularly Vietnam and Cuba, is what Dolgin and Franco have spent their careers documenting and at the beginning of *Daughter from Danang,* they continue to do so effectively.

Operation Babylift has always been controversial.[7] On April 4, 1975, a military transport plane associated with this "rescue" effort crashed, killing more than 100 children and at least 25 of the adult escorts on board. And although the Vietnamese children of Operation Babylift were labeled orphans, many of them were children with parents still alive in Vietnam. Upon arrival in the United States, many of these "orphans," including Heidi, talked about their families in Vietnam. As Heidi recollects in the film, "I used to ask [my adoptive mother Ann] for my mother and I would cry and cry and cry."

The US military context is important for understanding some of the macro-level dimensions of Asian international adoption; the beginning of *Daughter from Danang* adds an important micro-level dimension as well. As a mixed-race Amerasian adoptee in Pulaski, Tennessee, Heidi is an "outsider within" the black and white racial dynamics that dominate the American South. Adoptive mother Ann compels Heidi to remake herself to fit into the "white" side of this racial binary. Heidi says that Ann attempted to make her as "American" (i.e. white) as possible so that Heidi would pass an as American "with a sun tan." Heidi continued that Ann told her not to tell anyone that she was Vietnamese and to say that she was born in Columbia, South Carolina. Heidi's uncle also appears in the film, confessing that Ann was "a screamer and a hitter," alluding to the physical abuse Heidi endured at the hands of her adoptive mother. Thus, while Asian international adoption was popularly conceived as a more humane alternative to the threat of violence faced by Amerasians in Vietnam, and although poverty and violence in Vietnam were indeed real problems there, violence against Amerasian adoptees in the United States was also perpetuated through these demands for assimilation—these forced erasures and denials of formative aspects of adoptees' lives that are tantamount to emotional abuse—and through, in some cases, physical abuse.

According to the newspaper profile, Heidi's adoptive mother didn't "foresee any problems for the two of them," but these "unforeseeable problems" did come, indeed, and at a great price: Heidi's physical and emotional abuse and subsequent depression. Heidi relates that she felt she had to choose between her adoptive mother and other people who mattered in her life such as her birthmother and her friends. She had to be "all of [Ann's] or none at all," and when she could not fulfill Ann's ultimatum, they became estranged. "I've always wanted the feeling that somebody would love me no matter what," Heidi says while reflecting upon the very difficult years with her adoptive mother while she was in college. Heidi continued that Ann "told me that I owed her for the life she had given me." Note the violence informing this observation: the "life Ann had given her" was made possible by the end of Heidi's life in Vietnam.

Thus, film viewers learn that the "unlikely combination" between Heidi and her adoptive mother has since transformed into an "impossible combination." And Heidi painfully reflects upon how she has "lost two mothers." Taken together with the filmmakers' project of exposing the fallacies of war, the newspaper clipping's false foreshadowing of the failed adoption relationship reveals that humanitarian rescue through warfare is an "impossible combination."

Unfortunately, the important observations embedded in these beginning parts of the film remain undeveloped and, even worse, become overshadowed and forgotten as the film begins to chronicle Heidi's "joyous" reunion with her birth family in Vietnam. "It's going to be healing," Heidi says. "It's going to make those bad feelings go away." The main subject of *Daughter from Danang* truly begins where the newspaper profile ends, that is, with unforeseeable problems.

the not-so-innocent politics of filmmaking

In interviews, both filmmakers confess to having virtually no familiarity with international and transracial adoption, and thus claim not to have known what to expect in documenting Heidi's reunion with her birthmother, Mai Thi Kim. They admit to expectations that are more informed by a rhetoric of salvation and happy endings. "We went expecting to film a wonderfully joyous, healing reunion," Dolgin says.[8] Similarly Franco maintains that he and Dolgin expected "a simple celebration between mother and daughter."[9] Franco continues, "I knew so little about the Babylift situation that I didn't have preconceived ideas."[10] One begins to wonder, then, what could possibly have interested these filmmakers in expending the time, money, and effort to document Heidi's reunion. As the film progresses, this question leads to other critical questions about *Daughter from Danang.*

One of the most obvious questions is why the filmmakers didn't educate themselves about international and transracial adoption in the United States. Since the film begins with an appreciable amount of footage about the controversial Operation Babylift and about adoptive mother Ann's attempts to stifle any reference to Heidi's biraciality and Vietnamese origins, viewers are led to expect that Dolgin and Franco will continue to shed light on the phenomenon of Asian international adoption, which is an under-publicized ramification of the war. Such expectations are frustrated, however. Instead, a strange break occurs after the international and transracial adoption history is presented in the first half of the film—it is completely neglected in the second, with the documentary focusing instead on the dissipation of Heidi's happy reunion. What might have been an enlightening and insightful glimpse into the ways in which being an international, transracial adoptee has played a formative part in Heidi's feeling "a hundred and one percent Americanized" instead serves as perfunctory, and then forgotten, background to a personal drama.

As J. Hoberman wrote in a *Village Voice* review, "Whatever heartwarming scene the impressively discreet filmmakers may have expected to record with their mini DV, they show a remarkable ability to document both sides of this emotional car-wreck."[11] Ensconced in the context of documentary filmmaking, Dolgin and Franco claim to have had few, if any, directorial intentions when letting the cameras roll during the emotional and frustrating periods of Heidi's interactions with her family. Their seemingly innocent and objective stance regarding this development in the film is similar to the illusion of reality TV in the sense that whatever happens happens and will be naturally framed by the camera. As Dolgin explains, "It was not at all what we anticipated and we had to be there, moving along with it, as it revealed itself. It became far more complex than I think either of us anticipated." Franco adds, "As documentary filmmakers, we always have to do that. You can't have a preconceived notion of what you're going to be doing."[12] Dolgin and Franco would seem to have us believe that Heidi's story tells itself through the camera's eye alone.

Yet, to the contrary, in *Daughter from Danang* Heidi Bub is almost as scripted a character as one actually reading from a script. As much and as often as we hear Heidi's voice-over foregrounding, foreshadowing, and giving personal accounts of the events in the documentary, the storytellers behind Heidi's voice-overs are indeed Dolgin and Franco. While they claim not to have had a story in mind beyond a simple happy reunion of mother and daughter, their postdocumentary comments reveal otherwise. In one interview, Franco and Dolgin inadvertently discuss Heidi as a film-worthy subject.

> **Franco**: When we first met Heidi, it was, first of all, about getting to know her. We had known about the story for only a few weeks. Two days before we were to jump on a plane with her, going to the realization of the dream of her life, we had a lengthy interview with her to find out what she was all about. It was a very important interview. It gave us a chance to establish a

rapport with her, and also to find out how a Vietnamese girl developed in a place totally different from Vietnam.

Dolgin: We wanted to see what she remembered because we knew, as soon as we got off the plane, memories would start coming back and we wanted a real baseline of who she was before she landed in Vietnam, returning to a place she had lived for seven years. She didn't come to the US as an infant, so we knew there were memories locked in there that would be of interest as they were revealed, because in Pulaski they'd been shut down.[13]

Although Franco and Dolgin deny having had expectations in letting Heidi's story naturally unfold, they have also admitted in postfilm interviews that filmmakers do indeed have stories in mind before they even film. "We have a commitment to create an atmosphere of trust and intimacy with whomever we're working," Dolgin says in the same interview, "because otherwise we can't really tell a story the way we want to tell it."[14]

Viewers of *Daughter from Danang* should critically engage the film by considering this question: Just how *do* Dolgin and Franco "tell" their story upon Heidi's return to Vietnam? Dolgin and Franco are determined to remain off-camera, conceivably in an effort to naturalize Heidi's story by not cluttering it with their presence. There is also no indication that Heidi is speaking to the filmmakers during her on-camera monologues. However, the film camera's eye reveals scenes that foreshadow the impending tragedy—Heidi becoming overwhelmed by her birth family's appeal for her financial support. For example, when Heidi first arrives she presents gifts to her birthmother and other members of the birth family, such as a heart-shaped ring and a set of matching watches. At that moment, the camera captures the looks of awe, jealousy, and disbelief from a Vietnamese onlooker in the room, informing the viewers (but not Heidi) how such gifts might be interpreted as material evidence of the major socioeconomic disparities between First and Third World countries, how mythical stories like "money grows on trees" in the United States just might be true, and, more immediately, that Heidi herself is wealthy.

In other words, throughout this part of the film, Dolgin and Franco prepare the viewers for the West-meets-East culture clash, but during the film's making saw no reason to prepare Heidi. Tran Truong Nhu, the journalist who helped Heidi and Kim reunite, plays an important role in the drama as the translator who accompanies Heidi to Vietnam. The assimilation process Heidi's adoptive mother forced on her has resulted in her total loss of knowledge of the Vietnamese language as well as culture. Nhu pops in and out of the documentary at strategic moments, filling viewers in on the Vietnamese concept of the overseas family "benefactor," who functions as an economic "lifeline" for those left behind in Vietnam. But she does not bother to clearly inform Heidi, who interprets the continuous solicitation of money from her relatives as increasingly rude and insulting. Nhu fills *us* in on how "very upfront" Vietnamese can be about money, but again does not inform Heidi, at least not on camera.

Instead, viewers witness Heidi's increasing discomfort with and obvious ill-preparedness for such solicitations as "documented" by the filmmakers. Nhu says later in the film, "There was no way of really telling her what she was going to come up against, and I don't know if it was my job to tell her.... I tried to warn her about how things were different in Vietnam." Nhu even talks Heidi out of leaving Vietnam early. One begins to wonder in what ways Nhu, an old friend of Dolgin's and Franco's, was herself "directed" in the documentary to embellish the story Dolgin and Franco wanted to tell.

Dolgin and Franco are determined to tell their story through Heidi, and in doing so, they render Heidi less the teller of her own story than an unreliable narrator. She is a character to whom things happen, and viewers watch her reactions, at times in stunned disbelief. *Daughter from Danang* has elicited visceral responses to this constructed Heidi. In a question-and-answer period with the filmmakers after the film's screening at the New Directors/New Films festival in New York, one audience member wondered how Heidi could have been so naïve.[15] Film critic Vadim Rizov pans Heidi for her "entirely American-defined goals" and her "selfishness."[16]

How could Heidi have been so woefully unprepared? So naïve? So self-centered and inconsiderate? Dolgin and Franco seem to want us to wallow in these open-ended questions. What, after all, would *we*—as viewers, as *Americans*—have done in Heidi's place, without the benefit (which we had while viewing the documentary) of fluid translations simultaneously provided for us, particularly of the monologues in which her birthmother and brother make it plain that it is customary in Vietnam for *all* family members to be accountable for the entire family's financial burden? These questions speak to the underlying themes of the gross inequities dividing the First World from the Third World, inequities historically perpetuated and even furthered by US military intervention, such as in the Vietnam War. In *Daughter from Danang* Heidi is effectively portrayed more as a casualty of war than as an international, transracial adoptee in search of her identity and in the process of confronting a past that has been forcibly taken from her. While there is a fundamental connection between these two things, it is one that is not explicitly made in the film.

the new adoption studies: filmmaking as research, politics, and art

Given the proliferation of cultural production by and about international and transracial adoptees in memoirs, art exhibits, and anthologies, as well as documentary film, viewers can and should critically engage *Daughter from*

Danang in light of this new work. It illuminates Heidi's story as an Asian international, transracial adoptee—her upbringing in an area where she is the *only* Asian person and where she suffers from alienation, forced assimilation, and emotional and physical abuse; her decision to return to her country of origin and to reunite with her birth family; her longing for wholeness upon that return and reunion; and her experiences of disappointment and alienation—while not describing the experience of *every* Asian international adoptee, of course, is not so unfamiliar.[17]

What the new work will also highlight, however, is that in *Daughter from Danang*, adoptee Heidi Bub has virtually no agency. Compared to other documentaries about international transracial adoptees, *Daughter from Danang* appears much more polished, and part of what rankles a critical viewer is in what that polish obscures. Documentaries such as Deann Borshay Liem's *First Person Plural* and Nathan Adolfson's *Passing Through* portray their subjects—who happen to include the filmmakers themselves—as multidimensional human beings and as agents in the making of their own stories.

Furthermore, in *First Person Plural,* the viewers are confronted with the ways in which filmmakers and film cameras do not merely record what "really" happened, but rather participate in *constructing* the viewer's understanding of what has transpired. Borshay Liem's adoptive father constructs her happy all-American childhood through home movies of family vacations and other events. But we learn that in many instances he directs the family members on what they should be doing in these movies. Furthermore, in the film we watch Deann with film camera in hand turning the camera's gaze into the audience of film viewers, reminding us that we are a critical part of the politics of film.

Similarly, in *Passing Through,* Nathan Adolfson is both filmmaker and film subject. When he films the interviews with members of his adoptive family, the viewers are aware of Nathan's presence because we hear him talking with them behind the camera's eye. Like Heidi, Deann and Nathan reveal a range of difficult and disparate emotions on film—elation, alienation, pain—upon their return to their country of origin (in the latter two cases, to Korea) and their reunion with their birth families, but film viewers and critics do not belittle and castigate Deann and Nathan for their selfishness or naïveté.

By contrast, in *Daughter from Danang,* the complex range of Heidi's emotions upon her return to Vietnam is simplified as a West-meets-East culture clash. Heidi's voice-overs, inflected with a thick southern accent, strike a sharp contrast to the tinny, "Oriental" music that accompanies virtually every transitional scene to Vietnam. The otherness of Vietnam is magnified by scenes featuring Heidi's typically American descriptions of the lack of modern toilets, air conditioning, and privacy. She cannot tolerate the spiciness of the food or the pungent smells of the open-air marketplace.

Yet what lies beneath the surface of Heidi's strong motivations for returning to Vietnam and reuniting with her birth family is a complex set of desires—the desire to remember, to reconnect, to regain what has been lost, to love and be loved. Such desires compel Heidi to find her birthmother and to pursue what has by now become a familiar path for many Asian international adoptees—the Internet research and exchange of letters through various adoption and government agencies, the plan of the trip overseas, the multiplicity of emotions including joy, disappointment, and ambivalence. Viewers of *Daughter from Danang* would do well to reframe their interpretations of Heidi's character by paying attention to these desires, as would the audiences for other works by and about transracial adoptees. The new branch of adoption studies has much to offer those interested in engaging the problematic politics of filmmaking, so abundantly exemplified in the one-dimensional narrative of *Daughter from Danang.*

notes

1 *Daughter from Danang,* VHS, directed by Gail Dolgin and Vicente Franco (Berkeley, CA: Interfaze Educational Productions, 2002). See also the film's official website at http://www.daughterfromdanang.com/.

2 Here and throughout we refer to Heidi Bub, Ann Neville, and Mai Thi Kim (as well as other on-camera participants in this and other films) by their given rather than surnames simply because they function as characters within the narrative created by the filmmakers. Similarly, we use the filmmakers' surnames according to standard practice in referring to authors and the like. This usage is not intended to re-inscribe the powerless role the filmmakers have assigned these participants within the storytelling of the film.

3 See the *Daughter from Danang: American Experience* website at http://www.pbs.org/wgbh/amex/daughter/.

4 See Susan Gerhard, "Coming Home: *Daughter from Danang* Revisits War Wounds," *sfbg.com (San Francisco Bay Guardian),* March 31, 2002, http://www.sfbg.com/36/23/art_danang.html; Kate Schultz, "Interiview [sic]: A Tennessee Native Confront[s] Her Childhood Vietnam; Dolgin and Franco's *Daughter from Danang," indieWIRE,* October 31, 2002, http://www.indiewire.com/people/int_Dolgin_Gail_021031.html.

5 Reviews from the *Chicago Sun Times,* the *Kansas City Star, Hollywood Reporter,* and *LA Weekly,* as well as many quotes from reviews are posted on the film's official website. See also Vadim Rizov, *"Daughter from Danang," hybridmagazine.com,* http://www.hybridmagazine.com/films/0103/daughter-from-danang.shtml; Peter Crimmins, "SF Intl. Film Festival Showcases Berkeley Directors," *Berkeley Daily Planet,* April 27, 2002, http://www.berkeleydaily.org/artentertain_article.cfm?archiveDate=04-27-02&storyID=11631. A few negative reviews of the film have been published. See Soo Na, *"Daughter from Danang:* The Imperial Camera Lens as Documentary Form," *ChickenBones: Journal for Literary & Artistic African-American Themes* (2002), http://www.nathanielturner.com/daughterfromdenang.htm [note the irregular spelling of Danang in this url].

6 See, for example, the following texts that focus on various aspects of US adoption with close attention to the analytical categories of race and nation: Linda Gordon, *The Great Arizona Orphan Abduction* (Cambridge, MA: Harvard University Press, 1999); Barbara Melosh, *Strangers and Kin: The American Way of Adoption* (Cambridge, MA: Harvard University Press, 2002); Catherine Ceniza Choy and Gregory Paul Choy, "Transformative Terrains: Korean American Adoptees and the Social Constructions of an American Childhood," in *The American Child,* ed. Caroline Levander and Carol Singley (Rutgers, NJ: Rutgers University Press, 2003), 262–279; and Toby Alice Volkman, ed., *Cultures of Transnational Adoption* (Durham, NC: Duke University Press, 2005).

7 There are several websites that feature the history of Operation Babylift. One helpful website that contains information and primary source materials about Operation Babylift is devoted to adoption history more broadly. It is "The Adoption History Project," located at http://darkwing.uoregon.edu/

-adoption/.

8 Crimmins, "SF Intl. Film Festival."

9 Schultz, "Interiview."

10 Schultz, "Interiview."

11 J. Hoberman, *"The Weight of Water; Daughter From Danang* 'From Hanoi to Hollywood: The Vietnam War on Film'," *The Village Voice,* October 30—November 5, 2002, http://www.villagevoice.com/film/0244,hoberman,39490,20.html. Quote on the review quotes page of the film's official website at http://www.daughterfromdanang.com/.

12 Schultz, "Interiview."

13 Schultz, "Interiview."

14 Schultz, "Interiview."

15 The authors of this essay attended that screening and were present in the audience during the question-and-answer period with filmmakers Dolgin and Franco.

16 Rizov, *"Daughter from Danang."*

17 See, for example, Tonya Bishoff and Jo Rankin, eds., *Seeds from a Silent Tree: An Anthology by Korean Adoptees* (San Diego: Pandal Press, 1997); *First Person Plural,* VHS, directed by Deann Borshay Liem (San Francisco: National Asian American Telecommunications Association, 2000); and *Passing Through,* VHS, directed by Nathan Adolfson (San Francisco: National Asian American Telecommunications Association, 1998).

24 PROUD TO BE ME

Ami Inja Nafzger

When people of color grow up in a predominantly white society, it's difficult for them to realize that being different doesn't mean that one measures up any less—especially when there is little to explain why and exactly how one is different, and any reinforcement given about being different is negative. Recall the story of the ugly duckling. Imagine how an individual would feel after being hatched one day into a society where her appearance, mannerisms, and language were regarded as strange and distasteful by her peers; where, in public, her physical appearance became a source of embarrassment and shame. Despite her family's assurances, she would certainly begin to hate being different and avoid all reminders of her original identity.

In 1971 I was born in Chun Ju, Korea. At the age of four, I was adopted by a family and came to the United States, where I belonged to a Norwegian mother, a Swiss father, and four older homemade siblings. I grew up in Minong, Wisconsin, a small town of 500 people. There I was called racist names such as chink, jap, and nigger. I was even told to go back to my own country. I didn't understand what the words meant but I could feel the rejection by others, tied to my appearance. I always knew I was different and did not like it one bit. I wanted to explain myself, but I didn't have the knowledge of who I was myself, nor could my family teach me about my background.

When I was ten, my mother divorced my alcoholic father. For many years we struggled financially. My mother worked several jobs, trying to support five children on her own. At a young age, my siblings and I had no choice but to work and try to take care of each other, as well as help our mother as much as we could.

When I entered my teenage years, we moved to Minnesota, hoping to find better opportunities for our family. There I became more confused about myself. I encountered problems trying to find a true friend who would accept me for who I was. I also experienced conflict around dating; it was obvious people feared pursuing even friendship with a person of color—how could they even think about dating someone of a different race? I put myself through many extremes to feel acceptance, such as trying to dye my hair blonde, changing my clothes and mannerisms, and even thinking about facial operations to make myself more desirable. I thought this would resolve everything; I was only fooling myself.

A month before my high school graduation, my mother passed away from colon and liver cancer. During my mother's funeral, I realized the significance of my loss: I was abandoned once again. My siblings and I were devastated about losing a mother we believed embodied sainthood. After my mother's death, my siblings and I went our separate ways. I tried to finish high school. My siblings went back to their homes and led their own lives.

Years later, I look back and try to figure out what happened and how I could have changed things. Could I have saved my mother from dying of cancer? Could I have accepted my mother as a friend and felt more comfortable with my Korean self? Could I have done something other than cry when my peers put me down because of my race? Over the years, I have learned that when an individual is living life and is growing up in it, she doesn't always know what to do. But when she becomes older and looks back, she sees why things happen the way they did. I have found that my insights come from my experiences, and my strengths come from my will to endure.

a look in the mirror

In 1990, when my mother was in the hospital dying with cancer, I was invited to attend Augsburg College. My mother made me promise that I would attend this school, as she felt a connection to the college. She said, "Our pastor and many of my close church friends attended there. I feel Augsburg would be proper for your future." I kept that promise; I felt obligated, although I knew how expensive it was and how difficult my life would be as a student there.

However, I felt a need to quit school several times; I worked three part-time jobs to pay for my school and my living expenses. I wasn't able to have a normal college life like other more fortunate students. It really discouraged me in many ways. My promise was the only way I knew I could respect my mother and pay her back for her having raised me. I wanted to make her happy, knowing she watched me every day.

One day as a freshman I was walking toward my mailbox to retrieve my mail. Suddenly, I felt a tap on my shoulder. I turned around and there she was: the woman who changed my whole life. A middle-aged woman about 5'2" petite, with thick black coarse hair bouncing off her shoulders—it was *me*, only with slightly different features. She was an Asian woman, the Director of Augsburg Pan-Asian Association.

"Excuse me, Miss, is your name Ami?"

I looked at her in shock, not knowing what to say. I thought, *How does she know my name? Is she talking to* me*?* I looked around, then looked at her again. Then I turned around and started to walk away from her. I didn't mean to, and I couldn't help it. It's like I had no control of my feet. I just kept on walking. As I walked further away, I could still hear her encouraging me to meet other Asians and make new friends.

For two years after this accidental meeting, this woman never gave up on me. She continued to remind me who she was and that it was okay to join her. I was extremely frightened and I hesitated. Then one day, I took her up on her offer: "Um, He— Hell-lo… Hello, ma'am! Can I, um… I would like to, um, join your group."

With a big smile, she turned and said, "Well sure, Ami, I am so glad you have come around. I promise you that you will not regret this. I also assure you that you will make many friends and learn much about other Asians."

Relief passed over me when I saw how happy she was to see me join. I thought, *this is the first time I don't feel ashamed of being Asian.* Until that time, I had never talked to an Asian in the United States, nor seen one so close up. It was like looking in a mirror for the first time. I was a little overwhelmed and shy, but I was extremely curious at the same time. I began to realize I was not alone and learned a lot from the other Asians who attended my college. I became heavily involved in the Asian community in school and also joined the Adopted Korean Organization in Minneapolis, for people like me. I have never forgotten how this director broke through my isolation. She believed in me. If I hadn't met her, I would not be where I am today.

I didn't have a choice

Two years later, I realized that, although I had confidence about myself as an Asian American for the first time in my life, I really didn't know myself. I wanted to know more. Many questions occurred to me, such as, *Where did I come from? What is my country really about?* I had learned much about other Asian communities, such as the Vietnamese, Lao, Chinese, and Hmong, from the Pan-Asian Association, but I possessed very little knowledge of Koreans.

One day, I decided that I was not going anywhere here in America. I was missing something. I needed a change in my life. I intended to search for my biological family, find a piece of myself, and belong in a society without the kind of racial discrimination I had experienced in the United States. A friend of mine found a small magazine article about teaching in Korea. I thought, *This is a great sign. I should do this now. I don't want to wait years from now to make this crazy move.* I applied immediately. Within a week I got a phone call from the company in Korea that was going to be my future employer. The caller said my application was accepted, and he and his staff would meet me at the airport. I packed. I think my family was a little surprised and worried, and my friends thought I was just crazy. However, there was no stopping me now. I was pumped and ready for this change.

I arrived at the Kimpo International Airport of Seoul, Korea, and found myself pushing my cart with two large bags and a carry-on. As I walked out of the luggage claim area, I followed the crowd of Koreans. Large automatic doors opened and then there were hundreds of eyes staring at me. Shock and relief—I felt overwhelming emotion and elation to see all those Asian eyes. For the first time in my life, I didn't look different. I smiled with excitement!

I looked around for my name on a sign. There was no sign with my name. I kept looking for what seemed like an eternity. Hours later, as the airport was emptying out, I realized those people must have forgotten to pick me up. Overwhelmed with excitement yet unprepared for my journey and with only $255 to my name, I questioned myself: *How can I communicate? I don't even know the language! How can I catch a taxi, find a restroom? I don't know anyone. What am I going to do?*

That night, I found myself staying at a *yeogwan,* a cheap love hotel. I crashed there for the next three days until I was able to contact the school where I was going to teach. Little did I know that an older single man, Mr. Kim, and his 60-year-old mother were to host me for my stay in Korea.

When Mr. Kim finally came to get me, I questioned the man. "Sir, I thought a family with two children was going to be my host family. That's what my contract said."

He spoke with annoyance, "No! Your plans have changed and you will be staying with me for now on. I am your boss. You are in Korea, and you should obey your elders. You don't have a choice."

I looked down and apologized, "I am sorry, I didn't know."

About an hour later, we were still driving. "Where are we going?" I asked.

He said, "Home! Why?"

"Is this still Seoul?"

Mr. Kim chuckled and replied, "No, we are in Incheon."

"Incheon? What's Incheon? I thought I was going to be in Seoul. That's what my contract says."

Mr. Kim became annoyed again. "I said you are going to stay with me—you don't have a choice. I live in Incheon."

I went to Incheon. But after several weeks, I began to feel very uncomfortable living with Mr. Kim. He would open my personal mail; he would not relay my personal phone calls to me; he began to make passes at me, expressing how much he loved and wanted me. Within four months, I was completely frustrated with my living conditions. Approaching Mr. Kim, I told him how uncomfortable I was living with him. He became very upset and threatened me; if I chose to stop working and living with him, he would report me to immigration. The outcome would be deportation from my motherland for the rest of my life. It was obvious this man wanted to use me not only to make money for him but also to be his concubine. I was terrified, devastated. I didn't want to be sent out of Korea; I had barely arrived.

Shortly after, I approached a Korean man who was an acquaintance of Mr. Kim. This was a man I had met a few times, and I felt he was a good, trustworthy person. When I told him about my situation, he pulled me out of Mr. Kim's house and brought me down south to work for another company, under his name. Weeks later, I was living and working in a small town named Gumi.

Living in Gumi, Korea, is like living in small-town America. Gumi's people did not receive me well; life seemed to be more of a struggle than ever before. In Gumi, I was not aware of other overseas-adopted Koreans living in Korea; I never saw them or other foreigners. Day after day, I encountered rejection and constant negative reinforcement about being a foreigner and nothing more. As time went on, I began to feel out of touch with myself and didn't have the answers to identify who I was or where I belonged anymore.

Again, I was reliving the prejudice from my American life, but this time it took place in my birth country. And I wanted to be accepted so badly. I thought, *While living in Korea, live like the Koreans do. I must do this to survive. I don't have a choice.* I changed my style of clothing along with my mannerisms, and I even accepted the possibility of one day marrying a Korean man. In Korea, it is rare for people to remain unmarried, and I felt ready to settle down and accept the Korean social norm of marriage.

WHAT ADOPTION AGENCIES CAN PROVIDE TO OAKS POSTADOPTION

- The approval document of adoption within a week when adoptees request it for an F–4 visa. Also, explanations about the F–4 visa process for all adoptees who ask.
- Accurate and adequate information about birth backgrounds and biological families regardless of agency or orphanage. We understand there are inside policies for each adoption agency, but we need more accurate and adequate information. An explanation of why such information might not be provided would help adoptees understand this better.
- Counseling services for adult adoptees and social workers, who could gain a better understanding of specific problems that adoptees may have.
- More English speakers at adoption agencies, for improved communication.
- Work toward changing the attitude of social workers. Many adoptees have been made to feel they are asking too much from a social worker when requesting a copy of their adoption files. Social workers may forget or not realize that it takes years for many adoptees to have enough courage to decide to search for their birth families, or to want to know the truth about why they were adopted, and adoptees may also experience hardship in gathering the resources needed for the journey.

I did just that. I met a Korean man and decided marriage was what I must do to belong. But I was wrong. Falsely, for the first time since I came to Korea, I thought I felt acceptance for what I was and not where I came from. Yet while engaged to be married to a native Korean, I felt even more pressure and expectations to be someone or something I could not be. Day in and day out, I felt as if I had to speak Korean, cook like a Korean woman, quit my job, and stay home to clean for my fiancé's family—all to become Korean. I thought, *Hurry, hurry, speak Korean, and you will be a* real *Korean!* But I soon began to understand that speaking Korean didn't make one a real Korean, and getting married doesn't make one more accepted by native Koreans; only native Koreans could be so Korean. Still, I wondered what defined "real" for a Korean. My blood was Korean, did that not qualify? Confusion wrought havoc in my mind.

As time went on, I began to realize that behaving like a native Korean woman was only denying my true self. I was unhappy, and I could not accept the Korean way of life, so different from the American. I was hurting others around me, but most of all, I was hurting myself. For 21 years I had been brought up in an all-white American community with an all-white American family. I had only known one culture and one family; I was only fooling myself if I thought I could become 100 percent native Korean. I learned happiness comes from within us; one must find this inside and be at peace with it; one cannot choose to be someone else.

The longer my fiancé and I stayed together, the more we grew apart. He'd drink until 3:00 or 4:00 AM, and then he would call me and demand that I pick him up. Sometimes when he arrived home he would yell and scream at me. Seeing this other side of him, I realized that this was really not the life I wanted to live. Without regret, I packed all of my belongings and escaped to Seoul, away from my fiancé, without his permission.

Months passed, and we both agreed our cultures clashed. Now, as I reflect upon my life in Korea, I realize how frustrated I was with daily life and my fight to feel belonging, to be treated like a real Korean. Each time I'd encounter another Korean who was unaware of who or what I was, many questions were asked. Over and over, Koreans asked, "Are you Japanese?" "Are you Chinese?" Some people asked if I was from India. Then they looked at me in confusion, asking, "Are you Korean?" Or saying, "Oh, your mother's Korean and your father's American." Or prodding, "Is your grandfather Korean?" Or demanding, "Why don't you speak Korean?" (Snicker, snicker, hee, hee!) As they laughed at me, I just turned my head and walked away.

One time, I was approached by a Korean man who was unaware I was adopted and couldn't speak Korean. I shook my head mumbling the words, "I can't speak Korean."

The man jumped back and looked dumbfounded, as if he had just seen a ghost. He repeated in a loud voice (in English), "What you can't speak Korean, but you look Korean!"

I blurted, "I am Korean, but I was adopted and…"

The man cut me off, saying, "*Igo,* go back to your own country!"

I thought, it wasn't my choice my parents abandoned me. It wasn't my choice that I was adopted. It wasn't my choice that I could not speak Korean. Many things were not my choice. My life began to look very helpless and less free. I had thought living in Korea for two years would provide the missing pieces of my puzzle. But a year later, I was more confused than ever.

piecing together my jigsaw puzzle in gumi

I never knew anything about my birth family. My mother and father had told me everything they knew, which was nothing. Mother, father: unknown. Forever, as long as I can remember, finding my family has been my dream—a very good dream! However, now I know it will be next to impossible to fulfill that dream as I have such little information about myself.

The day I arrived in Gumi, I was 26 years old. I thought that Gumi would be a good place to start to try to find my identity. I strove to learn the Korean language and culture, and, although it was a big challenge for me, I conquered it. I felt my next challenge was to find my family. But despite my great ability to catch on and understand the language, my search was not to be as fruitful.

This is what I discovered: I was found when I was only a week old, in Chun Ju. A man who worked for the City Hall found me on the street in front of Chun Ju City Hall. On June 4, 1971, that man brought me to a temporary orphanage in Chun Ju. I was at that orphanage for ten days before I was sent to another one in Iksan along with ten other babies. I learned that I stayed at that second orphanage for four years, until I was given to the Holt Adoption Agency in Seoul. It was from Seoul that I was adopted.

After I placed an ad in a Korean newspaper, a man who thought he was my father came forward. It was really weird; we actually looked a lot alike. There were so many similarities: same Korean name, same location, both left-handed, which is genetic, his son left-handed, too. Everyone was convinced

WHAT THE KOREAN GOVERNMENT CAN DO FOR OAKS POSTADOPTION

- Provide updated international information on adoption, such as statistics, laws, and an explanation of overseas adoptees' rights in Korea.
- Provide financial support to the different groups and organizations working with postadoption services.
- Create one official adoptee-led resource center that is active in postadoption service. As we all know, adoptees have firsthand experience in adoption.

that he was my father. KBS (the Korean national TV network) was even convinced. They paid for our DNA test and brought me down to Pusan to film. They spent so much money because they were certain that he was my father. He turned out not to be.

After the reunion with the wrong father, KBS and I went back to my old orphanage again and found out that the staff had actually been lying to me. First they had my name right, and then it was crossed out, and then they had my new name, a different name, also crossed out, and then had changed it to my first name again. I thought that was really odd and asked about it. They said, "No, no, we changed it, we thought it was this, but no, this is it." So, I thought this was who I was. I came from that orphanage with ten different babies. Three died, one was taken back by the father, and six babies were left. They finally admitted on KBS that they had mismanaged my orphan files. They said that I probably was one of those six girls but they didn't know which one. I wondered if my name was really Jin Inja; could I be someone else?

If I wanted to, I could have done the research by tracing the lives of all of these people, but I just decided it was not really right to interrupt peoples' lives, their homes, just to find out what happened. So I just let it be. Ironically, another woman, Kimberly, with whom I am now friends, came to me for help with her search and we found out that we are both from the same place and that she happens to be another of the six girls. I wonder if she is Jin Inja?

It took me four years to do that search. I never did another. Anyone out there would have been bound to see me on TV or in the newspapers. After seven years, no one had come forward except that one man, the wrong father, and I never found out anything about my birthmother. Yet I'm satisfied with knowing that I actually tried; if I hadn't, I would still be curious. In the process of going through the search, you learn a lot about yourself and about other people. I've really grown inside and it's something I will never regret.

only we can help ourselves

In Korea I wished to find a friend, someone who could understand me, one who could relate to my experiences. At times, I began to feel alone and impatient because I always had to explain myself. After some time, I met several OAKs (overseas adopted Koreans) who could relate to me and understand me for myself. I have found OAKs are different in our own ways because our upbringings and individual experiences are influenced through our respective adoptive countries. I learned that a large number of OAKs were returning to Korea and experiencing just as many frustrations trying to find their identities as I did. Many wished to leave their motherland. And many did leave very disappointed and angry at Korea. I, too, felt this disappointment and wanted to leave, but I also had a part of me that wanted to stay. I wanted to do something to help other adoptees.

I didn't want other adoptees to experience the hardships that I had confronted, which had blocked my path to understanding my identity. I wanted to educate and help them so those hardships could be prevented. So, in 1997 I began to research Korean adoption in Korea. The Department of Social Welfare of Korea claims that international adoption has sent up to 200,000 Korean children overseas, and the adoptions still continue today. After so many decades and so many adoptions, I felt something needed to be established in Korea for adult adoptees returning to their birth country.

My mother always told me, "If you don't like something, don't complain about it, but do something about it; only we can help ourselves." That is exactly what I did, and that's how my involvement in adoptee activism all started.

ADULT OVERSEAS ADOPTED KOREAN ORGANIZATIONS AND HOPES FOR THE FUTURE

The existence of adult adoptee organizations in Korea and throughout the United States, Australia, Scandinavia, and Western Europe tells us that there has been a lack of postadoption services and an urgent need of support for OAKS in their adoptive and birth countries. Currently there are approximately 25 adult adoptee organizations worldwide. The model of adoptees serving other adoptees has been very effective. But we are also aware that we cannot achieve everything alone. We need help from sister organizations. Adoptee organizations and sister organizations can support each other with joint activities, summer schools and camps, motherland tours, international OAK gatherings, and a global network foundation of adoptee organizations. Benefits we could reap from working with each other include spreading the load in providing extensive postadoption services, thus lifting some of the burden from the Korean government, Korean adoption agencies, and other organizations. The Korean government and adoption agencies would be able to refer OAKS to an ongoing network and resource center when OAKS return to Korea. The Korean government and adoption agencies would get recognition and appreciation from the OAK community and their families. OAKS would have resources and positive experiences in Korea, as they would have a stable connection in, and a means to learn about, their native country. This could be beneficial for Korea in the long run. More OAKS and birth families could have the opportunity to reunite for the first time. And, finally, the shame and guilt of the birth families of OAKS could be alleviated, and they may be able to overcome their pasts.

goal: a home away from home

I envisioned a Global Overseas Adoptees' Link (GOAL)—a home away from home, an organization for all adoptees currently living in Korea, and for returning adoptees from overseas. By calling ourselves GOAL, we reminded ourselves that we have many things to accomplish in our global vision. Our idea was to change attitudes and to promote awareness of adoptee issues within Korea, as well as to solve differences between the native Korean community and OAKS. The organization would support OAKS by bridging the cultural gaps between their adoptive and birth cultures. We could inform Korean people and the Korean government about the existence of OAKS and about the meaning of being adopted, as well as use the media to break down the walls of prejudice, misunderstanding, shame, guilt, and pity that separate the Korean community from adoptees. I envisioned that the organization could not only benefit OAKS but also the Korean government, our communities, birth families, and adoption agencies as well.

So, on March 5, 1998, GOAL was founded.

Yet GOAL found it difficult to gain recognition in Korea. The Korean government denied our wishes to have either a voice or legal rights in Korea. Even though it was clear that there was a need for an organization to assist returning adoptees, I learned that founding one was not easy. I realized GOAL needed members of the Korean community to bridge the gap between OAKS and the larger Korean community. So GOAL is made up of Korean volunteers—the backbone of the organization—as well as Korean adoptees from Europe and the United States. We developed an infrastructure consisting of a president, a 14-member Board of Directors, and 22 subcommittee members.

The native Koreans have helped OAKS by providing knowledge about Korean culture, manners, and customs. They have shown a tremendous willingness to assist adoptees who are returning to their birth country. This support increases the awareness of adoption issues in the general Korean public and has helped make GOAL's presence in Korea significant to the Korean government, adoption agencies, and the Korean society at large. Some may wonder why native Koreans dedicate their free time for GOAL. I had the same curiosity. So, before I came to Washington, DC, for the First International Adoptee Conference in 1999, I interviewed several native Korean volunteers from GOAL. My questions were "Why are you involved in GOAL, and how does your involvement benefit you?"

Included in their responses were:

- We feel that we are not only helping adoptees but also helping our country's future.
- We have had some connection with adoption in our family. For instance, a cousin was put up for adoption.

- We know we have many problems here in Korea, and we feel this problem is a big issue in our society and we want to do something about it, because we know that there are few social welfare agencies in Korea.
- It gives us a sense of satisfaction.
- We used to volunteer at an adoption agency and could see this as a future problem.
- We lived abroad for a short time, but within that time, we recognized the difficulties in being in a foreign country as a foreigner.

In the past, many teenage or adult adoptees have been discouraged from coming to Korea because of their lack of connections in Korea. In response to this problem, GOAL has compiled a list of resources including lodging, translators, guides, birth search departments, and other support available *specifically* for Korean adoptees returning to Korea to visit or to stay. It is our hope that this information will reach adoptees and will give them the courage to visit Korea, as well as prevent isolation while in Korea.

searching for biological families

GOAL did not intend to create a registry but when so many adoptees and Korean birth families approached us, I realized that searching was a major reason adoptees come back to Korea. In March 1999 GOAL established a registry for all returning adoptees and Korean birth families. In 2000 the

WHAT RETURNING ADOPTEES HAVE AND NEED

- Adoptees have expectations, wishes, visions, and objectives in finding themselves and trying to fit into society.
- We need support from each other.
- We want Korean society to view us as adults, not as children.
- For adoptees returning to Korea, we need an ongoing, independent, adoptee-led organizational homebase that is legally recognized by the Korean government, not just a volunteer organization.
- We need funding so GOAL can work as a resource center, registry, and network link for established adoptee organizations.
- We need the opportunity to have an ongoing voice for acceptance, understanding, and human rights.
- We want a Korean education program or scholarship program for returning adoptees who want to learn to understand the Korean language, culture, and people.
- We need housing for returning adoptees who want to reside in Korea on a short-term basis.

website registry was established. This registry includes photographs and basic information that may help family members to identify each other.

GOAL aims to provide OAKS with opportunities to contact Korean media to assist their searches, provide OAKS with translation throughout their search process, help OAKS deal with matters both trivial and troublesome during their searches, uplift OAKS' status in Korea, improve OAKS' legal status in Korea (related to visa and citizenship status), and offer information about OAKS, which will draw public attention and improve the general perception of OAKS in Korean society. GOAL locates families through an online and paper registry; provides contact with adoption agencies and orphanages; provides contact with police stations, schools, and government institutions; initiates a media search (KBS, NBC, YTN); and obtains free DNA tests through the Mayor's Association (one per month).

GOAL received NGO status on March 17, 2004. As of this writing, GOAL Korea has two full-time employees and four volunteer staff (including the current secretary general, a Swiss adoptee). There are approximately 300 paying members and about 20 very active volunteers. In 2005, GOAL facilitated between 20 and 30 reunions.

other services

GOAL also provides assistance to OAKS by meeting them at the airport and offering necessary services, introducing host families who offer temporary housing or home-stays, extending information about job opportunities, supplying necessary information on Korean culture and language, giving free Korean language classes or private tutoring, providing temporary cellular phones, helping adoptees to network with each other and Korean nationals, and arranging Korean volunteers to assist adoptees at the immigration office. In addition, GOAL attempts to build community and awareness by publishing newsletters, providing monthly gatherings focusing on OAK issues, holding monthly seminars to educate native Koreans, maintaining a website, raising funds, holding conferences that bring awareness of OAKS to Korean society, arranging social activities (including sharing Western holidays with Koreans), cooperating with other organizations to coordinate major events like the 2004 International Gathering of Korean adoptees in Seoul, and holding seminars for Korean social welfare studies students.

the F–4 visa

Central to adoptees' ability to live and work in Korea is their visa status. The Overseas Koreans Visa (F–4), which came into effect in 1999, is a special visa for Overseas Korean residents, including adoptees who live in Korea. GOAL's volunteers, some Korean Americans, and I wrote proposals, received over 12,000 signatures for a petition, had a conference with a focus on this issue, and visited several government officials during the three-year process of getting the law for the F–4 passed.

Now thousands of Korean adoptees and kyopos (overseas Koreans who emigrated from Korea with their families) have the ability to reside in Korea without having to renounce their current citizenship. Korean adoptees and kyopos are also able to work as Korean citizens, do not need a sponsor or business to represent them while living in Korea, and are able to come and go anytime. All Korean adoptees and kyopos obtain this visa if they are going to reside in Korea or travel to Korea for a long time, and at the time of this writing (2005) the Korean government has officially made the visa mandatory for all Korean adoptees and kyopos employed by a Korean business. Those eligible for the F–4 visa include people of Korean descent residing overseas who emigrated after 1948; overseas Korean nationals (kyopos); and foreign national Koreans (OAKS, Koreans born overseas with a different citizenship, and Koreans who have changed their citizenship).

how the F–4 Visa benefits adoptees

We now have legal status in Korea for two years. Before the F–4 visa, every time we wanted to change a job, go back to school, or visit longer than three months, we had to leave Korea and travel to another country to renew our visa at a Korean consulate. This became very expensive and difficult for foreign Koreans who wanted to reside in Korea longer than three months. But the new F–4 visa may be renewed without having to leave the country. We no longer need a sponsor from a school, company, family, or friend. This means working, school, or family visas are not necessary. We may buy land, property, and housing, or open a business. And providing private tutoring, which requires no Korean employer, is now legal. However, the visa does not

FUTURE SCOPE OF GOAL

GOAL will continue to improve its existing activities by extending a range of services for OAKS who search for their biological families in Korea. Because Korean society does not offer equal opportunities for people who grow up in orphanages—such as employment, education, and eligibility to marry—GOAL plans to foster relationships between OAKS and orphans in Korea. GOAL also hopes to establish a Korean Adoptee Culture Center in Seoul, where all organizations that support adoptees could be together, adoptees could receive training for the Korean corporate environment, adoptees could teach their own languages and cultures to those who want to learn, GOAL could have a permanent home for its office, and artists could show their art.

In addition, members are currently planning a GOAL USA chapter for St. Paul, Minnesota. The US chapter will involve other Asian (non-Korean) adoptees and will collaborate with other adoptee organizations. The US chapter will also serve as another source of funding for the Seoul office.

(For more information on GOAL, visit their website at http://goal.or.kr/new/.)

guarantee us the ability to obtain an application for a bank loan or credit card; wire money overseas from Korea; or receive employment in jobs included in the "Three Ds," i.e., "dirty, dangerous, or difficult" work. (These jobs include street vending, factory work, and janitorial/housecleaning work.)

Among the documents required for the F–4 visa is the "hojeok," or Korean family register. OAKs must obtain the registry through their adoption agencies. Unfortunately, those who were adopted in the late 1950s or those who were not adopted through any current adoption agency may have a more difficult time obtaining this document. However, even if families are unknown, adoptees can often obtain a family registry from their adoption agency that states that, as orphans, they are the only members of their families. Using the model of the successful F–4 visa legislation, GOAL is currently lobbying for Korean adoptees to be able to apply for dual citizenship.

When adoptees ask for information on our backgrounds, we are not just looking to agencies for some meaningless documents. Those documents are our reasons for our existence—our histories, the reasons why we were given up. Those pieces of paper have a special meaning to us and may be the closest we will ever get to knowing our roots. That is why accurate information is so important. When accurate information is not provided, or information is claimed to be lost, it's the adoptees who continue to suffer inside, not the social workers. We need to be treated like people.

Hopefully the recommendations that have come out of GOAL's work (see sidebars) can help ease adoptees' entry into Korean society. And other transracially adopted people might use the recommendations as blueprints for setting up their own organizations. Our intent is to build a model of co-operation. Even though we are independent groups, we (adoption agencies, the social workers, researchers, adoptive parents, adoptee organizations, and others) all have something in common and our next step is to build a strong relationship so we can resolve problems together—now and in the future.

Conclusion

Over the years, I have met so many adoptees in Korea who have had troubles similar to my own. Many in my generation of adoptees did not have good placements. In our conversations, we have talked about our identities and how we felt about not belonging to either our adoptive country or birth country. We have also talked about how our lives lacked direction and Korean role models. I talked with and became close to a number of European adoptees; it was nice to be able to talk to each other and give support.

In 2003, before I left Korea, I wanted to make sure GOAL was stable. At the time there was a staff of five and about a thousand volunteers managing GOAL. It felt very good to have this strong following, but it was hard to actually let it all go—all my sweat and time I had spent fulfilling this passionate goal. I let it go to people I had trained but I hardly knew.

I felt a sense of loss when I returned to America. It was different not to have so many people depending on me. However, I am now working on establishing another nonprofit in the US, to raise funds to send back to Korea. I also have taken an active role on the board of directors for the Asian Pacific Cultural Center in St. Paul. This non-profit organization is not yet fully established, but aims "to create a *place* that will become a vibrant cultural resource for all the state's citizens." It is in the process of completing a large project that involves building a Pan-Asian Center in the US, the only one of its kind, to be completed in 2009. The center will provide opportunities for theater and dance, office and programming space for several Asian-focused organizations, conference rooms for both small and large gatherings, a visitor reception hall, and much more—it will be the first of its kind with a library. Within this center, GOAL USA will operate as a resource for all Asian adoptees, international and domestic.

Through my struggles, I have become a very strong person. I know that if I had never gone to Korea, I would not feel this way. My journey there has helped my longing—to actually be proud. When I look at myself, I see a Korean American adoptee. I do not see that I am only a Korean American. Korean Americans are very different, by upbringing and by belief. Nor am I just a Korean. I tried that one on—it didn't fit. I am a Korean American adoptee; that's how I define myself. I'm not ashamed of it. I'm proud. I can teach many people so many things.

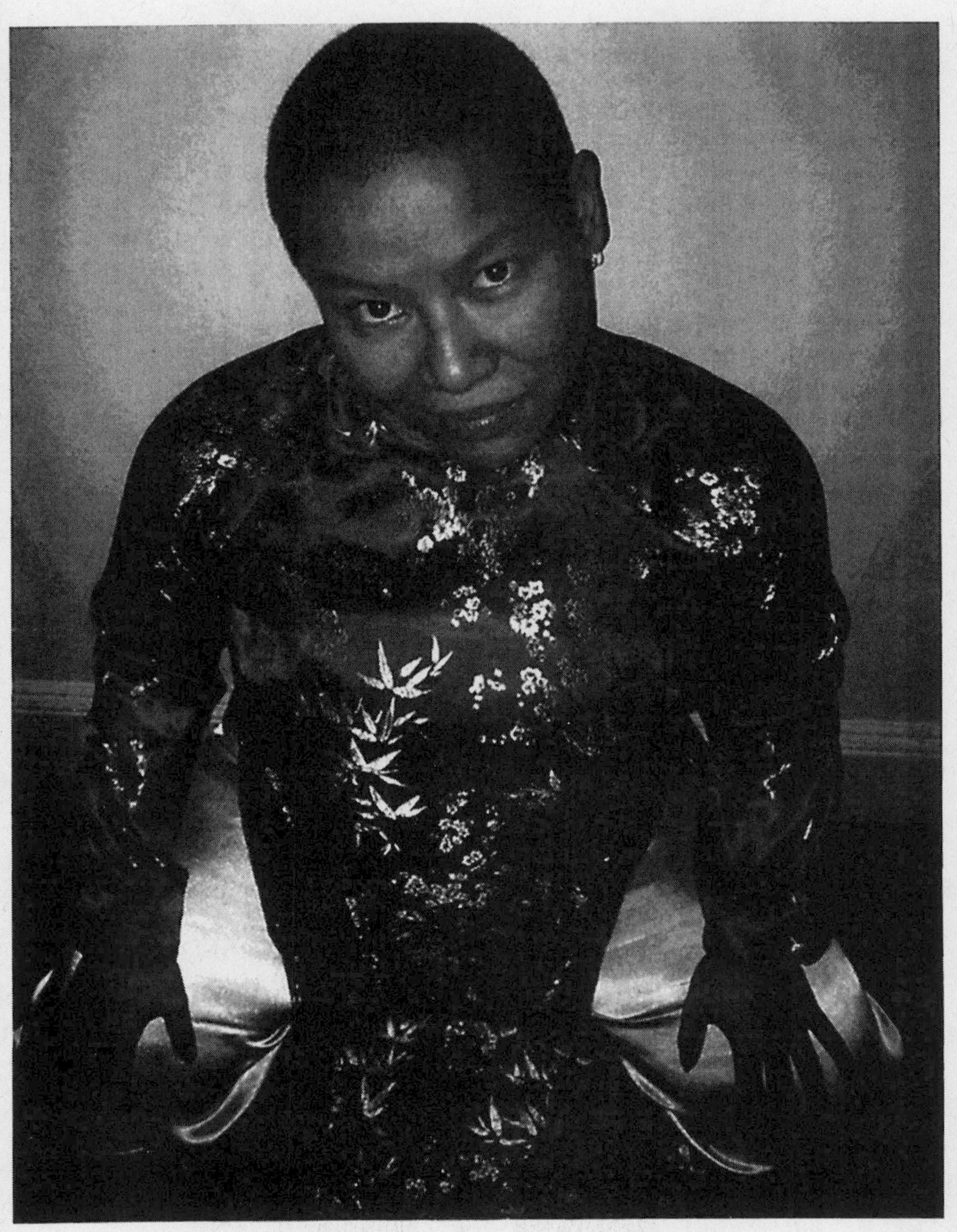

Raquel Evita Saraswati, *In Ao Dai*, 2004, digital photograph (subject Anh Đào Kolbe)

PRAISE SONG FOR ALA

Julia Chinyere Oparah

This red earth
claims me
runs through my veins
calling me to surrender
a lifetime of unbelonging.

Sinking to my knees
in my father's compound,
I feel the dark coiled roots of unspoken bitterness
loosen their grip on sinew and bone
releasing my ribcage.
I take my first breath
drawing the cicada-laden dusk
deep into my belly
Letting go of memories
of an ancient hunger.

Rich and moist
the red earth gives birth
to swollen yams
dusty and knarled and knotted
like my grandmother's hands
holding the day's crop.

I eat them boiled with stew
Like my Dad
My kid brother prefers them sliced and golden
Like his favorite French fries.

In San Francisco airport
my palms sweat
as the customs dogs
sniff by my suitcase
where the whole yam
my last taste of Mbierre
is wrapped in African cloth.

The rusty dirt
washes away in the rainy season
leaving gaping caverns in the road
my cousin hurls the car around them
with bravery verging on fatalism.
After they fill in the holes
the car throws up clouds
of choking red dust.
Dust creeps into my nose
reddens my eyes
I imagine it burrowing into my skin
settling into the strands of my dredlocks
I welcome its presence
longing for this landscape
to be etched into my body.

I have not claimed this red earth
She has claimed me
She has renamed me
placing unfamiliar consonants on my tongue.
Daughter of Umochoke
Blood of Mbierre
Child of Obazu.
She does not ask me to swear allegiance
does not demand that I choose
or forget.
She is not jealous or possessive.
In moments of stillness
I hear her whispering
words of comfort and solace
in a language I never learned.

PART SIX

SPEAKING FOR OURSELVES

Raquel Evita Saraswati, *Open Jacket,* 2005, digital photograph
(subject Anh Đào Kolbe)

26 RESEARCHING ADOPTION

WHOSE PERSPECTIVE AND WHAT ISSUES?

Kirsten Hoo-Mi Sloth

In April 2003 the Korea Club, the Danish association of Korean adoptees, hosted an international adoption research conference under the title *The Meaning of Roots*. The organizers' motivation was a desire to challenge the dominating adoption research paradigm in Scandinavia. The main objective of the Korea Club is to facilitate contact among Korean adoptees so they can share adoption experiences. Addressing research is, however, equally important because research influences—or should influence—adoption policy and practice. Research results interpret adoptees' realities. They inform our assumptions about what is right and what is wrong in adoption. Therefore it is vital that intercountry adoptees, as the "objects" of performed research, assess research results and compare them with lived experiences to ensure their validity and reliability. We cannot leave this task to nonadopted academics alone.

Until now Scandinavian adoption research has tended to exclude or minimise the issues of race, ethnicity, and biological family as relevant factors in explaining the well-being of intercountry adoptees. The consequence is that myths, ignorance, and prejudices still surround the subject of intercountry adoption. Its complexities are too often simplified into a question of adjustment, integration, and good or bad adoptions. Furthermore, most researchers in the Scandinavian adoption field are medical doctors, psychiatrists, psychologists, and social workers, so their perspective is clinical and they categorise people according to preconceived ideas of what is healthy and what is unhealthy, normal and abnormal. The basic purpose of this mainstream adoption research is to identify how adoptees deviate from the general population of the receiving country in terms of physical and psychological well-being, degree of education, job achievement, social relations, and identification with the national culture (in other words, feeling Danish, Swedish, and so forth).

The problem is that this approach—measuring deviation—is also loaded with a particular normative view of adoption that asserts the idea that it is only healthy and sound for intercountry adoptees to assimilate. Mainstream studies thus examine mainly whether adoptees have adapted to the adoptive family and culture of the receiving country. The outcomes of these studies have been interpreted as mostly successful. Having a different ethnic background is not considered to represent any severe impediment. The assumption is that adoptees are healthy because in general they identify themselves as Danes or Swedes and so forth; do not want to travel to, for example, Korea, Colombia, or India; live their lives in ways similar to the general population; and seldom experience racism—and even if they do, it is not considered very harmful.

This "Assimilation is Healthy" assumption conveniently corresponds to the ideologies guiding intercountry adoption, at least in Denmark: intercountry adoption is about rescuing children from a poor life in the barbaric Third World and making them objects in building nonracist Western societies. In other words, as I've written elsewhere, "Adoption is perceived as an international social commitment—equivalent to other humanitarian assistance activities. The rationale is that children are at risk in their home countries and adoption is considered an improvement of the child's possibilities. In this view, intercountry adoption is always in the best interest of the child. Another belief is that because intercountry adoptees are often non-whites they should be frontrunners in building a nonracist tolerant international society."[2] The research results on assimilation apparently show that the mission has been successfully completed.

According to this line of argument, any deviating behaviour—resistance to assimilation—must then be considered unhealthy and abnormal. Adoption professionals have thus claimed that, in general, only a minority of adoptees—those with poor mental health, low self-esteem, and bad relationships with their adoptive parents—wish to explore their birth cultures and search for their birth families.

If this is true, all the members of the Korea Club ought to be institutionalised; their motivation for joining the organisation is precisely an interest in exploring the meaning of roots and different ethnic identities, searching for biological family, and openly discussing the impact of racism and discrimination. These days we experience an increasing demand for our services, and I am sure that most members would object to being labelled "unhealthy" and characterised as having poor mental health, low self-esteem, and bad relationships with their adoptive families. On the contrary, many adoptees find it empowering to deal with these issues. It seems that a gap exists between the underlying norms of mainstream adoption research and the variety of lived experiences of intercountry adoptees. Instead of labelling behaviour healthy or unhealthy—which will lead us nowhere—professionals must explore the field in a more open-minded manner.

The *Meaning of Roots* conference organized by the Korea Club was an attempt to engage such exploration. One of the key speakers was the Norwegian anthropologist Ånund Brottveit, who outlined a theoretical framework for understanding ethnic identity development among intercountry adoptees in Norway. I want to highlight Brottveit's research because I think it is enlightening, particularly for the Scandanavian context, which is ethnically almost completely homogeneous and devoid of non-European immigrants.[1]

Brottveit investigated the identity development of young adult Korean and Colombian adoptees (mean age 25 years). Due to the lack of Korean and Colombian ethnic minority groups living in Scandinavia, he assumed that the Korean and Columbia adoptees were not able to develop Korean or Colombian identities as they might in the United States. Nevertheless, he still presumed that ethnic identity matters—both because of the adoptee's self-image and because white Norwegians might perceive and treat adoptees as foreigners due to their nonwhite appearance, subjecting them to what he refers to as external categorisation.

Based on this empirical research with adoptees, Brottveit identified three categories of intercountry adoptee ethnic identities. The categories are considered ideal types and he argues that both "secure" and "insecure" ways of adapting within them exist. The first category is *Norwegian* (and could be Danish or, if one could extend the theory to less homogeneous countries, Canadian, and so forth, i.e., the dominant ethnicity of the receiving country). Adoptees within this category feel completely Norwegian and are not interested in searching for roots. The secure adoptees feel confident about having a different appearance from their national counterparts, whereas the insecure have difficulty tackling comments about their appearance and origins. The second category is *Double Ethnic*. The secure adoptees within this group are characterised as having integrated elements from both the adoptive country and the birth country into their identities. The insecure, on the contrary, explore their birth culture as something to cling to, in opposition to the culture of the adoptive country. The third category is the *Cosmopolitan* group. These adoptees have a relaxed, flexible attitude to ethnicity and cultural belonging. The secure adoptees are open to new influences and stress individual identity more than national identity. The insecure tend to be rootless, constantly searching, and lacking any sense of belonging.

Brottveit stresses that all three identities are perfectly sound identities. Adoptees who feel they are Double Ethnic or Cosmopolitan are just as normal as adoptees who feel Norwegian. No ideal identity formation process exists, no identity is more mature than the others, and in real life the categories are often fluid and mixed. Brottveit's research shows that intercountry adoptees choose different ethnic identities. Many do not assimilate, and there is no clear-cut causal relation between a specific ethnic identity and well-being.

Brottveit's study therefore serves as a corrective to mainstream adoption research. In line with my claim that adoption research needs to be validated by our lived experience, it must then be asked whether his findings are applicable to other intercountry adoptee experiences. Since I will apply Brottveit's findings to the experiences of Korea Club members, I will first explain why they are a valid test sample. The Korea Club has often been accused of not representing all Korean adoptees. Certainly, there are 8000 Korean adoptees in Denmark and the club has only 250 members. However, through the organisation's 13 years of existence, it has been in touch with some 800–1000 Korean adoptees. Furthermore, the club's 250 members embody a wide variety of adoption experiences. The members are not some monolithic group of adoptees with identity problems, as people often think. The reality is quite the opposite, in fact; it is predominantly "strong" adoptees who become members, whereas adoptees with severe problems or even psychiatric disorders sometimes contact us but usually neither become members nor attend our activities.

That Korea Club members in general are "strong" is reflected in their socioeconomic profile. In 2001 I surveyed members to explore ethnic identity, impact of racism, and interest in searching for biological family. The results in no way represented a straightforward picture: adoptees claim different ethnic identities and deal with racism and biological family in different ways.[3]

The survey also indicated that the respondents are a resource-rich group. They are very well educated (33 percent had either completed or were studying for a master's degree). In comparison, only 7 percent of the Danish population aged 30–34 years old has completed a master's. In general, the respondents also reported that their relationships with their adoptive families were good. Thus, if achievement of high socioeconomic scores indicates healthy adjustment, the Korea Club members seem to resemble the adoptees portrayed in mainstream adoption research. But they also differ significantly, since while they appear to be well adjusted in socioeconomic terms, Korea Club members are still interested in exploring the meaning of ethnic and biological heritage in their lives.

The members' senses of ethnic identity shifted from childhood to adulthood. Almost everyone felt completely Danish as children, whereas in adulthood the adoptees presented a diverse picture. I found adoptees here who, to use Brottveit's categories, still felt entirely Danish, alongside adoptees who felt Double Ethnic—Danish and Korean at the same time. I also found adoptees who did not feel they belonged to any specific nationality and so may be characterised as Cosmopolitan.

Generally, the members indicated that in the process of shaping their identities, it made a difference for them to be able to explore Korean-ness and adoption. Becoming familiarised with Korean culture, eating Korean food, sharing experiences with other adoptees, travelling to Korea, and searching for birth family seemed to be meaningful activities for all the members irrespective of whether they identified with Korea or not.

The survey further revealed that racism and discrimination are a fact of adoptees' daily lives—both as direct discrimination and as more subtle racism; the latter is what many found most difficult to pinpoint and also most hurtful. Subtle racism is often not recognised by society at large. Many adoptees noted that their parents were not able to provide them with much useful information about Korea, but exploring and creating their own images of Korea as adults has strengthened their ability to cope with racism and discrimination.

Brottveit's study and the empirical data from the Korea Club member survey suggest that adoption is not only about adjustment. The need to explore roots cannot simply be dismissed as deviating, unhealthy behaviour. We must then ask about the implications of this alternative research perspective for our understanding of intercountry adoptees. Does it in fact constitute a more ample and accurate picture of intercountry adoptees than mainstream Scandanavian adoption research does? Some might question the objectivity and methods of the alternative research. However, research is never objective, and both the methodology and ideology of mainstream researchers must be called into question, too.

While psychiatry and psychology have arisen from a positivistic tradition that believes in objective knowledge, today it is widely recognised that researchers will always be guided by preconceptions that will direct their work in particular directions. A researcher is always constituted biographically and paradigmatically: biographically by gender, ethnicity, nationality, and life experiences, and paradigmatically by his or her scientific understanding and theoretical and methodological approach. But as researchers, what we can and must do is to reveal and clarify our assumptions from the beginning so that we can challenge them and ensure maximum openness throughout the research process. We can also ensure reliability and validity by documenting our methodology and analysis and by testing our findings. Testing can be done in many ways; I want to highlight testing through feedback from research objects. Findings are problematic if research objects cannot identify themselves with the findings, as is often the case in mainstream adoption research.

Furthermore, we must be careful not to pathologise specific behaviour or feelings, as mainstream adoption researchers have so often done. Does a universal healthy intercountry adoption experience really exist? I doubt it. While mainstream adoption research says that adoptees are healthy because they assimilate, the very different perspective presented by alternative research urges us to at least reconsider the assumptions guiding intercountry adoption.

The large-scale intercountry adoption we are witnessing today is a fairly recent phenomenon, but there is nothing indicating that it will either cease or diminish. Intercountry adoption is probably here to stay. We must therefore expand our understanding of the collective experience of intercountry adoptees by increasing efforts to record and study the experiences gathered by the objects in question—the adoptees themselves.

The most important implication of such research is that we re-evaluate current adoption policy and practice. Today we have enough testimonies and research results to enable us to specify what postadoption services are necessary. Now we should implement them so we can assist—without prejudice—all adoptees who want to explore the meaning of ethnic identity and biological family.

notes

1 Ånund Brottveit, "'Jeg ville ikke skille meg ut'—dentitetsudvikling, ekstern kategorisering og etnisk identitet hos utenlandsadopterte fra Columbia og Korea" ("'I Didn't Want to Look Different'—Identity Development, External Categorisation, and Ethnic Identity of Adoptees from Columbia and Korea"), (Oslo: Diaconia College Center, 1999).

2 Kirsten Sloth, "Adult Korean Adoptees in Denmark—Exploring Ethnic Identity and Making Sense of Adoption," in *Official Report of the Second International Gathering of Adult Korean Adoptees August 9–12, 2001, Oslo, Norway,* ed. Kirsten Sloth, the Korea Club, 2001, http://www.adopteegathering.org/2ndgathering/g2_report.pdf, 16.

3 Sloth, "Adult Korean Adoptees."

27 BEYOND THE VIETNAM WAR ADOPTIONS

RePresenting Our Transracial Lives

Indigo Williams Willing

Upon adopting a nonwhite child from Third World or marginalised populations, many white[1] adoptive parents living in the West[2] invest much love and effort in making their new family member feel that she or he belongs. In early childhood adoptees usually quickly adapt to their new family lives and flourish from the positive emotional, medical, and economic security provided to them. This trajectory is well documented in transracial/intercountry adoption studies conducted by white Western researchers in the past twenty years. Their work stands as an ongoing testament to the some of the postadoption benefits for so-called orphans.[3] However, as we will see, things can get a bit, what I will call tricky, as the adoptees grow older.

One reason is that race is still used to determine who is seen as an insider and who is seen an outsider. As this anthology reminds us, transracial adoptees come to occupy a space somewhere in between as the outsiders within. I am a Vietnamese Australian who was adopted and raised by a white Australian family. I share some of my own personal history and community work here to illustrate the tricky side of moving across national, cultural, and racialised boundaries. I then discuss how we can *all* re-engage with the complex politics of identity and difference of transracial adoptees.

from cute to tricky

The Viet Nam war is generally understood in Australia through the stories of soldiers and refugees. But what about those lesser-known stories of the children who were caught up in the chaos of war, removed from their country of birth, and taken into the hearts and homes of Australian families? There are many stories yet to be revealed.

In 1972 I was removed from an orphanage in Saigon and adopted by Australian parents. Although no official figures exist, Western humanitarian workers estimate that prior to 1975 Australian families adopted several hundred Vietnamese children. In 1975 approximately 280 more Vietnamese children were flown to Australia as part of Operation Babylift. White, middle-class Australian parents adopted the majority of these children.

The general expectation was that these children would grow up to feel they were the same as their new, non-Vietnamese families and peers. After all, most lacked memories of Viet Nam. They rarely arrived with birth certificates or mementos. Most adoptive families lived far away from areas populated by Vietnamese refugees and their families, so adopted children had little access to Vietnamese values, literature, songs, and language.

The Vietnamese adoptions also followed an era of Australian history when efforts to assimilate Indigenous and migrant populations into the dominant culture drew little mainstream protest. It is not surprising that adoptive parents were not encouraged by adoption authorities to provide their children with multicultural upbringings, with an emphasis on their culture of birth.

Ian Harvey's 1980 study of 109 Australian families with children adopted from Viet Nam concluded that the children, mostly still in early childhood, were successfully fitting in with their families. However, Harvey also acknowledged that it was "too early to establish by research in fact how ... inter-country adopted children adjust as adults and whom they identify with."[4]

Memories of my own childhood tell a similar story. For my first five years or so in Australia I did not feel different from my adoptive family and their social networks. When I look at photos of me as a child with my adoptive family, it brings a smile to my face and I am overcome with a warm feeling. I was tiny and wide-eyed, eager to embrace all the stimulants around me—new people, a mountain of cuddly toys, a seemingly endless supply of adorable children's clothes, and a picture-perfect middle-class home.[5]

But stories about Viet Nam would begin to affect me deeply as my world expanded from my immediate home to the wider society. I first came to learn about my country of birth from media reports on war events, such as young Kim Phuc, burned by napalm, running naked down the road. As the only knowledge I had about Viet Nam was built from images and stories of war and its devastation, I grew to fear my past. I imagined Viet Nam only as a land of hardship.

A 2000 study by the Post Adoptive Resource Centre in New South Wales, which included interviews with 13 adopted Vietnamese, found that some of those interviewed had also felt disconnected from their ancestry as they were growing up. Some had wanted to be white in order to fit in with family and peers and began to feel uncomfortable about looking different from them. The majority reported experiencing significant anti-Asian racism and had felt inferior as a result. Many felt embarrassed about their Vietnamese heritage because they could only associate it with derogatory images in

Hollywood war movies or stereotypical images in the media of "desperate" Vietnamese boat people or "deviant" Vietnamese gangs.

More disturbingly, as ABC journalist Siobhán McHugh revealed in her 1992 book *Minefields and Miniskirts*, one former Operation Babylift volunteer saw some of the adoptees she brought over as babies grow up to reject their adoptive families and end up living on the streets. In these cases, the ideal of "rescuing" children from poverty by giving them new lives abroad had been met with a very different reality.

There are, of course, other stories of adoptees with strong relationships with their parents, enjoying a lifestyle and opportunities that would, most likely, have been denied to them had they remained in orphanages. But I have often found from talking to other adoptees that underneath even these stories is a sense of loss and displacement. The complex forms of cultural discrimination, exclusion, and separation that adoptees experience are often masked by simplistic representations of their transformation from "rags to riches." These hide a much bigger picture.

It is only in recent history that those in positions of privilege (men and boys, white people, Westerners, heterosexuals, and so forth) have started to address the calls "Others" (colonized subjects, people of colour, women, and so forth) have made for recognition, rights, and respect. Without such due regard, the intelligence, civility, morality, and inventiveness of the excluded groups is stripped away, appropriated, or devalued as inferior simply because they are different from the so-called normal or universal standards dictated by the dominant group.[6]

Even further in the shadows are the disadvantaged birthmothers. Their voices are rarely heard. Without new attention to the voices of birthmothers and other people from adoptees' birth countries, the adoptees' backgrounds are often sadly and simply misrepresented. Adoptees' birth countries are all too often only described as lands of orphanages and poverty.[7] In contrast, the Western economic, military, and empire-building forces that have caused serious and permanent disruptions to families in the Third World are notably absent in many adoption narratives. Alongside this uneven representation of global affairs, adoptees' pre-adoption pasts are often portrayed without any acknowledgment of the versions of beauty, civility, or morality that exist in their countries of origin. For example, the loving parents, ordinary families working to make a living, community leaders, doctors, scientists, farming experts, artists, and poets (not to mention Booker Prize and Nobel Prize winners) who are often a part of the adoptees' origins are obscured from view.

This is not to say that there are no hardships in sending countries and that child poverty and homelessness aren't realities to be acknowledged. Women's rights, so inherently linked to the relinquishment of children, also need to be seriously attended to and supported. The benefits of adoption certainly exist. But adoption is only one of the strategic and ideally short-term solutions to the overall problem of disadvantaged children.

Furthermore, such adoption stories are questionable representations if they are described at the expense of the dignity, rights, and humanity of the sending countries and people. Adoptees' birth countries, so often robbed of their rich literary, professional, and intellectual traditions, are then usually redescribed as overwhelmingly inhabited by dehumanised, one-dimensional characters, including beggars, AIDS victims, unmarried women, and prostitutes. The children are then often portrayed as "better off" without their families and seen as easily portable objects without a need to know their own rich histories.

rethinking old knowledge

One of the dangers of the top-down approach of studying marginal experiences is that the peoples under investigation "have often allowed our histories to be told and have then become outsiders as we heard them being retold."[8] To highlight the comparative need for a *re*presentation of the transracial adoption experience *by* transracial adoptees, Vietnamese American adoption support group director Linh Lam-Song[9] refers to bell hooks's critique[10] of similar patterns of estrangement in the postmodern research of "difference":

> The suggestion that such work [by white scholars] constitutes the only relevant discourse, evades the issue of potential inaccessible locations, spaces white theorists cannot occupy. Without inscribing an essentialist standpoint, it is crucial that we neither ignore nor deny that such locations exist.[11]

Sunny Jo, Korean adoptee and author of "The Making of KAD Nation" (see Chapter 29), assesses outsiders' knowledge-making about Korean adoptee experience: "In the past and even today 'experts,' [adoption agency] professionals, and adoptive parents are often the ones who are telling KADs [Korean adoptees] what 'the adoption experience' is actually like" (p. 286). It is time to view transracial adoptees as expert documenters of their own lives, not just as informants for other writers and researchers to use as decoration to authorise their own views. But what does history, as *re*presented by those who have been adopted across national, cultural, and racialised boundaries, now tell us?

In 2002 I began to research the lives of adopted Vietnamese as part of a master's degree at the University of Technology, Sydney, continuing my studies as a Rockefeller Fellow at the University of Massachusetts, Boston, in 2003. Although most of the adopted Vietnamese I interviewed had enjoyed healthy relationships with their adoptive families, they also felt discomfort over their racial identity and estranged from their ethnic heritage. These new voices were adding to and expanding our understanding of the adoption experience.

One Vietnamese-Australian adoptee who participated in the study was raised in a rural Victorian town where racist views were common. She recalls, "I hated the way I looked [and] identified so strongly with my peers that I hated other Asians." This view was also reflected in her attitude toward dating; she admitted, "I never felt attractive enough as the boys saw me as too 'different' to date … and I would have felt too embarrassed to be seen with [an] Asian male."

Compounding this adoptee's own sense of difference was that she felt pressured to be "grateful" for being adopted and believed that this silenced her sense of grief and loss. It also denigrated her ancestry. She says, "I was forced to feel grateful, which I resented as a child. I guess it made me feel embarrassed about my country, that it was inferior, and I felt ashamed that I had to be rescued from it." As Korean adoptee and academic Tobias Hübinette writes, transnational adoption narratives send out a clear message that "life in the West is best."[12]

Throughout my own childhood and teenage years I struggled to find more respectful frames of reference to Viet Nam. Attitudes toward Vietnamese and Asians, filtered through mainstream representations of the war and boat refugees, were reflected in the attitudes of my peers. The kids in my local area were mostly Anglo-Australians and I was probably one of the only Asians they had ever encountered in the flesh. They often made jokes about my Asian appearance. We grew up in the same area, had identical accents, and each was as "typically Aussie" as the next, yet somehow I became different.

Other adoptees in the study also reported that they struggled to feel a sense of belonging in their school years. Many "felt white" but were constantly reminded by classmates and peers that they were not white: either through racism or being treated as foreigners and asked questions like, "Where are you from?"

It is only in adulthood that many adoptees have gained the confidence to re-engage with their heritage. This shift coincides with Australia's attempts to be more inclusive of difference. The recognition of second generation Vietnamese-Australians such as Tam Le, named Young Australian of the Year in 1998, and Khoa Do, recipient of the same award in 2004, has helped adoptees to feel a sense of pride in their cultural background and to acknowledge their multiple cultural identifications.

Some adoptees have experienced rejection from nonadopted Vietnamese as well as white Australians. One adoptee I spoke to expressed her disappointment in her interactions with nonadopted Vietnamese saying, "As we are adoptees, we are not considered as fully Vietnamese." However, many second generation Vietnamese-Australians are beginning to welcome adoptees. Vietnamese Youth Media, based at Footscray Community Arts Centre in Melbourne, has worked with adopted Vietnamese on plays such as *The Viet*

Boys from Down Under. Vietnamese adoptees are also featured by journalist and documentary maker Dai Le, whose work highlights the 30th anniversary of Operation Babylift.

Language barriers are a main source of tension between adopted and nonadopted Vietnamese. As adoptees, we either depend on translators or require others to use English. This can be as impractical as it can be painful. We are often unable to communicate with non-English-speaking Vietnamese in a deep and meaningful way. At the same time, we face the challenge of finding ways to resist the pressure to totally conform to notions of "Vietnameseness."

But there are spaces being created where such notions are combated and challenged. Adopted Vietnamese International, for example, is an online community that I developed in Australia so adoptees could build stronger ties with each other to explore their own senses of identity. Adopted Vietnamese International and other similar networks, such as the Vietnamese Adoptee Network, can assist adoptees in discovering how their experiences are unusual but not unique. Given the recent surge of interest from couples wishing to adopt children orphaned by the tsunami disaster and other crises such as the conflict in Sudan, it is timely to begin to reflect on the trials, errors, and successes of the Viet Nam War, and indeed, Korean and other transracial adoptions. The challenge for any family wishing to adopt a child from overseas is how to successfully integrate a healthy respect for diverse racial and cultural identities. We now know that adoption is a lifelong journey for the people involved, and the lack of appreciation of racial and cultural diversity in the upbringing of former waves of adoptees means that many are still struggling to make sense of their identities today.

starting new dialogues

The realisation and negotiation of transracial adoptees' own complex multiplicity, depending on how it is shaped, understood, and supported, can be a potentially empowering or an incredibly unsettling experience. We need to find ways to enable ourselves to achieve dignity through recognising our differences and incorporating them more positively into our identities, rather than allowing our adoptive parents or ourselves to deny or be confused by them. In other words, we should not feel inferior because we are different from both our white adoptive parents and most people who share our non-white and often non-Western pre-adoption ancestry.

Although transracial adoptee identities are potentially problematic and complex, I am not suggesting that they are destined to remain in a state of "terminal uniqueness."[13] As Grossberg reminds us, all "Identities are... always contradictory, made up out of partial fragments."[14] What might influence us is the parallel between the construction of identity in transracial adoptees and the "cut-and-mix processes" as well as "links and splits, connects and disconnects" that are also unfolding in the new generation of diasporas and migrant youth.[15]

It is also important to remember that no group is a monolithic entity; this includes white people.[16] There is a particular danger of "defining Whites as essentially oppressive, homogenous, immutable and intrinsically racist" rather than acknowledging "that all ethnic labels, including White, are historically sited."[17] Robbins warns us that a "reversion to the spurious authenticity of (ethnic or religious) origins" is also "a prevalent condition, and its consequences have been both damaging and destructive.... Cultural arrogance can become cultural violence."[18] In other words, adoptees need not give in to notions that cultural attributes are inherent or that one is better than the other. But where does such powerful knowledge leave these outsiders within?

Perhaps we can employ multiple strategies that allow us to make our mark in each culture that has given meaning to our lives by sharing knowledge. We can, for example, support organizations like Mam Non and the Catalyst Foundation, both in the United States, which provide Vietnamese culture camps for adoptive families *run by* Vietnamese Americans who understand that adoption comes with its own politics of difference. There are also many general gatherings and groups, such as US–based Also Known As and the Inter-country Adoptee Support Network in Australia, that offer collective gatherings where all transracial and intercountry adoptees can meet, seek and give support, and socialise. In most cases their friends, families, and partners can also become involved. Once again, these are spaces where the former "outsiders within" can draw attention to their own politics of difference and build new traditions. We can also keep creating new tools and associations that can help transracial adoptees develop and maintain a sense of pride in our differences through looking back at our own trials and errors.

Finally, in the past five years a new wave of researchers and writers who were transracially adopted have started to intervene, speak up, and produce valuable knowledge about who they are, what they feel, and what they need from their own perspectives.[19] The adoptees in this book are also creating a road map of what they need (or needed) by speaking in detail about their struggles as outsiders within. It may be too soon to make any final conclusions about "best practices," but the growing research by transracial adoptee scholars and community strategies evolving in adoption collectives who apply equal parts critique and constructiveness toward their circumstances will no doubt yield more and better pathways.

notes

1 The term "white" or "whiteness," also referred to as the "same," has been identified as "an unmarked or neutral category ... the unspoken norm" and given "a location of structural advantage, of race privilege" in the West (See R. Frankenberg, *White Women, Race Matters: The Social Construction of Whiteness* [Minneapolis: University of Minnesota Press, 1999], 197.) Other racial classifications, such as "Different" or "Other" refer to racial and cultural categories outside "whiteness" and are capitalised

to acknowledge that they have become a site of political struggle.

2 The West or Western refers not only to white European locations in Europe, North America, Australia, and New Zealand but also to "economic, institutional, political, ideological [and] cultural" practices (S. Hall, "Cultural Studies," in *The New Social Theory Reader: Contemporary Debates*, ed. Steven Seiderman and Jeffrey C. Alexander, [London: Routledge, 2001], 89). White culture, also described as "whiteness," refers to European-influenced traditions, language, religion, social practices, and values. However, white culture also "designates a subjective sense of identity as much as it designates activity or practice" (Frankenberg, *White Women*, 234).

3 See, for example, Ian J. Harvey, "Australian Parents for Vietnamese Children: A Social and Psychological Study of Inter-Country Adoption," New South Wales Department of Youth and Community Services, Australia, Sydney, 1980.

4 Harvey, "Australian Parents."

5 Class is not one of the key issues addressed in this study, yet it should not be entirely disregarded as contributing to the relative isolation from other Vietnamese people many adopted Vietnamese experienced growing up. Frankenberg argues that for children of colour with white middle- and upper-class parents, "Given … stratification of US society by race linked by class, the family's class and their racial or cultural identities were now in contradiction with each other: they could either live among their economic or their ethnic peers, but not both" (Frankenberg, *White Women*, 131).

6 Edward Said, *Orientalism, (*New York: Penguin, 1991); R. Stam and E. Shohat, "Contested Histories: Eurocentrism, Multiculturalism and the Media" in *Multiculturalism: A Critical Reader, Vol. 296–324,* ed. D. Goldberg. (Cambridge MA: Blackwell Publishers, 1994).

7 David Eng, "Transnational Adoption and Queer Diasporas," *Social Text* 21, no. 3 (2003), 1–37.

8 Linda Tuhiwai Smith, *Decolonizing Methodologies: Research and Indigenous Peoples* (New York: Zed Books, 1999), 33.

9 Linh Lam-Song and Indigo Williams, "Borders in Cyber Space and the Digital Divide Between Vietnamese Parents and Their Children Adopted Abroad Post War," paper, Generations: Continuity and Conflict in South East Asia Conference, Yale University, New Haven, (March 1–3, 2002), 1-15.

10 "Difference" is used in the context of the "Politics of Difference" to refer to the struggle for recognition rather than a belief in essential differences. It is a strategic identification against assimilation/"sameness" ideologies that "[structure] privilege and oppression" against differences that include racial and cultural identities (I. M. Young, "Justice and the Politics of Difference," in *The New Social Theory Reader: Contemporary Debates*, ed. Steven Seiderman and Jeffret Alexander [London: Routledge, 2001], 203–211.)

11 bell hooks, "Critical Interrogation: Talking Race, Resisting Racism," *Inscriptions* 5 (1989), http://humanities.ucsc.edu/CultStudies/PUBS/Inscriptions/vol_5/bellhooks.html.

12 Tobias Hübinette, "Adopted Koreans and the Development of Identity in the 'Third Space'," *Adoption and Fostering* 27, no. 4 (2003): 1–9.

13 Janet M. Bennett, "Cultural Marginality: Identity Issues in Intercultural Training," in *Education for the Intercultural Experience,* ed. R. Michael Paige (Yarmouth, ME: Intercultural Press, 1993), 115.

14 Lawrence Grossberg, "Identity and Cultural Studies—Is That All There Is?" in *Questions of Cultural Identity,* ed. Stuart Hall and Paul du Gray, (London: Sage Publications, 1996), 91.

15 Ien Ang and others, *Alter/Asians: Asian-Australian Identities in Art, Media and Popular Culture* (Annandale: Pluto Press, 2000), xix.

16 bell hooks argues, "Committed cultural critics—whether white or black, scholars or artists—or both—can produce work that opposes structures of domination (and) that presents possibilities for a transformed future by willingly interrogating their own work on aesthetic and political grounds. This interrogation itself becomes an act of critical intervention, fundamentally fostering an attitude of vigilance rather than denial." ("Critical Interrogation: Talking Race, Resisting Racism," *Inscriptions* 5 (1989), http://humanities.ucsc.edu/CultStudies/PUBS/Inscriptions/vol_5/bellhooks.html.) She suggests that it is useful for white people to focus on "whiteness" and for all individuals to more critically investigate and report their own relationship to the topic they are presenting.

17 Pnina Werbner and Tariq Modood, *Debating Cultural Hybridity: Multicultural Identities and the Politics of Anti-Racism* (New Jersey: Zed Books, 2000), 11.

18 K. Robbins, "Interrupting Identities: Turkey Europe" in *Questions of Cultural Identity,* ed. Hall and du Gray, 63, 66.

19 Hübinette, "Adopted Koreans"; Anthony Shiu, "Flexible Production: International Adoption, Race and Whiteness," *Jouvert Online Journal* 6, no. 1 & 2 (Fall 2001), http://social.chass.ncsu.edu/jouvert/v6i1-2/shiu.htm; Indigo Williams Willing, "The Adopted Vietnamese Community: From Fairytales to the Diaspora," *Michigan Quarterly Review* 43, no. 4 (2004): 648–664.

28 NO LONGER ALONE IN THIS GRIEF

SERVICE-USER-LED SUPPORT FOR TRANSRACIAL ADOPTEES

Perlita Harris

The loss of my birthmother through adoption has meant the loss of my birthright: of a way of life within the Indian community; of a rich and beautiful culture; of knowledge of my maternal history and ancestry; and of my ability to speak my mother tongue with birth maternal and paternal relatives.[1]

ᘎ

I feel like my feelings haven't really been recognized ... for example, I think losing, you know, your birth family, your parents, and your country and culture, and community and everything, and people don't think it's very relevant because you've never known it, and so I don't think people think you have a right to actually grieve any of that. (Lyn) [2]

ᘎ

I can't be alone in thinking that being transracially adopted, we have lost something: lost our languages, traditions, cultures, and most importantly the subtleties and nuances of those cultures. We have lost something we never had which we may not have even valued had we had it and, yet, we continue to mourn. Am I alone in this grief?[3]

ᘎ

Adoption of Black children by white families has been known in the United Kingdom for over 50 years, and yet the voices of transracially adopted adults are rarely heard. Indeed, very little is known about the childhood and adult experiences and the adoption support needs of this diverse, heterogeneous, and hitherto silenced group. This chapter focuses on the Association for Transracially Adopted and Fostered People (ATRAP), a UK-based Black social-service-user led and controlled organization, and the experiences of its members. In the United Kingdom, "Black" is a political term used to refer to people who originate from or are descendants of people from Africa, South Asia, and East Asia. All have a shared experience of oppression in British society. ATRAP uses this political definition of Black identity, which includes those people with one white birthparent. Unlike many adoption support groups, this organization brings together all those who have been raised in white families, whether by adoption or long-term foster care. The group recognizes that while there are some fundamental differences of experience between transracial adoption and long-term fostering by a white family, there are also crucial similarities, as this chapter will demonstrate. I begin by briefly examining the context within which the practice of transracial adoption has arisen and continues to flourish, followed by an overview of what we know from research about the experience of transracial adoptees. I then focus on the reasons members give for joining ATRAP and the difference that being a member of ATRAP has made to their lives. Finally, as the opportunity for transracially adopted and fostered people to voice their experiences and concerns is extremely important, I highlight some common themes and issues that arise in conversations among ATRAP members.[4]

setting the context

There are no figures available—either domestically or out of country—on the number of children who have been adopted transracially in the United Kingdom because the government has only recently started collecting statistics on the "race" and ethnicity of children who are adopted. However, we know that there is a direct correlation between social factors and the increase in domestic transracial adoption. With the decline in white babies available for adoption from the late 1960s onwards, from 14,000 in 1968 to 1400 in 1988, transracial adoption has become an established practice.[5] Prior to this, Black children, including children with one Black parent, were generally considered "unadoptable" or "hard to place." As a result, it was not uncommon for Black children to grow up in residential children's homes. However, in the 1950s and early 1960s, a small number of Black children were adopted by white families, often by their foster family caregivers. By the 1980s, the majority of Black children who were adopted were placed with white families. Today, one in five (20 percent) "looked after" children for whom there is an adoption plan are Black,[6] although only 9 percent of the general population in England and Wales is Black.[7] "Same-race" adoptive placements for Black children continue to be debated and challenged, while "same-race" adoptive placements for white children remain the norm and go unchallenged.[8]

Although government figures have only recently started to distinguish between intercountry and domestic adoption, we can estimate that intercountry adoption began in the late 1950s and early 1960s.[9] Intercountry adoption in the United Kingdom has been steadily increasing since the early 1990s. In the year 2000–2001, some 327 children entered England and Wales for the purpose of adoption. They mainly came from China, followed by Thailand, the United States, India, Guatemala, Russia, Vietnam, and Sri Lanka.[10] The adoption of children from the poor countries of the developing world to the rich countries of the developed world is an extension of global inequality that has its roots in colonialism.[11]

Adoption and "race" are quite politicized in the United Kingdom. In the 1990s, this politicization led to a backlash against the practice of same-race placements. This was epitomised in a Department of Health circular that outlines the government's position on transracial adoption. It included the following statements:

> A child's ethnic origin, culture, language and religion are significant factors to be taken into account when adoption agencies are considering the most appropriate placement for a child: however, such consideration has to take into account *all the child's needs.* (emphasis in original)[12]
>
> The Government has made it clear that it is unacceptable for a child to be denied loving adoptive parents solely on the grounds that the child and the adopters do not share the same racial background.

This position was reiterated in the run-up to the full implementation of the Adoption and Children Act of 2002.

However, despite the impression given by those attacking same-race placements—that white adoptive parents have been denied the opportunity to adopt Black children—the practice of transracial adoption has never stopped. In a national survey, the British Association for Adoption and Fostering (BAAF) found that overall, 17 percent of minority ethnic children adopted were placed transracially (with numbers reaching 50 percent in rural areas).[13] A Social Services Inspectorate report using a smaller sample found a higher rate, with 53 percent of adopted minority ethnic children placed transracially.[14] Current government policy emphasizes increasing the percentage of foster children who are placed for adoption and reducing the delays in placing children with adoptive families.[15] Coupled with a failure to recruit Black families to ensure they exist in numbers sufficient to receive the children,[16] this approach ensures that the practice of transracial adoption will continue, perhaps at even greater rates than in recent years. Furthermore, since June 1, 2003, the Hague Convention on Protection of Children and Co-operation in Respect of Intercountry Adoption of 1993 has been in effect in the United Kingdom. To comply with the Hague Convention, the UK government has arranged to be a state of origin as well as a receiving state. It follows that the adoption of "looked after" children by both a known (e.g., relative) or unknown person in another country will be considered as an option for children for whom an adoptive placement in the United Kingdom cannot be found. The government will maintain a list of children available for intercountry adoption. Inevitably, this list will include Black children.

Thus, the United Kingdom may be entering a new era in the practice of transracial intercountry adoption.[17]

There is a dearth of literature concerning the experiences of transracially adopted children and adults in the United Kingdom. The liberal paradigm that has dominated research on transracial adoption has been exhibited in researchers' tendency to whitewash any difficulties in such placements and to defend the practice of transracial adoption against the challenges that have been made against it, including downplaying the significance of "race" and racism.[18] Further, UK research has paid negligible attention to the experiences of adopted children and adults—either same-race or transracial—as described in their own words, primarily focusing instead on placement outcomes, such as disruption rates and allowing children's perspectives to be mediated through their adoptive parents. Nor has research looked at the adoption support needs of transracially adopted people or their experiences in receiving statutory and independent adoption support services. The overall effect has been to silence the voices of transracially adopted children and adults.

From the research that is available, however, we do know that younger foster children and Black children with one white parent are more commonly adopted transracially.[19] We also know that transracially adopted children tend to see themselves as '"white" in all but skin colour,'[20] with adopters taking a colourblind approach to parenting.[21] Many of these children have little or no contact with other Black people,[22] and engage in attempts to "whiten" themselves.[23] In addition, intercountry adoptees may experience post-traumatic stress disorder and unrecognized health problems.[24]

Adoptees report experiencing significant racism, sometimes within the extended family and school.[25] This includes widespread racist bullying during childhood, with both verbal abuse and physical violence, and with school the most frequent location.[26] They describe feeling "unable to cope."[27] Derek Kirton, in his pilot study involving interviews with ten transracially adopted adults, found these adults had "an uneasy ... relationship with 'whiteness' and an equally ambivalent one with 'community of origin,' characterized by a powerful gravitational pull but also by distance and discomfort."[28] Black adopted adults felt unsupported in countering racism and protected their parents from learning about their experiences of racism. Significantly, research has found that transracial adoptees are more likely than white adoptees to feel they are different from their adoptive family and report lower levels of closeness to their adoptive mothers.[29] Transracial adopters are generally less inclusive of birth relatives than Black adopters are.[30] Girls placed transracially appear to be at a slightly higher risk of experiencing disrupted adoptions than boys.[31] Further, not all long-lasting placements are successful when other outcome measures, such as satisfaction or "racial" and cultural pride, are taken into account.[32]

In addition, research has found that transracially adopted adults search for information at a younger age than their white counterparts (25.8 years compared to 31.2 years), with "racial" and ethnic identity issues featuring significantly in their reasons for searching.[33] More transracial adoptees search for their (usually Black) birthfathers, both initially and subsequently, than do white adoptees.[34] Some feel anxious or ambivalent about searching for their white birth families for fear of being rejected because they are themselves Black.[35] A Children's Society study of search and reunion found that, while transracially adopted adults are more likely to feel different from their adoptive families,[36] they are also less likely to feel "at home" with their birth relatives than their white counterparts, or to have had their "racial" and ethnic identity needs met following reunion.

In recent years, there has been an increasing interest in social-service-user knowledge and the recognition that such users are experts. The 1980s saw the emergence of service-users' own organizations, each with its own perspectives and demands for different, better, and more responsive services, highlighting the failings in social work policy and practices. Although there are differences within and between these service-user movements, they all demand the right to "speak for themselves" and to participate in debates and decisions affecting them, in their own movements and in society.[37] Transracially adopted adults can be seen as one group of service-users who have come together to speak about their experiences, to make demands regarding adoption and adoption support services, and, for some, to challenge the practices of transracial and intercountry adoption. Transracially adopted adults have also begun to write about their experiences. Personal accounts by transracially adopted adults in Britain and in other countries, along with the body of creative writing that they have produced, provide further insight into the day-to-day experiences of those Black people brought up by white families. Together they bring out the common themes of difference, belonging, and identity; loss and gratitude; racism and racial abuse; childhood depression and adult mental distress; loss of birth relatives, culture, and language; visiting countries of origin; and search and reunion with birth relatives.

current service provision

Although practitioners have emphasized the need for support groups for transracial adoptees, there are no comprehensive adoption support services in the United Kingdom tailored to meeting the needs of transracially—including intercountry—adopted children and adults.[38] Yet counseling services have found that these adoptees experience racism within the adoptive family, have feelings of "anger, sadness and bewilderment," struggle with a "negative self-image," and want to find their Black birthparent.[39]

The paucity of adoption support services for those who have been transracially and internationally adopted, both children and adults, is of great concern. In 1988 the Post Adoption Centre in London was the first agency in the United Kingdom to provide a service specifically for transracially adopted adults. This took the form of a series of support groups with two Black facilitators.[40] More recently, in 2001, the Manchester support agency After Adoption started a monthly group for transracially adopted adults. Following a study of service-users' views associated with a regional postadoption agency in the West Midlands,[41] the Birmingham-based Adoption Support is establishing a similar group, having made an earlier unsuccessful attempt in the mid-1990s. An appalling lack of importance attached to the needs of transracially adopted people is indicated in the failure of both the government and independent service providers to provide even one comprehensive adoption support system tailored to meeting the needs of this group of children and adults.

Not surprisingly, then, many ATRAP members have had no previous contact with any postadoption services and are unaware of their statutory rights and the services that do exist. Some of those who have used other services report difficulties, including long waiting lists for accessing adoption records, birth records counseling, and counseling services; problems finding a counselor or therapist, particularly a Black therapist skilled and knowledgeable about transracial adoption, search, and reunion; and a lack of information and guidance about searching for birth relatives who may live in other countries.

what is atrap?

ATRAP is run by and for transracially adopted and fostered people. ATRAP seeks to center the views and experiences of transracially adopted and long-term fostered people, and values their experiences as a basis for essential knowledge. ATRAP believes that members can take action to benefit themselves, learn from each other, explore and analyze their experiences, and identify actions and strategies to bring about changes that will improve the quality of their own and others' lives. Established in 1993, ATRAP evolved out of the series of groups for transracially adopted adults held at the Post Adoption Centre. The organization grew steadily, becoming a registered charity in 1996, relaunched in 2000, and in 2001 securing (minimal) three-year core funding from the Department of Health. Although based in London, ATRAP members have also developed regional groups and networks in Leeds, Brighton, and Bristol. Maintaining the organization has not always been easy and is impacted by the personal journeys that committee members are themselves undertaking, such as searching for birth relatives, making links with Black communities, and addressing emotional distress.

The primary aim of ATRAP is to provide peer support in order to reduce the isolation that transracially adopted and fostered adults feel. ATRAP aims to create a safe place for members to meet and talk, as well as social and educational opportunities to empower members. ATRAP seeks to provide a welcoming, supportive, and nonjudgmental space for all transracially adopted and long-term fostered people regardless of, first, their views about transracial adoption and fostering, intercountry adoption, searching, and reunion; and second, their sex, class, and whether they are users of mental health services, psychiatric system survivors, disabled, lesbian, gay, or bisexual, or they have experiences with the criminal justice system. It has been difficult to create a safe environment where all members will be accepted and valued by each other, but ATRAP has remained committed to challenging discrimination and oppression.

Membership in ATRAP is open to people who have been adopted transracially, both domestically and from another country, and to those who have been "looked after" in long-term transracial foster care or have been privately fostered. The Bristol ATRAP group (LAFTA) is also open to those who have grown up in predominately white residential children's homes. The ATRAP membership reflects the diversity of transracially adopted and fostered people, including those whose placements were disrupted and those who were abused or neglected by their adoptive or foster families. Members range in age from late teens to mid-40s and include people who have grown up in both rural and urban areas. Associate membership is available for interested professionals; family members by birth, foster care, or adoption; local authorities; and voluntary sector agencies.

Over the years, ATRAP has provided a range of services including social events; workshops; an email list; a website; a quarterly newsletter with members' poems, articles, and letters; referrals to legal advice; counseling and postadoption services; volunteer opportunities; and an informal support and friendship network. Social events enable ATRAP members to meet other transracially adopted and fostered people, to give and receive peer support, and to share and value experiences while socializing. The London-based ATRAP organization has provided support to those wishing to establish regional groups, and ATRAP produced a video, "Love is Not Enough: Experiences in Transracial Adoption,"[42] in which three transracially adopted adults speak about their experiences. ATRAP has also undertaken training and public speaking and has worked with the media.

why do people join atrap?

People join ATRAP for a variety of reasons. One of the main reasons they cite is to reduce isolation through meeting others who have been adopted or fostered transracially. ATRAP gives members the opportunity to talk about their experiences without fear of being ridiculed, silenced, judged, dismissed, disbelieved, or pathologized. Although some members have had contact with other transracially adopted and fostered adults in their childhood, including siblings, they say they were never enabled to talk about the experience itself or to question the practices of intercountry and transracial adoption. Many members report negative reactions when they attempt to speak about their feelings with adoptive and foster family members, friends, or acquaintances.

> I've told most friends that I go to ATRAP, and they, they really can't understand why, and I think they find it quite hard to understand that there is actually racism.... I just think it's really hard for them to understand ... you've got all these okay things in your life, so why should you be feeling down, depressed, can't make sense of your life? So it's, it's something that they've got no sort of conception of.... Then you end up feeling that you're just making a mountain out of a molehill. (Lyn)

> The only person that fully understands the experience is the person that's going through it. Everyone else has a different position from which they look into and upon that experience, and should your description ... not match with what they see ... then you'll get that reaction; that kind of hush, or that kind of, you know, ridicule, or you'll just be told to shut up, you know, "what are you talking about?, that's just ridiculous, that didn't happen, that couldn't have happened, it's obviously your problem." (Abayomi) [43]

Members have also spoken about feeling alone in their experience, or wanting to know what other Black people feel about being raised by a white family.

> I suppose I was hoping it might offer support in a way that I felt like I wasn't the only person that felt the way I did. I suppose reduce that feeling of being alone. (Lyn)

> I originally became a member of ATRAP because I was interested in hearing the opinions of other people who had similar experiences to myself, and I was desperate for a space to express what I felt about my experience without fear of suddenly feeling completely out of place or like an alien, or like I am from, you know, like I was suddenly on a different planet. (Abayomi)

The process of talking about these experiences is made more complex by the multiple losses and the pain, guilt, shame, self-hatred, confusion, gratitude, loyalty, and fear that so many members speak of.

> I sometimes have a feeling of indescribable sadness of losing my country, culture and family and wish I had the courage to shed this burden of feeling grateful. I want to express these feelings without fearing that people would reproach me for such contradictions and disloyalty since I don't deny having had a wonderful family, happiness, and more. (Mylien)[44]

why is atrap needed?

The experience of meeting another transracially adopted or fostered person is profound and powerful, for some exciting, for others overwhelming; ultimately, the experience can be healing. For many, it leads to the realization that they are not the only one, the "alien" they had previously considered themselves to be. Meeting others normalizes the experience of transracial adoption and fostering, with the potential to transform feelings about the self.

> I finally realized, after half a lifetime, that I was not ET, and my feelings about myself had been a normal reaction to the abnormal events I had experienced. (Anonymous adoptee)[45]

Some ATRAP members describe how meeting others has made a positive difference in how they feel about themselves and their ability to heal. This in turn has enabled them to feel more optimistic about the future.

> One's identity is affirmed by being with people who've had a similar experience, and that can help with my self-acceptance.... I feel wounded but the wound doesn't show ... that wound is taken care of somehow while I'm with those other people.... I can be myself, so it's healing. It's also part of myself that doesn't get a venue anywhere else. (Folusho)[46]

Members have also highlighted the important space that ATRAP creates in terms of a forum to talk, to share and express views, and to create a perspective that challenges self-blame and pathological views of transracially adopted and fostered people.

> When I'm talking about the space that ATRAP creates, I also mean the information that you come into contact with through ATRAP, and ... the philosophy that you ... can be exposed to as a result of having contact with ATRAP. That philosophy is one of it's not your fault, you know, you are not responsible, you should not feel guilty, you should not feel bad about anything. (Abayomi)

Some members report that for the first time they do not have to explain who they are and their circumstances.

> You just spend your life having to explain yourself and evading the need to explain yourself, and so you're not under that pressure when you're with people who've been through a similar experience. (Jo)

Others have spoken about how ATRAP has helped them to maintain their mental health.

> Discomfort about being in foster care and discomfort about being Black ... get addressed in ATRAP.... I wish I'd found ATRAP earlier.[47]

> For me it's important because there's very little alternative. Without this opportunity, I would probably have gone insane or be staring severe psychiatric problems in the face. (Abayomi)

Veronica Dewan, a psychiatric system survivor and an adopted adult of Indian and Irish parentage, has written about her involvement with ATRAP.

> In 1993, I met a group of Black adopted and long-term fostered adults who, like me, had been brought up in white families. Feelings we shared included loss, desolation, confusion, rejection and abandonment. When I heard parts of my story being recounted by other people, I realized I was not alone.... As our journeys converge, we are gradually working out different ways to support each other without getting overwhelmed. This has been a starting point for me to learn what it feels like to belong and draw strength from being part of a community.[48]

Sue Jardine, a Chinese woman who was adopted from Hong Kong, has described the learning that has gone hand-in-hand with her involvement with ATRAP.

> From listening to other people's experiences and being able to voice my own I have come to realize how much, from an early age, we felt it was necessary for us to take responsibility for our adoptive status. This situation was perpetuated because many of us had grown up in isolation and we also felt we had to protect our adoptive families from having to deal with our experiences.[49]

Involvement in ATRAP also helps members move from feeling powerless to identifying strategies for maintaining positive mental health and improving their lives. Personal difficulties are reframed as common concerns, while new explanations and perspectives may lead to a change in perceptions and renewed hope. Members receive collective affirmation of their experiences, and collective action may result in personal growth and increased self-confidence. They are able to listen to people at different points on their journey, empathize with each other, and learn from each other.

> It's helped me to come up with my own ideas, to sort of make my own situation a bit better.... Perhaps you listen to someone else's story and you identify with several, you know, several parts of their story, and it just shifts your perspective, because when you are not hearing stories that are similar to your own ... personally, I tend to see every door as being closed ... whereas when I hear a few more stories that are similar to my own, I tend to start to think a bit more positively, and I can rationalize, and.... I can at least attempt to make a difference. (Abayomi)

common issues

Despite differences in situations, members share a common experience of loss of birth family, community, and country of origin or heritage, of questioning their "racial" and cultural identity, and of racism.

identity

"Racial" and cultural identity is a key issue for transracially adopted and fostered people who have grown up in white families.

> There was a big shock coming to London. I felt dispossessed.... I wasn't cool with whatever Blacks were meant to be.... I'd grown up in all respects to be white. (Folusho)

> I think just walking around as a transracially adopted person you are struggling with that ... with liking yourself as a Black person.... It's been planted in your mind that to be Black is bad.... You have to adjust to what you are despite what you may have been brought up to think you are.... You go around assuming you're white perhaps, so ... you have to adjust to how people see you are. (Peter)

> There is an identity crisis that arises for most of us.... It's about remaking something of myself. (Folusho)

Transracial adoption involves multiple losses. One of the major losses for adoptees is the loss of culture.

> I feel that the Black part of my culture has been denied.... After all, how were my parents (... white, middle-class [adopters in their late 30s]) supposed to know how to introduce me to my Black culture?[50]

emotional distress

Members have spoken about having panic attacks around their racial identity, engaging in self-harming behaviour, self-hatred, trying to commit suicide, and becoming involved in the psychiatric system.

> I had first contemplated suicide at the age of seven, and such thoughts continued to haunt me throughout my childhood. I needed to get back to my roots.[51]

> Witness the high preponderance amongst us of feelings of self-hatred because we believed our white parents who while telling us we were "special" simultaneously demonstrated racist attitudes to other Black people in public and as portrayed in the media. Who wants love, if it's at the cost of low self-esteem or eventual suicide.[52]

lack of support around racial abuse and racism

Members often report experiencing racism within the immediate adoptive and foster family, as well as in the wider community and in society.

> It's there constantly as a child but you can't possibly acknowledge it if you're brought up by people that are white. (Jo)

> Maybe it was that my mother didn't recognize or understand racism, and so after the age of seven I would never mention it, and so that's something I would live with alone and never say to somebody until I don't know maybe early twenties. And I think that's really damaging. (Lyn)

the impact of adoption or fostering on day-to-day life

The experience of being raised in a white family impacts the self-esteem of transracially adopted and fostered people.

> The process whereby in order to be accepted by the family the [transracial adoptee] has to accept and take on (i.e., internalize) [the adoptive family's] possibly deeply racist attitudes.... In order to survive, the [transracially adopted] child has to grow up hating itself (for being Black)—the price for "love" by (even unconsciously) [a] racist family who doesn't respect [his or her] culture and colour. The self-esteem damaged at such an early age is difficult to recover throughout life.... Self-esteem ... is behind everything we do and achieve, and affects, for example, our relationships with others and our ability to love others and feel "lovable" by others. (Peter)

Adoption is a lifelong experience. Growing up with a white family and the loss of one's birth family and cultural, religious, and linguistic heritage continues to affect members in a myriad of ways.

> The simple fact is that most problems that I face nowadays one way or another I can pinpoint back ... to being fostered.... [It] has almost made me, I'm going to say proud of my ability to live without forming connections.... [Other problems stem from] separation from culture of birthparents and having to confront that on a day-to-day basis and having to think about that ... and just continuously sort of having to suppress that and then having it erupt all over you again, and then suppress it. (Abayomi)

gratitude and guilt

Many people speak about feelings of gratitude toward their adoptive and foster families, and of feeling guilty for saying what the experience of being raised in a white family was really like, or for questioning whether the practice of transracial adoption should take place.

> Because I feel grateful, I don't want to say anything negative to mum or my [siblings] about the life that I've had, and because of that you feel, you end up feeling angry or you end up feeling alone, and you end up feeling as if you're living ... a sort of fictionalized life because everyone's seeing you in a light.... I suppose you're not being honest with people because they're not allowing you to be honest ... and you feel guilty if you say anything negative. (Lyn)

> All in all, there is a lot of guilt and it does, it does get in the way, and it manifests itself in different, different ways, but there is a great deal of guilt. And it's quite hard to shake off. (Abayomi)

The guilt even operates among adoptees. Some members have expressed fear over how they will be seen by other adoptees, such that a self-silencing takes place.

> I don't ever say how I feel because I'm afraid they [other intercountry adoptees] are going to think I'm some traitor. (Lyn)

Few, if any, ATRAP members report being able to talk openly and honestly with their adoptive parents about their experience of transracial adoption or their views about whether transracial adoption should take place. Adoptive parents may also feel threatened by learning that their son or daughter is meeting with other transracially adopted and fostered people to talk about their experiences of growing up in a white family.

> I don't talk to my family ever about this. I managed to pluck up the courage to tell my [adoptive] mum that I was going to ATRAP and that was an experience.... She got quite indignant and defensive. (Lyn)

racism and abuse within the adoptive and foster family

Racism within the adoptive or foster family may be violently interwoven with physical and emotional abuse. Linda writes about physical and emotional abuse by her adoptive mother.

> All those years of humiliation, being beaten up and called "Black this and Black that," and then asked how much I loved her.[53]

Some members speak of sexual abuse within their adoptive family. These experiences of sexual abuse may be racialized. "L," for example, an adopted adult, has written about what she calls the "sexualization of ethnicity."

> For me there was being touched due to the curiosity that my ethnicity generated but then there was also the "access all areas." This never involved another child; it was just me on my own, though at times stuff happened when other children were present. The culprits in the main were parents, relatives, school teachers, and sadly, parents of friends.... My ethnicity seemed to provoke a response in adults that made them want to touch, stroke, feel, paw, maul, grab, and hold onto [me].[54]

Charmaine has spoken about emotional and physical abuse by her adoptive mother, and sexual abuse by her godfather, older adoptive brother, and a teacher.

> My memories of sexual abuse go back as far as I can remember. I couldn't tell you when it first happened.... I went from being very clever at school ... to playing truant all the time, self-abusing, taking overdoses.[55]

As a teenager, Charmaine ran away from her adoptive family repeatedly. A social worker visited, and Charmaine asked her to find her a new family, telling her that she did not feel safe there, to no avail. She felt nobody listened to her. Charmaine's experience highlights the reluctance by social work professionals to acknowledge and accept that adoptive families may be abusive and neglectful.

> There is no help. I've always been quite an assertive person and there was nothing. I was screaming out for help and all the signs were there—in church, in school, social services.[56]

Only as an adult has Charmaine been able to start to heal from her abusive experiences and to understand how they continue to affect her life today.

search and reunion

The desire to search for birth family members, although not shared by all, is a frequent topic of conversation among ATRAP members.

> I have yet to meet my birthmother. Each year Mothering Sunday comes around, I often wonder if I ever will. I do not feel able to celebrate my birthmother's life or properly mourn her death and may go to my grave without either experience.[57]

For intercountry adopted adults, this may be closely bound up with thoughts about the life and country they left behind.

> There is hardly a day that goes past when I do not think of Vietnam or about my difference as a Vietnamese person.... I am left wondering afresh about the family that I may have in Vietnam, and what my life could have been like if I'd stayed.[58]

post-reunion

Relationships with birth family members post-reunion are complex. Black adoptees with a white birthparent may have to deal with racism from their white birth family post-reunion.

> Yet, most of all she [birthmother] rejected me as a Black woman and I rejected her for her racism.[59]

Both domestic and intercountry transracial adoptees may have additional differences of language to overcome.

> But speaking to other people, it seems as if one of the reasons why they can't build a relationship with their parents is because they don't speak the same language. (Lyn)

Attitudes toward being lesbian or gay in the adoptees' families of origin and fear of a second rejection may also be significant issues. Meena, a transracially adopted adult of Indian parentage, has written about concealing from her birthmother that she is a lesbian.

> I am guarded about what I write, too. There is so much I wish I could tell you about myself, but everything I do is censored from my correspondence with you.... If I told you what I really do, perhaps you would disown me, and I am not ready to lose you again.[60]

survival

Some members speak about their struggle to get through each day and to make sense of their lives.

> I can assure you there are many transracially adopted and fostered adults attempting on a day-to-day basis to put back together the pieces of their broken lives, attempting to make sense of their place in the world, attempting to unravel what the hell has been inflicted on them—above all, attempting to survive.[61]

conclusion

Despite recent changes in UK legislation regarding adoption, the shift toward service-user involvement in social care, and the growing number of service-user-led organizations, adoption is one area where service-users, especially those who are Black, remain marginalized. The experiences of transracially adopted and fostered people, as told in their own words, have not been noted. Yet, as the experience of ATRAP shows, transracially adopted and fostered people have the ability to define their own needs, to set goals, to take action for change, and to work together to challenge injustice and oppression and to strengthen, support, and empower each other.[62] It is time that the social work profession paid due attention to the analyses and discourses of this group, and respected and valued their perspectives. Transracially adopted people must play a key role in the development of adoption support services if these services are ever to meet their needs. Unless professionals value Black service-user knowledge, they will fail to create adoption support services that are responsive to the needs and concerns of transracially adopted people, including intercountry adopted adults. Transracially adopted adults have the experience and knowledge to challenge the continued practice of transracial adoption and to show that far from prioritizing the needs of Black children, it is a practice that overrides their basic needs and denigrates their heritage, with serious repercussions.

acknowledgments

An earlier version of this chapter was published in *Models of Adoption Support: What Works and What Doesn't,* ed. H. Argent (London: BAAF, 2003).

notes

1 Shobha, "Mother's Day Service," *ATRAP Newsletter,* no. 1 (2000): 3–5.

2 Lyn (intercountry adopted adult, Southeast Asian).
3 M. Anderson, "Fish Outta Water," *ATRAP Newsletter,* no. 3 (2000): 3–5.
4 Unless otherwise indicated, the quotes are from an ATRAP focus group held on May 8, 2002, and an ATRAP Committee Meeting discussion held on May 25, 2002, attended by committee and other members. Some names have been changed to protect the participants' identities.
5 Beverly Prevatt Goldstein and Marcia Spencer, *"Race" and Ethnicity: A Consideration of Issues for Black, Minority and Ethnic and White Children in Family Placement* (London: BAAF, 2000).
6 United Kingdom, Performance Innovative Unit (PIU), *Prime Minister's Review of Adoption* (London: Cabinet Office, 2000).
7 National Statistics Online, "Census: The Most Comprehensive Survey of the UK Population," 29 April 2001, http://www.statistics.gov.uk/census.
8 Goldstein and Spencer, *"Race" and Ethnicity.*
9 K. Kinsara, personal communication, August 22, 2002.
10 Mary Mather and Marko Kerac, "Caring for the Health of Children Brought into the UK from Abroad," *Adoption and Fostering Journal* 26, no. 4 (2002): 44–54.
11 K. Kinsara, unpublished paper (presentation, ATRAP Social, London, UK, February 3, 2002).
12 Department of Health, "Adoption: Achieving the Right Balance." *LAC* 98, no. 20.
13 Cherilyn Dance, *Focus on Adoption: A Snapshot of Adoption Patterns in England—1995* (London: BAAF, 1997). Note: this survey had a response rate of less than 50 percent.
14 Social Services Inspectorate (SSI), *For Children's Sake: An SSI Inspection of Local Authority Adoption Services* (London: Department of Health, 1997).
15 PIU, *Prime Minister's Review.*
16 SSI, *Excellence Not Excuses: Inspection of Services for Ethnic Minority Children and Families* (London: Department of Health, 2000).
17 Department for Education and Skills (DFES), *Adoption Guidance: Adoption and Children Act 2002* (London: DFES, 2005).
18 Derek Kirton, *"Race," Ethnicity and Adoption* (Buckingham: Open University Press, 2000).
19 June Thoburn, Liz Norford, and Stephen Parvez Rashid, *Permanent Family Placement for Children of Minority Ethnic Origin* (London: Jessica Kingsley Publishers, 2000).
20 Owen Gill and Barbara Jackson, *Adoption and Race: Black, Asian and Mixed Children in White Families* (London: Batsford Academic and Educational, 1983), 81.
21 Derek Kirton, Julia Feast, and David Howe, "Searching, Reunion and Transracial Adoption," *Adoption and Fostering Journal* 24, no. 3 (2000): 6-18; Kirton, *"Race," Ethnicity and Adoption.*
22 Gill and Jackson, *Adoption and Race.*
23 Kirton, *"Race," Ethnicity and Adoption*; Kirton, Feast, and Howe, "Searching, Reunion and Transracial Adoption," 9.
24 Rene Hoksbergen and Cor van Dijkum, "Trauma Experienced by Children Adopted from Abroad," *Adoption and Fostering Journal* 25, no. 1 (2001): 19–25; Mather and Kerac, "Caring for the Health."
25 Kirton, *"Race," Ethnicity and Adoption*; John Triseliotis, Julia Feast, and Fiona Kyle, *The Adoption Triangle Revisited: A Study of Adoption, Search and Reunion* (London: BAAF, 2005).
26 Kirton, *"Race," Ethnicity and Adoption*; Kirton, Feast, and Howe, "Searching, Reunion and Transracial Adoption."
27 Sue Greenwood and Sarah Forster, "Tell Me Who I Am: Young People Talk About Adoption," After Adoption, www.afteradoption.org.uk, n.d., 19. No longer available.
28 Kirton, *"Race," Ethnicity and Adoption*, 90.
29 Kirton, Feast, and Howe, "Searching, Reunion and Transracial Adoption"; Triseliotis, Feast, and Kyle, *The Adoption Triangle Revisited.*
30 Stephen Rashid, "Diverse Reactions," *Community Care* 1244 (1998): 28–9.
31 Thoburn, Norford, and Rashid, *Permanent Family Placement*; Peter G. Moffat and June Thoburn, "Outcomes of Permanent Family Placement for Children of Minority Ethnic Origin," *Child and Family Social Work* 6, no. 1 (2001): 13–21.
32 Moffat and Thoburn, "Outcomes of Permanent Family."
33 David Howe and Julia Feast, *Adoption, Search and Reunion: The Long Term Experience of Adopted Adults* (London: The Children's Society, 2000).
34 Kirton, Feast, and Howe, "Searching, Reunion and Transracial Adoption."
35 Greenwood and Forster, "Tell Me Who I Am."
36 Howe and Feast, *Adoption, Search and Reunion*; Kirton, Feast, and Howe, "Searching, Reunion and Transracial Adoption."

37 Suzy Croft and Peter Beresford, "Postmodernity and the Future of Welfare: Whose Critiques, Whose Social Policy?" in *Postmodernity and the Fragmentation of Welfare*, ed. John Carter (London: Routledge, 1998), 103–120.

38 J. Shekleton, "A Glimpse Through the Looking Glass—A Summary of Personal Experiences and Reflections of a Group of Transracially Adopted Adults," *Post Adoption Centre Discussion Paper no. 8* (London: Post-Adoption Centre, 1990); M. Hayes, "Post-Adoption Issues in Transracial and Same Race Placements," in *After Adoption: Working with Adoptive Families*, ed. Rena Phillips and Emma McWilliam (London, BAAF, 1996); M. Hayes, "Transracial Adopted People's Support Group," in *After Adoption.*

39 Phillida Sawbridge, "The Post Adoption Centre—What Are the Users Teaching Us?" in *Signposts Adoption: Policy, Practice and Research Issues*, ed. Malcolm Hill and Martin Shaw (London: BAAF, 1998), 241.

40 Shekleton, "A Glimpse Through the Looking Glass"; Rose S. Dagoo, "Getting Together: Groups for Transracially Adopted Adults, and for Birth Mothers," in *Adult Counselling and Adoption*, ed. Alan Burnell, Diana Reich, and Phillida Sawbridge (London: Post-Adoption Centre, n.d.).

41 Perlita Harris, *"It Changed My Life Completely": West Midlands Post Adoption Services (Summary)*, (Birmingham: West Midlands Post Adoption Service, 2002).

42 The ATRAP video "Love is Not Enough" is available from Infactuation Productions at 020 7503 0509 or email: info@infactuation.co.uk. A percentage of all sales go to ATRAP.

43 Abayomi (transracially fostered, Nigerian).

44 Mylien, "Orphans of the Airlift," *ATRAP Newsletter*, December 2001, http://free.hostdepartment.com/a/atrap/html/newsletter.html#airlift.

45 Anonymous adoptee, ATRAP, http://atrap.port5.com/ (site discontinued at time of publication).

46 Folusho (transracially fostered, Nigerian).

47 Peter (transracially fostered).

48 Veronica Dewan, "Life Support," in *Something Inside so Strong: Strategies for Surviving Mental Distress*, ed. J. Read (London: Mental Health Foundation, 2001), 44–49.

49 Sue Jardine, "Transracial Placements: An Adoptee's Perspective," in *Working with Black Children and Their Families*, ed. Ravinder Barn (London: BAAF, 1999), 147–156.

50 Farrah Eldred, "Farrah Talks the Talk," *ATRAP Newsletter*, no. 1 (2000): 2–3.

51 Veronica Dewan, "The Pressure of Being a Human Chameleon," in *Speaking Our Minds: An Anthology*, ed. Jim Read and Jill Reynolds (Hampshire: Macmillan Press Limited, 1996), 23–27.

52 Anon., "Dear Editor," *ATRAP Newsletter*, no. 2 (2000): 11–12.

53 Linda, "Untitled," *ATRAP Newsletter*, no. 6 (2001): 3–5.

54 L, "Transracial Adoption—An Experience," *ATRAP Newsletter*, no. 9 (2002): 6–7.

55 Charmaine (transracially adopted, African Caribbean), personal communication with the author, August 22, 2002.

56 Charmaine.

57 Mary, "An Overwhelming Impact," *ATRAP Newsletter*, no. 2 (2000): 8.

58 G. Anthony, "Orphans of the Airlift," *ATRAP Newsletter*, no. 7 (2001): 3–4.

59 Dewan, "Losing and Choosing," *ATRAP Newsletter*, no. 5 (2001): 6–8.

60 Meena, "Letter to My Mother," *ATRAP Newsletter*, no. 3 (2000): 10–11.

61 Anon., "Dear Editor," *ATRAP Newsletter*, no. 2 (2000): 11–12.

62 At the time of publication, ATRAP was not operational.

29 THE MAKING OF KAD NATION

Sunny Jo

KAD: *Korean adoptee; a person who was adopted from Korea as a child and raised in another country, often by adoptive parents of another race, ethnic background, and culture.*

International adoption of (South) Korean children started after the Korean War, which lasted from 1950 to 1953. When the war was over, many children were left orphaned. In addition, a large number of mixed "GI babies" (offspring of Korean women and soldiers from the United States and other Western countries), were filling up the country's orphanages.[1] Korean traditional society emphasizes paternal family ties, bloodlines, and purity of "race," so children of mixed race or those without fathers were not easily accepted in Korean society. Touched by the fate of the orphans, Western religious groups and other associations started sending children to homes in the United States and Europe.[2] In addition, most Western countries had begun to face a shortage of healthy, domestic babies available for adoption in this period as a result of social welfare programs, legalized abortions, and the use of contraception. Thus, many Western couples opened themselves to the idea of adopting children from outside their own countries.

This was the start of a popular trend, which continues as the demand for foreign babies from infertile, upper- and middle-class couples in the West rises.[3] International adoption is today a growing and often favored method for couples to build their families and new countries keep opening up for international adoption, both as sending and receiving countries.

Korea was the world's number one exporter of children for decades. Some called it a national shame considering the country's economic prosperity, but domestic extra-familial adoption has traditionally been rare in this nation that clings strongly to patriarchal bloodlines.[4] Official numbers show that approximately 150,000 Korean children have been sent to North America, Europe, and Oceania,[5] but the actual numbers are most likely closer to 200,000. Most of these KADs have grown up in white, upper- or middle-class homes in suburban settings. In the beginning, adoptive families were often told by agencies and "experts" to make their children as much a part of the new culture as possible, thinking that this would override concerns about ethnic identity and origin. Many KADs grew up not even knowing about other children like themselves.[6] But the first generation of KADs has now reached adulthood and many have returned to Korea in search of their history, roots, and native culture, and sometimes also their birth families.

KADpropriation

In the past, and even today, "experts," professionals, and adoptive parents are often the ones telling KADs what "the adoption experience" is actually like. A number of social workers and counselors have specialized in adoption throughout their careers. Much funding, prestige, and power is entangled in this creation of "adoption professionals," and they have long been the ones setting the stage on which adoption policy and evaluation is being promoted, thus determining how it is framed. Even research done by KADs is based upon these criteria and draws heavily on former work done by "experts," as these criteria are needed in order for the work to be considered "credible."

Appropriation is when, within a situation with existing power differences, someone else speaks for, tells, defines, describes, represents, or uses the images, stories, or experiences of others for his own benefit and purposes, or when someone becomes the expert on other people's experiences and is deemed more knowledgeable about who they are than the people themselves.[7] In the KAD community, such experiences with "adoption experts" are referred to as "KADpropriation."

Adoption agencies run advertising and public relations campaigns to encourage people to adopt children, often from abroad. These campaigns work from the assumption that there is enormous "social benefit" for children, parents, and society as a whole. The dominant ideology of current "adoption professionals" is the notion that one can provide loving homes for needy children regardless of national boundaries, race, or religion—in other words, that affluent white couples in the "First World" can rescue poor, starving children from the "Third World," thereby giving them opportunities for education and a "good" life. The "blessings" offered by supposed authorities and experts are frequently used and highlighted by adoption promoters in their social marketing strategies, such as adoption-promoting publications like *Adoptive Families* and *Adoption Today.* Adult adoptees who question this notion are often portrayed as being maladjusted or having personal problems, meaning that the real concerns with adoption are taken out of the larger context and are reduced to individual, personal issues.

This belief is evident in the many professional adoption conferences held across the globe. Adult adoptees are not frequently invited, unless they also belong to a "professional" group. If adoptees are part of the events, it is often as participants in panel debates or presentations about their own lives and stories. As a result, adoptee voices are reduced to individual, personal experiences, which then can be evaluated and discussed by the "experts." This clearly reflects the disparity of resources available to various groups. Unfortunately, the associations formed by Korean and other international adoptees generally depend on volunteers and free publicity (to organize conferences, conduct research on adoption, provide assistance for searches, offer guidance on homeland tours, and so forth). They are poorly funded and organized compared to the adoption industry.[8]

organizations, associations, and groups

The first ever association to be created for and by adult KADs was the Swedish Adopterade Koreaners Forening, established in 1986.[9] Since then, similar groups have emerged in most Western European countries and various US locations, as well as in Canada, Australia, and Korea. Before this, most organized events and activities for KADs had been arranged and administered by adoptive parents and Korean immigrants. These events included culture camps and social gatherings and focused mainly on adoptive families and their children. But with the formation of the adult associations, KADs gathered for the first time with others who shared a common experience, on their own terms and by their own initiative. KADs were making a statement both to ourselves and to the public: We are no longer children, but independent adults with our own unique concerns and issues.

Together these various groups and associations have tried to work both locally and internationally to raise awareness about the unique position of KADs in relation to both Korea and our adoptive countries. In 1995 the first KAD conference was held in Germany, and in 1999 conferences were arranged in both the United States and Korea.[10] During the last couple of years, KADs have organized numerous adult KAD conferences and social gatherings in many countries, including world gatherings that drew participants from across the globe.

creation of a distinct culture and ethnicity

Based on discrimination and feelings of alienation both in Korea and in our adoptive societies, KADs have increasingly started seeing our culture as separate and different from the cultures of both Korea and our adoptive countries. We are dispersed around the world, either visible or cultural "minorities" within all societies, but we still own a unique culture (with multiple subcultures and factions inside) and a common identity. The creation of the KAD culture emerged through ethnogenesis, the evolution of a new ethnic group through the blending of other cultures, with the subsequent creation of a new and distinct culture made up of more than merely the sum of its parts.[11] In its simplest form, an "ethnic group" comprises members who identify themselves as belonging to the same wide category, which can again be subdivided depending on various classification systems. Identity is more about self-identification than clear-cut, scientific boundaries, and multiculturalism is inherently part of KAD "ethnicity." The experiences and even origins of each KAD are diverse, but we all identify as KADs (whether we're called KADs, OAKs, KOAs, or any other name).

The creation of KAD ethnicity and culture started with KADs reclaiming our own culture and heritage to get beyond the shame and inferiority that have been forced upon us by adoptive families and cultures from the start (e.g., attempts to fully assimilate us; the idea of our adoptions securing us "a better life"; removal and replacement of our names, language, and culture; lack of respect for our heritage and birth families; and ridicule, racism, and discrimination), or by Korea upon return (e.g., the pressure to be "more Korean" or to learn the Korean language—i.e., fully assimilate—and expectations of interest in Korea and Korean culture). Breaking out of these narrow frames and realizing that we are not inferior to the culture into which we were born nor the mainstream culture and society seen as "saving" us (from what?) is the first step towards self-acknowledgment and acceptance of our unique culture. Only when KAD culture is recognized as its own ethnic and cultural group (not only as "Korean" or "______") can a new identity and heritage be embraced with pride, freeing us from the stereotypes and expectations of both our Korean and our adoptive societies.

Since international adoption from Korea only started in the 1950s, KADs are still a very young population (despite the presence of some individuals who have reached their 40s and 50s). The current adult KADs are among the first generation active in the creation of KAD culture, so much of the path has to be made while walking it. Because adoptive parents raising the first generation of KADs sought our full assimilation,[12] many KADs did not become aware of or explore our Korean-ness until adulthood, meaning that even adult KADs have much to learn. One of the first steps for many has been to embrace Korean names. Some have legally reverted back to their birth names, while others use Korean names in their e-mail addresses and computer IDs.

Some cornerstones of KAD culture include being raised outside Korea (the majority of the time, completely isolated from Korean culture and people); attempting to assimilate into a new environment; and being given a new name and mother tongue. Many KADs experience common issues, including racism, negative stereotypes, feelings of alienation inside their own families, and having to deal with an unknown past and heritage.

We also share somewhat of a common history. Being surrounded entirely or mostly by white populations, many KADs avoided other Asians in childhood and adolescence in an attempt to deny our own race and heritage. Many had wished we were white like our families and peers, and strongly identified with white society. Meeting Koreans and Korean culture might have been a traumatic experience for some.[13] The result may be a sense of nonbelonging and rootlessness.

Only recently have adult KADs been able to unite and come together in order to claim a space and an identity for ourselves. Included in this unification is our reaching out to younger adoptees through such activities as volunteering as camp counselors and mentors at culture camps, even though many of these "home culture" initiatives were originated by adoptive parents with younger children.

Adult KADs are spread out across the globe, but there seems to be a tendency to cluster around certain geographic locations—often larger cities or areas where a high concentration of Asians/Koreans already exists. This has created a number of geographic anchors for the KAD community, among them Los Angeles, San Francisco, the Minnesota Twin Cities, New York, and Toronto in North America; Seoul in Korea; and Stockholm, Amsterdam, and Brussels in Europe. A few majority languages are used to tie the community together, such as English, French, and "Scandinavian," but in addition, a large number of other languages are spoken by subgroups.

Some KADs have come to see our KAD culture and identity as stronger than our ties to either the birth or adoptive cultures, often because we continue to be subjected to unfair expectations and ideas that we're inferior from both cultures, without ever being fully accepted by either. A sense of not fitting in, or of having no home, is also strong among many KADs.[14]

One thing that distinguishes KADs from most other ethnic groups is the fact that the majority of KADs are not raised by "our own" but instead by parents and families of another culture and background. This makes KAD identity and culture an individual discovery, not one shared by the family as a whole. In addition to being minorities in society, KADs are also minorities in our own families, making it hard for some to turn to adoptive parents for support and advice. We do not learn at home the essential survival skills needed to live as minorities in a racist society. Nor do most share our adopted status with our adoptive parents. For some, this has prompted a sense of loyalty and nationalism with other KADs and the KAD community.

This sense of belonging and loyalty with the KAD community has led some KADs to adopt children ourselves, either from Korea or elsewhere, while others have found spouses and significant others who are also KADs. Many make close friendships and ties with other KADs. This might indicate a strong need to identify with and bond through common experiences when creating our own families and social networks—and our coming together is creating KAD communities all over the world. These enclaves of tightly knit KAD organizations, friends, families, and couples are the foundation upon which future KAD nationalism and ethnicity will build.

notes

1 Hwang Jang-jin, "Adult Korean Adoptees in Search of Roots," *The Korea Herald,* December 10, 1998.
2 Jang-jin, "Adult Korean Adoptees."
3 Jang-jin, "Adult Korean Adoptees."
4 Louise Elliot, "Battling Pride and Prejudice," *The Korea Herald,* August 30, 2002, http://www.korea-herald.co.kr/SITE/data/html_dir/2002/08/30/200208300006.asp.
5 Elliot, "Battling Pride and Prejudice."
6 Isaac Dani Meier, "Loss and Reclaimed Lives: Cultural Identity and Place in Korean-American Intercountry Adoptees" (PhD diss., University of Minnesota, 1998).
7 Marianne Ignace and Ron Ignace, *First Nations Study Guide* (First Nations Studies, Simon Fraser University, 1998), 18.
8 Charles T. Salmon, *Information Campaigns: Balancing Social Values and Social Changes* (Newbury Park, CA: Sage Publications, 1989), 20–25.
9 Tobias Hübinette, "Korea—adoptionens historia (Um & Yang 3/1999)," http://hem.passagen.se/akf1/UmYang/Artiklar/historia.htm.
10 Hübinette, "Korea."
11 Ignace and Ignace, *First Nations,* 140.
12 Ryan Teague Beckwith, "Adopting a Culture: Woman's Struggle for a Korean Identity," *Columbia Journalism News,* November 11, 2002, http://www.jrn.columbia.edu/studentwork/race/2002/korea-ryan.shtml.
13 Meier, "Loss and Reclaimed Lives," ch. 5.
14 Meier, "Loss and Reclaimed Lives," ch. 5.

GENERATION AFTER GENERATION WE ARE COMING HOME

Sandra White Hawk

There is an outside and inside to a circle, an outside and inside of the self. There is an outside and inside of the heart, an outside and inside of a community. As Indian people, we believe we are all part of the Sacred Circle of Life that knows no beginning and no end. And when we are gathered in a circle we are quieted and know we are in a home away from home. There is a sacred energy that connects us in this circle of life. It is Our relatives. Adoptees are raised outside this Sacred Circle of Life, far away from this knowledge and understanding.

When we come back to Our relatives we stand outside this circle often in sadness, not knowing we can move to the inside. We don't even see there is a place waiting for us. A space that was left when we were taken.

To us there is yet another circle, a dark circle of shame, sadness, and discomfort. A circle so dark we often don't move through it the first time we experience it. We stand there frozen and overwhelmed. We are disconnected from the inside even though it is where our life began. On the outside we are disconnected from ourselves, a result of living "as if we fit in."

The connection of the self is a biological mirror. The biological mirror is our people; Our relatives. It is healing to see our image reflected to us in the circle of our people.

The connection from the outside to the inside of the heart is the drum, our songs, our ceremonies, Our relatives, ourselves. Let us help each other with compassion to know this sacred truth.

In American Indian languages, there is no word for "adopted out." The closest we have is "set aside."

My first memories of being told who I was and where I came from: standing face to face with my adoptive mother, her hands holding my shoulders, looking into her eyes as she said these words: "Your mother didn't really want you. She only wanted to keep you so she could have a welfare check so she could drink. If we hadn't gotten you, you wouldn't have had a chance. You have had a miserable existence. You should be very grateful we took you and gave you this chance at life." She told me over and over again, and as time wore on, these words became my identity. I was an ungrateful, dirty, ugly little Indian kid who needed to be saved from the reservation of people who didn't really want me anyway. After all I didn't even look Indian, she said.

The only positive thing I was told about my birthmother, Nina, was that she was pretty. She had two children before me, Leonard and Edith. Leonard lived with "an old Indian." My adoptive mother would say, "That old Indian wanted you too, but we got you. Leonard had TB. It's a good thing we got you, because they lived out in this old shack with no running water or electricity." She said, "You just wouldn't have stood a chance there." But I don't ever remember feeling "lucky" that I wasn't back on the Rosebud reservation. I sensed that my mom thought this "old Indian" was shameful for the way he lived. The tone of her voice and her body language always told me more than her words did.

In 1994 I found out that the "old Indian" my adoptive mom talked about was my grandfather. I also saw that the "shack" he lived in was still standing and that one of my relatives lived in it until 2002. That "shack" was home to my brother who was raised by our grandfather and uncles on our father's side. The house sits below my brother's house in Moser, South Dakota. There's a path that leads down to it. The men used the house during deer hunting as a home base, as a place to gut the deer and visit. When I saw the "shack" it still did not have running water or electricity. I stood looking at it and said to myself, "this would have been my first home." My relatives lived here. It was beautiful to me. I decided to let go of the resentment I carried. I saw it with my own eyes. The "old shack" was a simple and humble little one-room home. Many times in life when I have been consumed with fear, I picture my feet on the path to that house and draw strength from the land and our ancestors who walked there before me.

My adoptive mother always introduced me as her adopted Indian child. Her voice would change as she tipped her head and got a sad, distant look on her face. She would sigh deeply, and then she would describe the destitute place I was born into, and how if she hadn't gotten me I never would have stood a chance.

I always looked down at my shoes, feeling ashamed and ugly. My skin seemed to sting as if a blanket of shame covered me from head to toe. Each word she spoke would inch the blanket further over me, until I suffocated with shame. It was so hard to stand there as whomever she introduced me to would look me over, as if they were saying to themselves, "So this is what an Indian looks like." I felt so naked and on display when I was being studied by curious adults. I think some of them did feel sorry for me, recognizing that my mother was being inappropriate.

Any progress I made in building an inner world as a "normal kid" she would repeatedly crush with her standard distorted introduction: "This is my adopted Indian daughter. You should see where we got her," as if I were an animal she had rescued. She would go on and on to whoever would listen, recounting over and over the story of how she and my father were called to "work with the Indians" in South Dakota, and how they came to find out about this Indian baby, and how my Indian mother drank and didn't want me. She would describe my family as pagan people whose difficult life was of their own making because they were not Christians. This is what I was told and what I heard all my young years.

the farm in south dakota

I remember the house where we lived in South Dakota. I can still see the kitchen, where the sink was, where the kitchen table was, the living room, and the bedroom. How are these memories with me after all these years, the details, the sights, sounds, and smells, the energy in the room?

My adoptive parents lived on and worked a small ranch with beef cattle. My dad took me with him as he surveyed the cattle out on the range. I can still feel the excitement of riding in the jeep, hanging on as we drove over bumps and through the shallow parts of creeks. My mom has told me that I was eventually able to tell if a cow was ready to deliver her calf. What I remember is the joy I always felt with my adoptive father. He always wore blue, bibbed overalls with a blue work shirt. He was a tall, thick man with large hands. I remember his shy smile.

One day, the jeep must have broken down because we walked home from the field. I remember being lifted to his shoulders—and what it looked like way up there! His strides were long and strong, creating a rhythmic crunching and kicking-up of gravel with each step. I rode in complete comfort on his shoulders, my legs rubbing against the buckles on his bib overalls and tucked under his arms. The sun was warm, the grasshoppers were hopping alongside the road, and the magpies sang a song just for us. I remember feeling happy.

Then, the good feelings stopped abruptly, as they regularly did in my life. My adoptive mother sat in the chair holding me tightly as I struggled to get loose from her grip. Her breathing was a shallow pant that made my body weak with what I came to recognize as shame. She held me so close I could stare into the large pores on her skin and I was overcome by the smell. I left my body and became someone else, watching the small, naked brown baby struggle against the arms of the mother who scared her so. She sat in the chair and rocked, looking at me with an expression of excited desperation.

Just then, the door opened. The sun behind my dad's large frame shadowed his face. My mother startled, jumped up, put me on the floor, and ran to the bedroom. There were many of these kinds of times with my mother. Much later in life I would come to identify these times with her as abuse. All I knew then was how sick I felt in my body when she touched me.

There was a sale barn in Winner, South Dakota, and I got to go with my dad. I loved all aspects of the sale barn. It was full of the smell of cattle, manure, and grain, and the auctioneer's chant. My dad and I would sit on the bleachers in the arena watching as cattle were paraded around the center of the barn for all to observe and make their bids. I was with my dad and all was well again. Once he purchased a Scottish Highlander with very large horns. We transported him home in the red truck, the same red truck that carried me away with my adoptive parents several years before. The great Scottish Highlander thrust his body against the truck walls, and the truck shifted with his massive strength. He wailed with all his might, contesting the restraints of the truck bed. My heart pounded with excitement as I watched him. My mom used to tell the story of how his horns measured 32 inches from the tip of one horn to the tip of the other. He lost those magnificent horns one day. I don't know why they cut his horns off, but I do remember hanging on the fence, watching him struggle to no avail against the men who shaved them off.

So it went in my life in South Dakota. Times with my father seemed to be adventures full of all the sights and sounds of the land and all it had to offer. Times with my mother were secretive, terrifying times. As I grew older, I found ways to avoid being physically close to her.

i got a baby brother

One day we were riding in our car. I must have been about four. We drove slowly up a hill and down the other side, and then turned into a driveway. I looked into the rearview mirror and saw the collar of my dress. It was one of my church dresses. I felt good in it, admiring the little white scalloped collar. Then I looked up and saw a red brick building and a uniformed nurse carrying a small bundle to our car. My mother was walking with her to the car. They put the bundle into the back seat. This was to be my new baby brother. I got excited as I looked at him swaddled and asleep in the back seat. I tried to pry his eyes open; I must have thought they would work like doll eyes that closed when you lay them down. As I worked to pry them open he began to cry and I got a spanking. I don't remember much more about my brother until we moved to Wisconsin, but I came to know that he was my brother by blood. He was Nina's fourth child. I don't like to say "half brother." It seems to diminish his relationship to me. I believe that it was not our way as Lakota people to say "half brother"—you either were a relative or you weren't. The story my adoptive mother told was that "Nina signed him over before he was born. She knew she could not take care of him so she gave him to us."

Later, I learned that of the nine children my mother bore, all but two were adopted out.

the farm in cazenovia

In 1958 my adoptive parents sold their South Dakota spread and moved to Wisconsin. The farm there was tucked away in a wooded rural area about 90 miles north of Madison. It is beautiful there. The green is so green you can smell it. The house stood at the top of a quarter-mile long gravel driveway. I used to love making the trek to the mailbox on the main road. One day a garter snake scurried between my legs. I wasn't even scared—just in awe of how he seemed to appear, slithering on his way as if he had a destination. There was a wooden bridge that reached over the creek. I loved how the wood rattled when we drove or walked over it. I could get lost in my imagination for hours, playing on the banks of that creek. I saw a lone crane one time. I gasped, and since I didn't know what I was seeing, it was sacred to me. The creek held many adventures. Finding a crawfish under a rock, playing with toads, watching and listening to the pounding of a woodpecker and the buzz of the grasshoppers, then being reminded by the whippoorwill that it was time to head for the house—all this remains with me today. The peaceful song of the meadow creatures settled my spirit.

My dad often took me with him into the fields. To me riding along on the tractor watching the manure spreader was a great way to spend the day. The smell of the fresh brown green manure would draw the birds and bugs to a greatly anticipated meal. It was not until I was an adult that I learned manure "stunk." To me it was all part of the beauty of the time with my dad. He used to carry an old soup can on the tractor, and when we needed a break and were thirsty, we used that can to take water from the creek. It was a spring-fed creek so the water was always ice-cold. He showed me the mint plants. We picked them, held them to our noses, and sat in nurturing, peaceful silence.

The farmhouse had a coal bin in the basement. Once, my dad woke me and we crept down the stairs to see a hen with her nest of eggs. They were hatching and my dad wanted me to witness this miracle. We sat together quietly and watched as an egg slowly cracked. I could hear muffled peeping from within the egg. I studied the bantam hen's beautiful feathers to help resist the urge to pick up the egg and help the chick out. The mother hen sat nervously watching our hands, waiting to strike if we got too close. I don't remember the sound of my father's voice. I do remember the sound of the silence we shared. To this day I find myself reliving those moments when the spiritual became earthly just for a moment and was enjoyed by two respectful spectators, my dad and me.

"your daddy is never coming home"

The very things that I was to be "saved from"—poverty, abuse, and alcoholism—were thrust onto me by life's natural unfolding. My adoptive father died as a result of a farm accident when I was six.

My brother and I had just woken up and were sitting at the top of the stairs in our pajamas, giggling with each other. "When is daddy coming home?" I asked. My mother stood at the bottom of the stairs looking up at us. Her face was red, her eyes dark with sadness, and her voice cracked as she strained to get the words out. She looked away and said, "Your daddy is never coming home again." I don't remember if she explained that he had died or not. I do remember that my body felt heavy and afraid, and I was sad.

I am 50 years old. I only had a few years with my adoptive dad. He is buried behind the church we'd attended in Valton, Wisconsin. I have never had the opportunity to tell his story. As I write, I realize how he impacted my life. He taught me to get back up after falling. He taught me that sitting in silence is true spiritual intimacy. Because of knowing him, I know that men can be gentle and kind, and even though I don't remember what his voice sounded like, I do remember the silence we shared—it was pure love and acceptance.

My dad was gone and my mother was alone in the world with us, left to run the farm herself. Three scared souls—two children, one adult. She must have been so afraid and unsure. Many times when I recount my life story, I feel badly for my adoptive mom. We lost the house and farm; she lost her security. We had had a hired hand, but a hired hand's heart can't be the lifeblood of the farm. He worked for his pay, not for the land. Uneducated and emotionally unstable, my mother supported us on a minimum-wage job as she faded in and out of sanity. She was not diagnosed with a mental illness that I am aware of, although I remember her being hospitalized for "rest." We suffered a critical loss with the death of my father. My mother's emotional wounds were neglected, creating harsh behaviors as they scabbed over.

I was the target of my adoptive mother's pained, frustrated, broken heart and endured years of her verbal, physical, and sexual abuse. But I survived, graduated from high school, joined the Navy, got married, had two children, got divorced, and overcame the cycle of addiction to alcohol. I also began healing from the wounds caused by my adoptive mother. I have pushed through much of the anger.

I loved my brother tremendously; he was adorable, with a spirit both innocent and loving. We spent hours entertaining each other. I loved his laughter. But it all began to change when he was about 12. His relationship with our mother was so different than mine. When we were adults, I asked him if what had happened to me had also happened to him, and he looked shocked, surprised. I didn't pursue it further because I knew she was all he had. I had forged good friendships and had divorced myself from our mother. He needed her. So out of respect, I left it at that. My brother has his own story to tell; he will tell it if he so chooses.

In 1988 I went home to Rosebud for the first time. My family not only remembered me but I was told by one uncle that they have come to expect another relative to return each year. I was one of nine brothers and sisters, all but two fostered or adopted out. My mother, Nina Lulu White Hawk, was the oldest of 20 children, most of whom had endured the boarding schools. My family welcomed me home and encouraged me to keep coming back.

the path you are on

Growing up was difficult because of poverty and abuse, but it was the feelings of being "different" and of "not fitting in"—because I didn't look like any one around me—that led to unbearable feelings of isolation. I grew up without an Indian face to reflect my image and concluded that I was ugly and unwanted and did not fit in anywhere. At the age of 14 I learned to numb those feelings with alcohol and drugs. However, somewhere deep within myself, I had a sense—as small as it was—that I was Indian and that it was a good thing. I had no language for those feelings. I never discussed it with anyone. I did not know how I was going to get out, but I felt that someday I would. I was locked in years of isolation and confusion. It truly was the loneliest place to be, a dark time unlike any other time in my life.

The Lakota belief about how we arrive here on earth as children was told to me this way: We are all behind the stars in the spirit world. When it is time, we choose our parents. We choose who we know we are to be with. We choose knowing what our birth will do to and for our parents, and what we ourselves will do as we grow—all as a result of our being born to the parents we choose.

When I first told my adoption story to an elder he said, "You chose this path you're on." I was insulted and deeply hurt; all my life, I wanted nothing more than to make it back to where I came from, and finally when I met an Indian elder, he said *you chose this path!* I thought, if he only knew what I really went through, he would have never said that! I was abused, lost, lonely, confused, and deeply ashamed of who I was. *Who would choose this path?* I would not have chosen to be raised far away from Indian people! But because he was an elder, I listened politely, swallowing the sting of those words. *You chose this path.*

As time went on, I heard different tribes' variations of the same story about how when we are spirits behind the stars, we choose our parents. Then I heard an elder say, "Sometimes the spirits choose really young parents. They come into that family to help them. How many times have you heard of young mothers being so afraid to tell their fathers that they are pregnant?

The mother's father is enraged, and then the baby is born, and the father—in his transition to grandfather—is healed of his harsh ways and softened by the pure innocence of a grandchild."

Many years after meeting with elders and talking about healing our lives, I was struck by this question: If I chose my path—being born into a rigid, Christian family, knowing that my adoptive father would die, leaving me to be raised by an abusive, emotionally unstable mother—what purpose did it serve?

If I chose this path, I can only believe that it is because I knew I could do it. I knew I could survive, knew I could find resolution and let go of anger, resentment, and the shame that hides us from love. And if I could survive, I must have known that I could encourage others to do the same.

There was a time when I felt that my feelings of isolation, confusion, and shame were solely a result of the abuse. I know now that the deepest heart wound came as a result of being disconnected from my spiritual center as an Indian woman. I have since gained a sense of pride, dignity, purpose, and belonging in my life. This is a direct result of our traditional songs and ceremonies. I have had very good counseling throughout the years, but it was not until I first heard the drum that my heart began to open, and the shame, anger, and resentment began to leave. The healing effects of sage, sweet grass, and other medicines quieted my raging spirit and brought a sense of purpose into my life. Our ceremonial songs, given to us by our ancestors—those old songs sung in our language—encouraged the part of my heart that I had closed many years before to open. My spirit is Lakota, even though for a long time I did not know what that meant. The songs, ceremonies, and medicines healed me and brought me home to myself.

creating first nations orphan association

Today I see my purpose in life is to share my story with individuals, families, and communities to encourage them that we can heal from the grief caused by separation from our relatives and identity. It seems the time is right. It seems this is my purpose in life.

We know that between the years 1941 and 1978 (when the Indian Child Welfare Act [ICWA] was passed), up to 35 percent of all Indian children were removed from their homes and placed in orphanages, white foster homes, and white adoptive families. These institutions and homes were often brutal, which only added to the trauma of early childhood separation. Many immediate and extended families of these lost or stolen children still grieve their loss. These children are now adults and struggle with personal identity and a sense of belonging. The mental and emotional toll is evidenced in the high suicide rates and depression of adult adoptees. Many search for family ties but do not know where to begin, adding to the pain of their separation. The time has come to heal the wound of this forced assimilation by establishing adoptees' sense of belonging to a spiritually rich family.

The vision of a song for adoptees came to me, an honor song that would help those looking to find their way back. I shared this vision with Chris Leith, a Prairie Island Dakota Elder and spiritual advisor to the National Indian Child Welfare Association. He asked Jerry Dearly, an Oglala Lakota, to make the song. When many of us were taken away, there was no Indian Child Welfare Act to ensure family resources were used before an adoption took place. It was a time of incredible oppression; our families were in despair. Consequently, many families carry this pain with them today, praying quietly that their children are alive and healthy. I hoped the song would also help heal family members who have lost children to the system. We sang it for the first time in the Black Hills at World Peace and Prayer Day, June 21, 2000.

After the song was sung, Chris said, "We need to do a Wiping of Tears Ceremony to heal the grief caused by the years of separation from families and communities." He said that through singing this song and by using the Wiping of Tears Ceremony for those returning home, we are *okiciuywaste wablenica*—making everything good for orphans. After some time, we realized there was also a need for an organization that could network and assist adoptees, fostered individuals, and their families. Together Chris and I co-founded First Nations Orphan Association.

Today, even with the passage of the Indian Child Welfare Act, we still have many children placed in white foster homes. Our Indian families and communities are still healing from the intergenerational trauma of boarding schools, adoption, and foster care, a result of the systematic removal of our children that has it roots in the time when reservations were first formed.

In the 1890s the federal government, implementing its assimilation policy, began systematically

GOAL OF FIRST NATIONS ORPHAN ASSOCIATION

First Nations Orphan Association (FNOA) advocates for all adoptees/fostered individuals and their families in accordance with our traditional spiritual heritage and the policies of the Indian Child Welfare Act. FNOA serves to unite First Nations adoptees/fostered individuals with professionals, community leaders, other adoptees/fostered individuals, and spiritual leaders. FNOA's activities educate social-service providers in the cultural traditions and values of Indian families and their communities with the goal of bridging and enhancing services, and offer a ceremony to continue the healing from the intergenerational trauma caused by separation from family and heritage.

removing our children. Its agents took children and placed them in boarding schools. At the same time, missionaries came, followed by the social service system. Their response to the poverty on the reservations was to convince us that our children "deserved a chance at a better life." Many broken-hearted mothers did hand over their children to Lutheran Social Services, Catholic Charities, and similar agencies. Many were coerced with shame, being told, "You don't have anything to offer your child." The Child Welfare League of America (CWLA) had an Indian Adoption Project that focused on placing Indian children outside Indian homes. In April 2001 CWLA president Shay Bilchik made a public apology, covered widely by the media from Anchorage, Alaska, for the insensitivity and damaging effects of the project, which added to the near-destruction of Indian families

I find it ironic that these agencies looked at the concentration camp conditions of the reservations created by the US government and instead of saying, "How can we help improve their quality of life?" they concluded that our children—the only resource we had left to secure our future—needed to be taken from our families. Quality of life is not solely determined by money and possessions. Quality of life is family and sense of belonging. How many autobiographies have we read where people say, "We were poor, but we had each other"? As Indian people, we were denied the security of our families. Our communities are still recovering from the devastating effects of this era.

Today, even though there has been some improvement and understanding, I still see too many parental rights terminated and far too many children in foster care. Sadly, misguided social workers often continue to believe it is "in the best interests of the child" to place Indian

OBJECTIVES OF FIRST NATIONS ORPHAN ASSOCIATION

- Assist adopted and fostered individuals with applying for tribal enrollment.
- Assist adopted and fostered individuals with search and reunion process.
- Assist adopted and fostered individuals with post-reunion psychological supports.
- Assist adopted and fostered individuals with understanding and accessing their rights and benefits as enrolled tribal members.
- Assist adopted and fostered individuals with other issues that arise as a result of their lived experiences as adoptees.
- Assist adopted and fostered individuals with accessing their tribal spiritual leaders.

children in families outside of their culture. And while the Indian Child Welfare Act is a federal policy, we still have to be vigilant to ensure that tribes maintain jurisdiction over their children.

There are counties that have specialized Indian Child Welfare Act units staffed with ICWA attorneys, ICWA judges, and trained ICWA social workers. They learn the ICWA policy and understand that its purpose is to strengthen the Indian family using the extended family system. On the other hand, we also have counties whose workers ignore the policy and even actively work against reunification of Indian children with their families. I know because I hear the stories from social workers who witness blatant violations of ICWA policy and don't know how they can bring justice to the families they try to represent. I also hear from mothers, fathers, grandparents, and other family members about how extended families were not notified that a relative needed placement.

What is the solution? We need to come together to strengthen families. We need to find ways to keep families intact during crisis. And most importantly, states must recognize the Indian Child Welfare Act as a federally mandated policy and work with the tribes, following their lead in matters affecting child welfare.

There are people meeting right now throughout this country; minds are coming together trying to offer solutions for families in crisis. They spend many creative hours over the topics of "safety" and "permanency." Meanwhile, an adult adoptee/fostered individual who was raised in a "permanent home" is struggling to make his way back to his beginning, finding his people, searching for that sense of belonging. Are we looking in the right direction? The essence of who we are begins in the womb. How are we trying to honor that undeniable truth and ensure that wherever we place that child, he will be able to answer these questions: Who am I? Where do I come from?

As I have traveled and listened to stories on all sides of this issue, one comment stays with me: "When you take children from a family, you are taking them from their grandparents." (Chris Lieth, Dakota Elder)

Right now as you read this, a grandmother is praying for the return of her grandchild. The time has come to take back what was taken from us. Let us take it back in love and compassion.

Generation after generation we are coming home.

J. A. Dare, *Children not available for adoption, Peru*, color photograph

ADOPTEE ORGANIZATIONS

This list is for information purposes only and does not imply endorsement by the editors. We recognize that the list is not comprehensive and offer it as a starting point for adoptees interested in connecting.

General

Adoptees for Justice
https://adopteesforjustice.org/

Bastard Nation
www.bastards.org

InterCountry Adoptee Voices
www.intercountryadopteevoices.com

Mixed Roots Foundation (U.S.)
www.mixedrootsfoundation.org

African Diaspora

Adopted and Fostered Adults of the African Diaspora
https://afaad.wordpress.com/

Adoptés d'Afrique—La Voix des Adoptés
https://www.facebook.com/groups/lavoixdesadoptes.afrique/

Bolivia

Network of Bolivian Adoptees
https://www.facebook.com/groups/Bolivianadoptees/

Brazil

Adopted from Brazil
https://www.facebook.com/groups/233112333791234

Chile

Chilean Adoptees Worldwide
https://www.facebook.com/groups/861598220896254

China

China's Children International
http://chinaschildreninternational.org/

Chinese Adoptee Links International
https://chineseadopteelinks.wordpress.com/

Chinese Adoptees Sharing Stories (The WAI Society)
https://www.facebook.com/groups/ChineseAdopteesSharingStories

Colombia

Adopted from Colombia
https://www.facebook.com/groups/adoptedfromcolombia/

Ethiopia

Ethiopian Adoptees of Adelaide
https://www.facebook.com/groups/1772303432849144/

Ethiopian Adoptees of the Diaspora
https://www.facebook.com/EthiopianAdoptees/

Life Time Stories Ethiopian Adoptees
https://www.facebook.com/groups/LifetimeEthiopianadoptee/

First Nations/Indigenous

The Aboriginal and Torres Strait Islander Healing Foundation
https://healingfoundation.org.au/

First Nations Repatriation Institute
http://www.wearecominghome.com

Guatemala

Adoptados de Guatemala—Adoptiert aus Guatemala
https://www.facebook.com/groups/393522691177092/

Next Generation Guatemala
https://nextgenguate.wixsite.com/home

Haiti

Des Racines Naissent Des Ailes / Roots Are Born Wings
https://www.facebook.com/DesRacinesNaissentDesAiles/

Haiti Adopted Association
https://www.helloasso.com/associations/association-adoptes-d-haiti

India

b india belgen geadopteerd uit India
https://www.facebook.com/groups/503666156991523/

Lost Sarees
https://www.facebook.com/Lost.Sarees/

Voices of Adoptees from India
https://www.facebook.com/groups/indianadoptees/

Korea

As adopted Koreans are the largest and oldest diaspora of internationally adopted people in the world, many adoptee organizations with a variety of missions have been established. Please see the Korea Adoption Services (KAS)[1] website at https://www.kadoption.or.kr/en/root/adpt_org.jsp for a listing of most of them. Below are adoptee organizations that were not included on the website at the time of this writing.

Adoption Links DC
http://www.adoptionlinksdc.org/

Adult Asian Adoptees of British Columbia
https://www.facebook.com/aaabc2016/

ASK Los Angeles
https://www.facebook.com/AdopteeSolidarityKoreaLosAngeles/

The Korean Adoptee Association of Philadelphia
http://kaaphilly.com/

Network of Politicized Adoptees
http://www.npa-mn.org/

SPEAK
https://www.facebook.com/AdopteesSPEAKforJustice/

325 Kamra
https://www.325kamra.org/

Philippines

Filipino Adoptees Network
http://www.filipino-adoptees-network.org/

Rwanda

Les Adoptés du Rwanda
https://www.facebook.com/groups/480660615383413/

Vietnam

Adopted Vietnamese International
http://www.adoptedvietnamese.org/

1 Korea Adoption Services is under the National Center for the Rights of the Child and is an organ of the South Korean government under the Ministry of Health and Welfare.

Acknowledgments

Outsiders Within is a labor of love that has taken many years to complete. The editors would like to thank all the friends, family, and loved ones who have sustained us during this journey.

For championing the project and making it into a reality, the editors would like to thank Asha Tall and the collective at South End Press—including volunteers and collaborators Val Grimm, Josh Russell, Alexandria Straaik, Emily Tabor, Allie Compton, Maggie Hogan, Esther Cervantes, John Hulse, and the Design Action Collective.

Thanks to Jan Johnston for her excellent editing and administrative work at the University of Toronto.

Chinyere would like to thank her family in Winchester, Longbeach, Mbierre, and beyond; Chineke, Ala Igbo and her ancestors; members of the University of Toronto's Social Justice Cluster, Faculty of Social Work and Women and Gender Studies Institute; Mills College Department of Ethnic Studies and women of color community; Notisha Massaquoi, Margo Okazawa-Rey, Jacqui Alexander, Xochipala Maes-Valdez and Nadine Albert for their guidance, support, and inspiration; all the adoptees who have shared their experience and strength at Sankofa and ATRAP meetings; and the women in prison whose struggles for their children have helped shape the political vision of this book.

Sun Yung would like to thank her partner and fellow adoptee, Christopher E. Cross, and their two mixed-blood children, Jae and Ty, for their support and love. She would also like to thank Kim Park Nelson, Jae Ran Kim, Holly Hee Won Coughlin, Shannon Gibney, Beth Kyong Lo, Rich Lee, Gabrielle Civil, Meghan Flynn-Eusebio, and Ed Bok Lee for their support, ideas, and friendship throughout the making of this book.

Jane would like to thank her mother, whose life and death is the reason for one daughter's work in this world. To her sister who immigrated with her to the United States, and to the siblings who welcomed her back to Korea, where she lived during the final year of editing this book, she offers a heart-felt *komapsumnida.* And to the many transracial adoptees living in Seoul, Minneapolis, and throughout the world, who have challenged and educated her by courageously sharing their stories and thought, and who have generously provided the intuitive and emotional cornerstones for this book, she extends her sincere and deep gratitude.

Most of all, the editors wish to thank the contributors, who are the true creators of this book and so much more.

Permissions

The photo depicting Vietnamese children on page 74 originally appeared Sunday, December 2, 1973, in the *Minneapolis Tribune* article "Nurse helps troubled waifs in Vietnam" by Jacquelyn K. Jones, with the caption, "Rosemary Taylor, with children who have been adopted by families in Minnesota." Photo by Pete Hohn and reprinted by permission of the *Minneapolis Star Tribune.*

The photo of Mary R. Hyde, matron, and students at Carlisle Indian School on page 116 has been reprinted by permission of the Minnesota Historical Society.

The photos of the Apache children upon arrival at Carlisle Indian School in Pennsylvania, and the same children four months later on page 124 were taken by the U.S. Army Signal Corps and reprinted by permission of the Arizona Historical Foundation.

The artwork by Tracey Moffatt ("Early Theft, Draw a Map" on page 38, "Birth Certificate" on page 164, and the still from "Night Cries—A Rural Tragedy" on page 206) is reprinted by permission of the artist and the Roslyn Oxley9 Gallery in Sydney, Australia.

Anh Đào Kolbe was photographed by their wife, Raquel Evita Saraswati, for the portrait "Open Jacket" on page 252, first published in RunDontWalk Productions' 2004 Shades of the Rainbow Calendar and reprinted here by permission of the artists.

An earlier version of Laura Briggs's chapter "Orphaning the Children of Welfare: 'Crack Babies,' Race, and Adoption Reform" was published with coauthor Ana Teresa Ortiz in *Social Text* 75 (September 2003) and is reworked here with their permission.

Sunny Jo wrote "KAD Nation" in 2002. Since then, her article has been widely distributed, quoted, and cribbed online, and we thank the author for allowing us to publish this foundational piece here.

Quotes within Heidi Adelsman's memoir "Tending Denial" are taken from the National Association of Black Social Workers' 1972 policy statement on preserving families of African ancestry and are reprinted with the kind permission of the NABSW.

An earlier version of Perlita Harris's chapter "No Longer Alone in This Grief" was published in *Models of Adoption Support: What Works and What Doesn't,* ed. H. Argent (London: BAAF, 2003) and is reprinted here by permission of the publisher.

CONTRIBUTORS

Heidi Lynn Adelsman is a University of Minnesota graduate and a licensed pipe fitter. She is researching and writing about historical housing and school segregation in Minneapolis, as well as environmental justice. Her writing has been published throughout Minnesota in periodicals and newspapers. Her interest in transracial adoption stems from her experience in a family at the forefront of transracial adoption in Minnesota. Her brother was transracially adopted through the agency where her mother worked.

Ellen M. Barry has worked for decades with women in U.S. prisons and jails at risk of losing their children and with movements to advance racial and restorative justice and prison abolition. She was founding director of Legal Services for Prisoners with Children and cofounder of the National Network for Women in Prison, Critical Resistance, Coalition for Women Prisoners, and Circle for Justice Innovations. She is a MacArthur Fellow, a Senior Soros Justice Fellow, and was one of 1000PeaceWomen across the globe nominated for the Nobel Peace Prize in 2005 and 2008.

Laura Briggs is professor of women, gender, and sexuality studies at University of Massachusetts Amherst. She also holds affiliate appointments in history, anthropology, and Latin American studies. She is author of *Reproducing Empire: Race, Sex, Science, and U.S. Imperialism in Puerto Rico* and numerous other books, including most recently *Taking Children: A History of American Terror.*

Catherine Ceniza Choy is professor of ethnic studies at the University of California, Berkeley. She is author of *Empire of Care: Nursing and Migration in Filipino American History* and *Global Families: A History of Asian International Adoption in America.*

Gregory Paul Choy is continuing lecturer in comparative ethnic studies at University of California, Berkeley. He was previously a professor of humanities at the University of Minnesota and a professor of English at the University of St. Thomas in St. Paul. He has written on Asian American literature as well as on works by and about Asian transracial adoptees.

Rachel Quy Collier was born in Central Vietnam and adopted to the United States the following year. She has since lived in both her native and adopted countries, writing, editing, teaching, and doing social work. She now lives in California with her husband and two dogs.

J. A. Dare was born in Busan, South Korea, and adopted to the United States. He earned two bachelor of art degrees from Virginia Tech, as well as a master of science from California State University–San Jose. He currently lives in Germany, working as an engineer for a German-based multinational corporation.

Kim Diehl is deputy communications director at the National Employment Law Project and a master of divinity student at Chicago Theological Seminary. She has applied her communications experience to advance human rights and southern worker organizing for more than twenty years. She is a board member of Critical Resistance, a national organization dedicated to abolishing the prison–industrial complex. She serves as an editorial advisor for Organizing Upgrade, an online space where left organizers can discuss strategy and share organizing models. A native Floridian, she currently lives in Brooklyn, New York.

Kimberly R. Fardy is executive director of Young Women United for Oakland—a social and economic justice organization dedicated to the self-empowerment and self-determination of young women of color living in Oakland's lowest-income neighborhoods and highest-risk blocks. She is an outspoken activist, stud, visionary, and wordsmith. She shares her perspectives and knowledge of politics, freedom, love, pain, and history through a mixture of spoken word, rap, poetry, and narrative.

Laura Gannarelli was adopted from Korea at nine and grew up in a small Minnesota town. She now lives in Chicago, where she runs her graphic design firm Gannarelli (www.gannarelli.com). She has also started a not-for-profit organization, Paper Lantern Resource Center, to provide resources for parents, teens, and children. The center will help transracial adoptees navigate the unique and challenging circumstances that they face as children and as adults.

Shannon Gibney is an educator, an activist, and the author of *See No Color* and *Dream Country,* young adult novels that won Minnesota Book Awards. She is faculty in English at Minneapolis College, where she teaches writing. A Bush Artist and McKnight Writing Fellow, her new novel, *Botched* (forthcoming), explores themes of transracial adoption through speculative memoir. She coedited, with Kao Kalia Yang, *What God Is Honored Here? Writings on Miscarriage and Infant Loss by and for Native Women and Women of Color,* which was published by the University of Minnesota Press.

Mark Hagland is an adult transracial and international adoptee, born in South Korea and raised in the Midwest United States. He has had the privilege of contributing to several anthologies produced by teams of fellow adult transracial adoptees and speaks and writes widely on topics around transracial adoption. He is a professional journalist and lives in Chicago.

Perlita Harris was an academic in the field of race and ethnicity in adoption; taught at University of Warwick, Brunel University London, and Goldsmiths, University of London; and edited the collections *Chosen: Living with Adoption* and *In Search of Belonging: Reflections by Transracially Adopted People.* She died in 2018.

Tobias Hübinette (Korean name Lee Sam-dol) is senior lecturer in the Department of Language, Literature, and Intercultural Studies at Karlstad University, Sweden, where he teaches intercultural studies, Swedish as a second language, and gender studies. He has published within the research fields of Korean adoption studies and critical adoption studies and is currently engaged with Swedish critical race and whiteness studies.

Hei Kyong Kim (formerly publishing under the name Beth Kyong Lo) was adopted from Seoul, South Korea. She is author of *The Translation of Han*. Her poetry and prose have been published in numerous journals and anthologies, including *Parenting as Adoptees, Seeds from a Silent Tree, New Truths: Writing in the 21st Century by Korean Adoptees, How Dare We! Write,* and *The World I Leave You: Asian American Poets on Faith and Spirit.*

JaeRan Kim is assistant professor at University of Washington, Tacoma in the School of Social Work and Criminal Justice. Her research focuses on the intersection of adoption and disabilities, particularly exploring disability, race, and transnational experiences of post-adoption stability. Her blog, *Harlow's Monkey,* is one of the longest-running transracial adoption blogs in the United States.

Anh Đào Kolbe was born outside Sài Gòn, Việt Nam during the war and came to the United States via New York. They left two years later and grew up with their Greek and German parents in the Middle Eastern countries of Qatar and the Sultanate of Oman, spending a good part of their childhood schooled in the British system. Currently, AĐK is interim clinical director at a psychiatric residential facility serving adolescents with problematic sexual behaviors and has been a social justice activist and mentor to at-risk youth for over thirty years. For a sample of their photography portfolio, go to www.adkfoto.com.

Mihee-Nathalie Lemoine (now kimura byol-nathalie lemoine) is a Korean-Japanese-born, French-speaking Belgo-Canadian citizen. Ze cofounded Euro-Korean League, the first adoptee association in Belgium; E.K.L.-Korea, the first adult adoptee association in South Korea; and Global Overseas Adoptees' Link (GOAL). Ze has initiated workshops on LGBTIQ adoptees, artist adoptees, and adoptees returning to their birthland. During zer thirteen-year-long stay in Korea, ze has helped more than 600 adoptees in their searches. Zer first film, *Adoption,* won first prize at the Brussels Short Film Festival, and zer latest book, published in French, is *88 etc . . . (Je me souviens).*

Ron McClay was born in Glasgow, Scotland, and adopted at six months of age by Scottish parents. He and his family migrated to Australia. He currently works for the Australian Human Rights and Equal Opportunity Commission. He is active in adoptive issues in Sydney and regularly is a speaker at workshops for prospective parents of children from other countries.

Patrick McDermott is a student of Latin American and Latino studies at Salem State College in Massachusetts. He has presented his research on El Salvador–U.S. immigration at Harvard's Rockefeller Center for Latino Studies. He has worked with Pro-Búsqueda, a San Salvador–based NGO that reconnects families separated during the armed conflict in El Salvador. In the United States, he has been active with Central American immigrant organizations.

Tracey Moffatt was born in Brisbane, Australia. Of Aboriginal ancestry, she was adopted by a white family and grew up in a white, working-class suburb. She gained critical acclaim for her short film *Night Cries,* selected for official competition at the Cannes Film Festival. Her first feature film, *Bedevil,* was shown in Un Certain Regard at Cannes. She has shown her art in many exhibitions in Australia and abroad.

Ami Inja Nafzger (a.k.a. Jin Inja) was adopted from Cheonju, South Korea, at the age of four and grew up in Wisconsin. She attended Augsburg College in Minnesota, graduating in social work, sociology, and Native American Indian studies. She moved to Korea and cofounded Global Overseas Adoptees' Link (GOAL). She serves on the boards of the Asian Pacific Cultural Center, Children's Home Society, *Korean Quarterly* newspaper, and Dragon Boat Race Festival.

Julia Chinyere Oparah is a diasporic Igbo with family ties to Owerri, Nigeria, the U.K., and California who grew up in a multiracial adoptive family in the south of England. She is provost, dean of faculty, and professor of ethnic studies at Mills College in Oakland. She is author or coauthor of *Other Kinds of Dreams* and *Battling Over Birth* and editor or coeditor of *Global Lockdown, Activist Scholarship,* and *Birthing Justice.* She has been involved in abolitionist, anti-violence, and black feminist movements and adoptee of color organizing for over three decades.

Kim Park Nelson was born in Seoul, Korea, and adopted by white parents in St. Paul, Minnesota. She is an educator and researcher whose work has contributed to building the field of adoption studies and Korean adoption studies in the United States and internationally. She is author of *Invisible Asians: Korean American Adoptees, Asian American Experiences, and Racial Exceptionalism* and of several published articles and book chapters on the cultures and histories of transnational and transracial adoption.

John Raible identifies as a biracial African American and is an outspoken advocate for transracial adoptees. He currently teaches at the University of Nebraska-Lincoln. He has worked with teachers, social workers, clinicians, parents, and youth to support multicultural identity development. He has appeared on talk shows hosted by Sally Jesse Raphael and Joan Rivers and in interviews by the *Wall Street Journal, Essence Magazine,* and on the BBC's World Service radio. Many people recognize John from the documentaries *Struggle for Identity: Issues in Transracial Adoption* and *A Conversation Ten Years Later*.

Dorothy Roberts is George A. Weiss University Professor at University of Pennsylvania, with joint appointments in the departments of Africana studies and sociology and the law school, where she is the inaugural Raymond Pace and Sadie Tanner Mossell Alexander Professor of Civil Rights. An internationally recognized scholar and social justice activist, she has helped transform thinking on reproductive justice, child welfare, and bioethics. She is author of the award-winning *Shattered Bonds* and *Killing the Black Body*.

Raquel Evita Saraswati photographed Anh Đào Kolbe. She lives online at www.raquelevita.com.

신 선 영 **Sun Yung Shin** is award-winning author of three books of poetry, editor or coeditor of four anthologies, and author or coauthor of two books for children. With fellow Korean immigrant poet Su Hwang, she codirects Poetry Asylum. She is a full-time artist and cultural worker and lives in Minneapolis with her family; more at www.sunyungshin.com.

Kirsten Hoo-Mi Sloth was born in Korea and adopted to Denmark at the age of nine months. She holds a master of arts in political science and works as a project manager in a market research company in Copenhagen. She has been on the board of the Danish association of Korean adoptees, Korea Klubben.

Soo Na lived in Corea for six years before her migration through adoption to North America. Soo Na's life work includes working at unclotting the throat and loving without exploitation. Currently, she lives in the Republic of Corea, where she is working on a video and writing project. By day, she is a teacher.

Shandra Spears is an actor, singer, and writer who has performed or read throughout North America. Her poetry and scholarly works have been published in Native women's anthologies and journals. She teaches in the Assaulted Women and Children's Counsellor/Advocate Program at George Brown College. She is Ojibway, a member of Rainy River/Manitou Rapids First Nations, and a member of the Wolf clan. Raised in Chatham, Ontario, she now makes her home in Toronto.

Heidi Kiiwetinepinesiik Stark (Turtle Mountain Ojibwe) is a Ford Foundation Fellow and a doctoral candidate in American studies at the University of Minnesota. She received her bachelor of arts in American Indian studies at the University of Minnesota.

Kekek Jason Todd Stark (Turtle Mountain Ojibwe) is a Bush Leadership Fellow and law student at Hamline University School of Law. He has served as an Indian Child Welfare Act Court Monitor for the Minneapolis American Indian Center.

Sunny Jo is a KAD (Korean Adoptee) writer and activist. She was kidnapped from her birth parents and adopted to Norway at eighteen months and currently resides in Sweden. She founded Korean @doptees Worldwide (K@W), an online debate and information forum about KAD issues. She holds a bachelor of arts in communication from Simon Fraser University in British Columbia, Canada, and currently does communication work for the Swedish Police.

Jane Jeong Trenka was adopted from South Korea to Minnesota. She holds a master of public administration from Seoul National University and was instrumental in revising Korea's adoption law in 2011. She is author of *The Language of Blood* and *Fugitive Visions* and coauthor of *Child-Selling Country* (in Korean) with Kihye Jeon Hong and Kyung-eun Lee. She lives in Korea.

Sandra White Hawk is a Sicangu Lakota adoptee from the Rosebud Reservation, South Dakota, and lives in St. Paul, Minnesota. She is cofounder and director of First Nations Orphan Association. White Hawk is a spokesperson on the impact of adoption and the foster care system on First Nations people and has traveled internationally sharing her inspirational story of healing. She is also a traditional dancer and participates in powwows across the United States and Canada.

Indigo Williams Willing was adopted from Saigon, Vietnam, to Sydney, Australia. She is founder of Adopted Vietnamese International and a postgraduate research student at the University of Technology, Sydney. She has presented her work in conferences at Massachusetts Institute of Technology and Yale University and has been published in *The Review of Vietnamese Studies* and *Phoenix: An Anthology of Vietnamese Australian Writers.*

Bryan Thao Worra was born in Vientiane, Laos, and was adopted by an American pilot. One of the most widely published Laotian writers, his work appears internationally in over 100 publications, and he is the author of numerous books. He resides in Minnesota.

Jeni C. Wright is a biracial woman (Polish/German and African American) who was adopted at seven months by a white family from New England. She grew up with an older brother who was adopted from Vietnam, a white sister who was not adopted, and a sister of biracial background who was adopted when she was nine.

INDEX

D

E

M

Q

R